The Literary Correspondence of
Donald Davidson and Allen Tate

THE LITERARY CORRESPONDENCE OF

Donald Davidson

AND

Allen Tate

Edited by

John Tyree Fain

and

Thomas Daniel Young

UNIVERSITY OF GEORGIA PRESS

Athens

Special Acknowledgments

We wish to thank Mr. Allen Tate and Mrs. Donald Davidson for permitting us to publish these letters and for help in reading and interpreting the text. We are indebted to Frank P. Grisham and Susan Haddock of the Joint University Libraries in Nashville and Alexander P. Clark of the Firestone Library of Princeton University for aiding us in assembling the material and to the Penrose Fund of the American Philosophical Society, the University of Florida, and the Research Council of Vanderbilt University for financial assistance. We also have many reasons to be grateful to Martha Cook, Thomas Richardson, Patricia Rambo, James Fortuna, Kathryn McMillan, Thomas Daniel Young, Jr., and Jerry Brown.

Library of Congress Catalog Card Number: 73–88361
International Standard Book Number: 0–8203–0339–9

The University of Georgia Press, Athens 30602

Designed by Gary Gore
Set in 10 on 12 pt. Linotype Baskerville
Printed in the United States of America

Contents

Foreword

RE M A R K A B L E not only for its duration but for its consistency, intensity, and depth of thought about literature and society, the literary correspondence of Donald Davidson and Allen Tate, edited by John Tyree Fain and Thomas Daniel Young, is a record of no ordinary literary connection. It documents and explores a deeply experienced and indeed a covenanted relationship. The relationship now and again suffered from marked disagreements and even lapsed into times of silence, and in fact obviously did not endure in full mutuality of interests and aspirations for perhaps more than a third of its lengthy course. But it persisted until Davidson's death, the motive being no doubt an indestructible personal affection, but no less a compelling sense of literary community. If it was a community found and then partially relinquished, it was never wholly relinquished and never without meaning; for it was as large as the vocation to literature.

In its underlying aspect, to be sure, the literary correspondence of Davidson and Tate constitutes a dialogue about the nature of the literary vocation in the past two centuries. It represents in this respect a significant contribution to a discussion that—although it made its appearance in ancient times—had no reason to be continued in medieval times, when the orders of existence were subsumed under Church and State and the use of letters was largely a function of the Church. But out of the long process of the secularization of Western civilization that set in in late medieval times, there arose a third realm, the realm of secular letters. The meaning of the Third Realm is obscured by the complex relations it bore to Church and State. But its effort to emerge as an identifiable order of existence has been articulated by a series of literary intellectuals; beginning notably in the nineteenth century, when it became clear that still another realm, the realm of science, had erupted into history out of the realm of letters. And, moreover, that with its attendant technology this Fourth Realm was the culminating expression of the secularizing process and would—when the power it possessed was linked with the State—henceforth control history. It was at this point that the divinization of the secular word (a phenomenon accompanying the decline of Christianity and the rise of humanism from Petrarch on), together with the accompanying phenomenon of the divinization of the man of letters as a secular priest, began to be the shaping force of the literary vocation. It was recognized implicitly by every nineteenth-century writer of any depth who sought for the motive of his literary career. The articulation of the phenomenon of literary divinization was more difficult, however, and it has remained so down to the present day. One of the most direct attempts to set forth the phenomenon in the last century may be seen in Thomas Carlyle's *On Heroes, Hero-Worship, and the Heroic in History*—in which, along with the hero as divinity, as prophet, and as king, we have the hero as poet and the hero as man of letters. It is possibly not so significant that Carlyle presents the grand geniuses of the creative imagination, Dante and Shakespeare, as "Saints of Poetry"—"really, if we will think it, *canonised*"—as that he finds an "unexpected" shape of the spiritual hero in the man of letters. The specific shapes he appeals to are Johnson, Rousseau, and Burns, whom he considers to be "not heroic bringers of the light, but heroic seekers of it." Waiving the eccentricities and singularities of Carlyle's argument, we can see in his depiction of the "Man-of-Letters Hero" as "our most important modern person," the "soul of all" and teacher of the world, the burden of spiritual mission that the man of letters has begun self-consciously to assume by the middle of the nineteenth century or earlier. He does not necessarily assume the burden willingly or, for that matter, with a clear comprehension of what he is doing, but because men of letters, whether they know it fully or not, have become "the real working effective church of a modern country." But the organization of this Church—the "Priesthood of the Writers of Books"—is not yet effected. Men of letters have an anomalous, a "disorganic," position in society; they may wander through it like an Ishmael, the literary life in modern society being at times "a wild welter of chaos." In this disorder they seek to establish the rationale for the "organisation of the Literary Guild" which is yet to come: the teaching of belief to men who have become spiritual paralytics under the influence of the modern view that the world is a machine.

> But this I do say, and would wish all men to know and lay to heart, that he who discerns nothing but Mechanism in the Universe has

in the fatalest way missed the secret of the Universe altogether. That all Godhood should vanish out of men's conception of this Universe seems to me precisely the most brutal error,—I will not disparage Heathenism by calling it a Heathen error,—that men could fall into. It is not true; it is false at the very heart of it. . . . One might call it the most lamentable of Delusions,—not forgetting Witchcraft itself! Witchcraft worshipped at least a living Devil; but this worships a dead iron Devil; no God, not even a Devil!— Whatsoever is noble, divine, inspired, drops thereby out of life. There remains everywhere in life a despicable *caput-mortuum;* the mechanical hull, all soul fled out of it. How can a man act heroically?

He can act heroically by becoming a man of letters committed to changing the world view of modernity. "This must alter. Till this alter, nothing can benefically alter." The view of the world as "instinct with Godhood, beautiful and awful, even as in the beginning of days" must be restored.

The relationship of Davidson and Tate hardly began in a conscious awareness of Carlyle's grand vision of men of letters as the priests of a restoration of an age of faith in the face of an age of science. Yet such a vision, it becomes clear as we read their letters, can be taken as the context of the inception of their literary correspondence and of its long continuance.

They originally discovered their personal literary community within the small provincial circle of the Fugitive acquaintance—within, that is, the group of young poets who read and criticized each other's poems for several years before 1922, and in that year began publication of *The Fugitive,* a magazine of verse. A special communion between Davidson and Tate was established when Tate left Nashville in 1922. The two apprentices to poetry made an agreement to send their poems and accompanying criticism to one another. After the exchange had continued for something less than two years, Davidson's *An Outland Piper* was published by Houghton Mifflin. Tate looked upon this event both as tangible ratification of the value of their literary compact and as a revelation of its true significance: its implication of a spiritual community set against an alien world.

In the end it did not come to quite the same thing—this idealized community of alienation. It never came to quite the same thing. It is difficult to make a precise analysis of the root of it, but there was always a difference—a difference of temperament and personality, subsisting in part in a difference in family history and in personal experience, and resulting in a difference of outlook upon and approach to the meaning of the literary vocation. We see the hint of the difference in a letter by Tate of March 14, 1924. Tate refers to Davidson's conception of their mutual devotion to poetry as "the life of adventure" and glosses this with the remark that it is the life of adventure because "it is the life of the soul"—"the life of the soul despite the incidental frustrations we meet and the merely human foibles we display and the temporary misunderstandings of the flesh we may suffer." Thus, Tate exclaims to his friend, "to your bow of burning gold I bring, in my meager way, what arrows of desire I can make for us in the momentary cessations of clamor in the physical world." This is of course the self-consciously literary, the heady stuff of a youthful literary idealist, but it is not to be dismissed. In his response to the publication of *An Outland Piper* as "a kind of event of the spirit, a culmination of an adventure beyond the accidents of everyday life," Tate recognized, if not altogether explicitly, an impulse in his own vision of the life in poetry that his friend did not entirely share: the poem conceived both as a symbolic expression of the dualism of the material and the spiritual and as an emblem of a transcendent alienation from the material world. For Davidson the life of adventure in literature always tended toward a rather primary identification with its expression of the temporal condition of the mind—with the direct involvement, or engagement, of perception with the actualities of the mundane. Davidson did not basically tend to think of writing a poem as an act symbolic of the mind's capacity for the perception of transcendence. Tate tended always basically to do so. Although Tate might feel that he and Davidson were "approaching a common ground of principles, of which the fundamental one is that poetry must be the expression of a whole mind, not . . . a report of sensation, . . . a resolution of sensation through all the faculties of the mind," his emphasis on the subjectivity of the experience of wholeness opposes the essentially objective nature of the experience Davidson sought.

> I believe [Tate contends] that every person has a thought rhythm peculiar to himself, and this thought rhythm is identical with his special attitude to the world; hence a good poet is one who contrives an accurate symbolism for this special attitude. Nobody ever says anything about an external world; there are as many external worlds as there are persons (one is tempted to add that therefore there is no external world at all that we can know); all

that we are trying to do is to articulate the movement of thought, as if it were some vast snake which we must put together synthetically before we can look at the marvellous beauty and rhythm of the whole. The phrase, "poets are masters of life," only means that poets approach complete self-consciousness as a mathematical limit; they aren't mastering life, they are mastering themselves in the sense of understanding themselves.

Needless to say, such an attitude represents no more than an aspect of the struggle on Tate's part to establish a theory or rationale of the task of the poet. Seeking to find the reason for being a poet, Tate moved toward an acceptance of the "dissociation of sensibility" as a dominant, controlling, and irredeemable fact of modern culture. Or at least this seems to have been his direction as Davidson saw it in 1927, when he tells Tate that he admires his recent poetic performance but does so without passion. Davidson explains:

> I think the reason is this. Your poetry, like your criticism, is so astringent that it bites and dissolves what it touches. You have decided that the opposite sort of poetry (say, an *expansive* poetry) can no longer be written in an age where everything is in a terrible condition. But this attitude does not merely lie behind your poetry; it gets *into* it, not in the form of poetry but of aesthetics, so that poem after poem of yours becomes aesthetic dissertation as much as poetry. Wherever your poetry is out-and-out argumentative ... I follow you all the way and am nearly ready to say you are at your best; when you deal with *things themselves*, the things become a ruin and crackle like broken shards under your feet.

Davidson applies this observation in particular to Tate's newly composed "Ode to the Confederate Dead," a poem which, he says, in effect argues that no poem can be written on a subject such as the commemoration of the valiant dead. Davidson admires the beautiful execution of the "Ode," its "cold beauty." But, he asks, "where, O Allen Tate, are the dead? You have buried them completely out of sight—with them yourself and me. God help us, I must say. You keep on whittling your art to a finer point, but are you also not whittling yourself. What is going to happen if the only poetry you can allow your conscience to approve is a poetry of argument and despair. Fine such poetry may be, but is it not a Pyrrhic victory?" Davidson formulates the meaning of Tate's poetic course. It is a defection from the great cause of poetry in modern times, the cause Davidson obviously had

come to feel was implicit in their covenant: "I do not see how you think
the battle between poetry and science can be won in such ways as you
use, for do you not strive for and attain a rigidity as inflexible as the
rigidity of science?"

Tate's reply to Davidson's cogent challenge to the "Ode to the
Confederate Dead" is equally noteworthy. On the question of the possibility in modern times of an "expansive poetry" (a reference to poetry
in the heroic or epic mode), Tate observes that Keats did not bring off
either of his attempts at "Hyperion." In abandoning the second one,
he showed the "whole fallacy of injecting 18th century philosophy into
poetry, to take the place of myth." Tate adds significantly: "As for your
[Davidson's] poems, I don't mean that the material is irrecoverable in
the spatio-temporal sense; but that it is epistemologically—if this gets
across." In other words, Davidson's endeavor in his own poetry to use
the matter of the South as a means of conveying what Tate refers to
in the "Ode" as "knowledge carried to the heart" cannot be considered
wholly efficacious. The apprehension of this knowledge must be indirect. "Ode to the Confederate Dead"—ironically an ode about the
impossibility of writing such an ode, but at the same time "an attack
on those [i.e., the Victorian poets] who, some years ago, removed the
theme from the sphere of actuality"—dramatizes, Tate points out, a
quarrel within his own mind, or by extension, within the modern consciousness. But in this quarrel no issue is joined. It is dialectical. Tate
does not see his "Ode" as failing to project the battle between science
and poetry. "There is no battle.... Art is just as rigid as science."

Nonetheless Tate shared with Davidson a vision of reestablishing
in modern fragmented scientific and industrial society a sense of the
value of cultural wholeness. As he affirmed the loss of the heroic in
poetry, he was on the verge of joining Davidson (together with John
Crowe Ransom, Andrew Lytle, and Robert Penn Warren) in an active
engagement with modernity. This would take the form of a heroic attempt at an inquiry into the epistemological meaning of the South
and of an attempted recovery of the limits and validity of the historical
and mythic South as the ground of, the source of, a unified sensibility—
of "a knowledge carried to the heart." Tate had gone through a period
in which he had paradoxically been sustained by a faith in art as a
futile but necessary opposition to modernity, necessary if only as a
personal redemption. He had more or less lost faith in the ideal of
a community of alienation. But he had not, as Davidson feared, suc-
cumbed to solipsism. He had been seeking a way to make an effective

critique of the subjectivity of modernism. In "Ode to the Confederate Dead" he had found the way: The South understood as a traditional society afforded a symbolic reference of a world in which intellect and emotion are harmonized.

In spite of his very active involvement in the publication of *I'll Take My Stand* and in the Agrarian movement, Tate's approach to the meaning of the South remained symbolic in nature and relatively detached. Much influenced by T. S. Eliot, whom he considered to be the greatest contemporary literary intelligence, Tate, as Eliot does in "Tradition and the Individual Talent" and "The Function of Criticism," saw the meaning of tradition from a broad civilizational perspective. Tate's commitment to the South was that of the cosmopolitan poet and critic. It was his cosmopolitan intellectualism which urged him toward the formation of an "academy of Southern positive reactionaries"—an academy which would embrace the discipline and organization of a total movement and "create an intellectual situation interior to the South." This situation would be based philosophically less on "the actual old South than upon its prototype—the historical and religious scheme of Europe." Tate declares, "We must be the last Europeans—there being no Europeans in Europe at present." If Tate's assimilation of the history of the South to European history is mingled with an apparent Southern literalism, this should not be misinterpreted. He compares the Agrarian movement to "another and greater Southern movement," the Confederacy, which "foundered on the indiscipline of ideas." And he states flatly, "The Montgomery convention lost us the war." If this is a declaration of a neo-Confederate nationalism, it is as much or more an ironic metaphorical statement about the failure of the Old South to achieve a detached perspective on the logic of its position.

Tate's inclination to direct his engagement with modernity with a cosmopolitan intellectual austerity is to be seen in another instance, this in his reservations about Davidson's censure of Hemingway's writings as examples of "scientific ministration." Hemingway, Tate observes, "has that sense of a stable world, of a total sufficiency of character, which we miss in modern life"; and he possesses this "even though he has no historical scene to fall back on." If he "were a Southerner he would be just the novelist we are looking for—he would present us without any thesis at all. In other words, the ideal Southern novelist is the ideal novelist anywhere—I don't mean that Hemingway is the ideal novelist, only that he is nigh perfect in his own job—and ultimately there is no difference, for literature, between one thesis and another, in the sociological sense." Tate asserts that the Agrarian critics must be disinterested in literary judgments. In dealing adversely with any novelists, "we must attack them first as artists, and then show that their social attitude, because it is muddled, distracts the creative mind into mere propaganda and ruins the work of art." Tate concludes: "This could almost be made into a principle—that all great, or really good writers, must have a simple homogeneous sense of values, which incidentally are the kind of values we wish to restore." But Tate's dialectical imagination is not truly committed to seeking a restoration of a world established on a "simple homogeneous sense of values," save as the restored image of such a world (as presumably Hemingway's depiction of an ancient Spanish village like Burguete) would serve as an emblem of an integration of mind and heart, rebuking the dissociation of sensibility.

Up to a point Davidson was willing to accept Tate's cosmopolitan perspective on literature and society. He allowed Tate to correct his disposition to take a narrower view, taking to heart Tate's admonitions about Hemingway and "what you say about literary judgments in general, as not to be made from a sectional basis, but on the higher level." Davidson confesses, "I've felt for quite a while that I was in danger of losing balance and becoming merely a cantankerous localist, and your admonishment warms my conscience to its task." But Davidson drove toward a more absolute base of order than Tate envisioned—and this despite the fact that Tate turned at length to the authority of the Roman Catholic faith. The turning was a logical culmination of a quest for order conducted on the Western ecumenical premise, Western civilization being the context of Tate's quest and the preservation of the classical-Christian Western civilization its goal. Western ecumenicalism was not a premise of Davidson's thought. His cultural vision was pre-cosmopolitan; his mind harked back, we might say, to the time before the Stoics set forth the idea of a transcendent polity of mind. Davidson, Louise Cowan points out in her brilliant essay on his career, "conceives that the tradition exists among members of a society, who have a real, though spiritual, bond and a cumulative and undying history which they—and their ancestors—have created." Sharing in this continuity is made possible "by communion and pietas," not by "retrospection" or by "a mere program of wide reading." In "Why the Modern South Has a Great Literature" Davidson terms a traditional society one "that is stable, religious, more rural than urban, and politically con-

servative." But it must be more than the sum of these elements: it
must be rooted in "family, blood-kinship, clanship, folk-ways, custom,
community." The South, Davidson believed unrelentingly, not only
represented such a society in historical actuality but in a present actuality which was integrally a part of the past reality. He believed,
too, that the actuality could be preserved.

In a famous passage (in "The Profession of Letters in the South")
explaining the literary achievement of the modern South, Tate says
it was made possible by "a curious burst of intelligence" which occurs when a traditional culture and a modern culture come into conflict. But the burst of intelligence does not last and cannot be extended
beyond the inevitable passing of the old ways. Commenting in "Why
the Modern South Has a Great Literature" Davidson recognizes the
same motive in the South's twentieth-century literary demonstration,
but he is unresigned to the loss of the traditional society. He implies,
on the contrary, that the process need not remain "unchecked" if the
Southern writer will follow what he knows in his bones as much as in
his brain. The literary defense of tradition, Davidson always held, has
been inadequate or misguided. Poets and critics—men of letters—have
allowed the epic and ballad, the drama, and the lyric poem allied to
music to disappear. From Baudelaire to Tate they have compromised
with or yielded to the enticing but deceptive subtleties of modernism,
allowing the dictates of the literary intellect to corrupt or abolish the
basis of expression in the modes of oral narration and song. Davidson had a certain empathy for a kind of bedrock paganism. He had a
conception of the sensibility unified in a pre-print, even a pre-literate,
pre-historical age—in a culture existing in and through an organic
traditional consciousness, as opposed to an articulated historical consciousness; in a community formed long before the differentiation of
the realms of State, Church, and Letters. This vision, if never fully
developed and forever in conflict with his wide learning and his role
as a member of the academic polity of letters, constantly underlay the
activity of Davidson's mind. It accounts among other things for his
obduracy in promoting Agrarianism as a highly tangible cause. The
passion of Davidson's advocacy puzzled Tate, who sensed it before
I'll Take My Stand was published.

> There is one feature of our movement that calls for comment. We
> are not in the least divided, but we exhibit two sorts of minds.
> You and Andrew seem to constitute one sort—the belief in the
> eventual success, in the practical sense, of the movement. The

other mind is that of Ransom and myself. I gather that Ransom
agrees with me that the issue on the plane of action is uncertain.
At least I am wholly skeptical on that point; but the skepticism
is one of hoping to be convinced, not by standing aside to watch the
spectacle, but by exerting myself. In other words, I believe there is
enough value to satisfy me in the affirmation, in all its consequences,
including action, of value. If other goods proceed from that, all the
better. My position is that since I see the value, I am morally
obligated to affirm it.[1]

After the active Agrarian days were over, Tate was vexed by Davidson's conviction that the Agrarian group had failed to accomplish anything.

> You evidently believe [he wrote to Davidson in 1942] that agrarian-
> ism was a failure; I think it was and *is* a very great success; but
> then I never expected it to have any political influence. It is a re-
> affirmation of the humane tradition, and to reaffirm that is an end
> in itself. Never fear: we shall be remembered when our snipers are
> forgotten. I have had a certain disagreement with you from the
> beginning; you have always seemed to hold to a kind of mystical
> secularism, which has made you impatient and angry at the lack
> of results. We live in a bad age in which we cannot do our best;
> but no age is good.

Tate's assertion of a distinction in the Agrarian impulse between
reaffirming the humane tradition and a "mystical secularism" directed
toward specific political results suggests that he had comprehended in
his friend's motive as an Agrarian something approaching a will to
control history. Davidson would ironically effect a reversal of the secularization of history by virtue of a special and absolute knowledge of the
truth of the South. This knowledge, as much as the knowledge claimed
by the advocates of Progress, brooked no doubt of its efficacy. Tate did
not draw implications so drastic as these perhaps; but the term "mys-

---

1 Judged by the dispute over the title of the Agrarian symposium, which developed
   at the last moment before its publication, the division appears to have been Tate,
   Lytle, and Warren as opposed to Davidson and Ransom. The problem Tate saw
   was the failure to "appeal through the title to ideas." The title *I'll Take My
   Stand* left the authors of the symposium open to the charge of advocating a literal
   agrarianism, Tate says, and afforded critics an opportunity to ridicule poets and
   intellectuals for pretending to be farmers.

tical secularism" may well bear the import of an almost Manichaean version of history, and there is surely some justification for glimpsing in Davidson's mind the drama of a struggle between the forces of light (an organic Agrarian society of the South) and the forces of darkness (a dehumanized industrial society of the North). The drama took a poignant personal turn in 1945 when Ransom published in the *Kenyon Review* a renunciation of his Agrarian commitment, deeming it to have been an act of nostalgia. Davidson took Ransom's commentary on Agrarianism as an act of surrender to the enemy, if not of downright defection. "Anybody can now observe that Ransom of the North talks differently, if not oppositely from Ransom of the South; and can also see that Ransom of the North has put himself on the side of the strongest battalions. What next?"

The correspondence does not show what came immediately afterward. But a few years later Tate expressed his agreement with another criticism of Agrarianism by Ransom. He "alluded to our old views of the late twenties," Tate explains to Davidson, "when we were rebelling against modernism, and pointed out that we never got much further than Nostalgia because no historic faith came into consideration. I think there's a great deal in that. We were trying to find a religion in the secular, historical experience as such, paticularly in the Old South. I would now go further than John and say we were idolaters. But it is better to be an idolater than to worship nothing, and as far as our old religion went I still believe in it." Tate's identification of Agrarianism as a divinization of secular history may be understood as a clarification of what Tate had meant two years earlier when he had referred to Davidson's "mystical secularism." Tate was able to make it, we can surmise, because he had himself now embraced Catholicism and could see more clearly the phenomenon of the divinization of the literary mind, and the attendant desperate alienation men of letters undergo when they engage in the futile struggle to alter temporal history so that the Godhead may be restored. A differentiation between temporal history and supratemporal history became the basis of Tate's vision of the man of letters in "The Man of Letters in the Modern World" (1952). Men of letters have, he says, constituted a cult, an idolatry, "like the *parvenu* gods" of "decaying Rome." But their function has not been entirely impaired. Culture is dependent on the "use of the letter ... [,] in the long run our one indispensable test of the actuality of our experience." The man of letters has the "power of discrimination"—the power to choose between language which expresses reality and language which dooms men to a mechanical version of reality. The man of letters is primary in keeping open the possibility of man's apprehension of the truth of his destiny beyond time.

If Davidson replied to Tate's letter about the Agrarian idolatry, the reply is not recorded in the correspondence in this volume. The implication in Tate's letter is more drastic than in Ransom's statements about Agrarian nostalgia, for Tate suggests that the Agrarian perception was blocked off from actuality by its confusion of profane and sacred history. But, it may be assumed, Davidson did not grasp this suggestion with certainty. He saw no confusion in Agrarianism, his conception of actuality not truly including its dual nature in temporal and metaphysical dimensions of existence. Davidson's conception of the mission of the literary vocation remained nontranscendent. In fact, by the time he wrote "A Mirror for Artists," his contribution to the Agrarian symposium, Davidson had taken his stand on the function of the poet and critic. In order to survive in an industrial age the poet may retire "more deeply within the body of tradition to some point where he can utter himself with the greatest consciousness of his dignity as an artist. He is like a weaponless warrior who plucks a sword from the tomb of an ancient hero." But Davidson did not see the plucking of the sword as a secret and nonfunctional gesture. He indicates that as a critic of society the poet may come forth into "the common arena, assuming the guise of a 'citizen.'" He may become a farmer or he may run for Congress, but he must take a stand "against the industrial devourer—a stand that might prove to be a turning-point." A warrior-bard concealed in a Congressman—the image is not preposterous if we accept Davidson's view of reality. He wanted to join literature and politics, to create a viable Southern resistance movement against industrialism, and to take action. History can be changed, if the true source of the South's history in the ancient heroic society is understood.

In the first part of "The Man of Letters in the Modern World," Tate says: "While the politician, in his cynical innocence uses society, the man of letters disdainfully, or perhaps absentmindedly withdraws from it: a withdrawal that few persons any longer observe, since withdrawal has become the social convention of the literary man, in which society insofar as it is aware of him, expects him to conduct himself." He is suggesting, Tate says, "the melancholy portrait" of himself. He concludes his analysis of the man of letters, as has been indicated, by describing the capacity of the man of letters to keep open the knowledge of redeeming transcendence inherent in the discriminating use of the letter. This is his ultimate and only true function.

In his literary correspondence with Donald Davidson, and in his writings generally, Allen Tate's vision of the modern Priesthood of the Writers of Books derives from its major source: Tate's inheritance of the spiritual cosmopolitanism—the high culture—of Western Civilization. Tate has molded himself in the tradition of the great poets and clerks, from Dante to Eliot. This is the tradition of the heroism of the literary vocation we respond to most readily, for it is the one we are most familiar with. Still, the sense of the vocation of the heroic bard is not entirely lost to us. Davidson's struggle to recover it and to define for America a conception of the man of letters as bard demands our attention. Carlyle had intimated the importance of such a conception in his assessment of the various types of the man of letters by acknowledging the significance of Robert Burns. He was, Carlyle says, "a piece of the right Saxon stuff: strong as the Harz-rock, rooted in the depths of the world;—rock, yet with wells of living softness in it."

Lewis P. Simpson

Introduction

T H E present volume contains a selection of the literary correspondence of Allen Tate and the late Donald Davidson. The literary qualification is intended to suggest that the editors have tried to avoid personal matters. If the line is drawn strictly, however, much of the strength and convincing quality of the correspondents' criticism of each other's literary work would be lost. The source and context of their utter freedom and assurance of mutual confidence could not be revealed. Similar considerations arise when personal remarks are made about others. People do say things about one another. If some chips are not allowed to fall as they may, the record becomes unreal. Every time Hawthorne mentioned a good-looking woman or used a bad word in his notebooks, his wife blotted it out, and but for the discovery of infrared photography we never would have known his journals were written by a human being.

In a lighthearted moment in the spring of 1922 a group of friends, composed mostly of students and young teachers at Vanderbilt, adopted a prophetic name for their projected magazine of verse, *The Fugitive*. For the Fugitives soon began to flee, and Allen Tate was the first to go. It is possible to speculate that his unwilling flight from Nashville was an advantage—that his letters to Davidson, John Crowe Ransom, Robert Penn Warren, Andrew Lytle, and others enabled him better to realize his own creative purposes and to formulate his own critical principles. In what way or degree literary history itself was affected is only speculation. He did leave, so the conclusion from another premise is not arguable. Certainly his flight has enriched the *records* of literary history, for it made possible Tate's letters to Davidson and Davidson's letters to Tate. Approximately a third of this correspondence is contained in the present volume. The complete files are deposited with other Fugitive papers in the Joint University Libraries in Nashville and in the Princeton University Library.

There is no entirely satisfactory way to present or to read such a series, covering as it does a span of more than forty years. The first letter can be understood only after many later ones have been read. And if full annotation with cross-references to all proper places is attempted, some of the drama disappears. The fascination of discovery, of progressive confirmation of things only suspected, is destroyed. It is much better to read letters as we read fiction or poetry. As we begin to read a work of literary art, many things are said that convey little significance to us. We file them away close to the threshold of consciousness, where they lie until the artist, by a series of echoes and recapitulations, brings them to life for us, gives them meaning. It is the rhythm of life itself, the way our own thoughtless experience acquires depth and meaning, and indeed—shall we say?—the reason literary art as virtual life intrigues us in the first place. These brief introductory remarks would not be the place to launch out, like overzealous toastmasters, on such an essay concerning the art of reading; the present event should furnish its own proof. The reader, however, may be uncertain of the value of the suggested analogy, or perhaps uncertain of its application to the present set of letters. Let us, then, notice how the process works itself out in a single instance, the references to T. S. Eliot. And if by following this current as it flows through the letters the editors cannot induce the reader's suspension of disbelief, it will still be a good way to begin to get acquainted with the correspondents, with their special kind of mutual language, and with some of the problems of the group to which they belong.

In the very first letter of this edition—in fact the first letter in the complete file—Davidson says, "I have purchased T. S. Eliot . . . wondering very oddly whether my $1.25 was well-spent." At the time this letter was written the Fugitives had been meeting and discussing the poetry they had been writing for about five years. Tate, however, had been meeting with them only about eight months; and though they knew about Eliot and the modern movement, he was the gadfly that stung into complete awareness. So the quoted remark is in the tone of banter. When Tate answers, he does not have to let Davidson know that he understands the joke. In these written conversations everything is often taken for granted as if the participants were sitting together and could see the intent and the emotions of the moment in each other's eyes. Once in a while the donnée is forgotten—for things really do look different in black and white—and misunderstanding follows. Then once in a while real disagreement occurs, and the letters become sharp.

Intimate friends can be honestly angry with each other; they can seldom be just polite. But when Tate answers this first letter, without reference to the banter he returns to the characteristic subject matter: "I am not the least surprised that the D[ouble].D[ealer]. refused to take your poem." And then he says of his own recent publications, "You know how readily they took 'Euthanasia' and 'Parthenia,' and since I left, even 'William Blake'! All of these poems, with the possible exception of 'Parthenia,' are quite inferior to your 'Amulet,' but their tone is in unison with Eliot, Pound and Company." Tate's exclamation point after "William Blake" is there because Davidson had denounced that poem in both Fugitive meetings and private conversation. We must read not merely between the lines in this kind of conversation but around the punctuation marks too. Let us say that we approach these two friends talking to one another, and we wait to see what they are talking about. We catch onto tags and vague references. After a while we begin to understand the drift of things and can enter into the conversation.

The next month Davidson sends for criticism "Dryad," the first poem in what Tate came to call Davidson's Pan series, and he accompanies it with the following explanation: "I want to try out for a while, if I can, the idea of combining a certain satirical touch, or at least a certain hardness of texture, with an attempt at lyrical beauty. Do you think it is possible?" Tate replies that it is certainly possible but that he will have to fine Davidson for occupying his own posted ground, and in another letter he refers to Eliot as the master of the genre, who in "La Figlia Che Piange" and in "Love Song of J. Alfred Prufrock" will convince Davidson of the "consummate art possible in this direction." Later in the same year he says, "I have found the best statement of the problem of the artist in *The Sacred Wood,* by the demi-god T. S. Eliot. . . . Eliot is the most learned man writing now and the least musty."

This kind of talk, which was of a piece with Tate's opinions expressed in Fugitive meetings, was taken exception to by some of the members. Davidson reports as follows on Tate's editorial for the fourth number of the *Fugitive:* "Some thought you were a bit positive on the ultimate quality of Eliot's *Waste Land.* . . . A perhaps or two, or some such reservation, as John suggests, might help." The seemingly offhand reference here to John Crowe Ransom's suggestion is significant, since Tate's editorial was the beginning of what is known in Fugitive annals as the *Waste Land* controversy. This embittered quarrel between Tate and Ransom was an extreme case of conflict, but by no means the only one, among the Fugitives. It permits a vision of what happens when honest men of great talent band together and pursue with their whole hearts a common endeavor. But it seems to have convinced the Fugitives once and for all that it was unwise and misleading to air their differences in the public press.

Since Louise Cowan treats this matter at some length, only a brief notice seems necessary here.[1] Ransom had taught both Davidson and Tate. He was the only publishing poet when the Fugitive meetings began. He was the recognized intellectual leader of the group. But for these very reasons they resented the more vehemently any default of the expected noblesse. Actually nearly all of the references to Ransom in the present volume will remain slightly out of focus. The editors hope to be able to restore the proper focus in a future volume of the letters of Ransom to Tate, another voluminous series covering a lifetime of close friendship. Unfortunately a good deal of extrapolation will be necessary since Ransom apparently has not saved many letters from anybody. In such a volume a fuller background of the controversy under consideration will be more significant, but the reader of the present letters may need the bare facts. Ransom wrote an essay on *The Waste Land* for the *Literary Review* of the *New York Evening Post* in the summer of 1923. In it he said the same things he had been saying in Fugitive meetings. Tate, his demigod attacked, replied in a letter to the editor in the tough, no-quarter language he would have used in the meetings. And when Ransom replied in his own letter to the editor in the same kind of language, an open breach occurred, which had to be allayed by Davidson in his customary role of peacemaker of the group.

Two years later Tate is still voicing the same opinions about Eliot. But by now the other Fugitives are beginning to agree with him and he crows, "Of course I am demanding recognition as a prophet." He says he supposes it is obvious why he has always recognized Eliot as "the most intelligent man alive. . . . He writes up my own ideas better than my poor skill permits me to do for myself." The *Waste Land* controversy has not been forgotten but can now be taken in stride, as he says in the same letter, "I imagine that John rather regrets his aspersions of Eliot two years ago." Of course by this time Tate is living in New York, having discovered at the age of twenty-four that he can make a living as a free-lance man of letters. By the next year Eliot is asking Tate for material, and he writes to Davidson that he must get and read the

1   Louise Cowan, *The Fugitive Group* (1959), pp. 122–26.

Criterion, which he supposes he kept out of the library by recommending it two years before. His humorous remark here refers to Fugitive bickerings. Stanley Johnson and Tate were always opposed on the subject of modern poetry, and Johnson's wife was the head librarian at Vanderbilt.

There are not many references to Eliot in the later letters. After everybody agrees with Tate on the subject, nothing is left to argue about. An echo of old times occurs with the publication of Davidson's *Spyglass* papers in 1963. In congratulating Davidson on the volume Tate says: "You were a prophet in those days. . . . I believe you err in only one prophecy, that T. S. Eliot would write no more poetry." Davidson answers: "I'm happy that you like it, and will give me a good score on all but the Eliot prediction. . . . But I still can't help feeling, at times, the glassy stare of that monocle." His reference is to a passage in his review of *For Lancelot Andrewes* in which he had said, "One feels icily repelled, put in one's proper uncouth place; it is the same as being viewed through a monocle.[2]

Other such themes will be left for the reader to follow as they weave and interweave through the pages. Because of the intimate, allusive nature of the material, the editors have tried to keep this volume as free of editorial intrusion as possible. However, if we have neglected anything essential to an understanding of the letters, we have failed in our intent. The table of contents has been combined with an almost complete register of the letters, so that a reader may be able to see when the correspondence was fullest and most sequential, as well as to get some idea of the kinds of material omitted. Omissions of passages within letters are marked with ellipses. Most of these passages are trivial—reports on the weather and the state of health of correspondents and families, detailed plans for trips, and such matters. Many unimportant postscripts are omitted. Some of the omitted passages are important. For instance Tate's first letter contains a three-page description of Valle Crucis, North Carolina—an interesting passage but one that we considered expendable because everything could not be included. There are also omissions of material that those most personally concerned still consider private. Of course it would be informative for the reader to know what these passages are, but this is one of the hazards of publishing contemporary correspondence. All editors of such let-

---

2 *Nashville Tennessean,* June 23, 1929. This and many other Davidson reviews referred to in the text are available in *The Spyglass,* ed. Fain, Vanderbilt University Press, 1963.

ters are subject to some restrictions (including that of space). It is ad-mittedly better to include in the published record as much as possible while correspondents and their relatives and friends are still alive and care what is said than to delay indefinitely—lest the future reader be confronted with text and commentary complete but devoid of the breath of life which only the present can give.

In the chronologies and in the headnotes and footnotes we have tried to keep the informed general reader in mind, assuming that the literary historian can pass over what he does not need. Since both Davidson and Tate are masters of English prose and since they are precise and conventional in matters of usage—grammar, syntax, punc-tuation, and spelling—the editors have experienced few difficulties in establishing the text. (It should be added that the original letters are in good condition and that they offer almost no problems of legibility.) Because the errors of the correspondents are rare and are almost in-variably the result of haste or oversight, there is no point in reproduc-ing them. Naturally there has been no effort to change colloquialisms or otherwise to tamper with the prose style of either writer, but mis-spelled words (which are largely typographical errors) have been si-lently corrected. We have avoided the use of [*sic*] because, with the kind of material involved, this notation would usually be either tediously unnecessary or officiously irritating. Many of the letters contain mar-ginalia which have been inserted in the text at the most appropriate points. So far as punctuation is concerned it should be noted that both men occasionally use suspension points to indicate a shift of thought or a break in time or to emphasize an idea. Since the number of these points is purely arbitrary and since they are not integral to the sub-stance or style of the letters, we have dropped them so that we would not have to differentiate these suspension points from editorial ellipses. Since quotation marks sometimes occur before commas and periods, sometimes after them, and sometimes on top of them, we have regu-larized usage to conform to the American convention. Otherwise the punctuation remains unchanged. It will be obvious that the text itself has not been normalized. Note, for instance, the authors' varying use of quotation marks, italics, and capitalization when they mention the titles of books. Datelines have been regularized, however, as is consis-tent with contemporary editorial practice; and here, as elsewhere, in-formation supplied by the editors has been set off in brackets.

It will be seen that the letters between Davidson and Tate in-cluded here have been numbered and that the notes for the letters have been keyed to those numbers. Following each number is an abbreviation describing the nature of the document: for example ALS means auto-graph letter signed; TLS, typed letter signed; N stands for note (150 words or less). In the case of letters inadvertently left unsigned the no-tation s does not appear, and the signature is shown in brackets. The letters in the appendices are unnumbered; the abbreviation CC describ-ing some of them indicates that they are carbon copies.

In general we have endeavored to provide a text which is as close to the original as is reasonable and which retains as much as is possible of the original flavor.

John Tyree Fain
Thomas Daniel Young

Register

The following list contains nearly all the letters in the files used in making the selection for the present volume. Some short notes, fragments, and miscellaneous pieces have been omitted, usually because neither dates nor places of origin were discoverable. This register should be adequate for those readers who need to know more about the complete files than the text provides. The correspondents almost invariably give month and day of writing. The year is often omitted but can usually be ascertained from context. Brackets indicate all editorial additions except the year to which a letter is assigned. As for addresses and letterheads, the plan here is to give a complete address only once after a change occurs and thereafter to use a recognizable abbreviation. Since complete addresses can be followed in this manner, the text itself records only place of origin and date. The letters in the present volume of selections are here listed by page number so that the register can double as a table of contents. It should be noted that in this register Davidson's letters continue nearly two years longer than Tate's. The editors have been unable to obtain Tate's last letters to Davidson but hope to add a selection in a later printing if they can be found.

July 30	Davidson, [Forest St.], 860 words: thinks Tate can get a fellowship to work for an M.A. the next year at Vanderbilt.	
July 31	Tate, [Vanderbilt], 760 words: Bill Elliott "has a letter from T. S. Eliot complimenting the work of A. Tate. . . . I feel like putting a record on the gramophone."	
August 2	Tate, [Vanderbilt], 770 words: mostly on magazine business.	
August 12	Davidson, [Forest St.], 920 words: not sure he understands Tate's letter to the *Review*: "I just haven't enough philosophy to follow you always."	
August 14	Davidson, [Forest St.].	81
August 18	Tate, [Vanderbilt], 820 words: "Alas, I agree with you that my prose is gravid, but I do think I got the better of the [Tate-Ransom] controversy."	
August 22	Davidson, [Forest St.], 1820 words: mostly *Fugitive* business; since editor Davidson is out of town, associate editor Tate is in charge.	
August 24	Davidson, [Forest St.].	82
August 27	Tate, [Vanderbilt].	83
August 30	Davidson, [Forest St.].	85
September 5	Davidson, [Forest St.].	88
September 7	Tate, [Vanderbilt].	89
September 10	Davidson, [Forest St.].	91

1924

February 21	Tate, Lumberport, W. Va., 440 words: reports on his new job and on meeting Laura Riding in Louisville.
February 27	Tate, Lumberport, 270 words: says the students think he is a "good fellow" and the "smartest teacher" in Lumberport.
March 1	Tate, [Lumberport], 300 words: chiefly about

May 16	Tate, [Lumberport].	112
May 21	Davidson, [18th Ave.], 280 words: Warren ill and has gone home: "I doubt whether Red will come back to Vanderbilt."	
May 21	Tate, [Lumberport], 140 words: "I leave here in two weeks. Resurgam, etc."	
May 24	Tate, [Lumberport], 860 words: this and the next about Warren.	
May 26	Tate, [Lumberport], 70 words.	
May 28	Tate, [Lumberport].	113
June 2	Tate, [Lumberport].	117
June 4	Davidson, [18th Ave.].	118
June 5	Tate, Lumberport.	119
June 5	Tate, Lumberport, 220 words: reports he is leaving Lumberport and going to Washington.	
[June 8]	Tate, 65 Columbia Heights, Brooklyn, N.Y.	119
June 15	Tate, Columbia Heights.	120
June 23	Davidson, [18th Ave.].	122
July 11	Tate, Guthrie, [Ky.], 220 words: visiting Warren.	
July 16	Davidson, [18th Ave.], 240 words.	
August 6	Tate, [Guthrie], 520 words: reports he plans to come to Nashville with Warren.	
August 25	Tate, The Bancroft, 19th and Corcoran Sts., Washington, D.C., 270 words: reports he is staying with his mother for three weeks—or longer if he can find a job there.	
September 4	Tate, [1627 19th St. N.W., Washington, D.C.], 280 words: asks Davidson to recommend him to Dean Hodgkins, George Washington University.	
September 11	Tate, [19th St.], 370 words: mostly about reviews for the book page.	
[September]	Tate, [19th St.], 80 words.	
[September]	Tate, [19th St.], 200 words.	
[September]	Tate, [19th St.], 440 words: apparently a letter without a salutation, mostly on his reviews for book page.	

September 22   Tate, [19th St.], 130 words: asks to review
                 anything on Emily Dickinson.
September 25   Tate, [19th St.], 260 words: sends his transla-
                 tion of Baudelaire's "Correspondences"
                 and talks about it.
October 3   Tate, [19th St.].   123
October 3   Tate, [19th St.].   124
October 5   Tate, [19th St.], 80 words: note attached to
                 enclosed copy of letter to the editor of
                 Poetry.
October 9   Tate, [19th St.].   124
October 10   Tate, [19th St.].   125
October 11   Tate, [19th St.].   125
October 11   Tate, [19th St.], 60 words.
October 15   Tate, [19th St.].   126
October 23   Tate, [19th St.], 370 words: advising David-
                 son on article intended for the *American
                 Mercury*.
October 31   Tate, [19th St.], 170 words: asks for books by
                 Burke, Westcott, and Cabell to review for
                 the book page; says that he is leaving in a
                 few days for New York.
November 3   Tate, [19th St.], 180 words: states willingness
                 to give $25 to keep *Fugitive* going.
November 9   Tate, 55 Grove St., New York City.   127
November 16   Tate, Grove St., 170 words.
November 22   Tate, [Grove St.], 180 words: sends newsletter
                 for book page.
November 22   Tate, [Grove St.], 100 words.
November 29   Tate, Grove St.   129
December 3   Tate, Climax Publishing Corporation, 80
                 East 11th St., N.Y.C., 180 words: reaction
                 to Davidson's report that Laura Riding has
                 visited Nashville.
December 8   Tate, Grove St.   130
December 11   Tate, [Grove St.], 160 words: still thinks
                 "Aunt Harriet" Monroe is patronizing.
December 17   Tate, Grove St.   132
December 30   Tate, Climax.   134

1925

August 15	Davidson, [Wesley Hall].	177
August 20	Tate, Patterson, 310 words: "I am now running a page of books for *Charm*. . . . The worst sort of journalism, the best sort of pay."	
August 21	Tate, [Patterson], 160 words.	
September 4	Tate, Patterson, 340 words: this and several succeeding letters concern the Fugitive anthology.	
September 10	Tate, Patterson, 300 words.	
October 15	Tate, Bank St., 140 words.	
October 22	Tate, Bank St., 320 words.	
October 29	Tate, Bank St., 290 words.	
November 24	Tate, Bank St., 310 words.	
December 2	Tate, Bank St., 300 words.	
December 27	Davidson, Wesley Hall.	179
December 29	Tate, [Bank St.].	180

1927

January 5	Tate, Bank St.	182
January 19	Tate, Bank St.	183
January 20	Tate, Bank St.	184
January 21	Davidson, Wesley Hall.	184
February 15	Davidson, [Wesley Hall].	185
February 20	Tate, Bank St.	187
February 23	Davidson, Wesley Hall.	190
March 1	Tate, [Bank St.].	191
March 4	Davidson, Wesley Hall.	192
March 7	Tate, [Bank St.].	193
March 17	Tate, [Bank St.].	195
March 21	Davidson, Wesley Hall.	196
March 24	Tate, [Bank St.].	196
April 28	Tate, Bank St.	198
May 3	Davidson, Wesley Hall.	198
May 5	Tate, Bank St.	199
May 9	Davidson, Wesley Hall.	201
May 13	Tate, [Bank St.].	203
May 21	Tate, [Bank St.], 160 words: reports Harcourt,	

Brace has agreed to publish Fugitive anthology; next several letters mostly on details of contract, contents, etc.

May 23   Davidson, Wesley Hall, 530 words.

May 25   Tate, [Bank St.], 300 words: "The book will appear in January. All hail!!"

May 25   Davidson, Wesley Hall, 800 words: asks Tate to help Merrill Moore publish a volume of poems.

May 28   Davidson, Wesley Hall, 200 words.

May 29   Davidson, Wesley Hall, 600 words.

May 31   Tate, Bank St., 300 words.

June 1   Tate, Bank St., 350 words.

June 1 [later]   Tate, [Bank St.], 80 words.

June 7   Davidson, Wesley Hall, 300 words.

June 11   Tate, Bank St., 600 words.

June 22   Davidson, Wesley Hall, 700 words: Davidson apparently in Oberlin, Ohio, for the summer but is using his Wesley Hall letterhead; details of Fugitive anthology, title, jacket, etc.

June 24   Tate, [Bank St.], 230 words: "Stonewall gets more and more difficult as time passes, but more interesting."

June 28   Tate, General Delivery, Richmond, Va., 170 words; address puzzling: "I understand from Red that Dr. Mims is now one of my admirers."

July 1   Tate, Bank St., 100 words: preparing for "a month's motor trip in Virginia—battlefields, the kinfolks, etc. . . . I have purchased a sturdy 2nd hand Ford." Actually the family returned to New York on July 16.

July 11   Davidson, Wesley Hall, 330 words.

July 17   Tate, Bank St., 400 words: mostly describing trip.

September 5   Tate, Bank St., 460 words: "I have enjoyed Red tremendously and am much pleased with his nearness for the winter."

January 23	Tate, W. 26th St., 200 words: suggests John Peale Bishop as a contributor.
January 24	Tate, W. 26th St., 1000 words.
January 27	Davidson, *Tennessean*, 200 words: "Stringfellow Barr has signified his readiness to join up."
February 2	Tate, W. 26th St., 140 words.
February 3	Tate, W. 26th St., 450 words: suggests changing title of symposium to " 'Articles of an Economic Reform of the Spirit,' or something like that"; says he has decided to move South.
February 9	Tate, W. 26th St., 690 words: plans to be in Tennessee by the middle of March.
February 17	Davidson, *Tennessean*, 650 words: all about symposium; Tate has argued they should publish articles and then assemble them in a book; Davidson wants to get the book ready first before any publication.
February 19	Tate, W. 26th St., 520 words: Harpers offering contract for the symposium, and Tate does not want to consult on the terms of the manifesto any more: "Unless we can get this book out next fall, I must be counted out of it for good."
February 20	Tate, W. 26th St., 150 words.
February 21	Davidson, *Tennessean*, 510 words.
February 25	Davidson, *Tennessean*, 320 words: letters in this sequence concern a misunderstanding: both Harpers and Macmillan have offered contracts; they finally decide on Harpers.
February 25	Davidson, Nashville, 630 words.
February 27	Tate, W. 26th St., 350 words.
June 9	Tate, Route 6, Clarksville, Tenn., 240 words.
July 5	Tate, Clarksville, 140 words: in this and several succeeding letters they discuss the essays the Agrarians are writing.
July 18	Tate, Clarksville, 60 words.
July 21	Davidson, *Tennessean*. 250

July 21	Tate, [Clarksville], 170 words: pressing call for a book from Tennessee State Library: "Such is the fate of a writer living the Good Life in a bookless Eden."	
July 22	Tate, Clarksville, 480 words.	
July 23	Davidson, *Tennessean*, 900 words.	
July 24	Tate, Clarksville, 410 words: still urging prepublication of some parts of book.	
[July 25]	Davidson, Vanderbilt English dept., 520 words: planning a trip to University of Virginia, a conference of southern writers.	
July 27	Tate, Clarksville, 400 words: Warren has just returned from England, but they can't find him to talk to him about touching up his essay; Tate still objecting to *I'll Take My Stand* as title.	
August 1	Tate, Clarksville, 150 words.	
[Mid-August]	Davidson, *Tennessean*, 1130 words: "I'd be quite content to have you title the book; and I don't think any other contributor would raise any substantial objection. . . . Why not, then, just go ahead and fix the damned thing?"	
[Late August]	Tate, [Clarksville], 170 words.	
[Late August]	Tate, [Clarksville], 180 words.	
September 3	Tate, [Clarksville].	252
September 5	Davidson, *Tennessean*.	253
September 7	Tate, Clarksville.	254
November 3	Tate, Clarksville, 220 words: suggests they try to get a syndicated column in several southern newspapers.	
December 9	Tate, [Clarksville], 450 words: now that the book is published Tate wants to ask for a Guggenheim grant to finance other parts of the program; Davidson (in a letter apparently lost) objects, preferring southern money if possible.	
December 13	Tate, Clarksville, 700 words; Tate answers objections.	

1931

1933

January 18	Tate, [Guaranty Trust], 60 words, with an unknown enclosure, addressed to General D. Davidson and signed A. Tate (Colonel).
January 23	Davidson, Marshallville. 281
February 5	Tate, Guaranty Trust, 1420 words: detailed criticism of Davidson's *Hound and Horn* essay, "Sectionalism in the United States," which Tate thinks is overwritten.
February 6	Davidson, Marshallville. 284
February 19	Davidson, Marshallville, 850 words: despondent over Tate's criticism. Tate liked the essay better later.
March 10	Tate, Trenton, 50 words: announces return from Europe.
March 14	Tate, Trenton, 330 words: Seward Collins, editor of the *Bookman*, has written to Davidson proposing to change the name of his magazine to *American Review* and make it in part an organ for Fugitive-Agrarian views; Tate enthusiastically in favor of the proposal; next several letters on this subject.
March 16	Davidson, Marshallville, 440 words.
April 5	Davidson, Marshallville, 510 words.
April 8	Tate, Trenton, 1170 words: sends Davidson report on a meeting of "the brethren" with Collins.
May 14	Tate, Trenton, 230 words.
May 16	Tate, Trenton, 240 words.
June 7	Davidson, Marshallville, 450 words: leaving June 20 on way to Bread Loaf by boat from Savannah, "the cheapest way."
August 2	Tate, Cornsilk Plantation, Guntersville, Alabama, 420 words: visiting Andrew Lytle, who is living on and operating a farm owned by his family. "Andrew and I have been talking over the possibility of another symposium for next spring."

1934

1935

1937

March 27	Davidson, [Central Ave.], 810 words: Tate has apparently said that 100,000 copies of Davidson's recent review of Odum's *Southern Regions* should be distributed. (Several of Tate's letters of this period are missing.)	
March 31	Davidson, [Central Ave.].	300
April 8	Davidson, [Central Ave.], 520 words: thanks Tate for advice on the content of *Attack on Leviathan*.	
May 26	Davidson, [Central Ave.].	303
May 28	Tate, Clarksville, 560 words: the *Southern Review, Virginia Quarterly Review* and *Sewanee Review* are sponsoring a dinner for Ransom in Nashville, "whether he goes or not to Ohio, to witness his great service to Southern literature."	
June 20	Davidson, [Central Ave.], 150 words: getting ready to drive to Bread Loaf for the summer.	
October 7	Tate, Benfolly, Clarksville, Tenn. (new letterhead).	306
October 7	Davidson, [Central Ave.].	306
October 9	Tate, Clarksville, 500 words: has just heard that "Carmichael had said he didn't know why John left, that he thought the Kenyon offer had been met."	
November 16	Davidson, [Central Ave.], 450 words: planning next volume of verse and asks advice.	

1938

January 3	Davidson, [Central Ave.].	308
March 2	Davidson, Vanderbilt.	309
March 10	Davidson, Vanderbilt.	311
March 16	Davidson, Vanderbilt.	313
March 24	Davidson, Vanderbilt, 620 words: working	

on *Lee in the Mountains* text; revising Battle of Franklin poem, which was not included and has never been published.

April 12   Tate, 112 Arden Place, Greensboro, N.C., 530 words: reports on his lecture at Chapel Hill; likes the people he met: Paul Green "is in the long run a good Carliny country boy. They are all as good Southerners as you will find anywhere."

April 19   Davidson, [Central Ave.], 730 words.

April 22   Davidson, [Central Ave.], 320 words: Houghton-Mifflin wants to cut out more modern parts of his *Tall Men* poems; asks Tate's advice; sends new poem, "Sanctuary," for criticism.

April 26   Tate, Arden Place.   315

May 1   Davidson, [Central Ave.].   316

May 4   Tate, Arden Place, 330 words: "The end is definitely in sight" for *The Fathers*; spending summer in Connecticut.

July 31   Tate, West Cornwall, Connecticut, 200 words; reading proof of his novel.

August 3   Davidson, Bread Loaf, 900 words: has promised Scribners to finish his freshman composition text by November 1; sends proofs of *Lee in the Mountains and Other Poems*: "You certainly will not like all the poems, but I covet your opinion anyhow."

August 7   Tate, West Cornwall, 210 words: "I'm afraid you won't like my novel."

October 3   Davidson, Central Ave.   317

October 6   Tate, Woman's College, Greensboro, N.C.   319

November 2 Tate, Woman's College, 170 words: asks Davidson if he would take headship of the English department at Woman's College.

November 12 Davidson, [Central Ave.], 1100 words: Davidson's reaction to the proposal is interested but doubtful.

November 15 Tate, Woman's College, 380 words: further description of position. "Together we could really accomplish something. . . . We will talk it all over Christmas."

1939

March 21   Tate, Woman's College, 350 words: "I heard the other day from Howard Baker that your lecture and reading at Harvard was the most successful of the year."

May 12   Tate, Woman's College.   319

May 24   Tate, Woman's College, 130 words.

May 29   Davidson, Vanderbilt, 180 words: will help unofficially with a projected poetry series by the University of North Carolina Press but does not want to be on a board of advisers.

May 29   Tate, [Arden Place], 150 words: likes Edward McGehee's poems, about which Davidson had asked him.

November 26   Davidson, 410 Fairfax Avenue (Davidson's residence in Nashville for the rest of his life), 1100 words: thinks highly of George Marion O'Donnell, a graduate student who is helping him with the creative writing class.

1940

February 23   Davidson, Vanderbilt.   320

July 12   Tate, [Princeton University, Princeton, N.J.].   324

July 14   Davidson, Bread Loaf, 170 words: looking forward to reunion.

August 21   Tate, [Princeton], 150 words.

1941

January 19   Davidson, Vanderbilt, 500 words: "reading in early Tennessee Valley history."

February 13	Davidson, Vanderbilt, 370 words: the Vanderbilt Board of Trust has just put into effect a retirement plan, and Herbert Sanborn is vigorously protesting his own retirement and the arbitrary manner in which the plan was adopted; many of Professor Sanborn's friends are joining in the protest, which is discussed in several letters following.
February 20	Davidson, Vanderbilt, 440 words.
February 23	Davidson, Vanderbilt, 340 words.
April 6	Davidson, Vanderbilt, 750 words.
April 20	Davidson, Fairfax Ave., 1100 words.
May 12	Davidson, Vanderbilt, 660 words.

1942

April 3	Davidson, Vanderbilt, 670 words: Princeton is planning a Fugitive exhibit and asks Davidson to send some manuscripts; family planning his daughter's approaching marriage to Eric Bell of Montgomery; says he has heard Tate going into U.S. Navy.
April 9	Davidson, Vanderbilt. 325
May 22	Davidson, Vanderbilt, 1000 words: likes Tate's "reminiscence of Fugitive days" in *Princeton University Library Chronicle*; more about Sanborn.
May 31	Davidson, Vanderbilt, 950 words: account of the dinner for Sanborn, with Davidson as toastmaster.
June 23	Davidson, Fairfax Ave., 730 words: not pleased with the progress of the Vanderbilt plan to establish a "Fugitive-Agrarian Collection": "I am slow as a Swede to realize that I have been insulted. But damned if I don't believe I have been, really!" Leaving for Bread Loaf.
September 9	Davidson, Fairfax Ave., 650 words: more

June 23   Davidson, Fairfax Ave., a fragment of 350 words: letters in this period concern chiefly details of the projected Vanderbilt library collection, his perusing of old Fugitive records, etc.

[Early July]   Davidson, [Fairfax Ave.], 60-word note accompanying his poem "Refugees."

July 9   Davidson, Fairfax Ave., 430 words; Civil War section of Tennessee River book completed.

July 15   Davidson, Fairfax Ave., 340 words.

July 23   Davidson, Fairfax Ave., 800 words: Mrs. Davidson is finishing work for her Ph.D. in classics at Vanderbilt.

September 1   Tate, Library of Congress, Washington, D.C., 280 words.

September 7   Davidson, Fairfax Ave., 360 words.

1944

January 16   Davidson, Fairfax Ave., 260 words: pleased at news Tate is going to Sewanee to teach and to edit the review.

January 30   Davidson, Fairfax Ave., 740 words: gives requested advice on *Sewanee Review*.

April 26   Davidson, Fairfax Ave., 360 words: having eye trouble and his work on Tennessee River history has stopped.

August 6   Davidson, Fairfax Ave., 470 words.

August 13   Davidson, Fairfax Ave., 250 words: looking forward to having daughter Mary with them while her husband Eric is in the navy.

September 17   Davidson, Fairfax Ave., 800 words: not able to do much because of eye trouble; looking forward to first issue of *Sewanee Review* under Tate's editorship.

October 15   Davidson, Fairfax Ave., 380 words: in answer to Tate's request for reviews, says that he

	can do some that would not require research.	
October 21	Davidson, Fairfax Ave., 240 words: planning to come to Sewanee for an overnight visit to talk about article for the review.	
November 2	Davidson, Fairfax Ave., 630 words.	
November 13	Davidson, Fairfax Ave., 210 words: talks about his article on the Negro question for the review.	
November 23	Davidson, Fairfax Ave., 250 words: James Frank has just died at seventy-eight.	

1945

February 1	Tate, [Sewanee], 250 words: this and the next three letters concern chiefly a disagreement about the length of Davidson's article for the review.	
February 2	Davidson, Fairfax Ave., 330 words.	
February 12	Davidson, Fairfax Ave., 640 words.	
April 4	Davidson, Fairfax Ave., 350 words.	
April 10	Davidson, Fairfax Ave.	342
June 26	Davidson, Fairfax Ave., 600 words: talks about the vacation they have just spent at Sewanee.	
July 13	Davidson, Fairfax Ave., 800 words.	
August 8	Davidson, Fairfax Ave., 750 words: planning another short vacation at Monteagle: "If I should bring Homer along, would you have time to read any Greek with me?"	
August 19	Davidson, Fairfax Ave., 240 words: Theresa back at work on Roman law; she has a Guggenheim fellowship.	
September 4	Davidson, Fairfax Ave., 300 words.	
September 7	Davidson, Fairfax Ave., 200 words.	
October 2	Davidson, Fairfax Ave.	343
October 3	Davidson, Fairfax Ave.	344

1948

1950

Motor Court, Alexandria, Va., 700 words: a thank you note for visit in Princeton; on their way to Marshallville, Georgia, where they will spend December with John Wade.

December 15   Davidson, Marshallville, 350 words: Wade has gout; Davidson has heard from Chancellor Branscomb, who was "deeply impressed" by the Fugitive symposium.

1951

January 26	Davidson, Fairfax Ave.	353
March 14	Davidson, Fairfax Ave., 720 words: reports on Ransom's recent lecture at Vanderbilt: "It was one of his finest appearances. . . . So the success of the autumn literary program was repeated in a very telling way."	
April 8	Davidson, Fairfax Ave., 400 words: discusses Tate's offer of a professorship at University of Minnesota.	
April 29	Tate, Nassau St., 180 words: has decided on Minnesota and leaves June 18.	
October 17	Davidson, Fairfax Ave., 220 words.	
October 27	Tate, 1801 University Ave., S.E., Minneapolis, Minn.	354

1952

February 3	Tate, University Ave., 120 words: invited to lecture at Bread Loaf July 1: "I know you were the prime mover. . . . We still like this strange arctic place!"	
March 8	Tate, University Ave.	356
March 19	Davidson, Fairfax Ave., 200 words: acknowledges poems and promises to comment later.	

1956

April 26   Tate, University of Minnesota, 140 words:
                    planning to come to the Fugitive reunion
                    in Nashville.

May 19   Tate, University of Minnesota, 130 words:
                    deeply affected by the reunion: "Since May
                    5th there have been moments when I felt
                    I would like to come back!"

May 22   Davidson, Fairfax Ave.   372

1957

January 12   Davidson, Fairfax Ave., 350 words: chat about
                    Louise Cowan's *The Fugitive Group* (now
                    in press), the Fugitive reunion transcript,
                    and John Bradbury's *The Fugitives* (which
                    they think very poor).

December 11   Davidson, Fairfax Ave., 350 words: delighted
                    Tate coming to Nashville for Christmas.

1958

January 7   Davidson, Fairfax Ave., 380-word fragment:
                    more about Fugitive transcript; rereading
                    Tate's *Stonewall Jackson* to review reprint:
                    "How could a non-professional historian of
                    28 years ever write this book?"

January 26   Davidson, Fairfax Ave., 640 words: wants
                    Tate to think about coming "back home":
                    "It would please me greatly to hand over
                    my turkey-feather fan to you! You always
                    had the better wrist!"

February 18   Davidson, Fairfax Ave., 510 words: reading
                    completed transcript of the Fugitive re-
                    union, he sends a three-page memorandum
                    to all participants; diffident about publi-

December 9	Davidson, Fairfax Ave., 690 words: looking over old letters to help Virginia Rock again: "I was again—and more than ever —caught, held enchanted, stunned by your prescience. . . . How slow the rest of us were to catch on to what you somehow already knew—poet and sage, impudent though you were!—at twenty one!"
December 16	Tate, 2019 Irving Ave. S., Minneapolis, 390 words; likes Louise Cowan's book; tells about his marriage to Isabella McCormick.
December 21	Davidson, Fairfax Ave., 640 words: mostly about Cowan and Rock.

1960

| January 14 | Davidson, Fairfax Ave., 340 words. |
| February 18 | Tate, [Irving Ave.], 40-word card on Rock requests. |

1961

January 9	Tate, Irving Ave., 150 words: answering a missing letter, suggests Arthur Mizener, Morton D. Zabel, or John Hall Wheelock for April 1962 symposium at Vanderbilt.
June 7	Davidson, Vanderbilt, 30-word note at bottom of announcement to contributors that the Torchbook edition of *I'll Take My Stand* will be out in the spring. "Theresa and I are reading Oedipus at Colonus."
October 3	Tate, Irving Ave., 40-word card: "Your beautiful book [*The Long Street*] is at my elbow, and I dip into it daily."
November 23	Tate, Irving Ave.	380
November 29	Davidson, Fairfax Ave.	381

1962

June 7	Tate, Irving Ave., 400 words.
June 7	Davidson, Fairfax Ave., 360 words; has just read Meiners's volume on Tate, *The Last Alternatives*: "Meiners is good, there's no doubt about it. I regret his totally unnecessary deference here and there to Vivienne Koch, to Bradbury, to Babette Deutsch (Good God!)."

1964

February 8	Davidson, Fairfax Ave., 440 words: asks Tate's advice on what to include in volume of poems.
February 18	Tate, Irving Ave., 400 words: thinks Scribners should publish his collected poems: "Haven't you made them piles of money with your American Composition and Rhetoric?"
February 24	Davidson, Fairfax Ave., 1550 words: difficulties in the Vanderbilt English department; details of death of John Wade, through the years one of his closest friends.
February 28	Davidson, Fairfax Ave., 50 words.
February 28	Tate, Irving Ave., 500 words: more about Davidson's volume and troubles at Vanderbilt.
March 7	Davidson, Fairfax Ave., 100 words.
March 14	Davidson, Fairfax Ave., 700 words: depressed reading his old poems for the new edition: like Radames "one moment bouncing, the next dolefully warbling 'in questa tomba!' "
March 17	Tate, [Irving Ave.], 30-word card.
March 17	Tate, Irving Ave., 230 words: "My letter to Charles Scribner was very strong."
March 27	Tate, [Irving Ave.], 50-word card: planning to come to Tennessee first of May.

April 4	Tate, Irving Ave., 210 words: on chairmanship.
April 8	Davidson, Fairfax Ave., 400 words: discussing possibility of getting Lytle to come to Vanderbilt.
May 1	Davidson, Fairfax Ave., 200 words: reports Scribners rejection of volume of poems.
May 3	Tate, [Irving Ave.], 80-word card advising sending ms to University of Minnesota Press.
May 6	Davidson, Fairfax Ave., 300 words: "look for you next Thursday, the 14th," in Nashville.
June 2	Davidson, Fairfax Ave., 330 words: moving everything from office before leaving for Bread Loaf, as he is now Emeritus.
August 31	Davidson, Bread Loaf, 360 words.
September 5	Tate, Wellfleet, Mass., 200 words: has just returned from six weeks in Italy; on his way to University of Kentucky, where he is teaching the fall term.
December 23	Davidson, Fairfax Ave., 460 words: has sent his ms poems to Minnesota; is writing a short study of the English lyric for Random House.

1965

January 30	Tate, Irving Ave., 190 words: the reader for Minnesota Press "sent back a glowing report."	
February 5	Davidson, Fairfax Ave., 390 words: Young and Inge working on a Twayne series book on Davidson and want Tate's permission to read the Princeton letters.	
February 9	Tate, Irving Ave.	395
February 11	Davidson, Fairfax Ave.	396
March 1	Davidson, Fairfax Ave., 240 words: "Theresa and I will probably go to Europe for two months in the fall."	

March 7	Davidson, Fairfax Ave., 800 words: details of edition of poems in this and several letters following.	
March 11	Tate, Irving Ave., 150 words.	
March 13	Davidson, Fairfax Ave., 270 words.	
March 16	Tate, Irving Ave., 160 words: will be in Nashville the 26th.	
April 15	Davidson, Fairfax Ave., 400 words: has been in Columbia, S.C., working on a five-volume edition of the letters of William Gilmore Simms, for which he has promised to write an introduction.	
April 23	Davidson, Fairfax Ave., 430 words: mostly about edition of poems again; Tate helping him with selections.	
April 30	Davidson, Fairfax Ave., 210 words: report on trip to Hampden-Sydney College, where he delivered three lectures, in part on Tate's poetry.	
May 8	Tate, Irving Ave., 70 words.	
May 15	Davidson, Fairfax Ave., 310 words: promises to send his lecture on Tate's poetry.	
May 29	Tate, University of Minnesota.	398
June 4	Davidson, Fairfax Ave.	398
August 2	Davidson, Bread Loaf, 800 words: more about John L. Stewart's book; itinerary in Germany, Italy, and Greece.	
August 14	Davidson, Bread Loaf, 480 words: Stewart's book again; reading galley on collected poems.	
August 31	Davidson, Bread Loaf, 240 words.	

1966

February 1	Davidson, Fairfax Ave.	400
February 20	Davidson, Fairfax Ave.	401
February 21	Davidson, Fairfax Ave., 60 words.	
March 1	Davidson, Fairfax Ave., 250 words: "[Your	

	letter about Wilson is] a sign that you should begin writing those reminiscences without delay."
March 31	Davidson, Fairfax Ave., 190 words: looking forward to Tate's semester at Vanderbilt next year.
April 12	Davidson, Fairfax Ave., 440 words: going to Farmville and Williamsburg, Virginia, for lectures.
October 2	Davidson, Bread Loaf. 402
October 17	Davidson, Bread Loaf, 420 words: congratulates Tate on marriage to Helen Heinz; likes Marion Montgomery's "demolishment of Stewart" in *Georgia Review*.
October 29	Davidson, Bread Loaf, 430 words: priming Tate on Vanderbilt affairs.

1967

January 8	Davidson, Fairfax Avenue, 350 words: pleased that Tate likes John Wade's selected essays which Davidson edited; looking forward to Tate's arrival for the second semester.

The Literary Correspondence of
Donald Davidson and Allen Tate

I

Years of *The Fugitive:* 1922-1925

The correspondence opens in 1922, the year in which the Fugitive *began publication. The first letter in this section is from Davidson to Tate in Valle Crucis, North Carolina. Tate was in his senior year at Vanderbilt but had to leave school to go to the mountains for his health. In his third letter Davidson suggests that they trade poems while Tate is away: "If one sends the other a poem, the obligation will be on the receiver to transmit a newly composed poem in turn. What do you say?" The record does not show Tate's answer, but since he immediately began to act on the suggestion, he apparently thought none was needed. At any rate, this "compact," as it was later referred to, is the most important single event in the whole correspondence, since it forced them to write poems whenever they could and since it carried the assumption that honest criticism would go along with the poems. Tate speaks of it two years later as "that covenant which was more significant than either of us could guess on the day of its almost casual making." Many of Davidson's letters in this section of the correspondence have apparently been lost, probably because Tate was moving around so much during the period. Still the letters that we do have are full enough so that, in addition to a good deal of their mutual criticism, we can follow the main parts of the narrative: Tate's changes of residence and the reasons for them, some of the politics of* Fugitive *publication, the beginning of Davidson's* Spyglass *page, Tate's experiences as a young free-lance writer in New York, Davidson's thoughts on the possibility of leaving the South. This part of the correspondence ends in December 1925, the date of the last issue of the* Fugitive; *and Tate anticipates*

the event in his next to last letter of the section: "I await the last Fu-
gitive with much pleasure—not because it's the last—but because it's
the Fugitive!"

1 / TLS

Nashville, Tenn.

17 June 1922

Dear Allen:

Qua cursum ventus![a] In my desolated apartment I sit and vegetate,
unable to turn an idea over, witless as an animal. The Fugitives[b] have
certainly fled—at least I seem to have no communication with them.
And why did you not tell me that you were going Thursday night. On
Wednesday night, after seeing my wife off, I waited until 9:30 for the
purpose of giving you a Godspeed. You didn't appear—I am certainly
sorry I missed you—I am trying to make up for it by being among the
first to write you a letter (I know I won't be *the first*, but we'll say the
first typewritten letter, probably.)

The Amulet came back from the Double-Dealer[c] today, with a
yellow, very yellow, rejection slip on which was scribbled the word
"Sorry!" Now I don't know what interpretation to put on that scribble.
Does it mean that the editor was *sorry* in the sense of *regretful*, or does
it mean that my poem was a *sorry* affair? I call that double-dealing of
a deadly sort! Well, well! That's all I can think to say. But, considering
that you people put such a complimentary valuation on The Amulet,
I shall have to rank all the rest of my output down pretty low if The
Amulet gets many more rejections.

Did you see in the Literary Review[d] where Walter Clyde Curry
got jumped on? The reviewer, in dealing with Talley's book of Negro
Folk-Rhymes,[e] devoted quite a bit of space to Curry's introduction and
seemed to disagree with him rather heartily. But it's great for the Doc
to get so much notice, even if it only makes him notorious.

Those are my morsels of news! Except perhaps that I have purchased T. S. Eliot and wondering very oddly whether my $1.25 was
well-spent. I'll take him with me among the Philistines this summer and
try the effect. Perhaps in a less hot place he will be easier to unravel.

I have written nothing. It is too hot,—96 yesterday, the paper says
—cooler today. Besides, I have too much banal business on hand,—trying to rent an apartment, for instance—that's killing to the Muse.

Write me *at once* as to how you like your new place with the interesting name. I am particularly anxious to know whether the name fits and what the name means, but more anxious just to hear from you.

I will be here until Wednesday morning. After that my address will be Camp Kawasawa, Lebanon, Tenn. (accent on the first -*wa*).[1]

Fugitively yours, Donald Davidson

1   *a*. Tate would have read this in Vergilian context: "*Fugimus . . . qua cursum ventus . . . vocabat*" (We flee whatever way the wind directs), *Aeneid*, 3:268–69. *b*. The masthead of the *Fugitive* for October 1922, the first issue to carry the names of the poets, listed as "Board of Editors": Walter Clyde Curry, Donald Davidson, James M. Frank, Sidney Mttron Hirsch, Stanley Johnson, Merrill Moore, John Crowe Ransom, Alec B. Stevenson, and Allen Tate. *In absentia:* William Yandell Elliott and William Frierson. *c*. A little magazine published in New Orleans (1921–26), of which John McClure was an associate editor. The poem mentioned was published in the *Fugitive* for October 1922. *d*. Book page of the *New York Evening Post*, conducted by Christopher Morley (Kenelm Digby), a friend of Ransom's at Oxford University. *e*. Thomas Washington Talley, comp., *Negro Folk Rhymes, Wise and Otherwise* (1922). *f*. A boy's camp twelve miles from Nashville.

2/ALS

Valle Crucis, N.C.
20 June 1922

Dear Don,

Your letter came yesterday evening. I saw it coming over the hill in the squeaky, ramshackle buggy, which probably for the last century has carried the solitary, but fatefully certain, delivery of mail every day. I was delighted to get your letter and through it get back in touch with reality once more, for I'm not much of a rustic; though only a few days I've been gone, I have missed the old familiar faces and the daily literary gossip. I hope you will write often, for I fear that the bucolic environs of Valle Crucis are too full of sadness and repose for an urbane spirit like mine. I must have words with my old world if I am to keep my wits sharp, for losing one's self in the soul of nature brings sleep to the mind and makes one feel like a god of the Golden Age, careless of men and time. Letters from you and the other Fugitives will make me halt and say, "About my brain," and realize that I must not become one with the identity of the hills or cavort with Undine in the mountain river running through this valley.

I am not the least surprised that the D.D. refused to take your poem, and I'll tell you why. I don't think that John McClure really controls the policy of the D.D. as to verse, although he is the only poet of any distinction on their staff. You will remember he liked my "Scholar" and had practically accepted it until Basil Thompson[a] countermanded the acceptance, on the ground, I suppose, that it was not modern enough in spirit and technique. You know how readily they took "Euthanasia" and "Parthenia" and, since I left, even "William Blake"! All these poems, with the possible exception of "Parthenia," are quite inferior to your "Amulet," but their tone is in unison with Eliot, Pound and Company; and so they took them. I hope you will not let your evaluation of your own work be influenced by the short-sightedness and, often, the ignorance of magazine editors. What! Another poet, another Adonais, murdered by the critics? I think you saw the letter in which Hart Crane remarked that the present-day poet must look like a banker and be like a butcher, and I am forced to agree with him; for it is a grim fight, as I see it at the outset, with no quarter on either side. Why don't you try some of the Eastern periodicals? They are more catholic in their tastes and less given to the literary ephemerae of the time. Try the *Reviewer*[b] in Richmond. However, they are very leisurely in replying; they've had my "Old Maid"[c] poem six weeks. And try the D.D. again. I worried the very soul out of them before they took anything.

I haven't written a line, except letters, since I left Nashville. Fishing, horseback-riding, and walking, to say nothing of sleeping and eating, my two favorite sports. My appetite would put Hrothgar and his crowd to the blush, and Gargantua would sigh in envious admiration. I feel like a new man already, and I'm damned if I believe I have тв. Bass and trout are as plentiful as mosquitoes are in Nashville, and squirrels infest the woods everywhere. It would be a great place for Walter Clyde to give vent to his primordial thirst for cruelty; he could gloat over the daily hecatomb of squirrels as did Nero over the carcasses of dead gladiators. Still, I would like to see the review of W. C.'s Preface.[d] Have you a copy? I'm sending in a subscription to the *L.R.*,[e] but of course I'll miss that number. Anyway, tell me in which issue the review is to be found. Well, I miss all the crowd, and wish we were together again. I hope to write some verse this week, and if I do, I'll send copies around to all of you. . . .

Well, this prattle must cease. I am sending this letter to your rural address. It will take at least three days for it to reach its destination, so isolated is Valle Crucis from even the outskirts of civilization. I shall write to Stanley*f* this week, and to John Crowe as soon as I have a poem to send him.

Write me any news at all. Every item of gossip, literary or personal, will be like ambrosia.

Ave atque Vale! Allen Tate

2   *a.* Thompson was also an associate editor of the *Double Dealer.*   *b.* A magazine published from 1921 to 1925. James Branch Cabell and Paul Green were on the editorial staff.   *c.* "To a Prodigal Old Maid," *Wave* (December 1922).   *d.* Walter Clyde Curry.   *e. Literary Review.*   *f.* Stanley Johnson.

3/ALS

Lebanon, Tenn.
25 June 1922

Dear Allen:

I haven't time today for a long letter, nor much to say that would make a long letter, but I do want to scribble a line. Your letter, coming to me in these—like your own—rural solitudes, brought me right up to the fact that I mustn't forget brain for brawn as you indicate with respect to your own experience. Your letter was so delightful, and so many things in it deserve lengthy answer, that I won't dare to trust myself to an undeservedly hasty disquisition, such as fast coming darkness would compel, but will just jot down a few obvious things.

I am actually working about two hours a day—spending the rest of the time in an orgy of tennis, swimming, etc. My sole literary labors are the composition of a photoplay which I have evolved and which (to me) seems wonderfully promising. I am pegging away at the first rough draft now—it's to be in South America, with the W. H. Hudson atmosphere.*a*

Congratulations on getting "Wm. Blake" accepted—that is, personally and in friendly role, I congratulate, not *artistically,* for I still cling to my original mulish idea there. (It's very stupid of me, really.) When are you going to send something to the *Dial?* M. Moore said J. C. Ransom had sent his "Armageddon" there. I have no other literary gossip, nor have I a copy of the Lit. Review. The number that knocked W.C.C. was probably of week before last,—i.e. the week ending June 17. Am reading Gogol's *Dead Souls,*—one of the great Russian humorous novels (literally), for Gogol is the Russian Dickens.

Remember Horace at the Sabine farm and indite a few modern

bucolics at once and send them here. Best wishes for your health and progress in poesy. Write often. I promise to be more lengthy in a few days.

D. Davidson

3   *a.* Davidson wrote scenarios for about a year but never sold one.

4/ALS

[Valle Crucis, N.C.]
28 June 1922

Dear Don,

You certainly must write me a longer letter next time. It is not quite fair to let me taste the cup, but not drink thereof. I have grave suspicions that the sketchiness of your letter was due to the influence of your study of the iniquitous scenario! Dollars, dollars! It is dreadful that we should have to compromise ourselves for dollars. Of course I don't do it; I lie with supine graciousness upon the doorsill and stroke the wolf's head! But up here in the mountain fastnesses all economic exigencies seem of little importance. Often I liken myself to the hero of *Heart of Darkness*, but I doubt whether nature in these regions has the same hatred of man as the Congo-jungles; I suppose nothing tragic will come out of my stay here. . . .

As I say, I know no gossip. However I have just received a letter from Gorham B. Munson, editorial director of *Secession,*[a] a magazine of the literary expatriates; you will find some notice of it, I believe, in the back pages of the May *Double-Dealer.* I don't know why an expatriate should come to write me a letter; I've never thought of myself as being Shelleyan or Byronic. However, it appears that Hart Crane has been talking to Munson about me; and so the latter wrote me a letter asking for a contribution to his magazine. The magazine is being printed in Vienna, says Munson, the third number being in type at present. He sent me a copy to Nashville, which is probably lost. Unfortunately, I have nothing to send him right now, at least nothing that would rub his neck-fur the right way; I hope to send him something very soon. As to *The Dial,* I have the same lugubrious story. And furthermore, I confess I haven't written a line since I arrived in the land god forgot. I'm glad to hear that John-a-Dreams has sent "Armageddon" to *The Dial;* I hope it gets accepted. However, I have my doubts, though that poem is the most likely one for the purposes of *The Dial.*

Have you heard from Ransom? I am going to write him at this sitting, despite my lack of a "masterpiece" for his inspection, as he suggested before I left. Where is Stanley? I haven't written him yet—procrastination, my dear Don. I hope you will not fall into the scenario game too deep to write some poetry; I confidently expect you to enclose a poem in your next letter.

Are you sending out any poems to bait the editors? I hope so. Persevere. I haven't heard from McClure since I got here, but I do hope he will print "Parthenia" in the July *D.D.*, and "William Blake"[b] also. I will grant you that "W.B." is not artistic; it merely *sold;* that's the best I can say for it myself.

I suppose that the qualms you revealed to me concerning your prospect of the summer have all been dispelled. Two hours of work a day! You should be ashamed of yourself. Of course I don't do any, but then I'm not pretending to. Tennis and swimming! I wish I were there with you; no tennis here.

Please send me any gossip that crosses your path. I'm hungry for it, as usual. You've simply got to write me all about yourself; tennis is no excuse.

As for my health, I feel better than I have felt in several years. Took a seven mile hike yesterday. Yet, my progress in poesy could be accelerated without losing much wind. Get your lazy bones out of the shade and write that letter to me.

Sincerely, Allen

4   *a.* Published from 1922 to 1925. Some of the writers connected with it became friends of Tate after he moved to New York: Munson, Malcolm Cowley, Hart Crane, Slater Brown, E. E. Cummings, and Kenneth Burke. *b.* Both poems were published in the *Double Dealer* (July 1922).

5/TLS

[Lebanon, Tenn.]
2 July [1922]

Dear Tate:

I wonder if I *can* write a long letter! During two years in the army I wrote so many letters and such lengthy ones that I swore afterwards I never would indulge again. Three years of teaching have been three years of sparse correspondence. So you mustn't expect much. I am quite out of practice. Whatever I write will be mere chatter.

You'll find a little poem, herein enclosed. Let me have a criticism of it (I can anticipate some of your probable remarks and hereby forestall them, as usual, by swearing that the poem is still in an imperfect state). The style in this poem, as you will notice, is perhaps some departure from what I have been using. I want to try out for a while, if I can, the idea of combining a certain satirical touch, or at least a certain hardness of texture, with an attempt at lyrical beauty. Do you think it is possible? I have two or three more poems in embryo state, which I will send you when I complete them, if I complete them.[a] I would like to propose to you that we hereby agree to exchange *new* poems constantly,—that is, if one sends the other a poem, the obligation will be on the receiver to transmit a newly composed poem in turn. What do you say?

I think it is splendid that you are getting in touch with the "Secession" outfit as with other literary people. You must by all means make immediate use of the opportunity to break into the ranks of the secessionists, whoever they are. I haven't seen a copy of "Secession," but have read about it in the D.D. and somewhere else. What about that last poem you wrote?—I forget the title right now—it seemed absolutely of the modern note. Perhaps you might consider sending them that—I refer to the poem-answer to the Teague assault![b] But better yet, write something new. Here's a suggestion for you. Write a series of poems on "Repression," with a Freudian basis, showing in dramatic way how various repressions transform themselves into ex-pressions in various sorts of people. Perhaps it's a perfectly worthless idea, but it is characteristic of a great poet that he makes immortalities out of anybody's perfectly worthless ideas.

I would like very much for you to read my photoplay and give me a criticism on that, too. But I am sending my only carbon copy of the first draft to my wife, and haven't the chance just now of whacking out a new copy. Perhaps I had better wait until my correspondence school masters give me a dressing down on it,—and then I'll get you to pull me out of the hole. You don't seem to be much interested in photoplays, anyway. Believe me, the work is interesting, but it's hard. I've got the most bang-up plot you ever heard of, with an impractical young hero falling in love with the daughter of his father's enemy (quite an old theme, that), and a revolutionary plot in South America (not à la Conrad, however), and a noble villain who is three parts good and only one part bad. If Dr. Curry should read it he would say (as I wrote him), "HOT DOG!" But so far I have really succeeded in convincing myself that I can write photoplays, and if I find that I can sell them, I'll probably concentrate on that work for a while, in order to get the spondulix to sustain my further literary activities.

I have no gossip! I am isolated from *all* cultural influences except yours and other letters, and the New Republic. And as to your letters, "the evolutions and convolutions" of your ego are just the things that I am interested in, and I hope you will put lots of them into your future letters, as successfully as you have in the two you have written. There now, you have some bouquets on the brain! !xxxx! ????

Stanley's address is 310 20th Ave. North. I have not heard from him since I arrived here. I had a short letter from Blair[c] today. He is going to send me "The World's Illusion."

Am mighty glad to know that you are feeling so well. And here's the inevitable question—how about smoking? I am using nothing but a pipe now, and I don't smoke that very much. This air and exercise, etc., are doing wonders for me. I was in a more run-down state than you would suspect when I came here.

I live in what is called the Midget Lodge, with a bunch of little yannigans of the age of eight to twelve. They always make an awful row, and they are making a particularly fearful racket at this moment. Gallivant's[d] brains won't register. Guess I'll quit for the evening.

Sincerely, Donald

5   *a*. During this summer Davidson wrote a number of poems related in subject and technique which Tate referred to as the Pan series. They included "Corymba," "Dryad," and "Naiad."   *b*. "Parson" Teague was an editorialist for the *Nashville Banner*.   *c*. Lawrence Blair, a member of the Vanderbilt English department. *d*. Robin Gallivant was Davidson's pen name in the first two numbers of the *Fugitive*. Tate's was Henry Feathertop.

6/ALS

[Valle Crucis, N.C.]
5 July 1922

Dear Don,

I am certainly not going to write you over the length of this sheet; you don't deserve it; a post-card in answering my letter! If you let the bulk of the envelope deceive you, I'm not to blame; it is the four enclosed poems making the letter so obese.

I've been looking for the promised poems, but none has arrived.

I'm growing cynical. You'd better rehabilitate my illusions before this week is over.

The poems I'm sending represent my output of three weeks. They've all been sent to the Editors of magazines indicated. I ought to get a verdict in a week or ten days. I'm a little sanguine over "Elegy for Eugenesis";[a] I believe Munson will take it for *Secession*. Of the others my hope is on the descending grade, beginning with "Lady Fabulous" and ending with "Bored to Choroesis." I'm sending you a July *D.D.* in this mail; both "Parthenia" and "W. B." appear. *Be sure to read the first editorial.* Pretty good for Feathertop, eh?

Mail me those poems, or we'll be friendly enemies, at best!

Always, Allen

6   a. "Elegy for Eugenesis," *Fugitive* (October 1922); "Bored to Choroesis," *Wave* (December 1922); "Lady Fabulous" was not published.

7/ALS

[Valle Crucis, N.C.]

5 July 1922

Dear Don,

This is simply to retract the abuse of this morning's note! Your letter and poem have just arrived.

As for the possibility of combining in poetry lyrical beauty and the satirical touch,—well, I hope it is possible, for that's what I've been striving for, mostly, all year; of course there are exceptions—"A Scholar"—and the Sappho poems—of some success. But in the main my aim has been just what you set forth as yours at present.

"Dryad" is certainly not your "biggest" poem, but to me it makes an especial appeal, for an obvious reason. I think, after some revising here and there, it is the poem for the *D.D.* As for criticisms; the fourth line, second stanza, is weak and heavy when, I believe, it should be light—but the suspense of the interrogation has good effect; and why not shift some accents in an otherwise telling line—the fourth, third stanza? These are my sole objections. I should like very much to be the author of the first, fourth and fifth stanzas. The poem has a restraint, *the* restraint proper to satire. And the "ecstasy" of the last stanza quite elevates it above mere analysis. Keep it up, Don, I'm with you in this new line. As an afterthought: why not consider another title? Some abstract word, satirical in itself? The title in such a poem can often do as much as a stanza, and always gives the mood or color. Isn't *dryad* a bit colorless?

Now, I want a criticism, detailed and ruthless, of the four poems I sent you this morning. This letter is being hastily written and can't be half so appreciative of Dryad as I feel. I can't tell you how pleased I am over your new departure. Whatever the limitations of us Moderns, we are certainly exploring, and giving voice to, a vast neglected field; others may do it better in years to come—but so much for the originators.

Yours hastily, Allen

8/TLS

Lebanon, Tenn.
8 July 1922

Dear Allen:

I am delighted that you like "Dryad." Your criticisms are very searching and accurate. I am making changes in the lines which you indicated, although I must admit that the last line, second stanza, has given me more agony than any other line I ever wrote, I believe. The difficulty is mainly in the paucity of rhymes for "counter," a word which I cannot give up. As to the title, unless you can propose a better one, I shall probably make no change, for so far I have not been able to devise anything else that suits me. Perhaps, if you think hard, you may be able to detect a certain irony in the use of "Dryad" as a title—at least, so I intended. I hope there will be a companion to this poem later,—perhaps about a Faun, such as is commonly to be found in places where you would least expect. I surely do thank you for your criticisms. Give me some more on "Ecclesiasticus," which I am enclosing. This is Ecclesiasticus Number One.[a] Number Two has been started, but not finished. I realize that "Eccles." is not much of a poem as it stands. Perhaps it may develop into something if Feathertop will jump on it strenuously enough.

Now as to your poems. I can't render the same service you have rendered me,—being quite incapable of criticisms of these poems. You are rapidly going far, far beyond me. I have read your four poems several times,—word by word, line by line—and I have not a single change to suggest. I like every single one of these four poems very much; you are getting to be ultra-modern with a terrifying speed and sureness. Since I have an idea of what you are trying to do in poetry, I am in a position to extend all sorts of congratulations on achieving mastery in the sphere you have nominated as your own. In my opinion "Elegy" is quite as good, as far as method and style go, as any of Eliot's stuff that I have read (of course, the conception is not so big in *extent* as in some of his longer poems). "Bored to Choroesis" is almost equally good, I think, although I must confess myself quite puzzled as to what the title means. "Lady Fabulous" is beautiful and delicate, quite unlike most of your poetry, it seems to me, in language and method. And I like "Non Omnis Moriar,"[b] without being able to explain either my liking or the meaning of the poem. Perhaps if you have a fault in any of the poems it is in the direction of obscurity. "Bored to Choroesis" is the most obscure of the four. What is the application of Polynesian? I don't see it, though I like the word. And what about the "ritual of her lips?" What does that mean? Am I utterly stupid in asking? I can criticize you more, however, for what you don't do than for what you do. There is not, I believe, enough lyrical beauty in the two larger poems. Perhaps, while you are holding these objects up to analysis and to some sarcasm, there ought also to be an element of pity (Stanley's phrase) which would naturally express itself in beauty of a regretful, poignant sort rather than in hard, chiselled language. There should be a little more warmth (Curry's phrase) here and there, though it is not to be demanded every-where in this type of poetry. Those two things, I think are the greatest things lacking in Eliot's poetry. If you can fuse them with the other elements of which you have so perfect a command, you will infinitely surpass him. I have always heard a lot of talk about objectivity in writ-ing, but I have never been able to conceive how in the world it can exist, the only objectivity I know being the quality of being able to criticize one's own work. Beyond that, to my mind, it can be only an exceedingly slight approximation. One must have an attitude toward his object; one must pity or scorn or accept; one cannot *simply* analyze. Perhaps I have merely a fool idea, however. Nobody ever agrees with me on such subjects as this.

But talking about your poetry leads me to the next subject, where again numerous congratulations spring up at once. The Double Dealer is certainly doing you proud; and I am glad to know they have the good sense to do so; it makes me think more highly of them. If you develop as you should—and as I think you will—by this time next year, I hope, we shall have read your poems in other magazines. I see no reason, for instance, why the magazines you specified should not accept any or all of the four poems you are sending off. They may not—well, it's their loss and somebody else's gain, for you will certainly get them printed eventually. "William Blake" and "Parthenia" look great in print. I, personally, like them much better than the other poems in the issue. Maybe it's prejudice, but I think my reaction would have been equally favorable to them had I never read anything of yours or known of you before.

I am very eager to see your next poems; send them on as soon as you write them. There's nothing so exciting to me as to see these things growing up into black and white out of the inascertainable Kosmos of brain. And there's nothing so stimulating to my own literary efforts as to have such high objects of emulation. Write, write, write!

I am enclosing a copy of a clipping from Barrie Payne's colyum in the Tennessean. John C. R. is evidently getting some nice puffs somewhere. Presently, I imagine and hope, he'll be able to get an English edition on foot, and I have a sneaking notion that it won't be long before he will be trying out another volume in the U.S.A.ᶜ What do you think?

Sorry I can't give more detailed criticism. Really, you have knocked me cold. I'm speechless! Send me one you think I will surely like, and probably I'll amaze you by jumping on it as I did on W. Blake.

Am preparing to send off my first photoplay.

I write very rotten letters, I know. No style what ever! That's both laziness and inaptitude.

Had something else I wanted to say, but I've forgotten it. Thanks both for the poems and the D.D. Did you want me to return the D.D.?

Sincerely, Donald

8 *a. Fugitive* (February–March 1923); later included with "Ecclesiasticus ii" in *An Outland Piper. b. Fugitive* (October 1922). *c.* Both *Grace after Meat* (London) and *Chills and Fever* (New York) were published in 1924.

9/ALS

Valle Crucis, N.C.
12 July 1922

Dear Don,

Your fine letter and the new poem came last night, but I was too tired to answer them then. I had just returned from an all-day trip to Grandfather Mountain, next to the highest east of the Rockies, only a few feet under six thousand. I walked fourteen miles in all, and if you think I stood it like a milk-sop, you are much mistaken. Today I'm feeling fine and could do another fourteen without stopping for water.

Please believe me when I say that I like "Ecclesiasticus" even better than "Dryad." However, I may fine you for getting on posted ground. Not that it is the least like mine in style or method; but simply that the same attitude is in evidence. I don't like the second line, fifth stanza, because of the inversion. You know inversions for the sake of rhyme are my pet *a*versions; and this brings up "counter" in Dryad. If you can't find a satisfactory rhyme, don't rhyme that line. That is the secret of my new technique! I can't urge you too much to study the best example of the principle, "Praise for an Urn," by Hart Crane in the June *Dial*. You will notice that Crane uses an unrhymed stanza as the norm, and breaks it only in the one case of two stanzas in *enjambement*, and then he rhymes the first and third line of the first stanza in an apparently casual manner, but really for the purpose of greater rigidity, knowing that eight unrhymed lines in irregular quick tetrameter won't hold together alone. I can't use it so freely as Crane, but there is something of the kind in "Elegy—"[a] where, in the fourth stanza, I break the norm by rhyming the first and third lines as a surprise, but I pull it together again by the echo-rhyme "Protoplasm," on the first stanza, in the fourth line. This same general scheme was used in the last century by the French poets, notably Laforgue, and it is not lacking in English even in Samson Agonistes. And so I implore you not to ruin a good poem with a bad rhyme. I agree that "counter" is too good to part with, and don't you let it go. Leave the whole stanza unrhymed, or why not rhyme that fourth line with one of the unrhymed words of the preceding stanza? As for Ecc. I have only one other criticism which is really not that at all. I believe that your last stanza should be somewhat more pointed. It is not obscure as it is; perhaps you might make your climax more startling without making it less subtle. But this is only a matter of preference. Send on Ecc. No. 2.

I am glad you like my poems, but I am really sorry that you were so flattering. The two lyrics, you may be interested to know, were rejected by Mencken, who said that "they suggested things done by John McClure"! Still, he wrote me a very cordial note asking me to send him the bulk of my verse as he would like to go through it all. I didn't care to compromise myself that way; so I wrote him I was all out, sending only the newly-written sonnet, Long Fingers, a copy of which I am sending to you also. I have been unable to find the McClure prototypes; editors must be very clever. I think you over-praise "Elegy for Eugenesis." I must confess, though, that I rather like it myself, even if

Munson did return it. I fear that I can't compete with those Secession birds for all my ultra-modernism. I am sending you the copy of SECES-SION which Munson sent me and his last letter, both of which I must ask you to return. I have just received another letter from Hart Crane, and he tells me that Sherwood Anderson is now visiting him after three years of correspondence without a meeting. Munson is there too. Just keep the copy of the D.D.

I plead guilty to your charge of obscurity.[b] But let me expound somewhat. I made the word from the Greek which as you will recall means to dance. The title translated is something like this: Bored with everything else, the flapper, being somehow deeply religious, reverts to the most primitive manifestation of the religious emotion—the dance. "Ritual of her lips" is meant to express my feeling that in her labial twistings there is something reminding one of the most primitive religious ceremonies—phallic worship, etc. Polynesian is put in to suggest this still further. I don't agree with Stanley about the element of pity, never did. I feel that Stanley is to a certain extent prostituted before unworthy principles of craftsmanship entirely outside the sphere of art. He knows that fiction must have an "appeal" to the "emotions"—whatever that means—and dogmatizes similarly for poetry. I suspect that terms like "warmth," "feeling," are pitfalls of language. I haven't heard from the DIAL about this poem. By the way, do you get "eluding fallopian diagnosis"? Rather obscene, but rather expressive of the physiological interpretation of emotion, in this case erotic emotion.

Merrill Moore sent me copies of the poems read at a recent meeting of the Fugitives. They are all pretty good, but Merrill is bad, Steve rotten, and Ransom very good indeed. He asked me to return them. He said that Bill Elliott read his Mt. Everest poem—twelve pages.

I must end this. It's too long now. Please write me right away and send the Ecc. No. 2. Glad to see John's recognition in the L.R.

Affectionately, Allen

9   a. "Elegy for Eugenesis."   b. In "Bored to Choroesis."

10/TLS

[Lebanon, Tenn.]
15 July 1922

Dear Allen:

Thank you for the copy of Secession, which I am herewith returning undigested, and I think I never can digest it. In my last letter I believe I congratulated you on your new connection with Munson. Now I am inclined to congratulate you that your "Elegy" escaped acceptance for Secession. However, I don't propose to go quite that far. It is really difficult for me to give an opinion on the magazine. It rather strikes me as hokum,—very smart, very sophisticated, but nevertheless hokum. If the fellows who are guilty of that magazine went to Europe in search of art, it seems pretty obvious to me that they didn't find any. The article on the Dial and the prose excerpt from Aragon's[a] novel appeal to me as being the only things worth while at all. The explanations and interpretations of the poems contained in the magazine are only less ludicrous than the poems themselves, which are absolutely pitiful. Honestly, if you can throw some light on them—point out even one little bit of art in them—I will be very much obliged. I'm open to conversion always, but I must confess that my feeling is that I never will want to be a poet if I ever have to write stuff like that contained in Secession. But here's a constructive suggestion which you can forward to Munson if you like. If they are going to be so darn sophisticated as they seem to want to be, why don't they print their French poems in the original instead of translating them? The audience they cater to certainly ought to be able to read French. Now what is your opinion of the magazine? Come across.

I do not agree with you on "Peripatetics."[b] It seems merely a mess of almost meaningless words. I do agree with you as to the first passage you indicate on page 10,—that is, as far as I understand the language. What in the dickens are "idea-emotions"? And I don't know what abstract literature is—I can't imagine such a thing,—nor "abstract" painting, any more than I can conceive of abstract water or sand. I differ with you on the next passage you mark. I do not believe there have ever been periods when "the grandly serious things are of less importance." The grandly serious things are always important enough, but the writers are not always grandly serious enough themselves to get up to them. The periods when the grandly serious things have given way to smaller things have invariably been periods of decadence, so far as I know literature. And whenever you talk about the "exhaustion" of any literary form you are simply challenging contradiction, it seems, for literature is full of instance where a form has lapsed temporarily only to reappear in a better dress.

I thank you exceedingly for your suggestions about rhyming. They are very appealing,—right in line with a sort of subconscious conviction I have always had. And I am now figuring on that stubborn line in

"Dryad,"—I believe I have the goods at last. Will let you know about that later. You are right, too, in your criticism of "Eccl. #1." I have already altered it somewhat and strengthened the last stanza. Perhaps I shall strengthen it still more. And here is "Eccl. #2," for you. See if you don't think it a hot one. I am quite aware that I am treading on your preserves,—but I have had this stuff in my system a long time, and it has got to come out. And just see how much I am learning from you. To tell the truth, I think it is easier to write this kind of thing than the other that I have been dealing in more, and for that reason I am a little inclined to doubt the artistic sincerity of those who affect this style, including you and myself both! Now what do you say?

"Long Fingers" is a very oddly beautiful poem, but not, I believe, up to the standard of the other four you sent me. The only criticisms I have are peccadillish, probably. The first quatrain is immensely good; the second is not so good. I rather object to the "little eyes." I must confess I don't get it. Here, perhaps, you yourself had an impression which you did not convey adequately (notice I don't say clearly,—not being, like Stanley, an absolute stickler for pat clarity). The sestet is fine, particularly the closing lines. So the most that I object to is "long fingers that would stare— With little eyes; and then those eyes would crawl— Along the table's edge." Mencken is both right and wrong in talking about McClure in connection with the poems you sent him. I must confess that I myself thought of McClure when I read them. But, to judge from what I have read of McClure, I should not say they were *characteristically* McClurian.

It strikes me that you can well afford to cultivate Mencken, if possible. I think his offer to you might have been due, as much as anything, to a possible intention to write you up at the next favorable opportunity. You ought to send him a goodly batch before long; I trust you left the door open, so that you can take advantage of his request later, when you feel more like it. You are going at a fine clip, and must keep on hammering out poems by the car-lot. Produce! Produce! etc.[c]

If Secession had accepted "Elegy" the magazine would have been much strengthened, and I would have a better opinion of it. What are you going to send them next? I take back nothing of what I said before about your poems. I did not over-praise them—they are too damn good for a sheet like Secession, I know.

Stanley writes that Harcourt and Brace turned down "The Cage." Later I will send you a copy of their comment, which Stanley transmitted. He is figuring on the Harper contest now.

No other news. Have written Ransom, as yet no answer.[d] Have sent off my photoplay. Boy, it's a whopper! Do you want to see a copy? I can send you one, I think, if you'll be careful with it and kind to it.

Otherwise, I'm not feeling good mentally—dispirited—out-of-sorts— don't like people—feel like crawling in my shell and staying there—misanthropic blues!! The Reviewer sent back "The Amulet," but that's not the reason of blueness. I'm used to rejections.

Secession—Ha!

Yours for more poems, Donald

I got "eluding fallopian diagnosis"—having been a student of anatomy, lo, these many years. Also I suspected the others. Gosh, you're a dirty poet!!!

10   *a.* Louis Aragon, a dadaist.   *b.* A prose-poem by Matthew Josephson in *Secession* (Spring 1922).   *c.* An allusion to *Carlyle's Past and Present,* which was often quoted by Edwin Mims, chairman of the Vanderbilt English department, who had taught both Davidson and Tate.   *d.* A constant complaint also with the other Fugitives.

11/TLS

[Valle Crucis, N.C.]
21 July 1922

Dear Don,

Somehow I felt there would be a little fur flying when you read Secession. I can see the back of your neck bristling now. In many ways I feel the same way, checked only by an opposite tendency to sympathize with almost anything revolutionary, sensible or not, and at the same time to derogate conservatism of all kinds. This accounts for my attitude of sympathy for Secession. I agree that what they print as poetry is not poetry, but I can't feel that it is exactly hokum; perhaps we shall have to get a new term by which to designate this latest *genre* of literature. The chief point of my disagreement with them is their effort to get away from the connotative and ideational (idea-emotions) in poetry. It may be done successfully in music, I suspect, where the symbols of expression are wholly subjective in their effect, but in poetry it seems to me that our given medium of language, by its very nature, cuts us off from a complete intellectualism. These fellows are simply trying to do in poetry what has been done in the last twenty years in painting and music— abstraction. I, too, have little idea of what an abstract emotion is; or perhaps I had better say there are no abstract emotions, only certain symbols standing remotely for an emotion. For instance, a picture of a piece of cheese might be entitled "Envy," the cheese symbolizing a lady's envy of her neighbor's fur coat simply because she was eating pimento sandwiches at the same luncheon where the said coat appeared! You see, it is quite abstruse. But have no fear, my dear Don, I shall not write a poem to a piece of cheese. I don't believe Munson meant by *periods* literary history—merely periods in one's emotional life; and looking at it that way, I agree with his point of view. I don't think that one poem is better than another at all because of bigness of theme, i.e., philosophy. It is all style, method, diction, and a hundred other things. If I write a poem to my left foot it would certainly take precedence over some other thing to man's immortal soul—provided I am a poet. It's the man who writes the poem and not the arbitrarily chosen theme. I, for one, have secretly considered your bringing Christ into the conclusion of "The Scop"[a] a blemish, not because I have anything in particular against Christ, or against the mooted question as to Christ's attitude towards art—in other places; but simply that your purpose is too obvious and you do it up too thoroughly, leaving too little to mere suggestion. The diction of that poem is impeccable, but I think it is inferior to a more casual and perhaps less perfect poem in structure—"Demon Brother,"[b] which, upon reflection, I have always considered your best poem. While your phraseology in "The Scop" and in all your work is devoid of the cliché, I can't help but think that there is also a cliché of structure, of the too complete structure characteristic of the great English poets. If Keats had only had our modern view—as Dryden said of Shakspere!—he wouldn't have slipped so fatally in the last line of the Ode on a Grecian Urn, despite what Matthew Arnold said of it. I believe this same view is held to a certain extent by John Ransom. I heard from Ransom the other day after a long wait. He said we had gained quite a foothold in England through Bill Elliott, and some other gossip. I suppose you have heard from him by this time.

I must be frank and say that Ecc. No. 2 is not nearly so good as No. 1. Your Jeremiads are all clever, but there are too many of them. I agree with you that this particular poem was more easily written than your others. It's not that this vein is easy to write in; it's simply that it's easy to kid yourself that you've done something when you haven't. I don't mean that this applies to Ecc. No. 2 necessarily, because I feel that you *have* done something there; only it isn't so good as "Dryad" or

Ecc. No. 1. I would recommend the suppression of the fifth and the
seventh stanzas both for structural and doctrinal reasons. "100%" is
good.ᶜ This poem has none of the dramatic qualities of its precursor; it
is controversial, "tired with all these," polemical; hence limited, like
John's "Armageddon." This sort of thing is rather easy, like "William
Blake," which, except for revisions, I wrote in about an hour. However,
I came near spending two days in the actual writing of "Elegy for
Eugenesis," and a lot more time for revising. There is really a great
difference. Creating is of course much harder than destroying. One
more thing: I must object to your sermon in the last line. We could take
that for granted.

I *am* rather glad that Munson returned the poem. I have sent it to
John McClure for the D.D. The other day I dispatched two new ones
to THE REVIEWER; they rejected "To a Prodigal Old Maid"—justly. In
"Long Fingers" I tried to expose the psychology of paranoia; the man
is sex-crazed, and has made his Lady's fingers a fetish; read it again in
this light, and perhaps "little eyes" will be more comprehensible. Menck-
en turned it down too, but wrote another cordial letter, leaving all
sorts of openings if I can only hit him right. Send me the next poem.
I should like very much to see your scenario just for the sake of seeing
it; I could give you no suggestions for better or worse.

When will your time be up at Kawasawa? Do you intend to return
to Nashville directly you get away? Tell me your plans.

Sincerely, Allen

P.S. Don't wait so damn long to write. Well, it seems long anyhow.
From your sketch, I advise you to illustrate your first volume.

11   *a.* Not published.   *b. Fugitive* (April 1922); reprinted as "An Outland Piper."
     c. Not published.

12/TLS

[Lebanon, Tenn.]
24 July 1922

Dear Allen:

Your letter was immense. I haven't opportunity at this present
moment to answer it in full, as I will tomorrow. I am so anxious to re-
deem myself, however, from your indictment of Eccl. 2, that I transmit

herewith in great haste a poem written today. I intended it to be somewhat in the tone of DRYAD, but I am afraid I have missed it slightly.
Criticize particularly the final stanza, which I am very doubtful about.

Your two poems to OENIA strike me in the right place.[a] I like To
OENIA IN WINTERTIME better than the other one, which I naturally
rebel at for structural reasons which you will easily deduce. The first
one has the peculiar half-cold, half-warm beauty that marks your very
best work, although it is loose in form. I cannot yet decide how much
this looseness contributes to its beauty. I wish I could get that elusive
something or other which you are getting into all your poems. I realize,
I believe, that it lies largely in restraint which I don't frequently attain,
and also in not saying the pat, obvious things, which I incline to too
much, as in the case of the "The Scop." Well, I'll keep working.

My wife evidently detests "Eccl. 2," and doesn't like Eccl. 1 and
DRYAD very much. She says of Eccl. 2, "Your idea is all right—but any
one with a grouch and a little wit could produce something as good as
that." There you are!

I am just about half-crazy today. Have just finished reading "The
World's Illusion," by Wasserman. Not since I read Green Mansions has
a book so taken hold of me. Of course the two are utterly unlike. Wasserman's book is a terrible book,—almost unbearable in the emotional
pain it causes the reader,—a most awful tragedy. Have you read it?

John Ransom has not written me. Had a letter from Blair a few
days ago. No news of interest.

For obvious reasons, I refrain from illustrating this poem which
I send now. Will write more tomorrow, if I get a chance, and discourse
more at length.

Donald

12   a. Tate published a five-poem sequence "The Progress of Oenia"; the two poems
referred to here are "In Wintertime" and "Vigil."

13/TLS

[Lebanon, Tenn.]
25 July 1922

Dear Allen:

Don't put me down as a conservative because of my attitude toward
Secession. But, although I am in most ways sympathetically inclined

toward things revolutionary, (I even used to try to write free verse) I can't give *absurdities* any sort of standing, revolutionary or otherwise. What you say about abstraction tickles me immensely,—that is, I rather agree with it. I think I have all along had a general idea as to what the Cubists, the Futurists, the Imagists, etc., were doing—yes, even these Dadaists to some extent—but I can't allow these pure abstractions in any art but music, and even there I am doubtful. Music, in spite of its seeming abstract-ness, is so exact, I might say, so mathematical, a thing, that it has a definiteness quite peculiar to itself,—a definiteness that the poems in the magazine Secession by no means attain. Do you get my idea? I believe that most of the poems of the Dadaists, for example, have no meaning whatever, nor impression, except to their authors, who probably had something in mind to convey, but other people do not get that thing, whatever it is. However, a piece by Debussy, besides the conception it had for the author, produces a definite impression on every hearer, which to be sure will vary as far as interpretation is concerned with the individual culture and experience of the person listening. So I could not admit an analogy between poetry and music, except in the minor matters of rhythm and tone-color. There is where the Free Verse set went wrong, with that vague talk of "cadence." Their idea of a musical cadence transferred into a form of language-art pleased me very much until I found out how very unsatisfactory it was— it simply could not be done with words as a medium.

As to the matter of theme, I still yield not one inch. I still say that, other things being equal, if one of two poems has a bigger theme than another that poem is a greater, though maybe not a better, poem. For example, your "Elegy" is a much greater poem than To Oenia in Wintertime, because its subject is incomparably a bigger matter in the cosmos. And do not accuse me of arbitrarily choosing a theme for "The Scop," for that is just what I did not do. I followed whither ideas led me, as the poem grew, and you yourself know that it did grow very gradually. However, I have never had a very high opinion of "The Scop." It inclines to be turgid. And I have not yet been able to improve its weak spots, although I have pondered on it a great deal.

Your explanation of "Long Fingers" is helpful, but still leaves me partially unsatisfied. Don't you think it is a weakness that the poem requires such an interpretation—or rather *so much* interpretation? "To Oenia in Winter-time" is a much superior poem, partly for that reason, so I think. Am I stupid? Remember that I am declaiming against obscurity in particular cases, not obscurity in general.

Now about "The World's Illusion." I am very anxious to know if you have read it. If you haven't you must put it on your list. This book is, I believe, realism at its best, yet I hesitate to call it realism. It uses in general the realistic, modern method, but it is so suffused with great passion, gnawing idealism, and dignity of utterance that it rises above the mere disillusioned static quality of most modern realistic novels. It has plenty of sex-stuff in it, enough or more than enough for even such a modern as yourself. The book tore me all to pieces—and I don't know that I shall recover soon.

It has made me think of two poems,—one John's "*Epitaph*,"ᵃ and the other my "Demon Brother." You remember that last line of Epitaph, "For he conquered,—and the envious Caesars took it as tragic!" That expresses the denouement of the book exactly, to my mind. And also the hero was one who heard strange pipes when he was young, and was filled with a burning desire to learn the secret which kept eluding him to the end. Well, little I can say does justice to the book.

You will see that "Priapus Younger"ᵇ is a sort of companion piece to "Dryad." I have two more in mind now, which I hope I can work out,—a "Naiad," and perhaps a "Silenus."ᶜ The conception I have for the "Naiad"ᵈ almost frightens me—I fear that I shall not be able to do it well. Take a sort of a plot like this. A young girl, very beautiful of body, is bathing in a river with a group of companions,—men and women in the tawdry attire which custom imposes. She slips away to a place beyond a bend of the river, strips off her bathing suit, and goes in the water alone. There something happens to her,—perhaps the river god drags her down, but perhaps she merely drowns. Anyway, a certain insight comes to her in those moments,—something very mystical and beautiful. Sounds poor in prose, doesn't it? By telling you of it I am binding myself to write it, and though I tremble at the undertaking, I am full of a great desire to write that poem and make it exceedingly beautiful.

That's about all there is to write this time. Please specify what it is that we have gained in the way of a foothold in England through Bill. Ransom has not written me a word.

My time here is up August 16. I will go back to Nashville then.

Sincerely, Donald

13   *a. Fugitive* (June 1922).   *b.* Not published.   *c.* Not published.   *d. Double Dealer* (November 1922).

14/TLS

Valle Crucis, N.C.

31 July 1922

Dear Don,

There are just two reasons why I am not going to write you a long letter today; in the first place, I have nothing of literary interest to say, having spent every day of the past ten fishing; and in the second, I'm too tired to say it decently should an idea come. I enjoyed your letter very much; it was a good one; and you must forgive this unmeet reply.

"Priapus the Younger" strikes me right. Isn't it exasperating? Just as I want to write you a deadly criticism of the poem, the copy of it suddenly disappears. All the others are here, but not Priapus. Of course some dreadful neurosis may be responsible for my misplacing it—Freud would say so—but you will hardly be able to conceive my unconscious in the role of tricking me when it comes to the poetry of sex! However, I like the poem very much; it seems to have more finish than "Dryad," but your diction here lacks the "oneness with reality" found in that poem; by which I mean that your thrusts are not so direct and, if I remember accurately, you use contrast to less advantage. Incongruity is a big technical *coup* in this sort of stuff—like "gingham counter" in a poem called Dryad—and you employ it too little in Priapus, I think. Of course there are many roads leading to Rome; you may do the stunt differently and better. Priapus has certainly less roughness than Dryad and is a better if not quite so pointed a poem. I suppose you see by this time that this kind of thing isn't so easily written as you thought at first. Poems like Armageddon, W. B., and Ecc. No. 2 are fairly easy; but if you will consider a second time a few poems of the master of the *genre*, T. S. Eliot, you will, I feel, be convinced of the consummate art possible in this direction. Take "La Figlia Che Piange" or "The Love-Song of J. Alfred Prufrock." The latter will show to fine advantage beside anything of Browning in the same *genre;* it is far more subtle than any poem of the kind by Browning I can recall just now. Eliot avoids the trivial and devious paths—one of R. B.'s sins—and goes straight to the real thing; this is of course his "modernity," and I am with him. There is no beating around the bush.

After a long delay, several copies of the now defunct LITTLE RE-VIEW[a] have come to me from Hart Crane. There is much interesting stuff in them. One number is called the "W. H. Hudson Number," which I shall send to you directly I have read it through. There are some fine critical essays on Hudson by Ford Madox Hueffer, John Rodker, and Ezra Pound. It seems that Hudson is in high favor with the Moderns. In these copies also are to be found a few episodes of the much-talked-of "Ulysses" by James Joyce. An issue of 1917 contains a poem by Hart Crane; evidently he was going strong when he was only seventeen. If you are interested in these numbers of the LITTLE REVIEW, I shall be glad to send them to you. They go back to the beginnings almost of the Modern Movement in America. By all means send me the New Republic.

I haven't read "The World's Illusion." I should like to, but I don't know where I can get it. Whose copy have you? If it is yours, please lend it to me. I do very little reading. I haven't written anything in a week. I need somebody like you for my "pedagogue."

Now let me brag on myself. In the Literary Supplement of the N.Y. Times for July 16 the contents of the D.D. were discussed under the head of Current Magazines. I was mentioned as "a new personality, from whose pen interesting things may be expected"! Think of it! But isn't it strange that they didn't recognize my superior virtues when they knocked the Fugitive so hard? However, you all would never accept my *good* stuff. As to SECESSION, something John McClure wrote me about them may be illuminating. He says that their revolt is quite worthwhile, but that they haven't a figure big enough to put it over; he calls them a gang of weak sisters. He agrees with me that Crane is the best of the lot. We will have out that discussion of the abstract sometime at close range. I am confident that I can prove to you that music, though quite exact, like mathematics, is nevertheless perfectly abstract —like mathematics again. I am going to try to write a review for the September D.D., following a suggestion made by J. M.[b] in his last letter. If you know of any good new books—not *too* heavy—give me the titles.

I haven't heard from John Ransom again. He's an elusive bird. Think I'll put a little salt on his tail. A remarkable letter came the other day from Jesse Wills. He writes beautiful prose. In my opinion he is the finest talent in Nashville, and I think that we can hardly afford to reckon without him. I wish something could be done to get him into our crowd. I'm doing all I can. Why don't you write him a letter and start a literary correspondence with him? He knows more contemporary literature than any of us, Ransom included, and maintains a happy balance between the old and the new. His address is 217 Louise Avenue. I wrote to Stanley about a week ago—haven't heard from him so far. Have you heard from the Hirsch-Frank contingent?

I suspected that this would grow into a letter. Please write to me sine mora. Your letters do me good.

                                                                Sincerely, Allen

14   *a.* Published in Chicago, New York, and Paris from 1914 to 1929.   *b.* John
     McClure.

15/TLS

                                                            [Lebanon, Tenn.]
                                                             4 August 1922
Dear Allen:
    Like you, I think I haven't much to say this time. But, as in your case, this is liable to run into a long letter before I know it.
    Observe herewith another poem, the NAIAD I was talking about. I am also sending another copy of PRIAPUS, in case you have not found the one I sent. Please turn in at once and give me a detailed criticism of both poems. Just as I feared, I was hardly equal to the task of writing NAIAD. It is a delightful subject, but an extremely difficult one, at least for me. I don't feel that I am through with the poem by any means.
    I applaud the mention of you in the N.Y. Times. It looks as if you are coming along faster even than you yourself expected this time last year, say. Well, I certainly do rejoice in these beginnings of recognition that are coming to you and hope they will continue and increase, yea, manifold. . . .
    I had a letter from Stanley today, enclosing three of his poems, of which I will send you copies as soon as I get a chance to copy them. Stanley announced a Fugitive meeting for Saturday night with Bill Elliott, at which Wm. Frierson would be present. Also Stanley said that the "enfant terrible," Merrill Moore, had written twenty poems in a week.
    I should like to see the copies of the LITTLE REVIEW. Tomorrow I will mail you two or three copies of the NEW REPUBLIC.
    That point of incongruity which you mention has long since struck me as something peculiarly characteristic of the moderns and in many cases a thing quite poetically effective. In PRIAPUS, however, I couldn't feel justified in striking that note; the poem seemed to me too intense a thing. The incongruous note might jar too hard. I would like to hear some more from you on such points as this. And you *must* send a new

poem next time. Weren't you complaining about my leaving a long space between letters—you seem to be the guilty party now. Come across.

Sincerely, Donald

16/TLS

Valle Crucis, N.C.
8 August 1922

Dear Don,

From this time on you can't accuse me of laziness in correspondence. Your letter and "Naiad" came only last night. I am not only answering it at the earliest moment, but I am sending two poems, both of which will arouse your prosodical wrath to white heat.

Instead of writing a criticism of Priapus and Naiad in this letter, I have made copies of them for myself and am returning the originals marked with what cavil and punctures I thought they deserve. As I have said before, I am with you in this new stuff, and as good as the things are you have already done in the new vein I can't help thinking you haven't yet got into your stride, for before very long you will knock me cold—as it is, these two last have stunned me.

I have only scattering thoughts on the element of incongruity. It seems to me that surprise is the touchstone of the best modern schools. As you have seen, this technical *coup* is superficially merely incoherence and irrelevance; but the cerebral processes underlying what appears to be a mere hodge-podge are the main thing. The ordinary free association which characterizes our relaxed mental states certainly has no logical continuity, and a poem which exposes such a state should not violate it. In "Eulogium"[a] I have endeavored to do this trick. I can't believe that people are ever wholly "lost" in the contemplation of a piece of art; there is always something on the "fringe of consciousness" to distract; "street-cars" is the symbol in this case. Of course there is much traditional gushing in English Poetry—Wordsworth, Shelley, Keats (Sonnet on Re-reading King Lear), but I can see no reason for my being a liar even to emulate my great predecessors. This is what I would call objectivity in poetry, and I don't feel that it takes away at all from the emotional appeal, but rather adds to it in that it strikes directly at reality rather than at the creation of an artificial, unreal emotional world. I can't understand how emotion is put into a poem

(Stanley); emotion, as I try to understand it psychologically, is not a real division of the mind, but only an aspect of it, inseparable from any mental state, however "intellectual" that state may seem. It is simply that we are often the dupes of language and that there is nothing in reality to correspond to some good words as they are loosely used.

I had a letter from Stanley last week, a very good one indeed, enclosing three poems which I suspect are the same you have. Frankly, I don't think Stanley is doing much now in verse, if these latest efforts are typical. I don't think these are so good as many he did last winter. Perhaps he is wrapped up in his novel. However, there is a casualness about his verse that I like, and I believe he could write some fine poetry if he would only concentrate on it for a time—long enough to form a poetic, because I don't feel that any man can write without a theory of some kind, and a metaphysical theory at that!

I heard from Blair yesterday, and he told me that a meeting of the Fugitives was scheduled to come off last Saturday night. I do wish Ransom would let us know what's going on; he's a hell of a letter-writer; I wrote him a note last night intimating as much. Blair says that Dorothy Bethurum[b] has John's manuscript of his new volume—he is evidently doing it up in a hurry. I'm writing to Jesse at this sitting asking him for permission to get "The World's Illusion" from you. I shall ask him to drop you a card to save time.

I have sent the Duchess[c] poems to the D.D. If they reject them, I shall forward them to the DIAL. I have a regular route—I don't know what the emotion of discouragement is like. I'm also enclosing a poem by Hart Crane, which he sent me recently. Read it closely, even though you differ with him about structure—as I do on some points—for it is a fine piece of work of its genre. He may not be what we call a Poet, but he's a brilliant devil just the same. Don't show it to anybody else.

The copies of the New Republic are here, and I am enjoying them very much—especially Aiken's review of Prescott's "The Poetic Mind," and several others. The Little Reviews will come to you in a few days.

You must have a new poem for the next letter, but if you don't please write right away.

Sincerely, Allen

16   *a.* Not published.   *b.* Dorothy Bethurum Loomis, Vanderbilt class of 1919. The Ransom manuscript referred to is that of his second volume of poems, *Chills and Fever* (1924).   *c.* "Horatian Epode to the Duchess of Malfi," *Fugitive* (October 1922). The other "Duchess" poem was never published.

17/TLS

[Lebanon, Tenn.]
12 August [1922]

Dear Allen:

I am compelled for this once to dash off a short letter and will ask you to pardon me for not getting in a longer one, in spite of my lack of time. The circumstances of the last two or three days have been entirely unfavorable to writing letters of the literary kind. I faithfully promise that I will get down to business and indite a long letter either tonight or tomorrow, together with a criticism of the Duchess poems. I'll say a brief word on that line now. I admire them in this respect, that I believe you are achieving your poetical objective and living up to your theory. I am inclined to think that EULOGIUM is as good as anything Eliot ever wrote,—in fact, it is so much like Eliot, it seems to me, that that very circumstance may be a point of criticism. Another impression I get is that "Collateral Deviation," etc., is an extremely strong poem, but lacks the beauty and restraint of EULOGIUM, which I like so well that I write its title in caps., leaving the proletarian quots. for the other.

I leave here either Tuesday or Wednesday. Address letters to 1027–16th Ave. South.

Adieu, then, for a little while. Observe another enclosed atrocity.[a]

Donald

17   a. This is "Corymba," which became one of Tate's favorites among Davidson's poems.

18/TL

[Lebanon, Tenn.]
13 August 1922

Dear Allen:

First, as to your very acute criticisms of Priapus and Naiad. I am certainly glad that the poems made such an impression upon you. I am foolish enough to flatter myself that I have in some respects at least made considerable improvement in poetic technique in what you call the "Pan" series. I find that I enjoy doing this sort of thing immensely—perhaps too well. It would be funny if one of these "hot shots," say Priapus or Naiad, should be accepted by some magazine. That would amuse me immensely, for certain personal reasons. Now, you have gotten pretty well acquainted with editors' tastes, I suppose. Where do you think these poems might be sent, if they should be sent anywhere? I have had a notion to send the whole batch to the D.D. What do you think of it?

Your observations as to the rhymes in the first stanza of Priapus and as to *sheen* and *keen* in Naiad are quite correct, I think, and I was already aware of those weaknesses, though I really intended the first stanza of Naiad to be somewhat subdued and perhaps conventional to a certain degree. However, I disagree with you as to the line "All ancient beauty sang upon the flood," and am inclined to keep it. I do not see how you are going to keep the spirit of wonder (if I may use a hackneyed phrase) out of a poem such as this, and the line was inserted to that end. Of course it is very far from physical realities, seemingly, yet it is not as far as you think, for that line is intended to be a statement of the vague and indefinite forces which impelled this modern girl to strip off her bathing suit and go into the river à la September Morn. From this standpoint the line is couched in a significant symbolic form, the atmosphere of the poem is lifted just that much more into the realm of the *ultra mundum*, and yet in the other passages there is sufficient of the reality which you crave,—at least sufficient to keep the poem from flying off into space. That's my argument in behalf of the line, poorly stated. As to combining the two stanzas six and seven, I'm afraid to try it, though your suggestion sounds good. And I refuse to identify the God with the rustic,—at least not patently,—for I do not wish to destroy a certain vague, hovering supernaturalism. Perhaps the rustic was the God. The poem as it stands does not prohibit that view. You see I have striven for a strange combination in Naiad,—that's why I told you I was almost afraid to tackle the writing of it—supernaturalism, sarcasm, realism, strong lyrical beauty, all based on a theme of protest,—I tried for those things, even if I didn't attain them.

I must ask you a question. What do you mean by putting "Et tu, Brute!" on the sheet.[a] I must have done something you didn't expect of me. If you will state it more precisely I should be obliged, for I am at present wondering what sort of arrangement I am going to make between my past methods and subjects and these new ones. What vein am I going to continue to prosecute? Tell me something.

Pardon me for speaking so much of myself first. Now for the two Duchess poems. They do not arouse my prosodical wrath, for I realize something of what you are aiming at, I believe. My general view of such loose forms as you use here is not of absolute rejection, as you might surmise. I recognize the fact that one may write something which may be called literary and even poetic in such forms. But I do not believe you can ever write poetry of the highest type in this medium. I still stick to the old idea of "memorableness." These forms are too difficult, too deliberately casual, to bring artistic pleasure except to a very small group of extremely sophisticated people. You may be writing for them,—are you?

I am considerably handicapped in my judgment of these poems by lack of acquaintance with this "Duchess" and Webster. I am reminded strongly of Eliot's poems (or poem) in which Webster is mentioned. But for reasons of ignorance I find myself floundering about and not quite understanding either your poems or Eliot's. You are getting to be too brilliant and intellectual for me, Allen,—I can't follow you, as you will note from my marginal criticisms. I rather like these poems, but I am inclined to put them below "Elegy," "Bored to Choroesis," "Lady Fabulous" and the two to Oenia,—do you think I am thereby crazy. I believe I said yesterday that EULOGIUM ranked high in my respect. Today I am not inclined to put it quite so high, but nevertheless consider it better than the other one with the Cubistic title. The conception of EULOGIUM is as big as anything you have ever conceived. The language is beautiful, chaste, and severely chiselled (if I may use such a non-plastic word), its only defect being, in my opinion, that your "infusorian and trilobite" are too technical. I had to use a dictionary. After all, your presaging is probably correct,—I think a little less loose a form would help the poem. It might make it a great poem. I fear that you are stepping a little too far in the direction of Secessionism and Eliotism and Dialism. At the same time, I am equally afraid of being dogmatic about anything artistic, and assure you that I am quite humble and ready to receive all manner of information and theorizing.

Your philosophical discussion of incongruity, etc., runs me a pretty hard chase. I am such a poor philosopher and psychologist that you have the advantage of me in terms. I don't quite get your idea of emotion. What is the difference between saying that emotion is a division of the mind and in nominating it an aspect of the mind. Of course I do not think you can *put* emotion into a poem, but what you put there does or does not stimulate emotions. According as you select your conceptions and clothe them in language plus the emotional experience of the person reading your poem, an emotional reaction will result. Well then, what about it, Where's the argument. Does a poem have to arouse emotion? I would say—yes, at least a minimum is necessary. But I am totally unable to conceive just how much should or should not be present in effect to make that a fine piece of art. I am floundering in depths of speculation and will stop. I suppose this sounds like gibberish to you, you blooming intellectual.

Have not received the Little Review yet. Hope it comes on soon. I go to Nashville Tuesday afternoon.

Sincerely, Don

18   *a.* Tate is twitting Davidson for experimenting with his own kind of diction.

19/TLS
Valle Crucis, N.C.
17 August 1922

Dear Don,

Hail to thee, blithe spirit! CORYMBA is the prize poem. I beg of you to bring the Pan series to a close with this poem. It is the finest you've written, and the best you will write in a long time, or I'm much mistaken. A poem like CORYMBA isn't written every day. I salute you. If the D.D. doesn't take this poem, I'll write McClure that he is a damn fool. Send him the whole series. Why not give them a group-title?

I haven't time for a long letter. I'm four days behind on my correspondence now, and must write many short notes in order to catch up in one day. I have received a long letter from Stanley giving me hell from beginning to end. I'm glad he hasn't seen the Duchess; I shouldn't have survived his indignation. I'm just coming to as it is. He's down on us Moderns—you are now one of them—and is nauseated at our supposed liking for guts, slime, livers. If what he alleges were true, we should deserve his wrath, but I fear he misses the point. His letter was quite stimulating, and in my reply I shall do what I can to correct his false notions of the Moderns. He objects to our diction mainly and not without some reason. I suspect—may I say it?—that he is in the same difficulty as you are as regards the difference between intellect and emotion in art. He hasn't needed to consider this problem seriously in writing fiction, but it's a snag in poetry. However, if you can produce another CORYMBA, I should advise *you* not to worry about the question. Now I don't mean to imply that I have solved the question; I have a theory, not entirely original, and I work on that theory as a basis. Stanley alludes to McDougall for a discussion of emotion—certainly a blind

CORYMBA

Corymba has bound no snood
Upon her yellow hair.
But better so, no doubt,
Since the pale youths look elsewhere
At sleek curves and proud glitter
And flesh powdered and bare.

She has gone with a jaded youth
To a sudatorium.
The sweating there is of movement
To a cacophonic drum.
The bodies flex, the arms twine
In rhythmic delirium.

Her limbs seem delicate
For labors such as these.
Does her plasm breed toxin
From phonic ecstasies?
At the small hours, the gaudy hours
She projects new mysteries.

Who shall say in mockery?
"Cheeks were too hotly flushed!"
Or "That knee still touched too closely
After the drum was hushed!"
Over her eyes certain
And trance-like beauty has brushed.

She has heard a silvery jangle
From the slight harps of the moon,
The maddening sistrum shaken
For Isis' warm commune,
Seen arms lifted, bosoms bared,
In far other rig-a-doon,
Has of old spun twinkling feet
In a certain sacred way
Down the dark aisle where Shiva
Nods at his trembling ballet
Till the gongs peal, and the priests come
And Shiva breathes on clay.

Corymba has not rejected
Familiarities.
It is past noon. She dozes.
With half drawn-up knees,
Thinking of new stockings
And other such verities.

                    Robin Gallivant

Typescript of "Corymba" with Tate's comments and Davidson's replies.

alley for literary purposes. I have found the best statement of the problem of the artist in "The Sacred Wood," by the demi-god T. S. Eliot, a book of criticism which you must read forthwith. Eliot is a greater critic than he is a poet; the professors accuse the modern poets of superficiality; well, Eliot is the most learned man writing now and the least musty. You *must* read this volume. If you can't find it in Nashville, I will send it to you. In an essay on "Hamlet and his Problems" he states (p. 92) exactly what is the meaning of objectivity in art; you will be interested in this.ᵃ

As to the Duchess, I do wish you wouldn't profess so darned much ignorance. I'm returning the poem with my interpretation written in— a sad exigency! I'm glad you pointed out the inaccuracy in line three; trilobites *didn't* have molars; it's changed to dinosaur. In stanza four my mathematical figure means that whereas my native pessimism was infinite and without curve, that pessimism is doubled into two infinities after reading the great tragic struggle of the Duchess of Malfi as presented by the genius of Webster. I fear you exaggerate my borrowings from Eliot in this poem. The connection between the two poems is, briefly, this: Today I read the "Duchess of Malfi" with the impersonal aesthetic enjoyment stimulated only by the finest art (for D of M is a great play, better than many of Shakspere's) and then go to bed in the detached attitude of the appreciative critic. But tomorrow (Deviation) I take a walk and the ecstasy by that time is degraded to an assimilation with my own emotional experience, past and present, which is of course irrelevant to the pleasure proper derivative from art. The death of the Duchess finds a parallel in my own life. In my train of free association the two events, her death and the loss of a beautiful woman, are inextricably mixed, and the phenomena of the immediate external world— popcorn, a pile of bricks, worms—force themselves on the fringe of consciousness for the greater impurity (and realism) of my intuition. This second poem, incidentally, presents the way in which the inferior mind (the only way) appreciates art: the emotional content of the poem appeals only because it strikes a note in the personal experience of the reader; thus it is the content and not the art which is important to such a mind. This process is also characteristic of every mind in relaxation; and so the critic of the evening before becomes uncritical. My thesis, then, was this: (1) the exposition of the impersonal enjoyment of a piece of art, (2) and the subsequent identification and confusion of the art-content, the ecstasy having subsided, with mere personal experience. Now the question is, Have I done what I set out to do? Frankly,

I think not. These poems will undergo much revision. A theme so abstract (note!) as this is hard to handle, and it will take a long time to bring about the proper correlation between the emotion and the symbols expressing it.

I suppose you've seen most of the Fugitives ere this. Tell them all hello. Haven't heard from Ransom again. I will send the Little Reviews in the morning. By the way, I notice that spumy sheet has resumed activity. Look out for squalls! Let me hear from you right away. If you send me another CORYMBA, I'll fall dead of admiration. Don, I think you are a genius, and I say it without gushing. You know it isn't my habit to praise when I don't mean it.

Affectionately, Allen

P.S. Note on "memorableness." I should think that the ideal poem, which has not yet been written, ought to contain no single line more memorable than any other line. A phrase from a Cesar Franck symphony is perfectly meaningless outside its context; and a poem should be likewise. The whole poem should not be utterly dependent upon the presence of any single word, and each word should be meaningless without the rest of the poem; so that the reader would enjoy the piece as a unity or not at all. My chief quarrel with the English tradition is over the question of diffuseness. This is scattering and hastily written, but I think I can make my point.

19   a. Eliot's famous statement regarding the objective correlative.

20/TL

[Nashville, Tenn.]
23 August 1922

Dear Allen:

Here I am, right in Doc. Curry's old room,ª installed for the rest of the summer. As I have nothing else to do, I plan to do an enormous amount of writing, if I can only get started. So far I have been too indolent for anything. Yesterday, however, I did summon up strength enough to polish up DRYAD, PRIAPUS, NAIAD, and CORYMBA, and dispatch them to the D.D. I am really curious to know what they may think of them. I hope for the best, but one can certainly never tell about magazine editors. If these poems are published, I fear my numerous Puritanical friends are going to assail me as a pornographic wretch.

And what will Dr. Mims say to these poems?—GEE WHIZ. Do you suppose I'll be called on the carpet?

Your fulsome chant of praise on CORYMBA certainly makes me glad all over, though I rather feel that you are piling on more than the traffic will bear. Nevertheless, I appreciate your plaudits all the more because I know you are a hard-boiled rascal on criticism, and because I am quite sure that you are better posted on the particular subject-matter and technique that I have recently essayed than any others of our Fugitive group. Likewise, you have given me keener and more helpful criticisms than anybody that ever read my poems, and your ideas and theories have wonderfully quickened and leavened my rather stodgy mind. So I am greatly indebted to you. You will never find me unappreciative,—never, Jamais de ma vie!

Your explanation of the DUCHESS poems helped me enormously. I must apologize for my stupidity, but you'll find it an all-too constant trait, I fear. I'll say this for the DUCHESS poems (as for all of your more difficult recent ones)—I get a growing appreciation and liking for them, the more I read them. I see your idea in the DUCHESS poems quite clearly now, and I think it a very fine theme for poetic treatment. And the more I read them the more I am convinced that you have attained your ends mighty well on the whole, though I still stick to my original points about their extreme looseness and the over-use of technical (or extremely unusual and almost pedantic) expressions. But perhaps looseness is the only form you could use here. We had a great debate at the Fugitive meeting Saturday night,—the old controversy of the Moderns vs. Ancients—in which our guest, a Dr. Lockhardt[b] of Kenyon College, Ohio, declaimed against Modernism, supported mainly by Stanley, and opposed by Ransom and others. I took little part, for I am hesitant to crystallize my present vague and nebulous ideas into comments on theories of poetry, only ranging myself against the Secession bunch, the Dadaists, and the Dialists (of the extreme type). The debate lasted until past two o'clock, but left the combatants apparently unexhausted and mutually unconvinced. I read your DUCHESS poems, with an embarrassed smile, I must confess, when I came to the passages that floored me. (You had a poor reader; I really didn't read them well and felt very repentant. You would have been disgusted with my reading.) But nevertheless, they seemed to make a good impression, on the whole. They were more talked about than CORYMBA. The general opinion, much to my surprise, seemed to favor the second of your poems as the better one of the pair,—all except Sidney and myself, who favored I. But they did not render any criticisms worth while, either for you, or for me on CORYMBA,—except the point about the trilobite. I had not then received your letter. In fact, although we had a good meeting, the Fugitives didn't seem to get up much enthusiasm over any poem read. So you and I are in the same boat there. I fear that we are going to be looked on as the 'enfants terribles," the Turrible Two, in the Fugitive club now.

William Frierson gave a criticism of the poems read at the previous meeting none of which I was familiar with except Stanley's group, and my own, which I had mailed in. The Fugitives seem to like ECCLESIAS-TICUS best among mine. Really, I believe they are a little bit surprised at me, but they were complimentary on the whole, and think I have developed, apparently.

Ransom read a two and a half page poem of an extremely philosophic nature which sounded very good, but which I couldn't really form an opinion of, as he didn't supply carbons.ᶜ Steve's "Meditation"ᵈ I thought very good, and also Stanley's new venture, which ought to be a fine poem after some revision. It took well. Bill Elliott read a very short one about a tumble-bug laying the foundations of the Egyptian pyramids. It was terse and epigrammatic, and apparently excellent, though I didn't see a copy of it, either. Mr. Frank's and Sidney's were both too esoteric for me. I hear, however, that Sidney has written recently some very good stuff, none of which I have yet seen. Merrill's two poems were pretty fair, but too hastily done, I think. He needs to cultivate restraint. The rush of language carries him away. The Fugitives jumped all over one of his poems particularly. William Frierson read a sort of prose fantasy on Oxford which we all liked very much. He also read a paper on certain theories of poetry which was too much for me to absorb from an oral reading. I am going to get it and digest it, for he's a man of valuable ideas. I got too sleepy to be a good listener. Not used to being up so late. And that's about all I have to report of the Fugitive meeting. There is to be another Monday night. I hope you'll have a new poem here by then, so that I can read it. By the way, I wonder if your two poems to OENIA have been read there, and your others? Some of them have, I know. I'm determined to make a better reader for you next time. And while I remember it, I don't believe anybody at the last meeting showed any "prosodical wrath" in regard to the DUCHESS poems.

I don't see that the theme of the Duchess poems is abstract. Are feelings, state of mind, or attitudes, or experience (even art-experiences), ecstasy, etc., abstractions? Not to my way of thinking.

By "memorableness" I do not mean cheap epigrammaticism or staring poetical coups of language, but happiness and ultimateness of expression. Your idea of the perfect poem, I fear, applies only to the very restricted type of lyrical poem, that these Moderns (of whom you say I am one) are cultivating. I believe you are bound to have some looseness in a long poem, and I do not mean by that a long narrative or epic poem. The longer poems of Eliot strike me as weak because of the presence of the qualities you applaud. Maybe it's a cheap ideal, but I still can't help but think that it doesn't hurt anything for lines to be worth quoting (Pardon an interruption. A large kissam cock-roach is about to drag off my evening paper to his den, a thing which i won't permit even if he is bigger than me). Now what are you going to say to me? Another evil trait you are going to have to cure me of. Nurse, bring on the anaesthetic while the physician gets his instruments ready.

Since I have been here I have read W. L. George's A Bed of Roses, one of the best stories of a harlot I ever read, considerable Freud (thus alleviating my painful ignorance), and much stuff in the current Century; Double Dealer, Smart Set, and Shadow Land.ᵉ I can send you the first and last named if you want them,—I suppose you get the D.D., do you?

I'm sorry not to have another Corymba to send you. I have subjects in mind equally as good, but cannot stir a poetical finger at present. However, I'll have to produce something before Monday night, or lose my self-respect. I always work better when I am under obligation to produce something.

I am very much intent on writing another scenario now. My first one was sent back with a pretty good criticism. I'll send it on to you some time now, though you won't be much interested in it, I fear. I have got to write successful photoplays, for that's the only way I can figure out as a money-making scheme.

Come across with a new poem pretty soon, and I'll promise to do the same. Is there anything I can do for you in Nashville?

Affectionately yours, [Donald]

P.S. Had a long splashy letter from Curry. He has sailed by now. His talk was mostly about girls, and the good time he has had recently.

I wonder what he is going to do when those wild creatures in Paris, etc., grab his sleeve.

20 *a.* Mrs. Davidson was in Oberlin, Ohio, with her family for the summer, and Davidson was staying in Kissam Hall, where most of the men students and some of the unmarried faculty lived. There were no women's dormitories. Actually most of the suites in Kissam were designed for two students and included a study between two small bedrooms. Curry had converted one of the bedrooms in his suite to a bathroom, and "Old Room 19," as it was called, was inherited by a whole series of younger members of the English department and graduate students. *b.* Lacey Lockert. *c.* Apparently never published. *d.* Appeared as "Meuse Heights" in the *Fugitive* (October 1922). *e. The Smart Set* (1912–1923) was particularly important for modern letters under the editorship of George Jean Nathan and H. L. Mencken. *Shadow Land* was published from 1919 to 1923, later becoming *Classic* and *Motion Picture Classic.*

21/TL

[Nashville, Tenn.]
29 August 1922

Dear Allen:

Merrill says that you are coming to Nashville about Sept. 6. Everybody will be tremendously glad to see you and none gladder than I. The Fugitives were saying last night that they must have a grand meeting while you are here and so you must count on spending a portion of your time in that way while you are here. The meeting will be either Wednesday or Thursday night, whichever suits you better. I believe Merrill was appointed to write you and find out, so that things can be arranged accordingly. I shall certainly be delighted to bid you a welcome to the scholarly but lonely precincts of classic Room 19 and shall hope to engage you in many profound literary discussions for such time as you may be able to spend with me. . . . Be sure to bring numerous poems with you and if you can spare that volume of Eliot's criticism, I should be mightily interested in seeing it.

The Fugitives had quite a good meeting last night, which wound up in a duel to the death between most of the Fugitives on one hand and our guest, Dr. Lockhart on the other, who has been attacking us for being sloppy technicians, obscurantists, and too modernly modern. He likes us, but he doesn't know much about modern poetry and is hence very bitter against it. We certainly dealt him some wallops last night that would have done your heart good. I don't think the Fugitives are quite a unit on the question of modernism. You, Ransom, Bill

Elliott, Moore, and myself are certainly more or less ranged against Stanley, Stevenson, Hirsch, and Frank. I think the division is really a good thing.

Ransom read three excellent poems,—about the best of the evening, I thought. Stanley wrote what he called "his idea of *your* idea of a poem," and I must say he made a tremendous impression.[a] I suppose Merrill is sending you copies of the evening's productions, and you can see for yourself what was read. Bill Elliott read a very clever paper on modern poetic theories, and we all argued along those lines until it got so late that I had to leave and go to bed. I don't know what the final conclusions were. It was decided to bring out another issue of the Fugitive during the last week in September, dating the issue October. All the poets are to hand their contribs. to Ransom, who is going to make up the issue and submit his choices to the club for ratification. I think that is by far the best plan of all, don't you. Now I am going to take the liberty to hand in some of your things with mine, and if you have any objections or any new poems to submit, hurry up and send them along. Ransom ought to have a report ready by next meeting, when you can be here and look after your own interests. I believe you have sold the following, haven't you: Bored to Choroesis, the Prodigal Old Maid. Any others sold? I am going to turn in the rest of yours that I have, so that Ransom can make at least tentative selections, and have a final judgment and pow-wow with you when you arrive. Probably I'm taking a great liberty, but I am very anxious to see some of your latest stuff adorning The Fugitive,—we can't afford to be without it (nor can you), and I hope you haven't sold *all* of these poems somewhere else. If you have, you'll just have to get down to it and write some more right quick. This issue will be, I am sure, the strongest we have put out, by several times. I am sure that I have some better stuff,—so have you, so has Stanley, Ransom, etc., Sidney's Nebrismus is the best thing he has done. I don't think that either Mr. Frank or Dr. Curry will be represented this time, certainly not Curry, as he has contributed nothing for a long time. Merrill's stuff ought to be an improvement too. I haven't seen it yet.

Haven't heard from the D.D. as yet? By the way, for a group title,[b] what would you think of "Born in Arcadia"?

I am looking over Ransom's manuscript now. It makes an extremely impressive showing, I think. He has certainly written a lot of good stuff this summer. Holt and Co. turned down the manuscript,[c] with some remarks about the poor state of the poetic market. However,

John seems about half glad they didn't take it, as it appears from Graves' letter (which I saw) that Ransom has almost an absolute certainty of being published in England. In that case he can make the prescribed gesture with the thumb to Henry Holt and Co.

Have about finished the Little Reviews. Shall I keep them till you come through or send them? I haven't time to give a detailed opinion now, but I'll say this: the poetry is uniformly punk; the prose by Ben Hecht and S. Anderson is extremely good, though not great; the chapters from Ulysses are unique and interesting, but I am not inclined to accept them as art—My God, think of reading 782 pages of that blooming stuff. The reviews of Hudson and Eliot were extremely good. Why in the devil is it that these ultra-modern fellows think so much of Hudson (also of Conrad)? It seems that they would condemn him lock, stock, and barrel, if they adhered to their tenets. Hudson is a wonderful writer, but there is absolutely not a shred of ultra-modernism in him.

Voyez another poem? I am in a slump now. Write me information and instructions. I surely am looking forward to seeing you.

> Yours for the Moderns (excluding
> the Dada's, the Vers Librists, the
> Secessionists, and other ultra-ultra's). [Don]

P.S. Went to see Ransom Sunday. He thinks, as I do, that you are doing remarkable things, he likes about the same poems of yours that I do, and he also advises against going to extreme lengths in modernism.

21   *a.* This might be the burlesque poem which Johnson published in *The Professor* (1925).   *b.* For Davidson's Pan poems.   *c.* Of *Chills and Fever.*

22 / ALS

Valle Crucis, N.C.

31 August [1922]

Dear Don,

Just a note, so you'll get word from me by Saturday.

I shall probably be in Nashville next Wednesday, as I told you in a note which you probably hadn't got when you wrote me Monday, or Tuesday it was, I believe. But, still, I may be delayed one day; so don't have the meeting till Friday, if it can be held then conveniently. I'll let you know the exact day and time of my arrival just as soon as I can. By the way, are there *two* beds in R. 19? I don't relish much staying in the damn frat. house, even for a few days.

Haven't time to do justice to your dandy letter and get this off on time. The report of the last meeting was as thrilling as a western movie! Darn those conservatives! I'll harangue 'em till five A.M. The impudence of Stanley. I can hear his sarcastic rasp now. I'll give him a solar-plexus. Look out for squalls! I'm looking forward to the time of my life.

Thanks for giving Ransom my stuff. Don't forget the Oenia poems and *Long Fingers*. Why hasn't he copies? I've sent them all to him. I'm nearly sure. *Old Maid* is sold, and *Bored to Choroesis* contingently. McClure is holding it and will print it in the October issue if I agree to alter line 2, stanza 2, which I refuse to do. Munson also has a copy— one I sent Hart Crane—and may print it, but if Ransom wants it, I'll be darn glad to get it into the F. and then notify Munson; I've already written McClure of my mulishness. The D.D. rejected the Duchess because—so Mc says—of the first strophe of part two. He advised me to elaborate Eulogium, as he liked it. I agree with you and Ransom about the dangers of ultra-modernism; I hope you all will trim me down somewhat.

I am trying to produce a few poems now, but the obstetrics of poetry is great labor. I think I'll have some new ones for the Fugitive. By the way, I'm trying to do a review of Robert Graves' *On English Poetry* for the Oct. D.D., which, from what Mc. says, is pretty sure to get in if at all decently written. It is very interesting, though I take issue with his main contention.

Must close. Let me have a line by return mail. Can't afford to miss any news. Haven't heard from Moore recently. Give my love to the brothers. Am mailing Eliot's book, so you'll be prepared to line up with me for the assault as soon as I arrive.

Affectionately, Allen

23/TL

[Nashville, Tenn.]
8 November 1922
Dear Allen:

"Nuptials"[a] is certainly fine. Your best, I think, since "Parthenia," and perhaps a greater technical accomplishment than that masterpiece. I think you have achieved almost a perfect technique in "Nuptials." It has what I would call the proper balance—between the modern and the traditional,—the medium in which you are destined to do your best work. I like the unusual combination it has of both restraint and spontaneity, if you know what I mean. It may be "synthetic," but it does not palpably appear so.

Perhaps there is still too much of the Eliot tinge about it, yet not so much as I suspected there would be. It seems substantially your own original manner, especially the fourth section, which I admire with unstinted admiration. You have achieved great heights there. The conceptions and the language both bear the mark of genius. It is real poetry....

One more thing about the poem. Perhaps the subject is rather sordid. You choose rather an obnoxious symbol for your universal. That isn't really a personal objection: the writer of Corymba, Priapus, and Competition isn't casting stones on that score. But I believe, for my own part, that one really owes it to himself, finally, to pick more "elevated" material than the Brady-Jenny-Cephas set offer. This objection doesn't, however, qualify my admiration of the poem, which I deem *immense*. You are "coming back" now with a vengeance; not that you were ever in more than a temporary lapse. I have been reading Graves lately and agree with him that poets should wait and not force the divine afflatus. Here's to you and Jenny, and long may you "wear your new amethystine ring."

Sincerely, as ever, Don

23   a. "Nuptials (to JCR)," *Fugitive* (December 1922).

24/TLS

Cincinnati, O.^a
10 November [1922]

Dear Don,

I'm herewith returning the poems of the last meeting. Yours is not quite you, but Steve's, as you say, is a fine poem—the best from him in many months. I also return your critical paper with lucid marginal disputanda, according to my polemic custom. I am furthermore sending you a copy of the Editorial I am offering this time. I have already sent a version to Steve, but this one is the final one, containing a few minor alterations; and when you have perused it, please turn it over to him, indicating that it supersedes the one I sent him. Please tell me what you think of it in detail if you have time. I don't think I have said anything in a way to offend either faction. It's a pretty big mouthful for an editorial, but I hope I get the point over. It seems to me a rather timely thing, since we shall probably attract more attention than before through our visitors, and it might be wise to let the critics know that we are aware of issues beyond our own circle.

Write me soon and let me know what they all think of the Editorial. I'm just a little bit afraid of Stanley. I shouldn't mind him if I were there; I could out shout him—and perhaps come off even with him for all his "Logic."

Hastily, Allen

24 *a.* Tate is in Cincinnati, the headquarters of the coal company which his brother Ben owns.

25/ALS

Nashville, Tenn.
16 November 1922
Dear Allen:

Didn't you get my letter with comment on *Nuptials?* I wrote one. I liked *Nuptials;* and still like it,—and shall be your defender as well as representative Sat. night. My only criticism is the subject-matter, which surely is sordid. The sonnet you have just sent pleases me, too. The subject is a rather usual one, but your technique is different and distinguished. Where are you sending the sonnet?

The editorial is a hum-dinger.*a* Just the thing the F. needs. Ransom, Steve, and I are for it. Stanley hasn't seen it yet. I will show it to him before the meeting. I think the editorial is a brilliant piece of work; though I don't agree with it *in toto.* I am for putting it in as she stands—or practically so. John suggested that you might make it a little less of a general pronunciamento (objectionable to certain parties) by a change of pronouns. I don't know about that. . . .

Sincerely, Don

We are going to make a move for better organization—Sat. night. Wish you were here.

Bring down the price of coal if you can! I am a householder now!

25 *a.* "Whose Ox," *Fugitive* (December 1922).

26/ALS

Ashland, Ky.

18 November [1922]

Dear Don,

Your letter, that sweet draught of Araby across this cancer of nature, has just come, and I chuck work to answer. I can't tell you how good your letter makes me feel; it's the first from any Fugitive since I came here; and it will take many more like it to keep me from being submerged in the dulness of this city of my childhood. It is a strange feeling to drop back in here unheralded and unsung, having been away nearly eight years. There isn't a congenial soul hereabouts. I am marooned. So do your duty and keep the letters flowing when you can spare the time.

I am tickled witless that you all like the editorial. I spent much time and thought on it. The first draft was six pages; so you see to what strenuous pruning it was subjected. I flatter myself in thinking it good, perhaps, but I know it's the best bit of prose I've ever done—of *any* length. If you and John and Steve and Stanley, et. al., care to change the first person personal pronouns from the plural to the singular, it will meet with my approval, since the Ed., if printed, will be signed with my initials; so all responsibility for opinions therein expressed will fall on me, as they should on every editorial writer of the F. individually.

I'm sorry I didn't get your letter about Nuptials. I have needed considerable advice on it. Yes, it is sordid; but my purpose was simply to present the *mind* of a "proletarian," whose chief purpose in life is the procreative act somewhat fledged with the pleasures of eating and subduing in a crude way his fellow men. I fancy it couldn't be otherwise than sordid. Wordsworth's fallacy—"If thou appear'st untouched by solemn thought," etc. is hokum. There is an inarticulate clutch for beauty in the lowest men which is always futile and defies his expressive powers—"Suddenly had visions of beautiful dead hair." No! the poem isn't synthetic; but there's a good deal of psychology in it, I believe, consciously worked out. I wish the sonnet[a] were of a less trite theme; it is better than anything else in that particular form as to technique.

I hope you will send me a poem of yours pretty soon. You've had a *too* long vacation from the thankless and irresistible muse! Let me know the latest gossip and tell me what happened at the meeting.

Affectionately, Allen

Why not let me have a marginal criticism of the Ed.? It would be quite interesting to me to juxtapose our differences and agreements.

26   *a.* "These Deathy Leaves," *Fugitive* (December 1922).

27/TLS

Nashville, Tenn.

24 November [1922]

Dear Allen:

Heap not curses upon me for being niggardly in letter-writing. Though I am not grinding away at coal, I too am having my defeats in the matter of time to write. I am doing extra tutoring now,—trying to get ahead of the game so that the next two terms will afford me more spare time to write. I simply couldn't get around to this letter till to-night.

Your editorial is going in, it seems. There were no unfavorable criticisms of it at the meeting. In fact, it was well received, on the whole. Some thought you were a bit positive about the ultimate quality of Eliot's *Waste Land;* and it was also pointed out that you wrongly made a distinction between *artist* and *poet,* thinking no doubt of *painter* and *poet.* I rather agree with those criticisms myself. They are minor points, and it seems that it would be a good thing if you would consent to small changes in those respects. A *perhaps* or two, or some such reservation, as John suggests, might help on the Eliot business. But the mass of the editorial received no criticism. I think everybody took it as a brilliant piece of work; none of us, except John, could write such an editorial. The personal pronoun also might be effectively changed. That's the Double Dealer style, isn't it? I rather like that way.

Nuptials seemed to stump the crowd. Frankly, I believe that the subject-matter militated against an unprejudiced judgement. Steve seemed to want to express great admiration, but thought it was rather "hot." I think he admires the poem. John seems to regard it as a powerful feat of arms, but raises the question as to whether the thing is *en masse,* poetry. Sidney thought that it was a versification of a Ben Hecht novel. Stanley said nothing, said he would have to study it more. That was really the attitude of the group,—neither acceptance nor rejection, —a rather let's-see-now attitude. I myself remarked, and so did Steve, that the poem passed with flying colors the test of being read aloud. That's a great deal in its behalf. I believe this thought was in the back of everybody's head, "That's a damn good poem,—but alas, he has chosen a subject which raises this damnable Comstockian question in regard to publication in the Fug." I can assure you that it's going to be seriously considered for that same F., however. I believe it will pass between Scylla and Charybdis and go in.

Damn it, you did not send the Silent Room[a] in that letter, as you said. I am positive that Steve will want to consider it for the F. I'll rummage around to see if I have a copy anywhere. Don't think I have, though. Mail one to Steve, post-haste.

I am mailing some of the poems that were read. Jesse's two sonnets to his Aunt Minnie made a tremendous hit. He took my copies away from me for revision,—I made him promise to mail copies to you. Ridley's poems raised considerable debate. I don't know what to think of his "heart" poem, myself, and so told him. Both the Willses are going to be great additions. Ridley is slated for critic next time. Says he's going to rip us up. We had a fine meeting. No conclusions yet as to future organization, however.

Steve wants to know what it is going to cost to get those posters made of which you speak. I think it's a fine idea. I had already intended to suggest it, but if you can manage to get it done, so much the better. You know our exchequer is in bad shape. Still lack ten dollars of paying for last Fugitive. Moore consistently neglects to get in the money he is supposed to have available.

Bynner's poems have arrived.[b] He sends four,—"The Big White Bird," a translation from the French of Vildrar, about 60-odd lines; "Leave Some Apples,—To a Modernist"; and two "Poems to Poets," one to Carl Sandburg and the other to Edna St.Vincent Millay. All four are exceedingly good. Graves' four poems have arrived, as you know, and are also good. They are entitled: "The Birth of Poetry,"—"A Valentine," "Sibyl," and I forget what else. They are good, too. So Bynner, Graves, and Percy are our eminent visitors, and I figure that they will fill altogether about ten pages or more of our issue, depending on how many poems of each are used. The editorials will take three pages. That will leave possibly about eighteen pages for our own stuff,—the eleven Fugitives. The editorial committee will have to make quite a choice, you see. But let me tell you something, on the quiet. The Fugitive poems are by no means going to suffer by comparison with our eminent visitors' work. And that's o.k. for us. Hadn't you better write to Percy, as you promised him, and inform him what big company he has gotten into? I doubt whether Geo. Herbert Clarke[c] will appear, as Ransom

raised the question of his having submitted the poems under a pseudonym. Anyway!!!!—John Farrar and Milton Raison both promised but
did not turn up. David Morton has not been heard from.

I am going to get down to business pretty soon and do some real
stuff once more. I have a big poem in my head if I can get it off. Also
I want to criticize your recent poems more thoroughly, and the editorial, too.

Now for A SUNKEN GARDEN,[d] which I am not speaking of last because it's unimportant, but because I had to get these other things off
my chest. Now this poem is extremely good and quite in the direction
I want to see you take, except for the third stanza with its stale bellies
and the occasional too-deliberate choice of large, difficult and abstract
words of the Tatian breed: I'll write you a marginal criticism later, but
now, do allow me to rebel against the bellies, which *are* certainly growing stale, since you have used them in the last two or three poems, I re-
gretfully remember. That's too much belly for your poems, you'll
readily grant. This last poem will lose nothing by a certain abdominal
operation.

Now *otherwise*, the poem is right up with your very best work.
Although I readily suspect of myself these days that I am getting to
where I can like nothing exceedingly, I can confess myself without
reservation tremendously moved by the poem as a whole, and I do believe that you come near to recapturing the fine first rapture of Parthenia. Praise be to Allah! All the stanzas but the third are indeed tremendous, to my thinking. *Te saluto! Tu non omnis in illis regionibus
Ditis et Kentuckiensis morieris!*[e]

Faithfully, Donald

27   *a.* Not published.   *b.* Witter Bynner, Robert Graves, David Morton, and William
      Alexander Percy contributed poems to the visitors' number of the *Fugitive.*
      c. Clarke was editor of the *Sewanee Review* from 1919 to 1925; and Farrar, editor
      of the *Bookman* from 1921 to 1927. Raison was author of *Spindrift* (1922), a vol-
      ume of verse. Morton's poem "Presence" appeared in the *Fugitive* (December
      1922). *d.* Not published. *e.* "I wish you well! May you not entirely die in
      those regions of hell and Kentucky." (This is an allusion to Tate's poem "Non
      Omnis Moriar.")

28/TLS

[Nashville, Tenn.]
Thanksgiving [1922]

Dear Allen:

Find herewith the table of contents of Dec. Fugitive. Jesse would not submit his sonnets on account of their too personal implications. You will notice our old friend Nebrismus[a] listed. Yes, they went and done it! Now there you are. I criticized it to Stanley just before he went to the meeting, but refused to render a definite opinion as to what they should do, wanting to keep out of the game as far as possible. Nevertheless I guess he knows my attitude, which is solely based on what are to me obvious crudities in that poem and not on the merits as poetry—a question I would not raise under the circumstances. All in all, I suppose they did the best thing. For if the quality of the rest of the issue carries the poem, then all will be well; if the poem meets with scorn (as I am afraid it will), once for all then it ought to be demonstrated to the satisfaction of those concerned just where the chips have fallen. So don't be wrathy, especially since the committee did themselves proud by putting in your Nuptials. (I told Steve about that dedication.)[b]

Steve tells me you wrote him in more or less sarcastic vein about the editorial and the criticisms I mentioned. Pray be careful. The ice is thin. And don't disturb the already extremely delicate poise of the Fugitive skaters. You know what I mean.

That thing of Frierson's,[c] which I did not see but heard read, is, as its title implies, a reaction to the now famous "guts and slime" theme. It is free verse. I can't speak of it with any authority, not having gone over it, but it is clever.

The stuff goes to the printer Friday. I don't know when the magazine will be out.

That's good about the window cards.

Write me your reactions to the table of contents. I shall be interested to know what you think.

I am going to send some more stuff to the Double Dealer now that the Fugitive choice has been made. McClure wrote me a very cordial letter.

By the way, Merrill tells me that you and I are very prominently mentioned in the Richmond Reviewer. I haven't seen a copy. Have you?

Faithfully yours, Don

28   *a.* A poem by Hirsch.   *b.* The poem is dedicated to Ransom, whose attitude
toward it is not completely favorable.   *c.* "Reactions on Being Bitter" was later
published as "Reactions on the October Fugitive," *Fugitive* (December 1922).

29/ALS

[Nashville, Tenn.]
[Late November 1922]

Dear Allen:

I forgot to tell you that *The Fugitives* received a long letter from
Curry, anent the Oct. issue, both praising and criticizing us. He thought
that a number of the poems of that issue were as good as anything published in the U.S. of late years. Among yours he rated *Non Omnis Moriar* and *To Oenia* highest. His whole tone was enthusiastic. I will try
to get the letter from John and send it to you.

Dr. Lockert also writes, praising the Fugitive. He will be here
Xmas & wants to be with us in a meeting. Curry will be here Dec. 27,
probably en route to the Mod. Lan. Ass'n. at Chicago. So we are planning to have a big meeting for about that date. Will you by any chance
be here then? I hope so.

David Morton sent in two sonnets, both good, one very good, in
quite his characteristic manner. Now we have plenty of good material.
Perhaps enough to run over into later issues.

The committee should be making up the F. tonight, but it isn't.
With characteristic procrastination, said committee is waiting till Wednesday night. At the present rate of speed, the F. will *not* be out by
Dec. 10. I *hope* it will be out by the 15th, but I am never certain of
these damnably impractical poets.

Allen, the more I think of your last poem the better I like it. I wish
I could get down to business and turn out something decent once more.
My work saps all energy. Here is John McClure writing to ask me to let
them have first call on the revised "Priapus" poem or anything else I
may have to offer. And I haven't anything worth while to send him. As
soon as the committee finishes its work, however, I hope to touch up
some stuff and send it to him.

Faithfully, Don

I have practically no criticism of "A Sunken Garden," except that
point about "bellies." In the latter part, I question "posturous insom-
nolence, the horizontal surcease of a blind ken" as being perhaps too

heavy and abstract, while the rest of the poem is smooth-running and quite unartificial. You remember, it was a long time before I fully appreciated *Parthenia*. I find myself groping gradually towards complete admiration of this poem in much the same way. My slow wits! But I do see that of late you are accomplishing tremendous things.

30/TLS

[Ashland, Ky.]

29 November [1922]

Dear Don,

Just a hasty and brief reply to your very good note. Actually I'm getting so I simply live for your letters. Without them I should feel utterly submerged in the dulness of this dirty little town.

The festination of the committee is no surprise to me. I hope, though, things come through so that the issue won't come out just at Christmas—people won't have time then to read verse. Don't you think it would be best to use all the outside poems in this issue and make the best showing possible? Even at the cost of omitting some of ours? We ought to "strut our stuff," it seems to me.

For goodness sake, get the Priapus poem in shape for the coming Double Dealer. I have just heard from McClure that they are using Hitch Your Wagon[a] in the Dec. number, and it would do the cause good for us to appear together again; and, besides, it will add to the notoriety of the Fugitives to have two members coming out in a synchronous issue of another magazine. Fiswoode Tarleton[b] has noticed our stuff in the last D.D., and seems to be interested in the Fug. You may be sure that interest shall not wane for lack of attention on my part.

And please write something very very soon. I hope the new version of Sunken Garden shows an elimination of some of the very things you objected to. In place of the belly passage I've inserted one of mere horror—instead of nastiness; and "posturous" is gone, as if in anticipation of your criticism. Please let me hear from you on those business details I went into in my last letter.

Hastily, Allen

30 a. "Hitch Your Wagon to a Star." b. Editor of the *Modern Review*, which was published from 1922 to 1924 in Winchester, Massachusetts.

31/TLS

[Nashville, Tenn.]
4 December 1922

Dear Allen:

Don't expect me to answer *all* your respective letters, though I do wish I could, as each arrives. Time simply doesn't permit. Just allow me to do the best I can, and meanwhile don't let there be any cessation in the shower of your letters,ᵃ which I enjoy hugely. I'll answer as often and as much at length as possible under my damnable circumstances.

The meeting Sunday night was exceedingly enjoyable, though there weren't many poems. Your two were *the* feature of the evening. They were much admired. And I don't recall any criticisms. I certainly have none now, except possibly to question the syntax of your revised third stanza in Sunken Garden. The sonnet is indeed beautiful. I don't see why Mencken shouldn't take it. John's comment on the sonnet was that you showed up David Morton at his own game. And I like Sunken Garden more and more. The revisions help greatly, I think.

Another feature of the meeting was the reading of two new poems submitted by W. A. Percy, who writes that he likes us so well that he wants to put forward his best foot for us. The poems were tip-top.

Stanley read a poem, which I enclose, and I read one. Merrill read a very good one, but distributed no copies. There were no other poems. Steve read a very well-couched editorial for the F. (just the routine stuff, you know, but very clever). And then Enfant Terrible Willsᵇ launched forth as the evening's critic and attacked us all roundly. He claims there is not enough modulation and shading in Fugitive poetry, says we all have "anthologies of perfect phrases." Charges also that we do not often enough conceive poems as wholes and don't write in a unity of mood. Likewise says that we don't put our personalities into our poems. Well, there was a warm debate, in which Sidney and I finally locked horns again on old lines, but without rancor, and in which everybody took interested parts. The evening wound up with an argument on sophistication conducted with Stanley as leader. In short, we had a gay time,—quite in the old spirit. The F. crowd are on their feet now, I believe.

Look up the Dec. 2 issue of the Lit. Digest and see what a spread they gave us on page 33. Have you seen it? Pretty good for the F., eh? Shall I send you the clipping if you haven't a copy? I'm sure Ashland affects the Lit. Digest.

Plans for the Dec. issue include a cover of a different and lighter color, with names of *all* the contributors on it, and titles of one poem from each. Steve has it very attractively conceived, I think. The copy is with the printer now; proof is to be out Thursday, I believe. I daren't forecast when the magazine will finally come from the press. . . .

I will see to it that copies are mailed as you direct to Mencken et al.

I am rather surprised that the D.D. took Hitch Your Wagon. I would have thought it a little too hot for them. Evidently they are a game bunch. I admire their spirit, but congratulate you somewhat dubiously, bearing in mind what Mrs. Cole[c] is reported to have said to Merrill Moore,—i.e. that the Fugitives are a lot of dirt-daubers and triflers; that they ought to read Swinburne and find out how to write poetry. Hitch Your Wagon surely isn't the poem that Nuptials is, or Sunken Garden. I'm inclined to think these latter two, with Parthenia, the Scholar sonnet, Euthanasia, and Non Omnis M., are your best.

I am glad you wrote the Reviewer man. Blame the negligence on John, not on me, for John was the guy who received the first letter. If you want to say anything further to the Reviewer, you might write that we are considering the advertisement plan for our 1923 Fugitive. I am inclined to think that an exchange of literary advertising would be a good thing. I will transmit the Reviewer letter to the bunch, with proper lamentations on the subject of organization.

This organization question is about ready to come to a head now. *Something* has got to be done, and something will be done. I think the membership are in a better mood now for considering the question than they were last month and before. Perhaps we will wait till Curry arrives to work out a plan; I don't know, though. I have long been in favor of pushing things to a conclusion.

I am going to send some more stuff to the D.D. just as soon as I can make a little study of it. I don't want to send anything out inconsiderately. Already I am too late for their December number, but I'll get something off within a day or two, so that it will be available for the next number. I am going to send them a revised version of Priapus, Ecclesiasticus, and perhaps Competition or Cabined[d] (revised).

Don't take my enclosed poem seriously. I am going to reconstruct it, with the possible exception of the first, second, and last stanzas. The rest are forced. I have little time, alas, for poetry these days. Are you going to try for the Nation's poetry prize? I think I shall, if I can get off anything decent before Jan. 1.

Am anxious to hear your impressions on the table of contents.

Sincerely, Don

31   *a.* Most of which are missing from the file.   *b.* The epithet sometimes used for
Ridley Wills to distinguish him from his quiet cousin Jesse.   *c.* Mrs. Whiteford
Cole, whose husband at this time was president of the Vanderbilt Board of Trust.
d. None of these appeared in the *Double Dealer.*

32/TLS

[Ashland, Ky.]
7 December 1922
Dear Don,

Your letter has made me a new man, and I almost feel that I am
down there with the group, so replete with the very interesting details
of the meeting was your letter. I know you are busy and I shall not expect so many letters from you; but I am alone and have my evenings
invariably to myself; so I resort to letter-writing as a substitute for
conversation. . . .

Your account of the meeting is actually thrilling (and people say
poets are *so* dull), and all I can do now is mourn my own absence. It
must have been a great night—Stanley delivering his usual damnations
on the evils of sophistication or the pose of it, alias Me, as He would
probably say; Mttron*a* expounding his etymologies with a sweet contempt for accuracy; John sitting there with a cigar out of all proportion
to the man, amused often, bored occasionally, disgusted with such
thickness all the time; and then you, my dear Don, mule-like in your
standards of beauty and rhythm, which I am always trying to under-
mine with a blast of entrails and livers! I can't afford to miss many
more meetings; if I do, my nostalgia will become a disease and I shall
be a dear little idiot boy.

If Ridley's criticism was as good in detail as your summary of it,
I must admit that he uttered many truths. We *are* all after the perfect
phrase, I perhaps trying to lead the procession so bent am I on it. But
I do feel that there is a limit beyond which is sterility; and though, in
my own case, I am making some hazardous deviations from the conventional poetic phrase, I realize that across the line one also approaches
a convention as brittle and artificial as Austin Dobson another way.
An example would be the poems by E. E. Cummings in the current
Vanity Fair, every one free and spontaneous—superficially; but I immediately was reminded of the *Horatii curiosa felicitas,* so highly

artificial is the entire group of poems. Eliot is the only man who can
do the trick without detection. And we don't have enough "personality," either. I think Dr. Mims meant the same thing when he remarked
once that humanness in our stuff was lacking and urged that we create
"types." Ridley's point that our poetry lacks unity is also good; I think
you often start a poem and let it build itself line by line; but then I
fall into the opposite error of sometimes conceiving the poem as a whole
and then trying to piece the thing together, and the result is what you
call "synthetic." Doubtless the others have similar trials.

Mencken rejected the sonnet and said that he couldn't buy any
more verse till spring. I believe I sent the letter to Steve as evidence of
Mencken's interest in us. It may be he will write us up again soon and
more conspicuously than before. In spite of my love for the Augean
Stables, I still have some affection for the sonnet. I believe that in the
past five years I've written between eighty and ninety sonnets, five of
which are fairly decent. Your report of the reception of Sunken Garden
and At Dusk[b] got at the meeting pleases me mightily. I suspected that
the syntax of the third stanza of S G might not be clear—the participial
phrase on the end is the trouble; but by pointing the stanza differently
the difficulty, I hope, is solved. I submit it:

> Then the stage veers to a strange street,
> Where rutted eyes of old women glide
> Over the tender corpse its dainty feet,
> While the wind whistles,—a rat gnawing outside.

I preferred the absolute to the affirmative here for a nearer verisimil-
itude to the state of mind we are dealing with: when the mind is utterly fatigued, as in insomnia, I find that we do not think in verbs very
much, but almost always in adjectives and nouns, incapable of the
judgement to any extent at all; a succession of images, syncategorimatic
words, and uncopulated ideas pass through the mind. Now my stanzaic
norm here limited my freedom in this sort of thing; I had to use syntax
to interpret a state of mind which had no formal structure. Perhaps a
faithful literary reproduction of it would be quite lawless, and at this
point enters my contention that the emotion alone should determine
the framework. Just as the emotions of a girl of fifteen may inevitably
find artistic expression in the shallow mould of the triolet, so the terrible and devastating attitude of Eliot can be honestly conveyed only
in the form he has chosen. I don't see how either can be contested; both
are art if they *see* the Thing and make us see it. I shouldn't care to have

the way I have expressed the above dictum looked into too closely; it is hastily written, and it might easily be shattered by logic. But you get my drift.

Yes, I was surprised myself that the D.D. took the poem, but that's up to them! As to the advice of the lady you mention, I can't take that seriously. But her exhortation that we study Swinburne gives me an opportunity to moralize, and I shall. You will find that S is a favorite with many ladies simply because he talks about thighs and ruby lips and tempestuous passion in such a way as to make them beautiful to a mind at the stage of sophistication when the physical difference between the sexes is such a terrible thing. If the brutal is sentimentalized into a scheme of pretty flowers and birds, the ladies like it, for that adequately justifies a human element the unadorned truth of which they will not face. Sentimentality excuses all. The Moderns know that passion is vestigial of the brute and tell us so. They do not love it. Since Irony is the keynote to life, they throw, for this effect, the bare flesh into sharp contrast with mind. The flesh is the scourge of intellect, but art takes no sides, and so the result is simply spirit and body juxtaposed. I fear that the ladies show themselves up by preferring Swinburne. The lady patron of art usually doesn't patronize unless she can tell the artist what to write and how to write it. Maybe if we would only telephone the dear cultivated ladies before we write every poem and ask, "Please, ma'am, shall we celebrate today your eyes or your hair, or shall it be Uncle Henry's gout?" We should likely all of us be drawing salaries within a week, and have the loveliest poetry magazine in the world. I suspect the poet knows better than to compromise himself in this way. And sometimes the ladies don't wear skirts. Perhaps every literary or artistic venture has something like this to contend with, but I don't think art is the offspring of compromise.

I am very glad indeed to see that you have at last written the poem with the two first lines which were in your mind when I was in Nashville two months ago![c] I like the poem very much; it is quite in your best vein—perhaps a little too long to sustain the tenuous subject-matter, but a little shortening will do the necessary trick. Your first two stanzas are capital—only one suggestion in the latter: why not make line four read "Once wed in Avalon," repeating *wed* from preceding line? But no advice. You will make it come out all right. Shall you send this to the D.D.? I hope you have something for the Nation contest. I doubt if I will, unless I can get together a sequence of four sonnets—the kind of stuff they fall for!

The enclosed poems are very new, though I've been fiddling with Teeth some time.[d] I believe that poem is nearer the thing I'm struggling for than anything I've done. I like the last stanza. It is as serious a piece of work as I've attempted, and I hope fatuity doesn't lead me into the fond hope that at last I've done a *poem* without the old poetic machinery. Mary McDonald is a real live girl—in fact, a stenographer in our office, with a penchant for brutal-looking young men. I am forthwith sending her to the Bookman. I will mail you copies before the next meeting.

Must close now (at last!). Write me when you have a little time. Send me the press comment (local) on this issue. Give my best to all the brothers. Though I am usually represented in meeting by poems, I like to feel that I am also keeping up all round; so perhaps that is the reason for these long letters—and frequent. I try to contribute my bit to the harangue by mail.

Faithfully, Allen

32 *a.* Sidney Hirsch. *b.* Not published. *c.* The poem is "Avalon," *Fugitive* (June–July 1923). *d.* "Teeth" and "Mary McDonald," *Fugitive* (February–March 1923).

33/TLS

[Nashville, Tenn.]
14 December 1922

Dear Allen:

It isn't going to be possible for me to write a long letter tonight. I have never been so damnably and nastily busy with fruitless things in my life. Everything seems to pile up on me. But here goes for a few moments, anyway, snatched from the jaws of despair such as can come only after grading large batches of English papers.

Your last letter was a peach, and so were the poems,—peaches. Think of applying such a term to a poem of yours!

Your punctuation of the stanza in Sunken Garden helps. But I am doubtful as to your arguments in behalf of detached phrases. I have still a foolish idea that the object of language is not altogether to conceal thought. Syntax is required not because there is any virtue in it *per se* but simply because it has become so universal a mode of expression that a writer choosing a different mode will not put his idea across in 99 cases out of 100. No matter how adequate a form of expression may seem to you as a poet, you must consider that artistic expression in a void is a pretty poor proposition; that is where Eliot is going, in my opinion. He is as far as I am concerned talking in a vacuum, in Waste Land, which I have read three times, with no gleam whatever of comprehension. I would like, by the way, to hear your interpretation of that poem.

I liked what you had to say of Irony and the Moderns. But, you know, I am getting a little bit afraid of Irony. I believe Irony is giving me too much of a crabbed style. I seem unable to write anything distinguished that is also fairly simple.

Yes, I am going to try to send something to the Nation contest, though I have small hopes of getting anything. I hope you send something.

I am surprised that you like Avalon. It's a very imperfect poem at present. I am letting it mull awhile.

"Teeth" and "Mary McDonald" are both great. The first and last stanzas of "Teeth" are as fine as anything you ever wrote. The two middle stanzas haven't as yet quite dawned on my slow perceptions. "Mary" is rich,—I like it tremendously. I got the copies, and will read the poems Sat. night. Will withhold my criticisms till I have time to form a decent opinion.

Enclosed find my latest. It's not much. . . .

Hurriedly, but faithfully, as usual, Don

P.S. We had a nice letter from Alice Hunt Bartlett, who wrote the article (quoted in Lit. Dig.) in London *Poetry Review*[a] on American poetry. She also sent a check for subscription.

The Fugitives were guests at lunch this week with Hugh Walpole, and we had an interesting time, of which maybe more later. He hadn't seen the F. then, but we sent up a copy, & he told somebody that it was fine, that there was *"no mediocre poetry in it."*

33   *a.* "What America Is Doing for Poetry" (October 1922); cited in "The Rage for Poetry," *Literary Digest* (1922).

34/TL

[Nashville, Tenn.]
17 December 1922

Dear Allen:

Am dispatching to you 2 advance copies of The Fug. Will send your quota as soon as the batch is delivered.

I am pretty well pleased with the looks of the issue, though, like you, I have qualms as to Nebrismus. To carry three of Merrill's tinklers is perhaps a weakness, and I doubt very much whether in my case the committee made the best choice. On the other hand, the committee did make some very pleasing variations,—as in their selection, for the most part, of shorter poems in varying moods, thus avoiding the dangerous turgidity of some earlier issues. I think your *Nuptials*, Alec's *He Who Loved Beauty*, and Bynner's *Leave Some Apples* are the best poems of the issue, though I would not omit to mention also Percy's *Safe Secrets*, which I like more and more. I can't give Graves much, and I think your sonnet easily eclipses Morton's. Your editorial looks good, and so does Steve's. Steve has hit the right note very cleverly, it seems.

We are going to get together early this week,—maybe tomorrow or Tuesday—and mail out the issue. We have prepared a circular plea for renewals, which is also to be sent out.

It was the sense of the meeting (as far as Fugitive meetings ever attain practical business sense) that all members should at once make a concerted effort to obtain new subscriptions, in order that we may, if possible, finance next year's issue upon that basis without having to appeal to any damn club-women snifflers for a subsidy. Also we will work hard for renewals. We also are arranging to make the local book-sellers agents, and allow them twenty-five cents on every subscription they take for us. Besides that we will get a student representative to push things at Vanderbilt, on the same basis, and will endeavor to get other representatives in the city. I believe this is a good plan. If it fails to bring in the necessary funds, then we may consider the bootlicking proposition.

The meeting was very interesting, though few poems were read. I read TWILIGHT EXCURSIONS*a* and the ESSENE (which title I intend to change, probably to VICISTI); Sidney recited four poems of his own,—short ones. And Ransom read Max.*b* Mr. Frank delivered a criticism which called Plato, Socrates, Cicero, Webster's Dictionary, and other learned authority to witness that lofty themes, not simply technique, is what we want to lay hold of. It was a good paper on an old theme; he spent little discussion on individual criticism. Then I read your two new poems, which became the subject at once of a very lengthy discussion.

MARY MCDONALD received lavish encomiums. Everybody liked it, and particularly the last line. TEETH was the main subject of debate. I raised the point already mentioned,—i.e., that the first and fourth stanzas struck me as being as good as anything you had done, but that I got little reaction from the other two, particularly the third. Then Steve rose up as your defender, and explained what he thought the two stanzas meant. Stanley attacked the poem as being too cryptic, and questioned your now well-known stunt of sliding from the plane of artistic utterance into byplay and parentheses. Ransom defended you, particularly on the basis of fine diction. The upshot of the discussion seemed to be about this; on which there was a fair amount of agreement: that while it is admitted that the artist is subject, during the act of creation, to marginal impressions of reality and incongruous (seemingly) divergencies, he should not jot these things down too, but should wait until he has made a synthesis of his ideas, and should express this synthesis, suppressing the extraneous and unaffecting grosser material. Otherwise his expression is liable to be too disjected and incoherent, and I, for one, believe that your poem TEETH, with all its fineness of diction, and beauty, and dignity, is open to the charge of disjection and incoherency. The question arises also, in regard to the parenthesis, whether you have in this and other poems done the sort of thing you are trying to do in the best manner possible. Is a change in character of diction necessary, for example? Could you not make your form of expression more distinguished and thereby make your performance more convincing? I know I am expressing myself lamely, but I haven't time to give you more than a smattering idea of what was said. Personally, I think the poem one of your best, though I deprecate its disjection and lack of sequence between stanzas and regret the difficultness of the third stanza. The first and fourth, I repeat, are in your best manner.

Your NUPTIALS strikes me more and more. It is much better, I believe, than my CORYMBA, which you like so much. John seemed to like that dedication. He is writing you today.

The telegram of last evening was a suggestion of Sidney's, which we all eagerly greeted. I hope you can arrange to be here for the evening of Dec. 27, when we are planning to have that big Fugitive meeting. Doc. Curry has written that he will spend the night of the 27th in Nashville, en route to the Modern Language meeting at Chicago. So we will have him. Dr. Lockert is to be on hand as guest, and Dr. Mims is to be invited. I wish I could ask you to stay at my house while you are here, but we are so unfortunately arranged in this house that we can have no overnight company, ordinarily, except intimate members of the family. But if you can come, I herewith do invite you to eat dinner with me at home that evening. Then we can all go out to the F. meeting together,—you, and Stanley, and I. How about it? Let me know in advance.

Your work is evidently having a good effect on you, to judge from the fine quality of poetry you have been doing lately. I really think so. It's always better for one to be settled at least partially into a groove, even if one has to feel rebellious at it. So long as I don't have *too* much drudgery, I can always go to my real work with more zest than otherwise.

Sincerely, [Don]

34   *a.* "Twilight Excursions," *Double Dealer* (January 1923); Davidson published no
poem under either of the next two titles.   *b.* "First Travels of Max," *Fugitive*
(June–July 1923).

35/TL

[Nashville, Tenn].
13 January 1923

Dear Allen:

Vide report of last F. meeting herewith given. Mr. Shearon of the Presb. Bkstore was our guest of the evening. We enjoyed him; apparently he had a good time, too. Business was dispatched as follows:

1. Approved my schedule of publication for the year, which is to go to press by the 25th of Jan., Mar., May, July, Sept., Nov., and appear on the 10th of Feb., Apr., June, August, Oct., Dec. Each number is to receive a double designation by months,—as for example the coming number is to be known as the February–March issue.

2. Discussed advertising. The D.D. offers to exchange on a 2 to 1 basis. McClure writes that their circulation is 2,000 now,— hence his offer of inequal amount. We voted to agree to that, and to publish a full-page ad. in the F. twice, if he will run us a full page once. The Modern Review will take a half-page for similar return, and have sent copy. Others not heard from yet.

3. Question of the size of the magazine was again discussed, some arguing that we ought to continue the 32-page size instead of reducing to 24. After much argument, the club voted to try the 24-page issue this time. (Ransom urged it very strongly, though not

with very strong arguments, to my mind.) I am still rather dubious about the 24-page stunt. I would like to hear your opinion on it. Seems to me that—especially since we have all this visitors' stuff on hand—we must put out an extremely good issue next time, as much as anything else to make up for the lapse in the Dec. number. Can we come as strong as we are capable of coming in a 24-page issue, and won't it look a little bad? Of course, there are two factors against the 32 page–6 issue idea,—that we may not be able to meet the cost, and that we may not produce enough poetry. But there are equally good arguments on the other side. Why shouldn't we increase our circulation to at least 500—anyway?

4. The committee will meet Wednesday or Thursday to make up the issue. There is to be only one page of editorial matter this time. Stanley is to write that—no literary stuff, only the routine informative line.

5. Since the first of the year we have received approximately 18 new subscriptions and about 27 renewals. Money is coming in very slowly. Circulars will probably be ready to go out soon.

That's about all the business. Jesse, Ridley, Mr. Frank, Sidney, and I read poems. (Stevenson and Moore were absent, for reasons unknown—probably they are sick as Ridley has been.) I enclose copies of Jesse's, Ridley's, and Mr. Frank's. Please cast your eye carefully over the last-named poem and tell me whether or not I am going crazy. I do not like the poem much; it is pretty good for Mr. Frank or for anyone in the first puerile stages of learning to write poetry, but I consider it crude, conventional, old-fashioned, quite indistinguished. BUT John Crowe Ransom likes it, so it seems, and expressed what was to me an astonishing degree of approval, coming from one who is ordinarily chary of commendation. Of course Stanley liked it. Curry did not say much. But I am terribly afraid that this poem is going to go into the next Fugitive. If you have tears prepare to shed them now. I am beginning to see wherein you were right in doubting the committee. If John Ransom goes back on us, then where are we? I was more astonished last night than ever before at any Fugitive meeting. When I ventured to follow out that policy of open criticism which John has so often recommended and jumped on Mr. Frank's inversions and *did's*, John rushed into the lists in Mr. Frank's behalf and bowled me over. What d'ye think of that, now? That darn committee have put themselves into a place where they can't turn down the poem with a good face. They have bowels of compassion perhaps, but they need iron guts for such work. You and I seem to be the only persons possessing those essentials, eh? I got mine in the Army. I suppose you got yours from long residence at a frat. house,—or where else might it have been?

I have finally gotten a pretty clear idea of my function with regard to the magazine. As managing editor, I am to do all the damn detailed work for which I receive neither thanks nor credit, merely the beautiful thought that I am doing a wonderful "service" to the art of poetry, I suppose. It is rather apparent that the Committee on Selection expects me to corral the manuscripts offered, and, when the poems have been selected, take the stuff down to the printer and put it through. In other words, I am to do all sorts of indispensable work, without having any sort of voice as to the general tone of things, which would be reward enough. I am a mere factotum. It seems to be taken for granted that I will meekly take all the burdens of Atlas on my shoulders, while all the rest of the members here in Nashville are busily writing poems, writing novels, reading contemporary literature, and otherwise enjoying themselves.

You and I are both in the cold as far as our influence on the make-up of The F. is concerned. It was made clear to me last night that the so-called "advisory capacity" which I was supposed to possess does not exist. I am sure you and I will both agree that we don't mind the others choosing poems so long as they don't do any wild things. But do you agree with me, or not, that another mistake of the kind that marred the last issue[a] will give us a handicap hard to overcome,—a reputation in the eyes of critics that will be hard to live down? If you do, then let me urge you to bring what influence you can to bear on John (who is our sole hope) to accumulate some iron guts. I'll do all I can. You do the same. They don't have to run that thing of Mr. Frank's now, anyway. If they are so damn determined to put it in, why not wait for an issue or two, until we are well on our feet?

I have a terrible grouch on tonight, as you notice. But that's partly because I am feeling bad physically, as well as sick mentally—from the constantly recurring failure to achieve. But I'll try not to let my grouch lead me to extremities. I hope you'll be wary of extremities, too. Let's do our swearing in private, for the present, at least. The Fugitive is just on the edge of achievement now. Let's work hard to keep it going up Parnassus, and be careful that it may not topple back into the abyss.

Sincerely, [Don]

I read your Calidus Juventa.[b] I like the revised version better. The crowd seemed to like the poem.

35   a. The inclusion of Hirsch's "Nebrismus."   b. "Hot Youth"; in the letters Tate sometimes refers to himself by the title of this poem.

36/TLS

[Ashland, Ky.]
16 January 1923

Dear Don,

Your letter came late tonight and I can't wait to answer it even if I don't get a wink before morning. I want you to hear from me before the Committee on Selections meets this week. You know very well how I feel. Please don't apologize hereafter for your dudgeon; it will make me feel bad, because I am openly and blatantly enraged; and I shall not contain myself. But, of course, the way must be devious. It seems that you and I are alone and frozen out—as to the latter part of it, I don't care; it is the fact that it is incumbent upon us to deal with this matter that counts. Perhaps we had better put on an antic disposition. Lend me your ears!

I will withdraw from The Fugitive if the poem in question goes in the next or any issue. But I do not want them to know that, as coming from me, in advance. I will withdraw simply because I do not believe nor shall I ever believe that John Ransom sincerely thinks this poem worthy of appearing in The Fugitive. . . . GUTS are the sine qua non of art. Art is a grim dominion, and personalities have no place in it. Is the purpose of artistic creation merely the satisfaction of vanity? . . . There is only one thing in life to me, and that is the continual possibility of pursuing literature as an art, and I can therefore countenance no compromise in a matter which is of the utmost vitality to me. . . . I may be impractical and too unreasonable, but I will follow this course till I honestly believe I'm wrong. If Jesus Christ should come upon earth and present me a poem I sincerely thought inferior, I would tell him *just that* to his teeth if the issue at stake were as vital as this one. This particular poem is not merely inferior; it is illiterate and insipid. It is supposed to be clever?

If they decide to print this poem, please let me know immediately. I shall then write an open letter to the group, explaining very *calmly* (I can) just why I am withdrawing, and requesting, if they see fit, that they remove my name from the masthead and make such explanation editorially as they care to. I do not want them to know this now. It would seem that I am asking them to choose between me and the poem and that I am advancing egotistical threats. I assure you, Don, and I know you will believe in the sincerity of my attitude and motives, that there is nothing like that. If you want me to remain, and I know you do, this may be an added reason for your condemnation of the poem. My attitude has no resentment in it; I shall withdraw on principle.

I am less angry than I am heart-sick. In the realm of morals men are often crushed into compromise and littleness, but thank heaven we are not so determined in art. Don, this thing has a metaphysical significance to me. I believe that art is above life in a realm of freedom. We are determined in the plane of mortal existence, but in art we must be free or we shall have no art. I am too much worked up to answer your letter as it deserves. I will do better later. . . .

Yours ill and enraged, Allen

37/TLS

[Nashville, Tenn.]
23 January 1923

Dear Allen:

Having put The Fugitive to bed by the process of carrying it to the printer this evening, having answered sundry communications, returned sundry manuscripts, filed sundry letters, recorded sundry subscriptions, also having attended a luncheon meeting of the Vanderbilt Lecture Bureau, having run most of the way home in order that my wife might get over to Ward-Belmont promptly for her tutoring work there, having graded sundry themes, having cut out sundry paper dolls for my little Mary, having inserted an ad in the paper for a new servant, having fired the furnace sundry times (yea, even having burned the infernal thing out), having telephoned to sundry people about sundry things, having studied my lesson for tomorrow with the freshman, and having smoked sundry cigarettes while being engaged with these other sundries,—having done all these things, O Poet, O Allen Tate, O Hot Youth, I salute you, and close my twenty-six hours a day with this letter.

I can't tell you half of all that I could tell. There is too much. Every day in every way I'm getting fuller and fuller—of details. But here are a few things. Chattanooga News writes John C. R. for the full history of the F. for an article they are getting up on new Southern magazines.[a] Just had another nice letter from Witter Bynner, who has promised to look over my volume (if it is ever ready), and another note from Untermeyer, asking for an extra copy of the next issue to send to Edwin Arlington Robinson, to whom his Tangential is addressed. Merrill Moore has been in for a round of severe reprimand on all sides and seems to be straightening up a bit. He did not hand in any stuff for this Fugitive,—but he has now just written, so John says, some of the best stuff he has ever done. Sidney did not submit anything at all for the last F. Said he thought he had been given so much space in the last one that he wouldn't submit anything this time. Alec submitted two old things, but got turned down. Hasn't written anything recently, because he is expecting an event in his family (that's confidential, I suppose). The committee would have liked to use your Calidus,—John admired that particularly. Stanley, John says, wanted to put all of your poems in. You see how you have been misjudging his attitude. But you should see Stanley's one page editorial. It is a hot shot at the Moderns, a regular solar plexus of one paragraph, accompanied by a poem about his preference for the song of the bird rather than the garbage-heap and dung-hill outside.[b] It's all very racy and rather violent,—perhaps partly intended to set forth the other side of what you propounded last time. It's cleverly written and will please many of our readers. Though I, of course, like you, will not consent to all or most of Stanley's remarks, I think this divergency of expression in the F. is a healthy sign and one that will intrigue our readers, if not the critics, for whom you, my boy, have a keen ear.

I am glad the committee voted as they did on the list. As I indicated in my note, I was delighted to see you over your excitement, which worried me rather, all the more because I felt partially guilty of inciting you. I had a letter all composed in my mind, enumerating the various reasons why you could not afford to take such strenuous action as you mentioned. Not the least of my reasons was the responsibility which you along with the rest of us have incurred in starting off this magazine for another year,—an obligation to the public. The other obligation is that by which we are all bound,—an obligation to submit to the decisions of our editorial committee, which is probably going to do better than your dark suspicions led you to believe. In this connection it might be stated that the committee is going to present a report to the meeting Saturday night, Dr. Curry making the report,—which will be to the general effect that they don't want any more classical poems, or poems on classical subjects handled in the old manner, such as you know what. Curry, because of things he has recently said, seems to be in better standing than any of us at the old rendezvous, and I expect his statement to clear the atmosphere and make it possible for us to work with entire harmony during the year, as we ought. Sidney's spirit has been fine recently. Stanley's has too,—better than I ever saw it,—and he is most hospitable to your work, in spite of his editorial and his frequent argumentative attitude.

The mail of the F. has increased about one thousand percent since the first of the year, and is getting to be a real burden on my hands. Practically every day now letters are coming from far-off places, and I have to answer them all,—damn it!

Now as to Yellow River.ᶜ I am quite sure that it is the best thing in modern technique that you have done unless it is Nuptials. I can't as yet decide that. Neither can I give a complete criticism on the poem—until I have had time to study it thoroughly, which I haven't had. There is one thing that always strikes me about your poems,—they seemed completely purged of superfluities; they have a quality of clean-ness and sureness, like the lines of fine statuary, that appeals to my feeling for beauty. BUT I do not as yet know what Yellow River is about, —not entirely, only very nebulous impressions, outlines fading one into the other. I suppose that is a part of the intended effect. Unques-tionably the diction is wonderfully pure, beautifully hard in some places and lyrically musical in others, in spite of its elliptics and other ob-jections I might propose. But there's one thing that gripes me sore—I don't like it. How about those "soothing brackets"? They mean less to me than anything in the poem, and they seem to jar somehow in a diction that is marked for fine sense of word values. Allen, I can't endure the brackets. And I believe others will criticize you on that point. I'll have to think more on the poem before I can criticize it more in detail. I admire it tremendously, and I think it will surely be a fine poem to submit for the prize,—unless you had something of the Scholar to his Lady type, only longer. I'll believe Yellow River stands a great chance of turning the trick,—more so than anything I can submit, by far. . . .

Faithfully, Don

37   a. Caroline Gordon, "U.S. Best Poets Here in Tennessee," February 10, 1923.
b. Fugitive (February–March 1923).   c. Published in Fugitive (June–July 1923) as "The Screen."

38/TLS

[Nashville, Tenn.]
9 February 1923

Dear Allen:

Hey! Rub-a-dub-dub! Enclosed find a clipping from the New Republic which pretty well states my reactions on your Waste Land ikon. I rather agree with Conrad Aiken, and must say that I think it the best review I've seen.[a] Edmund Wilson's apologia to the contrary notwithstanding.

I am exhausted, dear poet,—absolutely. Instead of writing a poem for tomorrow night, I think I shall give an account to the Fugitives of how much time I have been spending on their business,—in effect, the major portion of the past four days, all other work having been crushed to nothingness by this Juggernaut of correspondence. My wails rise to heaven. Do you hear them?

I told Martin[b] that you were the cream of all Tartars. Be sure to write him your best and most brilliant letter,—and be as nice to him as modernity will permit you.

After Saturday night I shall have that clipping from The Tennessean. The Chattanooga News story is to appear tomorrow,—Saturday, and I will send it when I get it. Don't get impatient. You ought to be used to clippings by now. What are you, anyway,—not a publicity hound. You ought to assume a bored expression. Oh, these press notices, how vulgar they are!

I agree with you and John in a general way as to my poems. Still I doubt the greatness of ironic lyricism, as you call it. It seems to me that you, for instance, are distinctly limiting your possibilities by the Eliotish manner which you have to a certain extent adopted. Poetry is surely something broader than a rather sardonic, half-beautiful laugh. Why not let one's art include ironic lyricism, if you will, but not to the exclusion of other things, if one may attain them. Now you have an authentic manner, all your own, quite superior to Eliot's, though it may be occasionally faintly reminiscent of some of his things. It appears in Euthanasia, Parthenia, the next to the last movement of Nuptials, in the Scholar sonnet, in the first part of your first Perimeters sonnet, in Mary McDonald, some parts of the Yellow River (the part about the girl's face), and in The Happy Poet,[c] which I continue to like. I wish I had time to present you more of comment,—I have *much* to say. Lord, how I enjoy your letters and poems,—could stay all night to hear good counsel—and say somewhat myself, but for the condition of body-cells.

Mr. Harold Vinal[d] has just sent us a contribution,—something quite good. I believe we shall be able to use it; in the set of three poems he sends, beauty does not seem to hurt him, as some reviewer said it did. What did you think of Starrett's poem?[e] I am keeping it in the file for the present, and have not yet written him.

Faithfully, Donald

Yes, damn it, I found those other typographical errors in the F.

38   a. "An Anatomy of Melancholy," *New Republic*, 33 (1923), 294–295; Wilson, "The Waste Land," *Vanity Fair*, 19 (1923), 17, 92.   b. Herman Ford Martin, who published five poems in the *Fugitive*.   c. "The Happy Poet Remembers Death," *Fugitive* (April–May 1923).   d. An early editor of *Voices* (1921–25).   e. Vincent Starrett, editor of the *Wave*, published in Chicago (1922–24).

39/TLS

[Oberlin, O.[a]]
26 June 1923

Dear Allen:

Having read your letter several times with leisurely and pleasant digestion, having read Miss Swett's[b] letter with neutral stomach, and having approached your new poem with something approaching indigestion (or, simply, lack of digestion perhaps), I debouch from avenues of speculation and indite.

First for the infusorian managerialities (?)! Don't send Miss Frank[c] any magazines. In her last letter (see file) she indicated that she would rather not perform duties of distribution for us, and I think we have bothered her enough. So send copies to Brentano's (and bills) direct. No use bothering with Wanamaker and Washington Square Bookshop. The subscription is for my father,—W. B. Davidson, R.F.D. 1, Fayetteville, Tenn. You'll find his card among the old expired ones. *William* Davidson is my brother. I note that The Wave doesn't carry our one-half, -page exchange ad which they owe us. Perhaps they should be jogged up a bit. (I believe they are damned incompetent,—perhaps much more than we on the Fugitive ever were.) What about the Jacques Back arrangement?[d] Things moving slowly? You spoke of publicity on the poetry contest results. Have we had any good notices? I am tickled to death that H. Crane and Potamkin[e] sent in poems. What lured them? Money, for one thing, and besides it's an indication of increasing respect somewhere for the magazine. I believe that eventually we will have to arrange to pay for poems, if we wish to hold the best contributors. If we move slowly, do not bite off too much, and consolidate our position as we go, I think we can reach the proper point of prosperity without a great deal of agony. And I think we ought to plan for it.

Now for that letter from "Poetry." I am glad you answered them, and I think you said exactly the right thing. I haven't much to add, but I will write Miss Swett as soon as I compose my thoughts sufficiently. The letter indicates that the first purpose of the editorial has been fulfilled,—i.e., we have succeeded in stirring them up, and at least they will watch us.[f] As for what they may say in print (if they say anything), nothing they say, good or bad, but will help us. In some respects, the more belligerent they are, the better. I will write them, and send you a copy of my letter, with theirs, for the files. I suggest that somebody (you or I or whoever feels sufficiently moved) work up an editorial on the fallacy of the local color idea in American literature, going into the whole question at length,—and perhaps using this letter of Miss Swett's, which is an excellent jumping-off place for a vigorous attack on the seats of the so-self-called mighty. I personally don't care how mad the "Poetry" people are, but I do feel a little afraid that the South Carolina folks[g] may take some umbrage at our editorial. I should like a literary controversy, with anybody, but under the circumstances I think we should preserve, so far as is compatible with our own projects and ideas, courteous and friendly relations with the South Carolinians, who maybe are now finally waking up to a discovery of The Fugitive.

I should like very much to see a copy of that Southern "Literary" magazine. Will you send me one? Don't get mad over the eulogies of W. A. Dromgoole.[h] They are to be pitied. And if that's their line they have no chance in the general literary world of competing with The Fugitive, whatever deleterious influence they may have on Southern letters (I don't see how they can affect Southern letters at all, with that line, for they won't reach anybody but the Babbitts).

Looks bad for the Double Dealer, doesn't it? I should like very much to see a plan of consolidation worked on. Or I would like to see somebody buy them out. Could The Fugitive absorb the D.D.?

As yet I haven't heard from Houghton-Mifflin.[i] I am still very much afraid they'll turn me down when matters come to a final decision, for I knew all along that they would *think* me much more radical than I am. If I dared, I would write them and tell them just what I am trying to do in poetry, which is, as you know, to strike a balance between the best of the old and the new,—a balance I haven't as yet succeeded in getting, probably, but which I still aim for. However, even if they do turn me down, I won't feel bad, for I think now that I can surely find a publisher. But it would be a triumph to have Houghton-Mifflin take me, wouldn't it? And then I would have their interest assured on my future works!!!

I have three poems in the rough, but I won't send them until I have them thoroughly polished. Last week, on account of Commencement functions which I attended with my wife, I had no time for writing. Besides, I have been almost sick ever since I landed here,—partly change of climate, and partly my tonsils. I went to see a throat specialist yesterday in Cleveland, and will go up there Monday for an operation. When that is over, I anticipate having lots of pep and energy, which have been sadly lacking of late. I don't know that I ever felt much worse than I have of late,—drowsiness, lasting all day so that I would go to sleep over whatever I was doing; headaches, throat-aches, lassitude, a general nervous and wilted feeling. Next week, as soon as I get on my feet from the operation, I'll be able to get down to at least two months and a half of solid and I hope fruitful labor.

"One Wild Stag"[j] has much in it that strangely attracts me,—strangely, I say, because you know that I am fundamentally opposed to this type of poem. I could never grant to you or T. S. Eliot or James Joyce or anybody the right (the literary right) to decompose thought into these unwelded and amorphous combinations. Despite the singular beauty of phrase and conception which you attain here (you see, I take you seriously) I can well believe you have done little more, O Chemistry student, than apply a reagent to your compound of mingled experiences, from which you draw forth now a startling series of precipitates, gorgeously colored and well-formulaed, but understood and useful only in the textbook of the (in this case) psychological and obtuse specialist. To change the comparison: you have let your Genie escape from the bottle, and my dear Fisherman, he has swelled to fill your horizon, he threatens you, and how will you find the spell to control him for your needs, for he is anarchical. And now the plates of gold and silver which you have drawn up in your net are also of little use to a Fisherman who has not the Seal and the Word, which are alone deathless and supreme. Well, I have dropped into verbiage. Let it pass. As before many times I say,—I see what you are trying to do, I think, but bless me if I approve! Though I am sure that The Dial, for instance, would do better to use this poem of yours which is for the most part intelligible, than many of their unintelligibilities.

To more personal affairs now. I have a copy of the letter which Ben[k] wrote you on the strength of my letter to him. I am enclosing it to you in case you don't get your copy, which I note is addressed to Wesley Hall. I believe my letter to him must have had on the whole a good effect, though the tone of his letter is a little aggrieved still. Isn't the offer of tuition and fees quite a concession on his part, after all? I can well see that it is impossible for him, situated as he is, to understand your position as I do, and on the other hand, there is more than an atom of justice in his position, if one considers that in the final analysis it might have been possible for you to manage a little better than you did manage. I think you ought to arrange to take advantage of his offer. If you have already paid your tuition on borrowed money, you should get an approved statement (official) of your expenses for tuition and fees and ask Ben to reimburse you in order that you may pay back that money. I think he would do it. If on the other hand you can now manage without Ben's assistance for the summer, you ought to write him in such a tenor that it will make the way smooth for you to get a similar assistance from him next fall, in case you decide to work for a Master's. I think it is up to you, if for none other than material reasons, to preserve cordial relations with Ben. If you can demonstrate this summer to him that beyond the shadow of a doubt you can put things through when you have a just opportunity, you will have all the better basis for asking for a certain support from him in the future. As it stands, he probably looks at you as a rather bad gamble, and will be skeptical until you demonstrate the efficiency which the business man admires.

I hope I did not make any strategic errors in writing him. I wrote about four pages, I think, and went into your whole career (especially for the past few months) with whatever detail I could command. To make my analysis convincing I had to admit frankly your shortcomings, as I would expect you in a similar case to admit mine, but I took pains to make it clear that your position this last term was due to a large degree to circumstances outside your control. I painted Dr. Breckinridge[l] in the purple colors which I thought his attitude toward you demanded and said some uncomplimentary things about his actions, which I hope never reach his ears or the Dean's, though I said nothing that I would not be prepared to defend openly. I felt obliged to mention the Math, because there was no object in keeping back any part of the situation. I believe in utter frankness in a case like this. Ben would have had to know finally, anyway. But I told Ben that you probably were to an extent a victim in a sort of general immolation of unfortunate seniors who delayed their Math till the last year. I have the feeling that the Math department did decide to make a general slaughter as an example to future generations, though I may be wrong. And I said lots of fine things about you, which you have GOT TO LIVE UP TO. The point about courage and philosophy is an inevitable one, I am sure. One cannot be utterly unconventional and uncompromising unless one has tremendous resources, material or otherwise, on which to fall back. Your case, in my opinion, calls for adaptation, rather than defiance of the God of Things as They Are.

I want to suggest some ways of making money this summer. In the first place,—there's typewriting. You can get lots of it at Peabody. I used to. Find out who does the stenographic work there for students and profs.,—writing papers, lectures, etc. You might take the overflow. I used to make good money at it. Or you might bulletin yourself and go in independently. I practically paid my way through one summer by typing. Then you ought (if you have spare time) to try some potboilers for the magazines. I have often thought you might easily do the sort of ironical sketches which Smart Set and some other magazines use. Stories, too. There are lots of things you might try in the writing line which would pick up a little money. And of course there's tutoring. Above all, though, do GET that damned Chemistry and Math., and make everything cocksure for the degree. I am counting on you, and now that I have written to Ben I am more directly interested than ever in seeing you put things through in good shape.

As to teaching next year, that's up to you to decide. If you can by some hook or crook finance yourself, you might possibly do better by working for your M.A. next year. It's a toss-up as to which is better. You want the M.A. eventually, anyway. If you decide to go out for a teaching job, try J. W. Blair[m] in the Independent Life Bldg. He has a cold and steely eye, but he's efficient, absolutely. And he has a good line on teaching jobs in the South.

Whatever you do, too, plan right now to make yourself independent. It may have to come gradually, but you can do it, and until you are your own master in finances you will have to make more compromises and do more unpleasant things than you will after you have secured, if not a fortune, at least a salary.

Forgive me for preachifying. I'm very intent on this whole matter now.

This has been a long letter, hasn't it. Respond accordingly. Any news of Jesse and Ridley and Bill Elliott and Fugitive meetings? By the way, don't forget (pardon superfluous reminders) to notify John (absent-minded John) as to when poems have to be in. You can look for three new poems from me within a day or so.

I'm mighty glad manuscripts and subscriptions are coming in so well. Hurroo!

Yours for the peaks and pinnacles,

Faithfully, Don

P.S. Thanks for "The Wave." It *is* rather sad, isn't it? I think that poem by Kennedy,[n] "The Lake," is good. Did you notice how remarkably like my "Naiad" it was. Same theme & story, with merely the sexes reversed. I wonder—I suppose it's just coincidence. But I have a temptation to write whimsically to Starrett—enclosing a copy of my poem.

39   *a.* Tate is back in Nashville to complete requirements for his degree, and Davidson is in Ohio with his wife's family. *b.* Marjorie Swett, Harriet Monroe's assistant on *Poetry*. *c.* Sadie A. Frank of New York City. *d.* Later on this year Back takes over all noneditorial duties and financial responsibilities for the *Fugitive*. *e.* Harry Alan Potamkin, Philadelphia-based critic and poet. *f.* Although Harriet Monroe, in her editorials in *Poetry*, had noticed with acclaim other Southern poets, she had not mentioned the Fugitives, and they felt that her remarks on local color implied derogation of their kind of poetry. So Davidson tried to get a rise out of her in a *Fugitive* editorial, which ended truculently. Southern writers, he said, "will create from what is nearest and deepest in experience—whether it be old or new, North, South, East, or West—and what business is that of Aunt Harriet's?" *Fugitive* (June–July 1923). Ten more years of neglect by Miss Monroe followed this editorial. *g.* The Poetry Society of South Carolina of which Dubose Heyward and Hervey Allen were members. *h.* Miss Will Allen Dromgoole, an elderly woman who ran a column in the *Nashville Banner* in which she published some of her verse. *i.* Houghton-Mifflin is considering Davidson's first volume of poetry, which was accepted three days later and published in 1924 as *An Outland Piper*. *j.* Not published. *k.* Tate's brother. *l.* Head of the chemistry department at Vanderbilt. Tate had apparently refused to adapt himself (Davidson's word for it in this letter)

and was making up work in chemistry and mathematics at the George Peabody College for Teachers in order to be graduated. *m.* Manager of the National Bureau of Education. *n.* Thomas Kennedy.

40/TLS

Oberlin, O.
29 June 1923

Dear Allen:

The biggest news I have (at least from my standpoint) is that Houghton Mifflin has accepted my book, to be published early in 1924, for they say their fall lists are already made up. I am naturally jubilant. They wrote a very nice letter and sent me (contrary to their custom, they say) some reader's comments. I enclose the latter for the perusal of The Fugitives. As they are confidential reports, however, please don't make any other use of them.

I enclose a copy of my letter to Miss Swett. After thinking matters over I decided that it was foolish to argue much with a subordinate. Therefore I wrote only a short note, practically reiterating what you said. I wanted very much to say something about that "tone of condescension," but I thought, since she raised only one issue in her letter and apparently ignored the rude touches of our editorial, that we had better keep in reserve, for the present at least, any remarks we may have on Miss Monroe's smelly patronization. If Miss Monroe herself says anything further and gives us an opening, we can let go full blast.

I just got your letter which derives Paul E. More. Well, wherever he derives his ideas, his address was nothing but plain common sense, dealing with the well-known, but much overlooked, fallacy of extremes. I am quite sure you would agree with most of what he said. Indeed, his argument concerning standards was substantially what you and John and I, I believe, have generally stood for, and which Stanley has generally opposed. Unfortunately, I haven't as yet got a copy of his speech, but I had a nice short note from him, thanking me for the letter of appreciation which I wrote him.

By this time you will have my letter which treats of Ben, your brother, and of sundry other things. Please don't think I am trying to intrude myself unduly. I'm just trying to help out, if I can.

I'll send the S.C. Yearbook, and return The Wave.

Heave-ho, and a bottle of sass!

Faithfully yours, Don

41/TLS
Nashville, Tenn.

29 June 1923

Dean Don:

Hail! and hell, also. A wonderful letter, this last one, but how in the hell I'll answer it in one swoop I don't see just now. I'll go through your letter "pint by pint" and try to do it a decent pretense of justice anyhow.

The Fugitive is being well managed by me for Jesse, who calls non-chalantly every evening to approve with all the contentment of a complacent donkey after having watched another jackass pull a load up a hill. But it's good fun and helps to relieve the monotony from one to three P.M. daily, for which leaven I'm duly thankful. We note what you say anent Miss Frank, and also your father's subscription, which is now arranged. The Back proposition is all but closed; we expect, by next week, to transfer the business end of the journal to his hands. Steve is taking charge of the matter as the best, by virtue at least of being the only, business man in the group; so we're leaving all to him. Stanley voiced a syllable or two of dissention, *suo more*, on the ground that Back is often guilty of certain promissory inflations; but we've talked him out of his position; we have the thing in writing with Back's signature—the letter, only, to be sure, but Steve was certain that a formal contract would not be more binding. Subscriptions are coming in fairly well—about two a day—twenty-five in the past fifteen days.

Stepped out a moment and ran into Stanley. All hail! Thou art thane of Cawdor, that shall be king! He gave me the news. When will it be out? What did they say? Tell me all about it. Hooray! You're the boy, Don. Now don't be foolish and decide at the last minute to omit one of your best poems. I'll never forgive you if you don't let me see your final selection. More later and from now on!

Poems still come in at a staggering rate, and all of them are rotten. My selection for the Nashville Prize in this heat includes, provisionally of course, "Stark Major" by Crane, "The Last Renaissance" by Maude Elizabeth Temple, and the poem by Harry Alan Potamkin. Not many are coming in for the W–B Prize,[a] and the way things look now it seems that we shall not be able to print two for that prize in this heat. I'm highly in favor of not doing so unless we have good ones.

Now as to the prospective and somewhat projected controversy over the poor bedraggled Southern poet. I agree with you on every point; you know very well I would agree to almost any controversy. But your wise caution as to the South Carolina Society is well taken, and I would recognize the wisdom of that all alone, despite my fractious humours. I think that an Editorial quoting Miss Swett's letter, in part, is almost necessary as a courtesy, and if you want to write it, go ahead. We must be sure, at all costs, to place the Poetry Society of S.C. quite outside our proscription of the saccharine and grandmotherly, for even if we didn't have reasons for this, they would merit it anyhow because they're obviously an intelligent and talented group. I can't conceive that they will countenance this new literary (goddam) magazine. It might be a good opportunity to call public attention to the best poets now writing in the South, and if we think we could bring it in fitly, to the fundamental nature of the mistake behind such a venture as this new journal. It would certainly be the part of "dignity" to ignore it; but remembering that it is advertising heavily and widely, I think that something desperate might be hazarded for the sake of spreading broadcast the fact that there are groups in the South that do not feel themselves adequately represented by such an organ. It isn't the old South as material that we object to, it seems to me (all Greek literature is a throw-back to a fragrant and heroic past), but the fatal attitude of the South toward this material. I believe, as I wrote Miss Swett, that the Southern Literary Magazine[b] illustrates my point and proves it incontrovertibly. There's nothing wrong with local color, so far as I can see, except when it drops to mere colored locality—everything must be placed in space and time somewhere, and the South is as good a correlative of emotion as any place else; and so I think that the trouble is in the damnably barbaric Southern mind, which would be provincial in London, Greenland, or Timbuctoo. I am with you in not caring a microscopic damn whether *Poetry* is angry or not; our point was well-taken; and after all we objected to Harriet's patronizing attitude. I'm very eager to see your letter to Miss Swett; so please hurry it along. . . .

I'm awaiting the three poems with all the respect and eagerness due one so recently elevated into fame. They'd better be good after your late distinction. Jesse and I noticed at the same time the marked similarity between the poem in The Wave and "Naiad"; and I hope you do write Starrett that whimsical note, though of course the plagiarism is a good poem and justified on that ground—though not so good as yours, I believe. I'm on the point of giving up hope of ever winning you over to the One Wild Stag school of poetry, and I shan't send you any others of its ilk in the hope that you'll like them, but just to amuse you. I don't think it's a great poem, but I can't lay that to the form but to the one who formed it. You will be glad to hear that Shipley[c] has written me that I'm being considered for membership in a new group that will publish a magazine called The Folio. Membership will be limited to thirty-five, no editorial supervision, every member to have two pages per issue whereon to print anything he wants to, etc. Some of the members are Alfred Kreymbourg, Kallen the philosopher, Art Young the artist;[d] so you see it will cover almost everything in the way of art and letters. I ought to hear the verdict of their committee pretty soon—ten days or so. I'm excited. Nobody seems to be writing anything around here. I haven't got down to my poem as yet, but it's getting a little clearer; the general framework, a line or two, etc., are shaping themselves gradually. It will be my most ambitious attempt so far.

I've heard from Ben again, and we are once more on amicable terms. You may be assured that I'm going through with this Peabody work in fine style—haven't cut a class so far, up to the notch in all work in Chemistry, made the highest grade on the first test in Math., etc. As for livelihood, I've got enough to run me about ten days longer, and I have in sight several pupils for tutoring; and I'm glad to get your suggestion about the stenographic work, which I'll proceed to follow up. If I can only get through the summer. And I think I can. I shall show you, dear Don, that I can put things through; and I want you to give me all kinds of damnation whenever you feel like it, it will do me good. . . .

I've written all I can think of right now. Write me again, old boy, as you did this last time. It was a great letter. Go on with those poems and believe me

Affectionately yours, Allen

41   a. A *Fugitive* prize financed by Ward-Belmont, at this time a two-year college for women in Nashville. b. Published in Nashville and Atlanta (1923–24). c. Joseph T. Shipley, one of the editors of *Folio*, submitted a poem in the Nashville Poetry Prize contest. d. Kreymbourg, a critic, poet, and playwright, was later editor of the *American Caravan*; Horace M. Kallen, an advocate of pragmatism, was on the faculty of the New School for Social Research; Arthur Henry Young was best known as a cartoonist.

42/TLS

[Oberlin, O.]

Dear Allen:
14 August 1923

This is letter number two. Letter number one,—enclosed—was written before the mail came yesterday. After it came, with Jesse's letter and the current Lit. Review, I was again plunged into dubious meditation.

I deprecate John's letter in L.R., very grievously,—yet I hope that you will take the letter as not serious, rather as jocular, and either not reply (which would be preferable) or reply in a conciliatory and not controversial tone. The first sentence of John's second paragraph, which I myself at first overlooked, does indeed give ground for a non-serious interpretation. On any other basis, indeed, the letter is desperately injurious to the cause of harmony among the brethren. Though I think John's argumentum ad hominem grievously wrong and unjust to you, I also am bound to realize that the tone of your letter was less disinterested than it might have been,—just a leetle bit pert. That, however, shouldn't have drawn such a response from John—if it is really meant in a serious way, which I am inclined to doubt. You will play the better part by not answering at all, or, if you answer, by saying nothing that will widen the breach.

John's answer appeared under very unfortunate circumstances, it seems to me, inasmuch as K. Digby's[a] notation concerning the F. was published simultaneously. What ill conjunction of the stars is this, anyway? You know, of course, that I have just as many crows to pick with John as any one, but in view of the ominous trend of events this summer, I wish to lift up my voice for peace, and I urge that you join me in a policy of conciliation and do all you can to restore an atmosphere of genial understanding. I am willing to lay aside all vehemence myself, and hence herewith drop as unseasonable any further accusations, or fault-finding.

I enclose my letter of acceptance,[b] which is intended to be diplomatic, but which also is, I assure you, in every line sincere. I urgently desire that this letter may be read to or read by each Fugitive, and since I have not all addresses, I must beg you to take care of distribution. Especially must it be sent immediately to John, from whom I fear extremities, in view of recent events. Please be sure to do this, and I hope you will be moved to supplement my remarks by similar affirmations, in order that the tomahawk may be buried conclusively. You see it will be impossible or at the least extremely embarrassing to operate The Fugitive under a cloud of misunderstanding and controversial give and take.

Jesse sent me the mast-head.ᶜ I still think publication should have been deferred, though as I said before I believe the principle of the masthead proclamation wise and proper. The details, it seems to me, are not yet perfected. I enclose the masthead with my comments for you and Jesse to think over and talk over with the others, but I would personally request that all further debate on the subject be laid aside for the present. I wish to bring up the subject next fall, when these various winds of controversy have become if possible more gentled. . . .

Faithfully yours, by my halidom, Don

42   *a.* Christopher Morley, in *The Literary Review* of the *New York Evening Post* for July 7, 1923, praised "John Crowe Ransom's *Fugitive*." *b.* Acceptance of his election as editor of the *Fugitive*. Ransom opposed the election of an editor because he did not wish a change in the *Fugitive* masthead, which listed all Fugitives alike. Since this editorial disagreement occurred simultaneously with the *Waste Land* controversy, it increased the "ominous trend of events." *c.* In the masthead for this issue the heading "Published by the Fugitives" is followed by the names of members of the group. But Davidson is listed as editor and Tate as associate editor, followed by the statement: "The Fugitives choose annually from their membership an Editor and an Associate Editor, who work according to policies formulated by the group."

43/ALS

[Oberlin, O.]
24 August 1923

Dear Allen:

Just this a.m. received a letter from John. He writes in excellent spirit, accepting fully the principles of good will which I besought in my letter of acceptance. All in all, the letter is in a very conciliatory and reasonable tone, and affords a basis, I think, for bringing our various grievous difficulties to a peaceful close. He still declares against the present masthead, though not violently, and indicates that he will desire to discuss further the "Managing Editor" idea. Just as Sidney said and I thought, the question of *academic* position *does* figure, and he clearly intimates as much. When you have engaged a few years longer in worldly affairs, you will discover that it is even so with most men. His attitude allows me to judge, however, that the question may be now readily discussed and settled on its merits, without any issues of personality. So I feel much pleased, and reiterate my request in yesterday's letter,—that you do not make any further issue with John, but allow time and such healing influences as I may set in motion to take their course.

Faithfully, Don

P.S. More fully later, — of J's letter. He does not refer to the Tate-Ransom controversy!

44/TLS

[Nashville, Tenn.]
27 August 1923

Dear Don:

This letter, although it is likely to be very brief, you must appreciate more than any I've ever written you before, for it is being concocted in the most harrowing of pain. This week-end I spent at Stanley's and Will Ella's camp out at Woodale,ª and I had the best time I've had in months, BUT this damn sunburn, extending from groin to ankle in a formidable mass of blisters, is about to drive your Ass. Ed. insane; so that walking being next to impossible, he had to cut his class at Peabody this morning. But he is secretly glad that he has this opportunity to write to the Chief and make the best report he can under the circumstances.

Not of greatest interest perhaps, but certainly of the most practical interest, is your plan about the literary page in The Tennessean.ᵇ I must tell you that the idea is not quite original with you, for I have thought of it often, but only wistfully, for I have never had much hope that I could persuade anybody around here that I am competent to conduct such a page. Your proposal that we do it jointly strikes me as a great idea—but there are difficulties to overcome. I think it would be impossible to get the Banner at all interested in our project; Miss Dromgoole is eternal in her present position. The trouble generally, it seems to me, with the newspaper, is that it can never quite see that literature is a really serious business. At the present time James Comfort and Charles Moss,ᶜ both of whom you may remember, are running a little column every Sunday called Driftwood Flames; it isn't good, as you might imagine, for the two boys are frightfully ignorant, in the first place, and in the second they show a very sad lack of tact. And there are also book-reviews every week, written by a Miss Eggleston, which are little better than illiterate. These are in the Tennessean. And the point is: the Tennessean people will probably say that they already have the "literary" part of the paper taken care of; they aren't likely to see that there are differences between things literary. But you are the person to impress on them that now is the time for Nashville to take the lead in Southern letters, and that such a literary page, conducted by two distinguished literati, would be no small aspect of this leadership! I think that Mrs. Rankin[d] would be highly in favor of it, and perhaps the new city editor,[e] whose name I forget just now. On the practical side, it would help me no little—congenial work with some remuneration, making a rare combination. What steps do you plan to take before you return, if any? Or is there anything you'd like for me to do? I would hesitate to take any step myself without full advice from you.

As to the scholarship, I think I'll get it, though I'm not sure. Tolman and Sanborn have contributed strong recommendations; I hope Mims will do likewise when he returns Wednesday. Perhaps a personal note from you to Fleming might help out.[f] I feel that part of my claim to a scholarship rests on my recent progress in a literary way, but of course it is hard for me to make a point like that with the above gentlemen, with the exception of Mims. They don't follow the current movement, and they would take any mention of myself as wholly exaggerated egotism. Literature, to most of these Profs, is about as remote as Timbuctoo. If you feel like writing to Fleming about this side of my claim, or anything else you think proper, I should certainly appreciate it. It will of course be impossible for me to stay here this year without the scholarship; so you see I'm pretty much in an attitude of suspense.

The other points of your letter I'm observing closely, even though I'm feeling too damn rotten to go into them here. As to John, I don't know what to do about him, and will take your advice whenever you offer it. I'm very much interested in the secret pressure you may be able to bear; won't you tell me about it? I did send a letter to the L.R., but it was marked at the top, "Not submitted for publication." I couldn't resist a final word for the Editor's ears! So please go easily with me, for with that move I cried quits. I agree with you about the attitude John will have to assume, but I'm still wondering about the mystery you have in store. You have exactly the right idea about peace among the brethren, and I think you'll be able to do more than anybody else in the group to establish [it] with some degree of security.

Hibbard's column*g* interests me, and I hope he lets me see it. I'm send-ing Shipley a list of periodicals, as you suggest.

Must close now and try to amble over to get a bite to eat. Write me by return mail, and send your letter to 2019 Broad, as Stanley brings the mail over about every three days. I'm hoping you get back by the 15th at the latest, because I'm certainly eager to see you. Glad you like the new issue; it isn't as good as we will have from now on. By the way, we got a subscription from Joseph Auslander,*h* and a poem for the Contest too! Have you seen the current issue of Palms,*i* It says some good things about the Fugitive. Must quit *now* or I'll go on forever!

Yours affectionately, Allen

44   *a.* Johnson had a cabin ten miles above Nashville on the Cumberland River, as did Frank Lawrence Owsley and other associates of the Fugitives.   *b.* Davidson was editor of the book page of the *Nashville Tennessean* from 1924 to 1930.   *c.* Comfort, Vanderbilt class of 1925; Moss, class of 1924.   *d.* On the editorial staff of the *Tennessean*.   *e.* James I. Finney.   *f.* Herbert C. Tolman, dean and professor of Greek, was one of Tate's favorite teachers. On his death in Novem-ber of this year, he was succeeded as dean by Walter Lynnwood Fleming, profes-sor of history, to whom *I'll Take My Stand* was later dedicated. Sanborn is chair-man of the philosophy department.   *g.* Addison Hibbard, a member of the English department at the University of North Carolina.   *h.* Poet, later lecturer in poetry at Columbia.   *i.* A poetry magazine (1923–30; 1936–40), to which Davidson, Ransom, and Merrill Moore contributed.

45/TLS

[Oberlin, O.]
30 August 1923

Dear Allen:

Within are copies of revisions I have made. Tell me how you like them now. I sent "Serenade" and "Afternoon Call" to The Folio.*a* Work on these poems has been simply agonizing. I'm going to lay off poetry for a while now and give the muse a chance to recuperate from the fatigue which is at present so evident.

As to the column, it seems The Tennessean is our only hope,—of course. But there even—if I understand your letter correctly—my erst-while pupils are likely to prove an obstacle. As for the Eggleston lady,— I don't know her and don't mind contending against *that* rivalry. I don't see that much can be done till I return, and perhaps not much then. I suggest waiting, as on account of my former connection and my fairly good acquaintance there, I can gain the ears of the powers. I shouldn't much like to knock Moss and Comfort out of employment, however, even if I could, which isn't terribly likely. Are they working as reporters and doing this thing on the side, or are they doing just the column and getting pay for that? It would be a good thing to find out. If they are working as reporters, and just doing the column for fun, we can probably manage to get somewhere. You see, I shouldn't want to be in the position of tipping the boys the black spot, even though their work isn't up to what we could do. Perhaps when school starts they will drop it? If I had had any time last year, I would have tried long ago to start something. The Fugitive work, you see, was one of the main factors in preventing me from such enterprises, and that's one of the reasons why I found modest obscurity unpleasant. However, I am all for this newspaper column or page idea, and for you and me as col-yumists.[b] And I will do all I can to put it through, if I can do so without embarrassment to Moss and Comfort. If The Tennessean would give us a page, once a week,—say on Monday when the news is scarce, or on Sunday, or in their Sat. afternoon edition,—we might manage to retain Moss and Comfort, and incidentally direct and train their talents, which as you say, are still immature. Well,—no use bothering till we can get together and talk matters over. You might inquire as to Moss and Comfort, if you can. I don't think it worth while to make a move until we formulate a definite plan and proposition. But if you see any opportunities flitting about, nab 'em. Too bad the clever youngsters have beaten us to the colyum.

I'll drop a little note to Fleming at once. I hope with all my heart you get the scholarship.

I promised to tell you more about John's letter, didn't I? Well, John sends me felicitations on my volume and also on my new position voted me by The Fugitives. He follows that with this statement: "At the same time, I am not satisfied with our mast-head, and must declare my intention of agitating for a change as soon as I can attend a next meeting; but in doing so, I cheerfully engage to abhor strife and recrimination and to conserve my weak arsenal of tomahawks and war-whoops against a more appropriate occasion, and to approach the question with a feeling of good will." He explains that he is in favor of the Managing Editor title, and gives his arguments which he says he wrote somewhat too briefly in a former letter to the group. His arguments are, however, substantially the same as those you and Jesse outlined to me from John's former letters, except that he states more fully his feeling on the non-subordination principle. I quote: "In stating my personal and selfish attitude, I mean to pose only as an example of what I had heretofore conceived was the universal (or nearly so) Fugitive opinion. From the professional point of view, we all (with the possible exception of Curry) regard poetry as a potential source of profit. As an associate professor, specializing in composition, I know that *The Fugitive* is of direct professional importance to me. It is for that reason that I resent (if one can resent without feeling a personal grievance) a misrepresentation of the facts which permits the assumption that my own part in the magazine is of less importance than that of some other." He closes with a personal compliment to me, which I won't quote, and says: "Don't forget that there is no animus whatever in my position."

I think that letter indicates quite clearly how the land lies. John's academic standing is his bread and meat, as mine is to me. He is prepared to wage a fight on any elements which tend to injure that standing. That was why your phrase "super-annuated scholarship" bit deep. You might have been a *leetle* more tactful, though John should also have known that your assault was only your usual friendly battering. But, as I said in my note previously, I think that John's letter is conciliatory. At any rate, I wish to take him at his word, and I feel sure that the atmosphere of friendship will prevail. I wrote him, but not at great length,—expressing my gratification, etc., and also indicating my general attitude on the mast-head and organization. I did not fail to indicate that, while I believed the mast-head should make clear the true character of our group organization, I thought we ought also frankly to consider that *equality* has been and remains a fiction, a purely hypothetical thing among us, and that in practice, we do not make an equal contribution of time, interest, or poetry. I did not refer in bald directness to the famous Tate-Ransom controversy, but made unmistakable intimations which John will appreciate and I hope meet with the right spirit. So let's allow things to rock along for a bit. And perhaps I'd better not tell you what "influences" I might call in, for you might think me crazy, or give me the horse-laugh. I feel sure I can set things right as soon as I can see John personally. If you meanwhile should care to write John, you might possibly do so, if you think that you can navigate so as to close, not widen, the breach, but perhaps you would prefer, and perhaps it is best, to let matters ooze along until the atmosphere is subdued from its recent aspect of thunder and lightning. . . .

I am more and more impressed with the August Fugitive, as I continue to con its pages. Good stuff. I like the green cover, too. How are you progressing with J. Back? I have my eye on a good cover design for the magazine, which I am going to get my wife to copy.

Faithfully, Don

45   *a.* A New York illustrated magazine whose single issue, which appeared later this year, carried these two poems by Davidson.   *b.* As he explains in a later letter, Davidson had planned to turn over his book page to Tate if he had been able to get a teaching fellowship at Vanderbilt. But Tate did not get the fellowship and taught during the second half of the school year of 1923–24 in the Lumberport, West Virginia, high school.

46/TL

[Oberlin, O.]
5 September [1923]

Dear Allen:

Have you read Hibbard's article in the Lit. Rev.? Write me at once what you think of it. Hibbard asked me for a criticism, and I think I'll give him one. He put the emphasis in the right place, undoubtedly (i.e. no more Old South stuff), but I think he might have distinguished more accurately between groups. The inference from his article might be that there is a general pasty similarity in Southern poetry, which isn't true. Likewise, I shall certainly criticize his omitting to mention you. He told me, in a previous letter, that he had felt obliged to confine himself to those poets who had published volumes, which I feel is also a mistake. I don't know why he dragged in the mention of me, unless it was as compensation for giving him a lot of informative aid. And I don't care for the rather apologetic tone of his article. But on the whole, I think it's a very good piece of work, especially by way of giving to the public some information as to what is going on, in which respect the article is a valuable service. From the tone of the letter he previously wrote me I deduce, now that I have read the article, that he thinks we Fugitives won't like it much. Well, well. He might at least have distinguished us from The Nomad.*a* What do you say? When I get your opinions, I'll render him our joint criticism, since he asked for it.

Nothing new up here. My departure is still indeterminate. I shall probably leave here about Sept. 16 or 17, but it's impossible to tell until my mother-in-law gets back from the West, as our plans await her arrival. Witter Bynner has been urging me to come around via Santa Fe to visit him, but that's impossible in view of my bank account. I am going to try to persuade him to visit Nashville when he starts back to New York, as I think he intends to do some time soon.

Faithfully, [Don]

46 *a*. Published in Birmingham from 1922 to 1924.

47/TLS

[Nashville, Tenn.]
7 September 1923

Dear Don:

Your note of comment on Hibbard's article has just arrived; and it is a good time to answer it along with your last fine letter. I've been at loose ends more or less all week, or you should have heard from me, but I'm more unified now, and I can write with some perspective, perhaps. Frankly, my difficulty has been with Dr. Mims, who, it seems, has borne a grudge against me for some time. . . . He wouldn't recommend me for the scholarship until I offered him some sort of apology for past irreverences! Imagine confusing personalities with scholarship! But larger men than he have done so. The result is that I'm becoming a quite disillusioned young man, and strangely enough the prophets of faith and love contribute largely to my undoing.

As to the Tennessean proposition, we needn't fear about ousting Comfort and Moss from a job; they are reporters and do the literary work as a recreation. Nevertheless, they might cause a little trouble, especially Comfort, who is a rather sour and egocentric young man. But I have little doubt that we could get the paper to take the weekly page, and I eagerly await your return for the development of the project.

Stanley, more than once this past week, I have consulted about what I should do in regard to John, and after receiving his advice I decided not to send a letter I had written tentatively. I intended to tell John that I bore him no ill will and that the controversy was a closed incident, but that I regretted his failure to make his stand on the academic issue clear, saying that I would consider myself disingenuous if I didn't speak frankly of all matters, etc., etc. But I do believe that he should approach me first; it is due me, I believe; and more seriously, I can't afford to lose the tactical advantage of having him make the first move. Of course you may have your reasons for not telling me just what it is you have in mind to do about the recent warfare, and you know that I trust your judgement as I trust nobody else's, but I can't refrain from saying that I feel uneasy in the dark. You say I might think the method you have in mind absurd. My dear Don, nothing is absurd that works—in fact, nothing is absurd except those things that don't seem to be! As to John's letter of peace to you, I can only reiterate my former warning, backed up by Stanley's and Jesse's view of the same matter. If John persists in carrying over academic seniority from the University into The Fugitive and succeeds in doing so, I shall come dangerously [near] offering my resignation to the group. . . .

Hibbard's article is a good one, and I believe that it does more justice to Southern poetry than any other utterance in my memory. I agree with you that he should have distinguished groups more carefully, and we might go so far as to question his statement that there is nothing like a school in the South. But as you say, he placed the emphasis in the right place, and we should be thankful that we have a man in the South sufficiently intelligent to write from a critical point of view, so, all things considered, I believe that we have no complaint to make, but rather much appreciation to express. I am especially glad that John came in so prominently; it is the first time, so far as I know, that his Poems About God has received the praise it deserves, or even recognition; and if it weren't for the recent schism between us, which might lead him to misinterpret me, I should write him a note of congratulation. I think Hibbard could well afford to leave me out, but I can't deny that I should have liked being mentioned; it would have helped my volume along, besides the good it would naturally have done the Ego. But I am surely glad he mentioned you, and if your book had been out, I should have felt wronged somehow if your name hadn't appeared in equal prominence with John's and Percy's.

Please hurry back to Nashville, for I am much alone. Jesse left Wednesday for a trip of two weeks in the east, and now I am a reluctant eremite. The enclosed sonnet isn't to be taken too seriously; it is personal and I doubt its artistic qualities. By the way, Henri Faust (W. E. Spencer)[a] has been here for ten days: the most honest man alive; one of the most gifted; and withal, almost unlettered. He is returning home tomorrow, but will come back to Vanderbilt Jan. 1st. He was at the last meeting; we liked him. The copies of your poems were too late for the meeting Sat., but I will hold them for you; we agreed that we wouldn't have another meeting until the absent brothers were back in the fold. Write me FORTHWITH.

Yours ever, Allen

47   *a.* Another Fugitive visiting poet.

48/TLS

Oberlin, O.

10 September 1923

My dear Eremite:

Be not lost in lone splendor (or whatever it is) in the night of difficulties and buffetings. I hasten to answer your letter and sonnet,— first of all by saying that I will talk these things over with you personally next week, for I plan to debouch on the rocky hills of Nashville by either next Monday or Tuesday.

The first paragraph of your letter leads me at once to speak of your difficulty with Dr. Mims. Remember that I am, as always, on your side, and yet in this case I should have to be on Dr. Mims' side, too. As I have told you before (and so I believe has Curry) you and Ridley weren't quite fair in your attitude toward Dr. Mims last spring. I am sure he felt very much hurt and bothered by a belief that you and Ridley were in the ranks of the enemy, and that you were on occasion not losing opportunities to make sport of him. (Mind you, I'm speaking of what he *felt*.) I can't much blame him for feeling hurt and even aggrieved, though, at the same time, I don't think I would agree with his method of meeting the situation. You say "Imagine confusing personalities with scholarship." Yet that is exactly what you and Ridley did, or I am at least inclined to think so. I must confess that I can't see any dishonesty in his asking you to disavow past "irreverences." That looks like being perfectly frank. I am sure that he was not trying to humiliate you or to assert academic power beyond the point of honesty. Here's the way I dope the thing out. Probably he felt that in addressing the committee, however much he might praise your scholarship, he would in all conscience and justice be required to say that he had some doubts as to your seriousness with regard to academic matters. But, with a statement from you which cleared up that feeling of his, he would be able to give you an unqualified recommendation which would benefit, not injure, your case. That's how I see it. Now am I right or wrong. I think you could well afford, without any qualms whatever, to do whatever Dr. Mims asked toward setting things right, not even considering the issue of a scholarship. I infer from your letter that you have met the situation already, and if you hadn't I should certainly urge you to do so. I am honestly glad you have. And now, adopting a Reginald Wright Kaufman[a] pose, I am prompted to declare a principle of life,— Young man, if you wish others to be charitable to you, you must be charitable to others. Thus do I moralize, and damme if it isn't true.

You are having lots of troubles these parlous days, aren't you, and no one grieves more than I for that. But look back and ask yourself, if stones have bruised you, whether that is not often because you have, forsooth, deliberately butted your head against them. I don't know much of Plato's world of ideas, but my slight perspective of the universe leads me to think that acts and attitudes are assuredly among the realities of the world. They have *beings*, it would seem, of their own,—once they are born. They become individuals, rampant, coursing to and fro, practically indestructible, and one may at least recognize them by their track of consequences. Hinc illae lacrimae,—again. I hate the role of preacher. I would not adopt it in this paragraph but for my honestly tremendous desire to see you get on. Discount my preachments all you wish, and forgive me on the score of the aforesaid desire, but leave dishonesty out of the charge against me.

You didn't say whether you had gotten the scholarship. Has it been awarded yet. I hope you get it,—by george I do.

I think the best method of persuading peace to the warring parties in the late controversy would be to invite you and John and Stanley to a good dinner with plenty of liquor on the side, to warm the cockles of the heart. But since I can provide no liquor, other means must do. I agree with you and Stanley absolutely on the academic business. Have no fears as to my attitude on that score. I think the greatest trouble with several of us, including myself, has been our vindictiveness. Vindictiveness will gain nothing,—will only make more trouble. My plan of procedure is simply to go to John at the earliest possible moment and talk things over with him very frankly. I am foolish enough to think that I have a good chance to succeed in restoring amity. I am inclined to think your letter would have helped. But let's wait until I arrive to talk these things over. Much writing gets nowhere. I am most eager to be with you again and see the Fugitives re-assemble. With both John and you subscribing to the principle of no tomahawks and all good will, my task as intermediary won't be hard.

I'm glad you liked Hibbard's article. Now that we have conferred, I'll write him our reaction, giving the criticism a subordinate and casual place, and making the letter in the tone of congratulation.

Also I'm glad to hear about Henri Faust. I was always interested in that fellow's things, and shall be glad to learn more about him.

Wasn't that review of Driftwood Flames[b] a corker? I'm glad for our junior brethren. They deserve good mention. I am for the boys through and through (always praying against cranial enlargements), and besides, that review is a great boost to Vanderbilt. Do you realize how much publicity Vanderbilt, Nashville, and The Fugitive and Fugitives have been getting of late in the Lit. Rev.? Somebody has been in there off and on all summer.

With this letter I close the letter season, but not without mentioning that your sonnet, whatever its personal implications, is in every way superb as a poem. I have no criticisms. I admire it,—I just admire it.

Faithfully, Don

48 *a*. A prolific popular poet and novelist. *b*. An anthology of verse published by the Nashville Poetry Guild in 1923 and dedicated to Ransom.

49/ALS

[Lumberport, W.Va.]
3 March [1924]

Dear Don:

Thanks for a fine letter at last;*a* it is quite an occasion. And for the poems, too, which I am very glad to see. I don't like Stanley's "To an Aged Pall-bearer," although it has fewer "bad lines" to the square foot than "A Matter of Record," which I like better. John's poem*b* is extremely deft, and I like it; but I should like a little more time before venturing what would be an objection to it as representing an order of poetry that doesn't strike me at all. Very soon, I hope, I'll get around to a letter to John and make my case to him personally.

While I think of it, let me mention the advisability of my offering a resignation of my present title of honor among the Fugitives. I didn't have time to go into it before I left, I went so precipitately; and I knew it would be all right to settle the matter at almost any time before the April issue. I can see only one reason for a refusal of the group to accept my resignation,*c* and that is the vivid possibility of my return to Nashville in June. I certainly do not care to go to New York and waste many of the very sparse moneys at my disposal in the best of times; I'll need them, wherever I am, next fall; so Nashville, if I can eke out a physical existence there for three months, and I think I can, is the best because, all things considered, it is the most congenial place. You see just how the matter lies; and I am depending on you to give me the advice that will prompt me to act most agreeably for all concerned.

I wish I could reproduce the *Best Poems* review,*d* but I'm afraid I can't. The main point of it lay in picking out particular poems, and now I can't remember them. But no harm done! It was a trifling piece, and after all one fewer among the hack jobs to be held, finally, against me by my literary conscience.

I sent my mss. to Seltzer,[e] and today an acknowledgement of receipt came saying a favorable word or two and promising a decision in a very short time. But I have little hope of success with him. Indeed, the more I look at my copy of the mss., the worse—or, rather, the more absurd even the best of it seems. But I'll try to get it published, at any rate, in deference to the simplest and most clamorous of vanities, but with no sense of having achieved anything even when it is done. As I look back on the past four years of my verse-writing, I recall that I was aware that I might have worked any of two or three tendencies I experimented with and to as much success as attaches to the average volume of "good verse" (cf. Parthenia, Scholar to His Lady, etc.); but intellectual unrest over formal problems and an impatience with the meager statement imposed by the demand of intelligibility have about undone me. I suppose a philosopher, like Santayana, can plunge directly into complexity, because it is his business as a philosopher to explicate, to explain and describe the manifold elements in any intuition or idea, to say, "One thing bears a certain relation to some other thing." But, alas poor Yorick, the poet amputates his intuition for the sake of some sentiment so general that every naive commoner may use it for a hitching-post; for if he doesn't do this, but flings out a pattern of intuition unexplained and unsung (!),[f] he writes what you call gibberish, while actually he is only offering the very datum the metaphysician tries to place in some kind of "order" and not to much end, at that. Heigh ho! the holly! but that's enough of this stuff!

After Seltzer returns the mss., I'll send it to H-M. I certainly appreciate your offer to write them about it, and I'll notify Cobb,[g] who I believe will write too. I have every conviction you'll have the chance to do me the kindness!

I'm glad to hear that *The Tennessean* is going to pay off,[h] not so much for the amount, which will be small, but for the thrill of getting paid for "literary" writing! Just forward check to me!

I've written too much already to ask you to read more of this pencil scribbling. Write soon—just a line or two if you can't write more.

Yrs. ever, Allen

49   *a.* Nearly all of Davidson's letters of 1924 and 1925 are missing from the file, possibly lost because Tate was moving around so often during this period. *b.*

"Ada Ruel," *Fugitive* (April 1923). c. As associate editor of the *Fugitive*. d. This was an intended review for Davidson's *Spyglass* page, which had now begun to appear in the Sunday *Tennessean*. e. This is the manuscript of a proposed volume of poems. f. The exclamation point is for Davidson, who had criticized modern verse "because it does not sing." g. W. C. Cobb, class of 1923, now working for a publisher in New York. h. Contributors to the *Spyglass* page were paid by inches of newspaper column during the first seventeen months; nobody remembers how much an inch.

50/ALS

[Lumberport, W.Va.]
8 March 1924

Dear Don:

This is simply to ask you to make *one* revision for me in the Cummings review,[a] to ask you very meekly, almost submissively after my quite Tatian spume of day before yesterday! Ah, mon frère, you must—well, not indulge me, but bear with me. If you think I was too enthusiastic about Cummings, remember that he, like some others, is in the minority, and may need an extravagant word or two to strike a fair average with the opposite extreme of prevailing unfavorable opinion against him; actually, my review is more favorable than a more technical presentation of him would have been; I see much that is only magnificent charlatanism, but if I made that statement in a popular review, the public would be sure to misunderstand, thinking I meant he is insincere or something equally absurd. And particularly the reference to "Hero and Leander" was ill-advised except for the purpose of the moment; it was uncritical, but the analogy will seem fairly accurate to "poetry-lovers."

The revision is simply this: paragraph one, last sentence,—"practitioners of *the* arts," instead of "*three* arts." I'm going to do my best to write the reviews as you require them, and if they don't suit you, send them back with the wicked parts of them marked; I'll revise and try them on you again.

Thanks for the copy of page Feb. 24 and of Mar. 2. They are very good, both of them. Durn you! I see you came back at me for knocking Vinal off. Do you want *my* come back at you? Well, here it is: the fact that Harold is a minor poet makes the need of impeccable technique all the more imperative; Eliot, who is an extremely minor poet—minor in the critical but not therefore unworthy sense, just as Housman is in his way—has only one defense, perfection of technique. We can excuse bad craftsmanship only in a titan; therefore, Harold, to my mind, is negligible. Now, aren't you routed?

I enclose a clipping of some titles I'd like to review. This doesn't at all mean that I expect you to make an *effort* to get them; if they come your way, turn them over to me if it's convenient.

Farewell—while I go on planting thistles as other men plant corn!

Affect. Allen

P.S. Teaching gets more pleasant every day. My seniors are taking *The Rape of the Lock*, and I don't know when I've had so much fun. I rouse 'em in approved Mimsian fashion; and would you believe it? They seem to be getting something out of it besides *lessons!*

50   *a.* Tate's review of Cumming's *Tulips and Chimneys* appeared in the *Spyglass* page for March 23, 1924.

51/ALS

[Lumberport, W.Va.]
14 March 1924

Dear Don:

How shall I tell you of the many emotions of delight and satisfaction that rose up in me when I suddenly discovered that one of the packages contained *An Outland Piper*? It was a kind of event of the spirit, a culmination of an adventure beyond the accidents of everyday life. Seeing your very own name on the book and the familiar poems, whose writing I had followed from the first one to the last so attentively, in its pages brought up the past two years of our joint procedure in this lonely but exciting business. I almost feel that the book is partly mine; and you will forgive my saying this, for you know just why, out of what feeling, I say it.

Perhaps you wonder why I speak so seriously—I, who always seem to vacillate between gaiety and bitterness—but really there are very few things in experience (in mine) that are worth being called serious; this is one of them. It is uncommonly serious; your note to me is the meaning of it. It is the occasion for a renewed consciousness of the meaning of our compact, that covenant which was more significant than either of us could guess on the day of its almost casual making. For my part, its significance is quite separate from any idea of the greatness or immortality our different, yet identical, efforts may or may not achieve.

It is a compact of the understanding, the seal of a love unsuspected by those who are so inured to the mere materials of life that they cannot speak of it impartially in art, either out of love of it or out of hatred. This attitude, however divergent in its projections, this attitude grown out of loneliness in an alien world is so secret that it must exult a little when it recognizes a brother. You may think of it differently, in other terms, but I swear it must in the end come to the same thing.

As you say, it is the life of adventure, and I say that the reason of this is that it is the life of the soul; and it is the life of the soul despite the incidental frustrations we meet and the merely human foibles we display and the temporary misunderstandings of the flesh that we may suffer. And so to your bow of burning gold I bring, in my meager way, what arrows of desire I can make for us in the momentary cessations of clamor in the physical world.

Let this letter be apart from our others, as a type of what might be said if there were no days and nights and worlds to be considered.

Yours in the compact ever and with all affection, Allen

52/TLS

Lumberport, W.Va.
26 March 1924

Dear Don:

The page of March 23 came this morning, and all I can say is that it holds up an already fine standard in the usual style. Mrs. Rankin's review is surprising—better than I thought she could do—but it is too bad that a certain limitation of taste permits her to think Percy Mac-Kaye is a worthy dramatist; do you intend to run much of her stuff? But hooray for the Spyglass! It's tip-top. You hit an excellent stride in the column. May it continue. I am very glad that Nye[a] likes my work just for the practical end of it. Don't you think I'm just about hitting the level I should maintain?—improvements in ease and "charm" always to be desired? I rather think if I should write as I'm naturally inclined to, Nye would find it not only highbrow, but positively incomprehensible; probably I have enough leeway now. However, when some particularly austere thing comes along, I might like to do it up uncompromisingly, but of course by previous arrangement and discussion. But his (Nye's) remarks, and Alexander's,[b] don't they go to show that perhaps we underestimate the capacities of the merely intelligent reader?

There are probably hundreds of people about Nashville with as much appreciation as they.

I have a new candidate to propose for your staff of reviewers, Laura [Riding] Gottschalk. She recently remarked, by way of humorous comment, that she was not exactly wealthy; I humorously suggested that she might write for The Tennessean; and she quite seriously fell in with the idea. I promised immediately to write you about her, and I hereby fulfill the promise. I know something about her prose; you may know a little. I have read her novel, I have read a good many letters; and I do not exaggerate when I say that her prose is quite as brilliant as her verse, and, what is more, it is always perfectly translucent. I have already informed her of the rates, space limits, mechanical make-up, etc. If you favor her, all you have to do is to drop her a brief note. And I rather believe it would be a good thing to get her with us (it would tie her more to The Fugitive), and for this reason: she writes that Harriet Monroe, rejecting all recent offerings, gives a reason that can only be interpreted as a dislike of her friendship with us; and at the same time, L. G. comes forth with the confession that she thinks The Fugitive is quite the equal of Poetry (and she's a competent judge, by the way) and for many reasons would prefer to appear with us. So wouldn't it be good to sorta affiliate here with us by way of the book-page? She will be thrilled over Graves' liking for her work; I pass on the news. I feel almost paternal!

I suppose you have my note telling you about Seltzer's rejection and my decision to send the mss. to H. M. I sent it this morning. I made an entirely new mss., omitting two poems—To a Dead Citizen and the soft little sonnet, You Left. In my letter accompanying it I simply stated that I am editorially connected with The Fugitive and pointed out the possible wisdom of changing the title of the book, and then signed my name; I felt the less I went into myself the better it would be. I have little hope of acceptance, but there's nothing like trying. I shall send it to Brimmer[c] or Knopf next. You see, I'm perfectly cynical about the present pilgrimage! I suspect it will get a hearing at all only because of your letter and Cobb's, which I suppose he will write.

The table of contents for the coming issue looks mighty good. I don't at all blame you for not taking to the poem I offered. It was a trifle, although I do think now, since later revisions, it is a good trifle. I'd like to offer it again next time, if I don't place it elsewhere—which I probably won't. If you will read it carefully, I believe you'll see that it just about sums up what I say in my editorial.[d] With all its faults I rejoice over the editorial, for it keeps me from being entirely out of the issue; I should hate to miss out now after the flow of the past two years; 'tis the weakness of sentiment, but a forgivable one I hope, for occasionally I get a bit sentimental over the old Fugitive!

I think your observation on the strictures of my aesthetics upon my practice is a very just one. I know my aesthetics dictates too much. I'm coming round gradually, I think, to a realization that all art, in its lyrical forms, is an immediate and direct expression of an irresistible vision or conviction, and implies, or rather has as its necessary motivation, a fundamental mysticism. In writing of Cummings I tried to simplify the point by calling it "passion," which I said he lacks. Hart Crane has it (he's a mystic in his way as thoroughly as Blake; a close look at his work would prove it even to *you!*), and that is why I think he's the best poet of his so-called group—which is really as varied within itself as we are, perhaps more so. If Crane should offer us an exceedingly difficult poem, do you think it would have a chance with the Committee? I suspect he's under the impression we're hostile toward him, and naturally you can see he would hesitate unless some encouragement were indicated; and I know he feels that a poem by him would embarrass me, knowing I should be for it, if it was distinguished, in an uphill fight. I have a copy of the poem, and personally I can vouch for it; but what the Committee might think is probably another matter!

(Yes, John does it with a disarming flourish, but that doesn't mean the public understands it; it simply means that he writes better than I— which is irrelevant from the popular viewpoint.)

I see I'm rambling, although there are at least a million things more I'd like to tell you, if I could only focus them to the present moment. Shortly you will receive, since God works in a mysterious way, a mysterious parcel from H. M., and it will contain a copy of your own book: this, as per agreement!

By the way, if you hear of a job I might get in Nashville for the summer, newspaper work, etc., please let me know at once. I'd like to spend the summer in Nashville; I'll probably never be there much again.

Farewell for the nonce!

Yr. ob't serv't, Allen

P.S. Consider this point in your editorial capacity: we are interested in getting the best of the present generation. We are at present holding up people like Laura Gottschalk as proof of our interest in getting an audience for the best Unknowns. Well, why not Hart Crane, whose medium is just now Secession alone? I doubt seriously if Francis Jeffrey or, before him, Dr. Johnson would have looked with favor upon a poem suddenly appearing from William Blake; while now we are deeply certain he was a very great poet. My point isn't that it's as good as proved that Crane is as good as Blake; it is simply that Jeffrey (or even Coleridge) wouldn't have understood Blake, throwing him out therefor, and that we dismiss people like Crane for the same reason. Of course the judgement of posterity is a capricious thing, and might never justify our approval of a man like Crane; so it is a gamble, but I think, as "farsighted editors," we ought to consider the point I am lamely making. Remember that Harriet Monroe in her dotage makes much of her liberal youth: the discovery of a crowd of idiots who later turned out to be wise men. Please read, or report, this to the Committee and others, won't you? I may say that it isn't a "radical" propensity behind this; Crane is the only one I feel this way about. And to clear myself, I can easily be so vulgar as to say that Crane has found nothing good in my work for over a year, but has condemned it all heartily![e]

Expect reviews of Camilla Doyle, King of the Isles, and M. L. Woods on Sunday.[f]

52   *a.* John H. Nye, managing editor of the *Tennessean.*   *b.* T. H. Alexander, one of the editors of the *Tennessean,* wrote a syndicated column "I Reckon So," to which Davidson occasionally contributed.   *c.* The B. J. Brimmer Company of Boston.   *d.* "One Escape from the Dilemma," *Fugitive* (April 1924).   *e.* Three of Crane's poems appeared in later numbers of the *Fugitive.* His "Starke Major" appeared in 1923 as a prize poem.   *f.* Tate reviewed Camilla Doyle's *Poems* and Margaret L. Wood's *A Poet's Youth* for the *Tennessean* on April 13, 1924; his review of J. V. Nicholson's *The King of the Black Isles* appeared there on April 6, 1924.

53/TLS

Lumberport, W.Va.
2 April 1924

Dear Don:

The damn mail has been delayed for two days because of floods, but at last the reviews of your book are here, and I'm greatly excited. I think I can understand your own emotions over them; but let me say right here, that they aren't really half-bad, considering that first volumes, however good they may be (remember Robinson's first reception), only serve to give the reviewers a chance to exploit their stupidity. The Times[a] review is the sheerest piece of nonsense I've ever seen, but what else do you expect? Of course they quoted the wrong poem, and I hazard the notion that they did simply because you are "new" and they didn't want to take the trouble of reading your volume carefully; and if you aren't the superior of Heyward, then I'm a caviar-eating catfish. The Nation[b] does better by you, but where they find the obscurity (great God! what would they say about me?) I don't see; I think you're as lucid as the dawn. As for Hibbard, he's obviously an ass, I regret to say, and if it weren't for the popular blow it administers your volume, I should think you could thank him for his judgment as an indirect tribute to your book; it is quite a tribute to be misunderstood by some people. Altogether, such are the adventures of a first volume, I should think, and doubtless you have more comment to come! No, I don't think you get a reflex through The Fugitive; it's the other way round. Shouldn't the general comment in the Times about the Southern re-nascence, which distinguishes The Fugitive, be given some publicity in Nashville? Especially if we are going to ask for patrons? These reviews bring up many things, but out of them emerges most clearly my exhor-tation that you ignore them for the most part. You know that a few of us are with you and understand.

The situation seems to be about as I expected it to be—John, Stanley, and Curry against continuance. Let me say forthwith that I don't think Curry counts; I think he would admit it himself, because of his very slight interest personally in creative writing. So there are Ransom and Johnson, only, to be considered, for it appears that every-body else is enthusiastic, at least not indifferent. With this in mind, what is to be done? If you intend to continue till December, we have eight months to provide ways and means, and God knows I have enough of the sanguinity of youth and of the spirit of adventure not to give up this soon.[c] John, of course, would be a devilish loss, but I don't think any one person is a decisive factor; besides, we should probably get most of his work, anyway. Stanley, I believe, could be made to see things differently; he doesn't consider the thing in its broader aspects—the magazine as a small but probably important service to American po-etry, etc. I should imagine that any one with the pride of the profession would sooner or later consider this point. I don't think literature can be merely a medium of individual satisfaction; I believe that truly hon-

orable men work for the fine abstraction called Literature, as a contribution to another abstraction called Civilization, and I think there
must be some unanimity however individualistic the separate contributions may be. This sounds pretty far-fetched in connection with the
poor Fugitive, that humble little journal; nevertheless, the idea has
been with me throughout as a concept which gives our small endeavors
a dignified significance. If our members are going to retire into the
crypt of self-interest, I think they are defeating themselves, for foresight
might tell them that their greatest interests may lie in keeping intact
the idealism behind our venture, although immediate satisfactions may
not be greatly in evidence. I wish I were there to offer my eager, if
unheeded, word to the discussion. Of course, in the face of complete
insolvency, what I say must sound merely pretty; but we have a year,
and I, for one, will not have given up till the last minute; I may have a
more practicable word to offer at a later date. If you care to pass on my
views, do so by all means. I might add that the excuse of insolvency
won't be fully convincing if all the while we show ourselves as utterly
cold; only the extremest efforts will justify our suspension. I doff my
hat to you and Mr. Frank.

I understand the point about reviews by L.R.G.,[d] and I think Nye's
point is in many respects well-taken. But do what you can without
embarrassment to yourself.

John's review of the Oxford volume[e] is full of interest, not least
because of the nice lift he gives me—which I am enabled to accept at
its face value. Offer him my appreciation.

I await the letter of your earliest leisure. Damn! How I curse our
separation at this time, when so many high things need to be discussed. . . .

                                                    Expectantly, Allen

P.S. Reviews of Robinson and Heyward ought to arrive Sunday. I'm
going to do a *bold* thing incidental to Heyward review; you may not
like it—well send it back then!

53   *a. New York Times Book Review,* March 30, 1924.   *b.* April 2, 1924.   *c.* The December 1924 issue of the *Fugitive* announced that the group was resuming "financial management of the magazine" and expressed to their readers their sincere
appreciation to Jacques Back, without whose "assistance and generous interest,
it is doubtful whether the magazine could have survived during the past eighteen

months." *d.* Laura Riding Gottschalk. *e.* D. C. Thompson and F. W. Bateson, eds., *Oxford Poetry* (1923); Ransom's review appeared in the *Tennessean* for March 30, 1924.

54/TLS

Lumberport, W.Va.
14 April 1924

Dear Don:

I doubt if I can gather up the things out of your last few notes that I want to answer; but I'll try.

Anyhow, the new Fugitive came today, and it looks mighty good. ... Your Prelude in a Garden[a] ... is a hell of a good poem, but will you forgive it, Don? When I had finished the first stanza, I glanced to the top of the page, thinking there must be some mistake, that your name shouldn't have been there, but John's; however, I began to recognize you as I went on. But I'm a jellyfish if line four isn't John's! But, as I say, it's a fine poem—more composure than you usually achieve, more flexibility of line, better phrasing—less strained. Are you looking in a new direction? It seems promising. As I re-read my article, it *does* seem a bit hectic—and very bad prose, but indeed much better than I wrote a year ago; I hope to improve with age, like Bourbon.

H-M have returned my mss.,[b] but wrote me a splendid letter. As I thought, they were afraid of the modernism; they said the poems were brilliant and original, and that they'd like to see my collection a year from now if I hadn't placed it elsewhere—which I take to mean that they liked best the poems at the end of the book, the less radical forms which are of fairly recent composition and seem to indicate my present tendency. I swear I haven't the incentive to send it anywhere else, but I may if I can think of a likely house. Can you suggest one? Thanks again for your letter to H-M!

I'm glad to see that the Double Dealer is out again; this last issue is almost in their old stride. Oughtn't we send them something? I think I'll review some of these books *again* for them! Let me have any news, especially Fugitiviana.

In haste, Allen

54   *a. Fugitive* (April 1924).   *b.* Tate's first collection of poetry, *Mr. Pope and Other Poems,* did not appear until 1928.

55/TL

Dear Don:

This is just the second section of my letter of yesterday—not the dining-car, my dear Don, for there's nothing here to feast on, but the sleeper.

Here and now I testify to my pleasure in your Spyglass of last Sunday. Your defense of Bridges was extremely well-considered. Let me resent with you the linotyper's gauche error—the idea of such an octogenarian dignitary in a debauch is quite shocking; but I don't think your readers will indict you, despite the unlikelihood of an unfamiliar word like debouch occurring to them. The reviews were very good, yours of Gibbs' book especially, and also John's of Zona Gale—John throws a very wicked style, indeed.

I'm glad you are liking my article. If I had had the necessary space, I think your initial objections to its style would not have been made, for I had to concentrate too much; I couldn't expand my points. I think the issue is a very good one, and I will write the critique, in light vein, at my soonest leisure. But I wish Red had cerebrated a little and got titles for his poems; there's a falsifying impression of connection given as they are printed. That boy's a wonder—has more sheer genius than any of us; watch him: his work from now on will have what none of us can achieve—power. If he can triumph over that hellish environment of his for another year, I have no fears for him. Incidentally, I hope Dr. Mims won't keep nagging at him (I doubt if you know whereof I speak), for he's very sensitive, and while the Doctor's solicitude is well-meant it is wholly irrelevant; he no more understands Red than he does the fourth dimension.

It's damnably good news that Benet is doing your review. While I think he's at bottom a lightweight, I realize he's influential; so here's praying for panegyrics. . . .

Adieu! [Allen]

56/TLS

[Nashville, Tenn.]
23 April 1924

Dear Allen:

I wish I could answer adequately even three or four of the thousand or so matters you indicate. But I'm tired, sick, disgusted, bored, distracted, nervous, apprehensive, worried, busy, oppressed, and am really not doing any of my work efficiently. Here, however, is a poor essay, random and disparate in anguish.

The Fugitive situation is still beclouded, at least to my ken. A motion was passed at last meeting to this effect: i.e., that Mr. Frank inform J. Back that we carry out the schedule of publication planned for this year; that we will probably terminate the contract at the end of this year; that, though *without guaranteeing* anything, we will *endeavor* to aid him financially, *possibly* to the extent of financing two numbers—the two final ones.

I view this as absolutely indefinite and even disgusting. However, mine was the only dissenting vote, and Mr. Frank is the one appointed to see Back because I begged to be relieved of the painful duty of such a conference.

At the next meeting I advocated requiring Mr. Back to publish the two next numbers, then taking it over from him and publishing the last two ourselves—this proposal being based on the indication given by him that he would be glad to see us adopt a quarterly basis for the rest of the year,—i.e., publish two more numbers.

Mr. Frank stubbornly opposed this, on the ground that we should retain the advantage we have over Mr. Back; that, as partners, not being a corporation, each of us is individually liable for total debts; that Mr. Back might have legal basis, if we "failed" (Mr. F's word) to fulfill our part of contract, for recovering damages from us; and that accordingly the immediate discontinuance or midsummer discontinuance of contract was dangerous and an unsound business step.

He may have other reasons. He was not very communicative,—but held on like a bull-dog. When I said that, since I had gotten much out of the magazine, I was willing to stand the sacrifice of a financial assessment, Mr. Frank retorted that others, who had not gotten so much out of the magazine, might not feel that way about it. You see, don't you? I tried hard to press the issue to the point where it would be clearly evident who would and who would not support the magazine out of their pockets if necessary. No use. The issue is still vague.

Neither Stanley nor Curry was at meeting. This morning Stanley, Ransom, and I had a lengthy conversation on Fugitive matters. Ransom's stand now seems to be about the same as mine, though he didn't uphold me in the meeting. That is, he does not like to see Back going on at a dead financial loss; he sees discontinuance as almost inevitable, but wishes to carry out this year's schedule; he is willing to dip into his pocket. Stanley is full of schemes which I think are perhaps impracticable,—such as the stock company idea. Do you think, for instance, that fellows like Potamkin, Shipley, Spencer, et al, would be willing to enter an organization with us, paying ten to fifteen dollars in return for certain privileges?

But Stanley's attitude is tinged with bitterness. You know why. I finally found out this morning, upon questioning him, that he feels he has been unjustly treated. He says that the Fugitive has been just about ruined because the standard of the majority has been forced upon the magazine; minority poems have had no chance. Says he isn't in the minority with Hirsch and Frank,—that's a different one. His own "bloc" was composed, say, of Ridley, Elliott, and himself. Now he's the only member here. And he thinks that our policy in regard to poetry has largely been the cause of the very evident disruption of Fugitive spirit.

I am not any more in a fighting mood. I am indignant, but I do not wish to fight if there is nothing worth fighting for. It becomes increasingly evident to me that my position is too thankless to be comfortable, and I am thinking very seriously of presenting my resignation at once. This is of course confidential.

Today John and Stanley had the effrontery to say to me that if I did not continue as editor another year the magazine was doomed anyhow, since nobody else would care to do the work. That is as much as to say that I am the poor goat; I am to do the work, to pull and haul and heave, while there is a spirit of disunion abroad and a lack of interest which renders my work with this failing enterprise daily more difficult and disheartening.

I am tired of the business, body and soul. So long as high spirit was uniform, so long as the enterprise possessed nobility, it was truly a happy labor. I feel disgracefully compromised now. I have no heart for the work. (Though I realize, all the while, the very fine attitude of a portion of the members.)

Enough of that.

I'm sending you the poems read last meeting. Please be sure to return them. Jesse's was the hit of the evening. Mine is punk.

Enjoyed your recent comment on the new Fugitive. I agree with you in the main. But you miss terribly on Merrill's sonnets, I think. I admire them very much, because he is doing spontaneously just what the radicals shout they should have privilege to do,—i.e., violate a form for the sake of their individualism, their damned self-expression.

I don't think that your withdrawal from the group is in point at all. Nothing has indicated that anybody felt hostile to you. I think such a stand would hurt, not help, matters. Don't think of it.

I'm awfully sorry you didn't get the fellowship. The whole business makes me sad. What will be your plans now?

I had rather you'd review *only* the Morand[a] book I sent. I'm making it a rigid policy to review no books we don't receive,—we have enough of them, Lord knows. You can *mention* the other in your review, won't that be sufficient?

I wish you all success with Brimmer, though I don't know whether it's a wise step to send them your book.

We got a batch of poems from L. R. Gottschalk, but had to reject them. Committee's unanimous opinion was that they wouldn't do. Three were almost good enough,—Golden Plover, Last Women, All Right. But the last was too long, Last Women was over-drawn, and Golden Plover wasn't as good, we thought, as any of the other stuff we published. We are sending them back, with a request to return the Plover together with others, later on. This batch of poems was, I thought, very diffuse. If these are the poems Harriet Monroe rejected, I can't say that I blame Harriet. Don't my boy let your admirations color your aesthetics, which I thought you were constantly submitting to a regular litmus test!

Heigh-ho, the holly, most friendship is feigning, most loving mere folly.

                                                                    Yours, Don

I have said nothing of resignation to the members, and shan't until I'm ready to offer it. What is your attitude?

56   *a.* Paul Morand's *Green Shoots* was reviewed by Tate in the *Tennessean*, May
      18, 1924.

57/TLS

[Lumberport, W.Va.]

26 April [1924]

Dear Don:

The two bad novels and the Morand book came last night. Reviews will reach you within a week. I note your advice about the Morand book; I'll simply allude to the other one.

More importantly, the Fugitive poems and your letter came this morning. Your poem I take to be an expression of your temporary dissatisfaction with the things that are. Cheer up; and even if the devil isn't dead, rejoice in his devilish presence. This, too, old boy, is part of the Great Adventure.

The other poems are not very good—except Jesse's. Lend me your ear a moment. Now I suppose I'm always espousing a new enthusiasm; but at this time I call to your attention that Jesse's poem is confirmation of an enthusiasm I've had all along. John has surprised us all with his originality; you have uttered the romance of disillusionment in a fine lyrical strain; I have shown that irony may possibly be diverting; but none of us is in full purity a poet. Jesse is; and if anything ever written by a Fugitive deserves the appellation of genius, Jesse's poem does.*a* It is the finest poem yet written by a member of the group. I have read it again and again for nearly three hours. The subtlety of the conception of the poem, the power of its imagery, the complete subordination of every part to the whole, and, withal, the profundity of thought unconsciously informing the entire piece stamp it as the superior poem of the group. More than that, I doubt if there's to be found anything more satisfying anywhere else. Don't say that my personal feeling runs away with me this time; I think Jesse has written in the past some quite negligible poems. But this is poetry at its purest. I can't tell him all this; it would embarrass him. Perhaps his humility, in this connection, is significant.

I understand how you feel about things. As to Stanley, I think his attitude is positively fantastic. Ridley? Great heavens! I don't see his connection with him. There's no humbug about Stanley. Fair treatment? Let him think of me. Of course I've always been represented generously in the magazine, but I doubt if anybody else's work has so continually provoked violent opposition. If I've been represented more often than Stanley, it is simply due to the fact of my having written more. Why not ask him to consider this point? I'm with you as to the financial policy for continuation; I'll be in position to meet an assessment along with the others. I see behind the screen of Mr. Frank's point, but aside from that I don't think his stand tenable.

In haste, Allen

57   a. "Snow Prayers," *Fugitive* (April 1924).

58/ALS

[Lumberport, W.Va.]
26 April [1924]

Dear Don:

The note I wrote you earlier in the day was too scrappy, did but scant justice to your good letter.

First, the matter of your resignation. It's simply unthinkable at this time. I realize with some little sympathetic bitterness myself just what your position is and almost precisely the very natural resentment you feel. You ask my attitude. Well, it is against your resignation although I must admit that I see everywhere a justification of it. Clearly, the group, represented at the moment by John and Stanley, want the magazine if it involves no labor of theirs; on the other hand, they resent the idea of any one else's having full control who does all the work (last summer's issue), they would let it die, rather. In other words, if they can't get something for nothing, they aren't going to let anybody else get it even though he works for it. It is disheartening, I confess. After the present contract of publication, you may be in position to dictate, for if no one else will take the editorial duties, you can take the journal to yourself. In this way, you could function without the carping of the group. Of course, this only means such an avenue would be open to you; for financing it alone would be another matter indeed. Don't think I'm the witches prodding ambition in Macbeth; I say nothing I wouldn't eagerly make public at a suitable opportunity. But despite your just indignation, the disloyalty, the almost ingrate callousness of the members to your fine work, I pray you continue for the time being. As for myself, I do not hesitate to resign my small job; but I can offer my resignation without any appearance of ulterior motivation, on the ground of absence; it will cause no speculation. But you are the pivot of our activities; you mustn't unseat us suddenly. But I repeat that you have every justification for doing so. My own resignation I am offering at once. I send it to Sidney as President. My reason for this method is a devious one. In resigning I wish to make a few points as impersonally as possible; in a formal, official letter I can do it; in a letter of resignation to you such a procedure would be too obviously forced. I enclose a copy. Write me your opinion of it when you can.

I don't understand why it may be unwise of me to have sent my mss. to Brimmer. I wasn't aware that Braithwaite[a] is president of the firm till I saw their stationery. What are your reasons?

Going back to Stanley; how does he make the "majority rule" account for disruption of spirit in the group? It may account for his own. After all, I suppose a harmonious community of poets is a contradiction in terms.

The comment on my sonnet was about as I expected it to be. The only sane criticism in detail, as I see it, is your objection to "brittle." John's painfully literal speculation as to the actual thalamion misses the point entirely. Does a poem named "Prothalamion" have to base itself on the possibility of a real nuptial? I merely took the nuptial idea as a momentary vehicle of my own attitude; any other might have done as well. I repeat again a bit wearily that perhaps poems aren't literally *about* things; *that* sort of aesthetics was held naive even before Kant, who discusses the point specifically. As to affectation, that seems ridiculous. It is depressing to reflect that the only real piece of affectation I've committed, the only emotional *tour de force*, is the very poem that was cherished best by the group—A Scholar to His Lady. I was simply posing; but "mob" sentiment, *cliché* emotion, never seems affected; it seems sincere because "everybody" feels that way. But I don't feel that way, and so it's insincere in me. "Horation Epode" is more accurately *I* than the poem I've mentioned. Some day I'll write an essay on Sincerity in Poetry. Of course, you may not like this serio-comic person I put in my poetry; but that's what I am, and I can't change it. Blame Koschei! Or lament that I scorn terms with Mother Seredon! . . .[b]

De profundis, Allen

58 *a.* William Stanley Beaumont Braithwaite, poet and anthologist. *b.* Characters in James Branch Cabell's *Jurgen.*

59/TLS

Lumberport, W.Va.

14 May [1924]

Dear Don:

It *is* a good page. And you particularly do yourself up proud in the Byron review.[a] I had thought of asking you to let me do the Byron book, but your comment makes me glad I didn't. I would only have belabored him after the current fashion. I like Byron tremendously— he was one of the first poets I read as a child; but I must confess that I can't read him now without fidgeting. Your point at the end, which you ask me about, is very well taken, but I don't think it will hold water with Byron. At this time I imagine we could accept a careless worker only if he should be a Shakespere. We are an age of Minors, and our only raison d'etre is good technique, it seems to me. Our poet must be a sort of Eugene O'Neil of verse if he wants to get by without crafts-manship. Mustn't he?

I am greatly pleased, as I have already written John, that the Fu-gitive esprit de corps has taken such a rise; and of course quite tickled in that it seems that my letter has had something to do with it. But I do regret that the wholly ironic character of the thing wasn't per-fectly clear on first reading. As it is, I fear, from what both you and John say, that it appeared to be a personal complaint for ill-treatment and a pharisaical assumption of virtues the others don't possess. I meant nothing of the kind. You know I called it a Poem; I merely took to myself, for lyric purposes, the various attitudes of the various brothers, so as to avoid calling names. I am perfectly sure that aspects of my Fugitive conduct have been just as absurd as the others'. If I may award myself any distinguishing virtue at all, and characteristically I don't at all hesitate to do so, it is simply honesty of opinion and the courage to express it. Frankly, I don't think anybody else except yourself has pursued such a policy; that is what I wanted to convey in my letter. But lest you think I am trying to be "nice" in completely exonerating you, I proceed to say that I think you fell short on the matter of candid criticism at meetings; I have often felt that you resented a candid sever-ity. I make bold to say this merely because you will appreciate a sincere remark from one of your best friends; otherwise I shouldn't be able to count myself such. Of course there is a certain presumption in saying it at all; but you will have to take that as one of my manifold short-comings. I can't help saying that if we were all a bit more presumptuous we might be less dishonest. . . .

I'll probably be near Nashville this summer, near enough to get into Nashville in an hour or so; so I can attend a meeting occasionally, anyhow. I may be a gentleman of labor for the summer. More later.

I know how you feel about that one line in the last stanza. But sacrifice a line for a poem any day, my dear Don. And let me see those reviews, letters, etc.

I've already sent in my poem to S.C.[b] I had no choice, as I saw it. I had only "Procession"; there wasn't another thing after I had looked them all over carefully. But not the Procession as it is in the Fugitive. He's a new man! Much better, I think. I hardly know what to tell you to use; but I should think your choice would be among these three, in the order named: Drums and Brass, Dryad, Redivivus. The last is an unbeatable little poem, but it *is* small, and you deserve fuller representation. What do you think of my selection? I considered The Happy Poet Remembers, in much revised state, but couldn't get my own consent.

Graves missed you entirely. Showing that a critic may spin fine theories of genetic criticism and yet know nothing about the poetry itself. That's the trouble with men like Graves and Prescott, and Brooks, and Babbitt; they tell you all about the glandular disturbances that produce poetic Urges, but they don't know a poem itself from an egg.

Write soon.

Amore, Allen

P.S. McClure's essay in the Mercury is good, don't you think? But I don't believe his conclusion—"sound-form"—will hold up. It's fusion of images quite as much as sound.

59   *a.* H.J.C. Grierson, *Poems of Lord Byron*; reviewed in the *Tennessean* May 11, 1924. *b.* The Poetry Society of South Carolina.

60/TLS

[Lumberport, W.Va.]
16 May [1924]

Dear Don:

The fulmination hath descended. But I turn it off easily. Behold the enclosures.

I didn't have the slightest idea how you wanted the reviews of the cheap books written. I see, though, that mine was very bad. I do them as you prescribe; I am just as glad to do them that way as any other. Compromise my "artistic principles"? Hardly! You take me to be more foolish than I really am. Why, oh, why (to use your own words) do you get so excited?

After looking over the first paragraph of the Cournos[a] review, I look see that your objection is pretty well founded, although the "reader's inference" which you draw isn't, I believe, the correct one. I meant no condescension at all; I was merely trying to write journalistically, according to my notion of that genre. But I see your point perfectly, and I have revised.

As to the possibility of some one's getting something personal out of the review, all I can say is that I had nothing personal in mind when I wrote it, and if any one chooses to take it to himself he will simply have to do so. With your caution in mind I am, of course, able to find such an interpretation possible, but that is post facto; and I therefore see no reason for toning it down. If anybody is hit by it, he will seem to me to reveal a very damning sensitiveness.

You can simply paste the new first paragraph over the top of the page. I have re-written the last, but I don't think it is pruned much; but it may sound more general in its intention; however, you don't need to use it if you don't want to—you can keep the last paragraph as it was originally. This is up to you.

I know I give you a lot of trouble over these reviews; and you may lay by it that I appreciate your sending me the books at all. But I really don't think there would be such confusion if I were present in Nashville, where you could save time by cautioning me personally. Of course my jejune obstreperousness makes it worse!

The Houghton Mifflin page is very good—for you, but what company you are in! But it ought to sell a few copies. By the way, are you a millionaire yet? (!)

Hastily, with more coming next week: Allen

60   a. John Cournos, *The New Candide*; reviewed in the *Tennessean*, May 25, 1924.

61/TLS

[Lumberport, W.Va.]
28 May [1924]

Dear Don:

I am certainly glad to get your long, fine letter; and although I can't do more at this moment than acknowledge it (I am swamped in work), I can at least tell you that I appreciate the full discussion you have given your attitude concerning your position among the Fugitives.

I've always maintained that a free expression of inner difficulties, when these difficulties bear upon our relations with others, will do more toward the harmony of spirits than anything else in the world. I know this isn't an original observation, but the application of it is extremely rare. I can say that, even as closely as we have been thrown together and as well as we've known each other, I never till today quite understood your position, and therefore failed to accord you a full generosity of feeling. It is quite as satisfying to feel generously toward another as it is to be the object of generous feeling; so what you have said makes me feel very good indeed, for I don't like to carry a residue of unfaith about a person with me indefinitely. I say I understand your position: I mean that I understand fully your real position and also the position you think you occupy, for there is a difference here due no doubt to your sensitiveness, although as usual there is some foundation for your present feeling. But this foundation is really very slight, and probably is only your share of a general state of disaffection among the members: I allude to a profound jealousy that exists, which makes us all rather unwilling to applaud achievement in one another. It wasn't that the brethren were so surprised at your success with Houghton Mifflin (Mims is one of the hero-worshippers of literature that think literature is very godly and hence must always be written Elsewhere)— they weren't so surprised as disappointed! I would be tempted to explain it this way under any circumstances; but I am compelled to now since I observed very closely the reactions of the group when the news of your acceptance came: my theory was simply forced on me by the facts. You are not the unique victim; I remember the expression on John's face as he read my letter of acceptance from Lieber[a] over a year ago. We all have the inferiority complex, every artistic person has it, but I think you give it the wrong turn in analyzing your position—just as I do in analyzing my position among the members. But it *is* devilish hard not to get twisted up in looking at one's own self. I may say that I feel that I am held in much the same bad esteem you discover for yourself, but I daresay neither of us is greatly contemned. My own feeling of course prepares me to understand yours, since you have expressed it so frankly, and I am damn glad to know that some one else feels similarly, for it renders plausible a much-desired suspicion that we are both wrong. Furthermore, I suspect that the opposition you have met is merely a concomitant of the office, without regard to the personality of the incumbent. It is jealousy again. John, or any of those you denominate intellectual leaders, while they (or *he* to be precise) might not have met such positive opposition, he would have been thought of even more evilly, for the group fear of John would have become ingrown and a compensatory, secret malice would have ensued. I really don't think you can explain the situation by any possible connotation of your personality, by anything peculiar to you. However, I think their attitude toward you has been damnable, as I have always said, but the more I think of it it seems just a function of the group muddle-headedness and recrimination.

It is certainly a good one on me that I attributed Stanley's poem to Steve; a very hurried reading of it is no excuse at all. Really, in a sense, it was a compliment to Stanley as well as to Steve. I noticed in the poem a very smooth rhythm, and a delicacy of image that Stanley usually eschews. Damn! But I'll have to look more sharply after this! I don't think your poem was unintelligible at all; it was simply impure; but I think I got your intention, I only thought you failed to work it out completely. The charge of unintelligibility indicates the state of critical commentary in the group. If we had more ruthless, sympathetic analysis and less ruthless, unsympathetic and irrelevant ambage of comment, we might pursue poetry more profitably. I'm for brutal criticism—but let it be *criticism*.

I didn't tell you about my plans because they weren't mature at that time, as they really aren't now. I didn't want to spread a false rumor of my approach; there have been too many false rumors about me recently—and a few true ones, I suppose! If you are going to be away right after Commencement, I may possibly not see you till you return, but we'll see each other before June is out, whatever happens. It occurs to me that unless you leave before the 11th, it will be only a little over a week till we meet, for I leave here a week from tonight. Whether I shall go to Tennessee, of course, depends on Red's success in getting us both jobs. Although this job will only pay expenses, I'm willing to take it: anything, so long as I don't have to spend what I'm trying to keep hoarded. If I don't come to Tennessee, I'll go to Washington, and later, New York; but this is very unlikely—at least, the New York end of it. But you'll hear from me again on this point very soon. (Speaking of Red: Vinal wrote me on his very hour of leaving for Europe that he was taking two of Red's poems I had sent him, at Red's suggestion; I'm extremely glad.)

The Table of Contents looks very good. The two strangers thereon, Dye and Gilchrist, stir much curiosity. All the others offer an expectedly fine pabulum. And I notice Gilmore again![b] Ah, my dear Don. I think Jesse's poems display the finest Fugitive offering this time; they are both unbeatable; but your Swan and Exile (which change in title I like) will rival anything in the issue if you got those kinks flattened out. As to your article, you may well imagine that I'm all eagerness to see it. Your feeling of timidity is quite foolish, my dear Don; don't make apologies before they're proved necessary!

I am very glad indeed that you have given me the bit of information about Brimmer. I wasn't aware that they were addicted to such nefarious practices. My letter to them of last week was therefore wise; I wrote them that if I didn't have their decision by June first I would have to withdraw the mss. You see, I want it free for the renewed consideration of the Bonis.

The page of the 25th is one of the best. Steve's review of Anderson is all one could desire; he certainly writes well: another good man gone wrong. But for the life of me I can't see Dr. Mims's review of Van Doren. He speaks of the "wealth of sentences and phrases," but he doesn't anywhere try to expose, precisely and critically, Van Doren's critical method; and then the pot-shot at Mencken at the end is about the weakest thing I've ever read. He doesn't like Mencken, but why doesn't he call him an out-and-out satirist, which he is; he still upbraids him for not being something he never intended to be in the first place: Mencken doesn't pretend to balanced judgment, any more than Swift did in A Modest Proposal, but I daresay we can't chastise Swift because he didn't write the Sermon on the Mount. Might as well object to Michelangelo because he wasn't another St. Augustine. Such muddled thinking rouses my ire; and it can only reveal a neurosis that expresses itself in a hatred of anything that doesn't contribute to the making of a Sunday School superintendent. This, with John's insincere review of Phelps,[c] is enough to make Hamlets of us all.

In two installments, this hurried letter has become horribly prolix. But I am very splenetic these days, and you're one of the very few whom I dare speak all my mind to. Write me a note in the next few days, telling me your final plans for the first part of June. And if the new Fugitive comes out by June 2nd, send it here, please; otherwise, hold it.

Farewell for the time, and amore, Allen

61. *a.* Maxim Lieber, of the publishing house of Lieber and Lewis, agreed to publish
     a collection of Tate's poetry but declared bankruptcy before the final manuscript
     was submitted. *b.* John Homer Dye of Andover, Massachusetts, and Marie Emilie
     Gilchrist, of Cleveland, Ohio, appeared in the *Fugitive* for December 1924; Louis
     Gilmore, associate editor of the *Double Dealer*, had poems in the issues for April
     and December, 1924. *c.* William Lyon Phelps.

62/AL

[Lumberport, W.Va.]

2 June [1924]

Dear Don:

Begorra! If Shipley isn't right! It *is* a damn good page. I don't
often speak of it, but I'm continually admiring this added fine feather
in your cap. (Mayfield[a] writes like a repressed spinster, but well for his
purpose).

I note verdict of S.C.[b] No: *I*, for one, shouldn't have entered if I'd
known Harriet had her proboscis in it. Thank God, we are [not]
truckling to any of the Powers, as the P. S. of S.C. often does!

Won't be in Tennessee, I'm afraid, till after 25th, but then most
surely. Leave here for Washington Thursday, but address me here;
mail will be forwarded right off. Will [be] in Wash. one week, N.Y.
two, Nashville after that.

Hope you like the Strong[c] review (second version); I think it's the
best I've done. The ethics abstruse? My dear Don, it's a monument of
simplicity! (This shows what a bad judge I am; but get John, who is a
philosopher, to read it and see if he thinks it's hard. I'm really anxious
about this.)

Farewell for a day or two. Will write again before I leave here, and
hope to hear from you. You'll certainly get a daily bulletin from me
in N.Y.

[Allen]

62 *a.* George Mayfield taught German at Vanderbilt. *b.* The Poetry Society of
    South Carolina held a contest for several years and published the prize poems
    in a yearbook. Both Davidson and Ransom won prizes in the contest. *c.* L.A.G.
    Strong, *The Lowery Road*, reviewed June 15, 1924.

63/TLS

[Nashville, Tenn.]
4 June 1924

Dear Allen:

It's downright mean of you to run off to Washington after getting our hopes so high. We are all truly spifflicated, if you know what that means, for we postponed Fugitive meeting till Saturday night on the chance of having you and Red here. You say you're going to Washington, then to New York???????? Well now!!!!!!! This will have to be looked into. I must admit that my hopes ebb. I'm turribly afraid you'll get to New York and find it difficult to tear yourself away. My faith in you endures, as always, though, and I hope you can overcome the siren attractions of Gotham, Gorham, and the Ghetto. I'll be disappointed if I don't get to see you, but I'm hoping for the best,—that is to say, even if you don't get to make us a visit that you'll find compensatory arguments, rewards, and excitements for not doing so. Gee-whiz. Have you suddenly gotten rich from school-teaching. Or have you been in a crap game? People who travel must have money.

Vide Idella's[a] letter within. You answer your part; I've answered mine. As to that philosophy review—I can't understand it, and I don't believe there are six people in Nashville who would,—those being the various professors of philosophy and their most highly advanced students. I am going to hold it until I can confer with you, in the hope of getting you to translate it into words of one or two syllables. John by the way, confesses defeat on certain portions of your vocabulary. My dear beetle-browed philosopher, you forgot you were writing for a newspaper. The Strong review is good,—but beware,—you'll have to exercise constant caution to keep your style from becoming too heavy.

When you do get to New York and the Secessionists, kindly point out to them that the Tennessean is (I believe) the only Southern newspaper that has given Secession a mention. And keep notes on everything that's said, and come back burbling with impressions,—we must have them,—all the literary talk—and write bulletins by all means. Good luck for your jaunt, enjoy yourself, don't fall off the Woolworth Bldg. Write me. If I leave here, it will be about next Wednesday, and I'll be back within a week.

Faithfully, Don

63   *a.* Idella Purnell, who published four poems in the *Fugitive.*

64/ANS

Lumberport, W.Va.

5 June 1924

Dear Don:

Your note of the 2nd came just in time. I leave here tonight, but alas, I go East—to Washington. My plans were altered suddenly the first of the week; Red informs me that the job he thought he had for me will not materialize before the end of June, and it isn't certain then. So you see how I'd be if I came South right now. However, I'll be down that way IF the job becomes certain later on; I simply can't pursue an *ignis fatuus*, especially in the South, a region none too friendly at best.

I can't give you my address for a few days yet. I don't know how long I'll be in Washington or whether I'll go on to New York for a few days. But write anyhow, and hold the letters till you hear from me; it will be by the first of the week.

I'm damn sorry to miss the goodly meeting of this Saturday night, but 'tis always thus. Where shall you live this summer? Will you be a bachelor *pro tempore?*

Hastily, Allen

65/ALS

Brooklyn, N.Y.

[8 June 1924]

Dear Don:

Having been in N.Y. all of two days, I now proceed to an exhaustive exposition on that subject, an exposition I proceed to but don't write; you are spared.

Crane is a peach of a fellow and is treating me royally. He's a 160 pounder, strong as an ox, looks like an automobile salesman (at a slight distance) and is proud of his looks; talks incessantly of trivialities and laughs all the time; but confessed to me late last night that he was a mystic! He took me to dinner earlier in the evening, where I met Cummings and the Lit. Ed. of The Forum, whose name I've forgotten. Cummings reminds me of John in his reticence; he never talks literature unless he introduces the subject and is opposed on principle to Poetic Theories; has none, he says; just writes the way it seems good to him (likewise Crane; and here let me say that it's apparent this gang is much less theory-ridden than we Fugitives). The Forum gent is very

Austrian looking and had with him an actress, with whom he lives (this lady admitted very graciously that she was a Lesbian!). Met a few others but no notables; most of these, it being Monday, hadn't yet got back from week-end outings.

Munson, a much married young man, couldn't be present last night, but he sent me word to call on him; so I did this morning. He's a very nice fellow and excessively fantastic of visage: petite spiked mustaches and a huge tuft of hair on the back of his head; rather fat, mainly amidships. Like most uncompromising critics, he is very meek in conversation, but very precise in his statements—no fumbling; he knows his own mind. Said some good things about you and then some bad ones—likewise of me and of John; is extremely interested in Warren—has noted his progress since last summer. Etc., etc.

Will write more later—that is, after tonight. Am calling Shipley by 'phone this evening. Went by to see Mullins, but she was out. May be in Nashville next week, but not unless I miss a job Munson has put me on to. More later.

Allen

P.S. Tell John that Yvor Winters is a kid of 21 in the West, whom the crowd here has never seen. He's a brilliant devil!
P.P.S. I'm greatly thrilled at the mere *physique* of this great city! The subway is simply marvellous. Fancy going under a huge river at the rate of 40 miles an hour! The sheer wonder of it is almost atonement for its significance as a phase of the triumph of the Machine.

66/ALS

Brooklyn, N.Y.
15 June [1924]

Dear Don:

Many thanks for sending me all the accumulated mail; I hadn't had any for so long I was getting very lonesome in this big and desolate and hectic city.

I may say that despite the fine time I've been having, which is due to the courtesy of Crane and company, I am already aweary of New York. I am hankering to leave; so you may find me in Nashville when you get back there; but this is uncertain.

I postpone till we meet any description of personalities, who are numerous and confusing. Suffice it that everybody has been very good to me, quite beyond expectations, and that's saying much, for one usually gets less than one expects. Today offered me my first rest, and I took it with Malcolm Cowley who escorted me through the Bronx "Zoo." We discussed the coming Anthology, in which my inclusion is now a certainty: discussed it quite casually, for Cowley refuses to talk literature, looks like a truck-driver, and was educated at Harvard . . . the type of snob that becomes a snob himself by giving one to under-stand that he deprecates all other snobs: but a very keen and refresh-ingly unpretentious person withal. But Crane, despite my fears, is the most considerable personality I've met among the younger men.

It seems that after all, as I wrote you, the Bonis may publish my book. Although I shouldn't feel like exerting myself to embarrass them, they are nevertheless legally bound to publish it. Cowley advises me to make them publish or sue them for $500.00, which he says it is certain I could get.

It will interest you that nearly everybody here, even Josephson, knows and likes your work although without exception they complain of your "*lack of* structural sense" (!) Don't think these people are an organized group of aesthetes. They're the simplest and least given to "organization" of all people I've seen, and are far less conscious of being "poets" than we are as a group.

It may interest you to know that the "outer circle" of *The Dial* (Cowley, etc.) have so strongly urged me to offer my Baudelaire transla-tion to that journal that I am mailing it in today. I called at the Dial office Saturday, having been previously recommended, and got a prom-ise of some reviewing in the coming four weeks.

There is a lot of gossip and impressions fairly shouting for record here; but I am too tired. I close with prayers and supplications that you write me immediately!

Calidus juventa, Allen

. . . Saw "All God's Chillun" at the Provincetown Thursday night, Mrs. Edmund Wilson in the leading role. It is an extremely powerful thing; the literary version conveys none of it essentially. Went with the wife of the artist who designed the masks of the recent staging of "The Ancient Mariner"—Mrs. James Light, a nice and acute person.

Am going to visit Burke at his country place next week. It seems, by the way, that Crane, Burke, and Slater Brown are the large boys here. Cowley said this, naturally leaving himself out; Cowley is now having a feud with Munson. Cowley ridicules Waldo Frank, Munson worships him.

67/TLS

[Nashville, Tenn.]
23 June 1924

Dear Allen:

Though I would that my tongue could utter the thoughts that arise in me after reading your letter (found on arrival here) and also the one to Jesse (we made a mutual exchange), I find I really have nothing adequate to say except again to volley forth my salutations as you make the rounds of Gotham and to pray that you will find all good things wherever you wander.

Since you probably haven't seen them, I'm sending two Tennessean pages,—they'll look a little pale by the light of the metropolis, but you shall see that we are still here, though I'm having to hustle considerably on account of the undisciplined manners of my reviewers' staff. I'm particularly anxious to get your opinion on my review of Auslander.[a]

The new Fugitive will be on its way to you speedily. Why Jesse hadn't already sent it is something I can't quite figure out,— but I recall his diffidence. I hesitate to put my poor little article[b] at the mercy of your friends, but let 'er go. I included Cummings in a certain mention, you will note. I did not include Crane because I do not know his work well,—have seen only two or three specimens—and therefore can't rate him.

The latest news (This, dear Cosmopolite, is Rural news but none the less news) is that L.A.G. Strong selects two of John's poems for his anthology,—Captain Carpenter and one other. We have all been invited to contribute to the Southern Magazine,[c] which is putting on a program of literary improvement. I have promised a poem and an article.

I enjoy hugely all your comments on New York and the persons there. But I don't know what to reply exactly,—so I'll just continue to peruse your bulletins with extremest interest. This is a high point of experience for you; utilize it to the utmost, especially if you are going to stay only a short while. And again I want to *urge* you not to leave New York without calling on such people as Benet, Farrar,[d] and all worth while folks of whatever group. I beg you to do this on behalf of the Fugitives,—to pay our respects. This is the first time we have really had a representative in New York (Ridley doesn't exactly count), and do make the most of it. Charming as your friends of the Left may be, you will not be treating yourself right unless you manage to stir up an acquaintance also with some of the Right.

Your prognostications as to return or stay (we can't figure out which) confuse us somewhat, and I gather, indeed, that for the first time in his life the redoubtable Tate may be a leetle bit confused himself. Don't let 'em get you down, old man. Stand up to 'em and tell 'em what's what. Soak up all you can (other than liquid refreshment), but don't forget to emit a hearty and sufficient blaze—and toot the old horn *judiciously* by putting up a thoroughly Fugitive front wherever it is meet!

Salutations again, and I await your next bulletin.

Faithfully, Don

Do call on Louis Bromfield at Putnam's—

67   *a. Sunrise Trumpets* was reviewed in the *Tennessean*, June 22, 1924.   *b.* "Certain Fallacies in Modern Poetry," *Fugitive* (June 1924).   *c.* Also known as the *Southern Literary Magazine*, published in Atlanta and Nashville from 1923 to 1924. *d.* William Rose Benet and John Farrar.

68/ALS

[Washington, D.C.]
3 October [1924]

Dear Don:

Thanks greatly for the Fugitives—and the page. I'm having them bound after the Dec. issue; so I will complete a volume then. I'll try not to lose them.

The Fugitive news sounds mighty good, though I'll miss your name, Editor, on the masthead. But continuance was the main thing. I think I've written my glee over the plans; I can only add my satisfaction at their adoption.

As for reviews, I'd like certainly the forthcoming book of Kenneth Burke's. And the "Tattooed Countess" by Van Vechten. And Tagore's book.*a* I don't mean I'd want *all* of them; but I would like any of those named—or any others. I enclose a note from H. M. Kallen; it does the reviewer's heart good; and Kallen is no mere exchanger of courtesies. I'm much complimented.

I'm glad you like the recent poems. Your comment, as usual, was greatly to the point. But I can't change "puke and rind"! With you I think *Homily* is the best; *not* with you I think it is my essential style—remember *Euthanasia*. By the way, Mark Van Doren has taken the poem I dedicated to Red for the Nation. I think I'm making friends there—both Irita and Mark Van Doren are for me, I believe. He wrote an excellent letter.

Tell John to write me. I'll begin to think he's mad at me for my letter combatting his recent essay on Freud. Wasn't it beautifully written? But he surely betrayed himself as a classicist in speaking as he did of obscenity. It is sentimental Romanticism that has thrown obscenity out of literature! But—"shantih"!

Write when you can. And feel better as soon as possible!

Yours, Allen

68   *a.* Sir Rabindranath Tagore's *The Eyesore or Letters from Abroad.*

69/ANS

[Washington, D.C.]
3 October [1924]

Dear Don:

I've just read McClure's review of your book in The Double Dealer;[a] and I can't wait a moment to hail you with congratulations—and him, too, for that matter, for having sense enough to give you your due. It's by all odds the best you've received, I should think. See what he says about ye Fugitives! You bring honor to us all. I think the local public should be made to read the high points of that review—in The Tennessean, perhaps. The hell with your damn modesty!

And let me once more remind you of my own acumen in pointing to the Corymba group as your best, by showing how it's confirmed yet again. Recapture that vein!

Yours, Allen

69   *a. An Outland Piper.*

70/ALS

[Washington, D.C.]
9 October 1924

Dear Don:

I'm glad you're so pleased with McClure's review. It certainly shows up the rotten and prejudiced notice in *Poetry;*[a] and if it needed any outside justification my letter to Harriet has it in McClure's praise. However, my letter could be thoroughly justified on "general principles." The complacent old hierophant ought to be attacked from all quarters.

I'd be glad to review "Chalk Face" and the play you mention. By

the way, Canby of The Saturday Review has promised me some books!
I only hope he sends me some I can be lucky enough to hit a good opening stride on; I suggested several, in response to his note, that might
help me in this. I had sent him some of my best reviews in the recent
past, for inspection. If I can get beyond the starters and make a real
connection, I'll be much gratified. Who wouldn't? I've asked for Vai-
hinger's "Philosophy of 'As If,'" among other books, because I want to
make a display of "foundations" in an effort to impress him! Thus, the
subterfuges of aspiring writers.

Write me when you feel like it. Get out of the Slough of Despond.

Allen

70   a. Tate's letter protesting Harriet Monroe's treatment of *An Outland Piper*
     was published in *Poetry* (December 1924).

71/ANS

[Washington, D.C.]
10 October 1924

Dear Don:

I have a note from Harold Vinal asking me to become a Contributing Editor to *Voices*, and it seems he would have me function immediately by writing an article on the Fugitive group. *Voices*, he says, is
changing into a critical journal—much space, it appears, to be devoted
to harangue.

Naturally, I would like your advisory remarks before I begin the
article; for, as I see it, it's quite an opportunity for us, and thus I'm
already determined to write it.

Let me hear from you, if possible, by return mail. He goes to press
the 20*th*. What leading points would you suggest? I would naturally
have to omit myself from the discussion and write as an impersonal
observer, of course stating the assumption of that attitude.

Yours, Allen

72/ANS

Washington, D.C.
11 October 1924

Dear Don:

Your letter anent the attack on Harriet is just received. I must
say that I wrote the attack really anticipating most of the objections

you see to it; but I sent it ne'ertheless! There is *one* thing, however, that I completely overlooked—a statement to the effect that *you* knew nothing of the letter; I cover that point in a note to Harriet today. Yes: I confess; I had more diabolical fun writing that letter than I've had since God knows when! I'm willing to accept any consequences the letter may bring; in fact, I'd glory in the debacle! But I do want to spare you the wreckage. But if all the casuistries you suggest were ob- served in this kind of literary warfare, if we hesitated till we were sure, there would be no warfare, for you can't *prove* things like *revenge*, etc; you have to divine them and let loose. And what is life without war? Bellum omnium contra omnes, said Hobbes in "Leviathan."

And so forth, Allen

73/ALS

Washington, D.C.
15 October [1924]

Dear Don:

Your letter is excellent, and I'll try to reply to all the questions, arguments, etc., but there's a regular avalanche of them, and I may omit one or two.

As to my Fugitive article, after corresponding further with Vinal I've got his permission to put it off one issue;[a] I couldn't get it done this week if life depended: I'm too immersed in reviews, etc., and a new poem, tentatively completed, the writing of which has caused me the agonies of the damned. I agree with the recommendations you make for the article; but there is one point, one not too important perhaps (I may not even broach it), that is subject to various emphasis and inter- pretation; namely, the matter of adverse criticism. Such would not imply disunity; it would indicate a healthy condition within the unity; unity exists on other terms sometimes than mutual admiration. I don't mean that I would single out people individually for destructive com- ment; I simply mean that it seems necessary to convey the notion that not only I, but the group as a whole, aren't suffering from megalomania and believe they are all great poets; for we're not, not a damned one of us. And then, too, I have to think of my own integrity; besides and furthermore, "unselfish praise" would actually redound as a libel on the group; there's no greater slam than too much praise. However, my whole tendency is to extravagant encomium; so I naturally propose these safeguards.

I'm greatly thrilled that you're doing an article for Mencken.[b] And I'll get out after those magazines tomorrow or the next day; today I feel like a picked chicken—calomel, etc., pulling me down to the thoughtless bone. I have only two ideas: (1) Classification of magazines — what are "little" and what not; (2) A warning not to dismiss the "radicals" before you find out what they're all about. As to (1) I'd say those you mention (Stratford, Guardian, etc.) are *little*, but it might be well to define *little* as meaning *non*-commercial, as distinguished from Century, Scribners, etc., which let their policy be dictated largely by thought of circulation. As to (2), take the Little Review; when you see a mixed gibberish of French, etc., signed by Picabia and Tzara, you'll dismiss it. *Don't!* The Little Review, unlike The Fugitive, is under no illusion that it's publishing a near-great poem every time, but publishes a lot of candid experimentation (which is preferable to the Isabel Conants and Louise Driscolls)[c] and then occasionally prints first class stuff; since 1917, the first poems of Eliot and Yeats' finest work,— "On a Dying Lady," etc. I offer this point as a parable.

I've had some very recent communication with Mencken myself; and if you don't use the article I sent you the other day, I'm going to re-write and enlarge it for The Mercury. I've got a lot of *data* I left out for brevity, but it would be pertinent, all of it, in a more thorough piece. . . .

Your always, Allen

73   *a.* This article was never published. *b.* Never published. *c.* Isabella Fiske Conant, poet and author of *Puritan* (1925); Louise Driscoll, author of *The Garden of the West* (1922) and *Garden Grace* (1924).

74/ALS

New York City
9 November [1924]
Dear Don:

Crane brought over to me the various mail of the day, last night; and glad I was to get the good part of it which was yours. I can't do the letter I'd like just now; if I got started on "impressions" I'd never stop; so suffice it that I like N.Y. this time both more and less than I did last summer. Expecting to be here rather permanently, I can take my time seeing people and things, and excitement is thus only moderate after the first few days and cocktails (you'll be interested in this) are quite infrequent and hilarity practically not at all. N.Y. isn't so different from Nashville, but it certainly permits one to be alone in the proper way and nobody, fortunately, is his brother's keeper. I go to work regularly tomorrow morning—a rotten grind, but I'm sure I'll prefer it to teaching.[a]

The sundry proposals and projects of the Fugitive interest me greatly. I am in total agreement with one exception, but that exception is a weak one. I'm willing to contribute as you propose, but I shouldn't like the act of our contributing money to stand for a step toward permanent support by us; only as a temporary relief. In short, I don't believe in our paying to publish our own verse, and that's to be the purpose, or the *main purpose*, of continuance. I think we could pay to publish *other* persons, but I think somebody else should pay for our own. On this principle I declined the invitation to join *Folio* for the second issue, despite its proud company of Amy Lowell, Bertrand Russell, etc. (the Bonis are printing it at the *authors'* expense). Not that I go so far as to *want* money for my work; I gladly give it away; I just don't like to go so far in the opposite direction as to pay to get it printed. But, as I say, anything up to 25.00 is all right with me, as temporary relief, looking toward patrons, subscriptions, etc.

I'm much pleased that The Fugitive is getting such praise. Any of it from the South? I doubt it. Praise is a fine thing, but don't have too much respect for authority! . . . The hell with the critics! If they afford publicity and get us subscriptions—well and good; but otherwise they're all the things Mr. A. Pope said they were. And speaking of critics—I've just read the chattering inanity which is S. P. Sherman's Book Section in the Herald-Tribune. Why give up one's job as a professor if one can't do better than that?[b] And so on.

Write me a letter *very* soon. In a few days I'll send a list of book shops where the new Fug. should be displayed. And I'll send poems before the 15th. Best affections to yourself and the gang.

                                                                        Allen

74   *a.* Tate is doing editorial work for the Climax Publishing Co., a publisher of pulp magazines. *b.* Stuart P. Sherman (1881–1926) resigned from the University of Illinois in September 1924 and became editor of the *Herald Tribune* literary page. Tate later thought highly of him.

75/ALS

New York City
29 November [1924]

Dear Don:

Your several notes and letters have been greatly enjoyed, and I regret that the confusion of life here keeps me from a full reply at the moment. I like especially the Table of Contents of the coming issue. I am also greatly pleased at the prize awards; I couldn't have distributed them better myself! All in all, I'm much elevated at the renewed zest of the Fugitives; and believe me that I miss the fine company of you all a great deal.

As to the magazines, I went this morning to Brentano's and had $4.35 worth sent to you; there may be duplicates of some you already have; if so, forgive me. I had them send the things to you C.O.D., in order to simplify the transaction. I strongly recommend having The Fugitive placed at Brentano's, without regard to the business end of the matter. Every other magazine is there.

I'm nearly rushed to death for time. I have five books on hand for review, one for you, the others locally. God knows when I'll get them done. There are always people to see—talk, talk!

Your new poem, Boudoir, hits me squarely *atween* the eyes! Fine stuff! There are some great imaginative lines in it. I have no criticism in detail of it. However, I do believe you show *your* typical weakness (each of us has his own) which is lack of real structural sense which permits you to become diverted from the aesthetic problem into irrelevancies; I refer to the last stanza—a tag stuck onto an otherwise excellent poem. Think it over. You are again hitting your old stride. I think you've written much verse out of a mere sense of duty to the "art"; but [when] you permit yourself to feel properly savage and primitive you produce *poetry*.

Write soon. I'll do better a little later. Regards to the Brethren; and my congratulations to Stanley.[a]

Allen

75   a. Harcourt Brace has just accepted *The Professor*, which was published in 1925. Stanley Johnson resigned from the English department before it came out. The chief character in the novel was said to be a burlesque of Mims and Curry.

76/ALS
New York City

8 December [1924]

Dear Don:

Please forgive, even yet again, the trite plea for indulgence in my hectic correspondence. But, after all, you must grant that I am prompt—if not adequate. Therefore—

Hurrah for *The Fugitive*, in the past, and emphatically for 1925. I can say, and with much sentiment of which I'm so little ashamed that I am positively proud of it, that although I'm swamped in the maelstrom of literary N.Y. I feel myself to be a Fugitive, in our special sense of the term, as I did in the spring of 1922. I hope, naturally, the emotion is reciprocated.

For there are particular symptoms of the resurrected Fugitive spirit that I admire extravagantly. I like the spirit of chaste publicity. I like the apparent absence of timidity, the unblushing courage which determines, at last, to brag about us—the lack, in short, of the false conception of dignity which has heretofore confined us to what is after all the most middle-class, *bourgeois*, of attitudes: the derivative notion, of people uncertain of themselves, that *Silence* is something aristocratic. There is nothing more dishonest or affected; for the vanity usually comes out *ridiculously* in the end.

Again, hurrah for The Fugitive! In particular, send me ten (10) *more* copies for my personal distribution. And send me a dozen or so copies of the pamphlet, and as many of the boiler-plate sheet. As to my Southern essay, forgotten by you, my dear Don, I am not solicitous of it. I shall not write it for Mencken—having seen him. He's a perfect ass. He became exceedingly vulgar and admonitory, whereat I politely, yet vehemently, suggested that just because he is an emancipated Methodist he needn't try to bluff other people into being equally cheap; that I never intended to be a journalist and that he couldn't *be* anything else; that I couldn't write the article for him because I refused to imitate his style as the other contributors to *The American Menagerie* do; in short, that, while he is doubtless a great man and can kill my literary reputation with one vulgar blow, he is ultimately an ass; whereupon the gentlemen got into a taxi, minutely intoxicated, and I went home to bed. Amen. Mencken is the flapper of Amer. lit., i.e., he gives typical expression to female sophomores in Southern and Middle Western universities. His journal is a two-ring circus of which the squeamish intelligence, which is often mine, grows extremely bored.

This, of course, brings up again the magazine I previously alluded to. I can only say, if it crystallizes, that it will be as aloof as the English Criterion and not cranky as the American Dial. It will realize that an essay on Sophocles is probably more significant than one on Ben Hecht or Joseph Hergesheimer; that Whibley's articles on the *arcana* of Greek literature, or Burke's aesthetic theory, are more important than Dr. Canby's struggle for freedom from the influence of Professor Sherman (who, by the way, conducts the best weekly review in America). And so on; but more later. Suffice it that the magazine will want *your* CRITICAL articles and John's—but none of, say, Curry's—who writes, not for literature, but in order to get a better job. The point, while dealing in personalities, at the same time elucidates significantly the attitude of the proposed magazine: no academic arse-kissing or journalism allowed, but intelligent erudition greatly desired. But, as I say, more later.

There are so many things I could write about that I don't know where to begin or leave off. I've seen at least 4,976½ persons since I got into New York a month ago. My summary of it all, if you are interested, is something like this: there is no criticism in this country; there is only one journal that isn't journalistic—The Dial, but even it is a personal toy for Thayer*a* rather than an unprejudiced critical organ. However, there is much that commands respect—Sherman, for one, who, although a journalist, isn't a fool and dishonest—as Canby is, cutting parts of reviews (or revising them) which are unfavorable to the cheap fictionists he admires, or the good novelists he likes for almost invariably the wrong reason or none at all. In other words, one feels as desperate here as elsewhere; one may be anathema or ostracized in a year (though one is discreet as possible); but one refuses to give in in order to get a review published which may please the American People but pleases its author nowhit. However, I ought to say I'm in good standing everywhere so far; I am merely anticipating the usual tragedy. Forgive this; I merely feel I haven't done you a *letter*, a real one, since I came here. Write soon.

Yours, Allen

76   *a.* Scofield Thayer, editor of the *Dial* (1919–26).

77/TLS

New York City
17 December [1924]

Dear Don:

Your excellent letter is just to hand, and after my custom I prefer promptness to adequacy. I must say that it is the first good letter, the first real Don-ish letter, in months. Accept my thanks and hearty wishes for another like it soon.

I don't know where to begin; you open up such avenues of discussion! But for this time I fear I shall have to content myself with the merest circumstantiality—the things you ask; but even there I may miss a few of the myriad manifestations of your interest and curiosity in me, the New York scene, and the mingling of them both. . . .

No, I can't *guess* what Dr. Mims' comments were, but I *know* damme well. One doesn't necessarily agree with a person just because he shares with that person certain antipathies. It isn't the fact that I prefer Sherman to Mencken which is significant; it is *why* I prefer him. As to literary situation in general, I may say that I am a person admirably constituted to succeed very badly; it happens that most of the people in power here inspire worse than my contempt, and if you rejoin that this is merely a continuation of the familiar Tatian arrogance, I must retort: So be it. I can't see my way clear, whatever my limitations and prejudices may be, to accept offers of reviewing from the Post or the Saturday Review or the Bookman; what little time I have for reviewing will go to The Nation and the Herald-Tribune (although Mrs. Van Doren and the Paterson thing are little better than club women; but Sherman is all right and, at any rate, doesn't cut out paragraphs of the reviews which he happens to disagree with, like Canby and Tewson). As to my activities here, I must say further that I didn't come to New York to conquer it; merely to live as a civilized being in a place where it isn't important whether you drink liquor or are a virgin, and to see a few congenial people when I care to; and thus to concentrate my energies on my own work, for which I have ample time—three or four evenings a week and the entire of Saturdays and Sundays. My companions—at not too frequent intervals, for they are absorbed too—are Hart Crane, a very fine person, Malcolm Cowley (whose review of White Oxen in the Dec. Dial I urge you to read, for fine, simple, lucid prose), Kenneth Burke, J. B. Wheelwright, James Light, director of the Provincetown Theatre, and only a few others—I should mention Slater Brown:[a] there is no wittier, more charming, more learned person; and lately, Cummings, just returned from France. The other "personalities" whom I come in contact with I do so more or less for convenience. . . . It is exciting. But most of all, the tremendous physique of the great city of New York. One can be utterly alone—in some cheap Italian restaurant, dining alone for seventy cents, with a sense of intimacy with oneself that I have never felt before; one feels independent and, at the same time, humble.

YOUR praise of my recent verse, and Jesse's too, pleases me extremely. Good or bad, more is forthcoming; I feel like a geyser. I pray that you feel likewise.

Everywhere The Fugitive is getting a lift. People who have been deaf to us are perking up. I regret deeply the exhaustion of this issue. Those I desired to distribute it to are mostly critics and never subscribe to anything; it is our loss. If you get back any copies from bookshops, let me have them to place in shops here—personally.

And this ends the epistle. Write soon. My voluminous correspondence takes two evenings a week, at least; but I wouldn't sacrifice it for the world. It is an outlet for my enthusiasm of all sorts; and I confess, without blushing, that through the hells of all sorts that I've been through in the few years that are so far mine I have never been able to stifle my enthusiasm for life and literature; although I have successfully hushed an early liking for ethics and Dickens.

Farewell.

Yours always, Allen

P.S. I am replying to Stone's letter at this sitting. Thanks. I must respond to your characteristic kindness and love in telling me how I am missed by you and the few of the others. This means a great deal to me; I can never forget you all. But really I shall never return to Nashville; so you must come up here when you can. And I beg you to begin planning now to come up for a month next summer.

One more thing. As to a volume, I have lost all interest for the moment. I am pretty well acquainted with Huebsch and have had friendly conferences with the Bonis; but the longer I think of it, the fewer my worthy poems become; I haven't more than a dozen or fifteen poems that satisfy me—and personal satisfaction is after all the only aim. Any other is of course a form of prostitution.

77 a. Brown, Wheelwright, and Tate were among the young writers who produced *The Aesthete* in February 1925, a satirical response to Ernest Boyd's charge in the *American Mercury* that young writers were "repeating the attitudes . . . of the aesthetes of the '90's."

78/ALS

New York City
30 December [1924]

Dear Don:

Your note of the 23rd came this morning. Thanks for the Page. And if you can't find that Krutch review, be sure to let me know.

There is no news here. Except that I'm enjoying life tremendously and have never felt better. It's great to get up at eight and feel so good you have to take callisthenics to calm yourself. Have gained ten pounds, too. There's nothing like being happy. One can do any amount of work under that circumstance. I'm not getting so much writing done; very little, in fact. But I'm making valuable friends, and that, as I've found, is very important in New York.

But I get more done here than I ever did in Nashville. Numerous poems are in my notes; more gestating. How do you like the last one I sent you?

I'm surprised to hear of Stanley's resignation; somewhat disgusted. But he is where he'll likely be happier; he is a man of action essentially.

For God's sake slow up on your work. You'll kill your fool self! It isn't worth it. I can see how a man can put *literature* before life, but I'm damned if I see how he can put the *grind* above it. But we're all different; so that's that. But I *am* distressed about you, and I hope *you* will listen to *my* advice.

Write me that promised letter soon. I know how impossible it is to write letters when one is all run down. Be sure to *go easy* from now on as much as you can.

Yours always, Allen

79/ALS

New York City
7 January [1925]

Dear Don:

Thanks greatly for the check; such trifles are always needed.

I am darn sorry I raised such a rumpus over the Roller review; but then, as you say yourself with charming jesuitry in the Spyglass, I never seem loath to do so! It was of course none of my affair. However, my dear Don, you call for a finer distinction than ever I could conjure up: you say he probably isn't guilty of "serious cribbing"; what is *un*serious cribbing?

As to your answer to my letter, you took it more seriously than I did! Just a little fun! I wrote it at the office in a spare moment. Now, *if I were* replying to your reply it would go like this:

Literary Editor of The Tennessean:

I have greatly enjoyed your comment on my recent letter objecting to remarks of yours concerning Wescott's "The Apple of the Eye." The result of the controversy is simply zero: you still think it unimportant to call an American book European; but in persisting in believing in the rectitude of that error you really tangle yourself further in the difficulty. "European flavor"? Czech, French, Russian, Finnish? Of course I grant you that to an Olympian men might not be greatly distinguishable from monkeys, and to him the difference would be unimportant; only a vague knowledge of the *genus* wouldn't afford him particular knowledge of the *species.*

Your analogy of the taste of the apple will convince some while to the sticklers for logical preciousness it may be inadequate. Of course there is nothing legally to be done about people who taste American books and find them "European." But for those who may insist upon tasting an apple only to call it an olive the State has provided institutions where they may indulge that delicate perversity in isolation. Granting that you were merely describing the book: can you defend a wrong description? Could you say that *Louis Quinze* furniture is like early English and be applauded? More seriously, you give yourself away: "Its carefully chiselled language, its great sophistication"—these qualities are European and praiseworthy!

Then, on another account, I think your duplicity in bringing in my epistolary habits was somewhat disengaging. It disengaged one's affection for the moment; it also disengaged the attention of the reader to a matter beside the point, while at the same time it won his sympathy because it was an *argumentum ad hominem.*

Finally, it was unbecoming of one who could advance very shaky logic to assume the attitude of bored patience and superiority. Was it not? Especially when I was jazzing up the scene a bit and free of charge at that!

Let's have another controversy!

Sincerely yours, Allen Tate

So it might run! But after all my own sins, I am thankful for "letters to the Editor." My bow to Dr. Mims! I really don't see why John has all along permitted Graves to make a sort of cult out of him—an interesting barbarian. I daresay John is quite as civilized as Graves; from what I've seen of Graves' writing I suspect he is more so. Graves didn't really touch John's poetry—certainly no more than my review did; and I do think he went me one better in dealing in the personal issue.*a* Is Graves so much interested in John's verse as in the anomaly of an educated man appearing in the wilds of America? However, John may care to be insulted by a second-rate Englishman; so it's none of our business. I suspect John was touchy about my review (he hasn't written me since it appeared), but really it was meant favorably, in spite of the fact that, unlike Red, I didn't call him a "genius." . . .

Salutations! Allen

79   *a.* Tate's review of *Chills and Fever* appeared in the *Guardian* (November, 1924); Graves's review, in the *Saturday Review of Literature* (December 27, 1924).

80/ALS

New York City
16 January [1925]

Dear Don:

Your good letter has lain about on my desk for two days. At last I have a moment. Such a moment these days is rare, so rare indeed that my letters must seem very abortive and hectic.

I am very glad you don't feel too disturbed about my "letter to the Editor." My dear Don, please don't think I was trying to patronize you —for God's sake! I was only attempting to *twit* you a bit, and I hope you really didn't take it *too* seriously, (I suspect you did take it *somewhat* seriously, but I can see how you might, at the moment.)

The news of Fugitive enthusiasm is good news. Let me have more of it. Around here there's nothing much of interest going on: just the same struggle and rivalry, punctuated by frequent meetings of good fellowship; but there's a tendency to become insulated—united we stand, etc., and thus there are a thousand groups in New York. Ours is more or less solid and consists of these people (you may be interested to know what company I've finally and definitely become a part of):

Cowley, Burke, Brown, Crane, Cummings, Dos Passos, Josephson, Mitchell, and the several wives of those that have 'em. But even these are subdivided into twos and threes; ultimately, it's every man for himself, as it should be.

I do hope you come to like the last poem I sent down for inspection. I don't think it's too good; but it represents my tendencies as they've gathered into a single direction from the Woman Mountain several months ago. In the end it will amount to a complete rehabilitation of technique: it will consist mostly in establishing a method of presentation, of my own (in other words, a new form), within the traditional prosodical patterns. I can't expect much understanding or approval just now; but there's no hurry; for I ought to be at my best ten or fifteen years hence! At least I'm determined not only to *think* it through—which might be done in a comparatively short time—but also to work it through; so that in the end I shall certainly have something of my own, good or bad, poetry or non-poetry. But "what is man to say what poetry is?" . . .

Write! Allen

81/TLS

New York City
21 May 1925
Dear Don:

. . . I can proceed to the interesting contents of your letter. As to my future status on The Fugitive, you have ere now been apprised of my pleasure, expressed in a letter to Ransom, at the new arrangement whereby those absent fall into inactivity rather than disconnection. I am very grateful to the Group for wanting to give us some sort of qualified standing. My desire for this, as you know, bore no deprecation of the work the magazine is doing; only a disagreement with it; and I didn't expect any one to submit to my views; I only wanted them recognized. They have been recognized in an excellent way.

I have received your Conrad article and read it with considerable pleasure.[a] Since I know practically nothing of Conrad, having read only some five or six of his books at intervals, I can offer no criticism; although I have a suspicion you didn't quite get enough out of your points, failing to follow them through. And, in style, such phraseology as "the book has an experimental air," instead of looking like incapacity, looks like haste, and deprives your article of distinction in form;

the "air," after a little more thought, could have been condensed into a precise observation. But surely this one instance isn't enough to talk about; it seems the touchstone to the weaknesses of your style. With a little more attention that article would have looked mighty good in The Yale Review. It's a thorough piece of work.

I was damn sorry Ranson didn't get that prize; he was the only one who actually deserved it. But the Committee could be safe in giving it to Robinson[b] and didn't have to exercise the cortex in order to pick him out. As for me, when it comes to contests, I'm never going to enter another one—unless the sum is in thousands and I'm promised beforehand I'll get it.

Your summer plans interest me a great deal. I wish I could get out of New York for a month or so; but it is impossible. However, I have a very comfortable apartment, with plenty of room and air; so it won't be so bad after all. I'm thinking of working on half time for a while at the office, and then I'll get something done—perhaps.

Your plans for further graduate study are worthy ones indeed; and I think your chosen field, the 18th century, is excellent. After the Elizabethans, that age is the only sensible age in English literature. When we get over thinking that all Poetry must be like Shelley, we will see that some of our greatest poetry is in Dryden and Pope. I could hardly suggest a subject for you; but there is certainly an important one that could be pursued if the university authorities weren't opposed to exhibitions of intelligence, preferring its absorption in pretentious nonsense. (Although you might avoid this at the Sorbonne.) This problem is one that interests me even if I shall never work it out, lacking the leisure or the prospect of it: an analysis of fictional methods in the 18th century, particularly Swift and Fielding and Sterne, as they have influenced certain moderns—Joyce, Wyndham Lewis, Mary Butts,[c] a few others; for this seems important now since the breakup of the novel and the necessary return to older methods. Eliot has indicated one of these returns in discussing Joyce, but he hasn't elaborated the point: a repudiation of the exhausted narrative form for a purely conceptual form which in Joyce is simply a special application of the Ulysses myth. You can readily see that other thought forms in the past can be appropriated for similar use. I speak of this not because you might be interested; I'm sure no university would think it worthwhile; but because I've been thinking about it a little recently, and I'd like to see somebody examine the subject thoroughly.

I get a little writing done occasionally. I am absolutely not going to publish another poem for months, maybe a year or so; the two out now are the last—one to the Guardian, the other to The Nation. I'll not stop writing poetry, however. I'm doing about 2000 words of prose a week, in addition to about one review in two weeks, on the average. I haven't yet sent out my southern article; I'm keeping it about me till I'm sure of it; changes, minor ones, occur to me every few days. But I am certain it will not appeal to Mencken; so I'll not try him. He wants a sledge hammer in every paragraph; and I can't write that way. I'm sorry I missed Wood's book for the Herald Tribune; it's the goddamdest nonsense ever displayed in the name of criticism; he's a person of the most astonishingly stupid opinions and has no ideas, so far as I can discover, whatsoever. . . .

Write me soon. I always like news from Nashville. And remember me to the Group.

Yours ever, Allen

81 *a.* "Essays on Conrad's 'Supense,' IV," *Saturday Review of Literature* (November 21, 1925); Davidson's essay won fourth prize in a contest for the best suggested endings to Conrad's unfinished novel *Suspense.* *b.* E. A. Robinson won the Pulitzer Prize in 1925 for *The Man Who Died Twice.* *c.* Lewis, well-known man of letters, was editor of the short-lived little magazines *Blast* and *Tyro;* Mary Butts, English novelist and short story writer, the author of *Ashe of Rings* (1926), *Armed with Madness* (1928), and other titles.

82/ALS

New York City
23 June 1925

Dear Don:

The June Fugitive has just come. Although I can't get enthusiastic about much of the verse—except For Example, one of Ransom's, and one of Red's—the issue was worthy of print for your review of Eliot's book and for John's note on irony.*a* It is very interesting: an issue of the Fugitive containing some of the most important critical writing in months, with no chance of being read at all. Yet time, it is to be hoped, will do you justice—even if New York won't. If you were up here and could see in what hands the immediate fate of American letters lies, your quick tendency to despair would lead you to forthright suicide (I'm thinking of such persons as W. R. Benet, Herbert S. Gorman, Elinor Wylie, Ernest Boyd,*b* etc., because I happened to pass a dull evening with them last week at Edmund Wilson's. Wilson is an excel-

lent man and critic; it astonishes me he likes those fat-heads: Elinor
Wylie, a good poet, isn't an exception; she's the dullest talker I've ever
met—but one of the most beautiful women, to be sure).

It does seem, after all, in spite of dissention among ourselves, that
you, John, and I have been looking toward the same conception of
modern poetry; and Eliot, in England, is with us! You will remember
an editorial of mine in The Fugitive a year ago or more:ᶜ my point, not
so well put, was Eliot's identically although I stated it historically,
i.e., I said our dissatisfaction with the 19th century led us to an attempt
to restore poetry to the tradition, *via* late 19th century French poetry
because that poetry represented an integration of the sensibility—the
only available one whose technique was adequate to a new and complex emotion. I can't help but think that persons like John, for instance,
who has, I believe, been a little suspicious of the French, after the
fashion of the last American generation and all English generations
since the 18th century, are a little short-sighted, or have been; for
whatever one may think of this French poetry *per se*, it has served to
restore the tradition to lead us back to the Elizabethans whose formula,
under differing surfaces, was much the same as that of Corbiere and
Laforgue: the formula which Eliot states—an integral activity of emotion and intellect.

Right here I'm offering you one of my gems before it comes out
in the New Republic in the next month or so! It has been a superstition
that emotion alone is the material of poetry, but the 19th century in
England shows that emotion without mind is a falsity, for the neglect
of mind, the critical check, permits not only real emotion to emerge
but also faked emotions. Over half of Tennyson is faked, much of
Browning. The social consequences of this in our own time are interesting, for society, following literature, is burdened and distorted
with a spurious emotional equipment, all the emotions being *ec*centric,
and so the modern poet must not only surmount the great difficulty
of eliminating the emotional falsehoods from his own attitude, he must,
in the lack of a criticism to prepare his audience, do his own pioneering
—he must not only make, he must sell his article, which is nearly impossible. If Eliot had cared to explain the reason why modern poetry is
difficult (it *isn't* intrinsically) he would doubtless have written something like the above: an audience with one set of emotions, the poets,
in advance, with another set, and this means nothing else than a currency of two different languages. What do you think of the idea?

I believe you owe me a letter, but I'm so full of this idea this morning, and so pleased to see other Fugitives in my way of thinking, I couldn't resist writing.

What are you doing this summer? Write me that and other things.

Yours, Allen

82   a. In the *Fugitive* (June 1925) Davidson reviewed Eliot's *Homage to John Dryden*, and Ransom published a brief but significant essay "Thoughts on the Poetic Discontent."   b. At this time Benet was associate editor of the *Saturday Review of Literature*; Gorman was on the staff of the *New York Herald Tribune* and had published *James Joyce—His First Forty Years* and a volume of verse; Elinor Wylie, a well-known poet, was Benet's wife; Boyd was a regular contributor to the *Literary Review* and other periodicals.   c. "One Escape from the Dilemma," *Fugitive* (April 1924).

83/TLS

New York City
8 July 1925

Dear Don:

Your letter has just arrived, at the end of my lunch hour, which is three hours long, but I will try to answer it to an extent now because if I don't it may be several days before I can get to it. Your letter is too good to neglect that long.

I am greatly surprised to hear of the travails you have so sorely been afflicted with; I had no idea your troubles were so heavy, for your card seemed to indicate only a slight and very temporary indisposition. But I am certainly glad you are through it safely. I can sympathize; I had a tooth taken out in February; I walked the floor for a week.

It pleases me immensely that you are again seeing the light in your work. I am perfectly sure you will do something large in the next year. Everybody gets into a slump, either of ideas or of creative impulse. I was in the former dreadfully about two years ago; I am in the latter now, but it doesn't worry me, for I think I see where I am going all the same.

I am also much pleased that you liked Eliot's book. I imagine that John rather regrets his aspersions of Eliot two years ago—called him immature, etc.—for Eliot—*I* have known it all along!—is the most intelligent man alive, and there's no possibility of doubting it. Of course I say that because he agrees with me; more so, because he writes up my own ideas much better than my poor skill permits me to do for myself.

But frankly, Don, I do feel a bit aggrieved that it had to be Eliot who at last convinced all of you, that I was scanned with lifted brows for several years as a person with "radical" ideas. For three years I have defended the kind of poetry that integrates emotion with intellect, and the entire basis of my admiration of Hart Crane's work has always lain there. Of course I am demanding recognition as a prophet; I admit it.

But there is always something—in addition to Bodenheim[a] and other imposters—to keep me up in the air. The latest is the Virginia Quarterly Review. I will say no more. I only wish I had seen it before I wrote my article on the South; the galley proofs are returned; it is too late. . . .

Yours always, Allen

83   *a.* Maxwell Bodenheim, Mississippi-born poet and novelist.

84/TLS

New York City
25 July 1925

Dear Don:

I have read over again your fine letter many times. I am greatly complimented by your extensive remarks on my work. Believe me, it is the most complete statement on it I have ever received; it is also the most penetrating, and I think I am not deluding myself in saying that, simply because the drift of your commentary was favorable. There is not one thing in it that I should disagree with, and you must know I am much gratified to be understood by somebody at last. That, of course, is different from being merely praised; praise is more available than understanding, but when they arrive together the combination is irresistible!

But besides your comment on my work, this letter contains some of the most lucid and penetrating remarks on poetry in general I have ever got from you. They easily go to show that we are rapidly approaching a common ground of principles, of which the fundamental one is that poetry must be the expression of a whole mind—not gurgles and spasms and ecstasies over every wayside hawthorn bush; in other words, it is not, as you say, a *report* of sensation, it is a resolution of sensation through all the faculties of the mind. Poetry to me is successive instances of the whole rhythm of thought, and that includes reason, emotion, extralogical experience, or as I put it a year or so ago, the entire phantasy of sensation. And the only rule of good writing that deserves respect is simply that not a single phrase should be admitted to a poem which doesn't exist organically in the rhythm of thought. Robert Graves is right (for once) when he says that thought isn't simply reason or logic; it is everything that goes on in what we call the mind. I believe that every person has a thought rhythm peculiar to himself, and this thought rhythm is identical with his special attitude to the world; hence a good poet is one who contrives an accurate symbolism for this special attitude. Nobody ever says anything about an external world; there are as many external worlds as there are persons (one is tempted to add that therefore there is no external world at all that we can know); all we are trying to do is to articulate the movement of thought, as if it were some vast snake which we must put together synthetically before we can look at the marvellous beauty and rhythm of the whole. The phrase, "poets are masters of life," only means that poets approach complete self-consciousness as a mathematical limit; they aren't mastering life, they are mastering themselves in the sense of understanding themselves. But such a phrase gets much corrupted by popular usage; nearly all Victorian usage was popular usage: there was no other age in which every thing was so vastly misunderstood.

I must say again how grateful I am for your letter. I do wish you had had time to expose my personal metaphysics. I doubt if I know it myself, except to say that I am a pluralist, whatever that means; there are hundreds of pluralists, yet each of them has a pluralism of his own. No rationalized system of philosophy can hold within its terms the particular individuality of a mind; the historical systems are simply reductions of groups into types: they can do nothing for individuals of any one type. Hence the superiority of art over philosophy!

By this time you have doubtless seen my review of the Sitwells.[a] The damn proof reader ruined a quotation I inserted, making the third line the first, reducing it to utter nonsense. My next will be a two thousand word article on Marianne Moore. It's hard writing, the hardest I've ever done; and it goes slowly—only a hundred or so words a day, even those to be revised, many cancelled.[b]

By the way, I happened to see your selection of the Best Line in the Evening Post. It was very well put. Have you been writing for the Post? I never read it; it isn't worth reading except for gossip, and one gets plenty of that here first hand. But there are occasionally good contributors, and you may be one of them.

Crane has offered, at my suggestion, three poems for The Fugitive.[a] I am sending them to Ransom immediately with a brief and, I hope fitting defense. I am asking him to read them over through a period of a few weeks before he decides against them should he be inclined that way at first. I think John has fine ultimate judgment, but I remember he has missed out several times in exercising his immediate taste. He didn't care for Laura Gottschalk's work at first, but I understand he is very enthusiastic about it now. I have every reason to think he will like Crane just as well. Frankly, he didn't like Crane two years ago because I liked him first. Likewise, with T. S. Eliot! Suppose the Forty-niners had refused the California gold simply because somebody else discovered it!

The poem Idyl is much revised since I sent it to you, and since you took so much kind interest in it I am sending the new version.[b] You will see that one of my revisions was prescient of a criticism of yours. But I do think the poem on the old woman is the better poem.[d] I am also sending carbons of the three poems by Crane. If you like them speak for them; if you don't like them, just hold your peace!

Write soon.

Always, Allen

84   *a.* Osbert Sitwell's *Out of the Flame* and Sacheverell Sitwell's *The Thirteenth Caesar* in the *New Republic*, July 29, 1925.   *b.* Never published.   *c.* The September 1925 issue carried two poems by Crane—"Legend" and "Paraphrase." *d. Virginia Quarterly Review* (July 1928).

85/TLS

New York City
30 September 1925

Dear Don:

I was about to begin this letter without telling you a vastly important piece of news anent the Tate family in New York; you see, I've written so many family letters in the past week to announce it, that the news seemed very old to me as news, though its fact will likely remain a stupendous novelty for some time.

That fact is nothing less than proud fatherhood for Allen Tate. A very fine daughter, Miss Nancy Meriwether Tate, was born unto us a week ago today. You have a little girl, and I can't very rationally parade a superiority to you; but I suspect you are my only equal extant

Nancy pleases me much. The damned nurses will hardly let me near her; I come off the street germ-laden, they say! But I did see her today, and I rejoiced to observe the absence of her original very wicked and angry expression, which I took to be a protest against the hard riot of unrequested sensation from an extremely undesired world. She has fine blue eyes, a perfect chin, and amazingly prehensile fingers. What more could one wish?

And so I pass with reluctance to gratitude of a most cordial sort for your trouble in having cut out all those clippings for me. And I wonder why I asked you to do it. There are only two decent reviews among them—that is, decent according to changed standards. The writing is monstrously bad throughout.

I am much pleased to see your comment on Miss Sitwell's essay, which should become the Pater Noster of every college professor and the editors of the following magazines: Harpers, Scribners, The Century—but why name them all? As to the Van Doren book, we disagree. I have just perused Wilson's copy, and there isn't a total of twelve pages of intelligence in it. I am sure that Mark had little to do with it. He could write more accutely than that of Yeats: the old rot about the "Celtic dreamer," a supposed lack of common Anglo-Saxon sense, etc. And by the way, if you'd care to have me review C. Van Doren's Other Provinces, I'd be pleased to do so.

It is great to have Laura here. I've been informed, to my exceeding pleasure, of her coming success in England. I saw Graves' letter; it was the highest praise. I'm betting on the young lady, and when she gets over thinking every poem she writes is great because it's hers, I'll bet everything on her. Laura is great company, and we've had a fine time since she arrived. She reported an excellent visit in Nashville. I think you all need her constantly. She seemed to feel that everybody in Nashville was congenitally depressed; but she would put life into—well, into anything. She is a constant visitor to the Tates, and Carolyn finds her very charming, if strenuous!

Write me when you can. I'm buried as follows: Home, Reviewing, Office, Friends. And God! What happiness to be so immersed!

As always, Allen

86/ALS

New York City
15 October 1925

Dear Don:

Your fine letter was an excellent eye-opener this morning; I read it with great pleasure and luxury, in bed. The poem in free verse is a masterpiece! It will probably be preserved to posterity. And, as I read, the subject of the poem lay blissfully sleeping in the next room. In fact, she does everything blissfully: she blissfully sleeps, she blissfully eats, she blissfully eliminates. Indeed, she is a triumphantly inspired oesophagus! And all our spiritual judgments of her are the vainest pathetic fallacies; she heeds them not at all, but Great Digestion lords it over the Tate apartment so that of the 2½ persons there, the half takes the whole place! But the literary influence remains, not only through her parents, but through her accoutrements: everything she uses was passed on by various literati whose children have outgrown them. For instance, she is daily tossed into scales presented by Edmund Wilson; and one may say that she is thus weighed in the literary balance, though it's as yet impossible to determine whether she's found wanting in that respect. She will not be a poet; she will be a society lady or a chorus-girl, and the choice will not be between extremes, the same qualities being requisite to both! But I fear I bore you! Vixere fortes ante Agamemnon![a]

I've an arduous list of fall reviewing which will swamp me for six weeks. But I'd like to do the Van Doren book for you if you can wait that long; forget about pay! By the way, I've haughtily quit working for The N.R. Littell resigned six weeks ago, and his successor to the Book Dept., Lovett, and I fail to get along. He likes my work, however, for I've had testimony to the fact. But he's very neglectful of keeping his word about books; hence, my resignation. But something always happens; Canby has asked me to do a couple of articles on the criticism of poetry, which I hope to write before the winter is over. The invitation resulted from my essay "Poetry and the Absolute,"[b] which was too long and technical for his purposes. So it goes in Literary N.Y.

Laura, incidentally, is destined to great fame before two years are out. She'll be the most famous of us all, and she deserves to be; she's the best of us all. There are two poets I'm betting on—Laura and Hart Crane; if I'm wrong about them, I'm wrong about everything. As to the Sept. Fugitive, there were *two* good poems in it—Virgin of the

Hills and History of Two Simple Lovers.[c] It was a kind of shock to see some other and rotten stuff by Ransom along with the masterpiece!

Write soon. Allen

86   a. "Brave men existed before Agamemnon!"   b. *Sewanee Review* (January 1927).
     c. The second poem was later entitled "The Equilibrists."

87/TLS

New York City
26 November 1925

Dear Don:

This is a fine letter from you. I would I could answer it as it deserves to be answered. But my time, alas, since I quit my office work is less my own, in a sense, than ever before. I am now thoroughly a slave to reviews. I suppose I ought to be happy in that state, for I have waited a year for the confidence and the advance capital to enable me to become an independent free-lance. I quit three weeks ago; they tried to give me extra work without extra pay: it was a good opportunity, for if something like that hadn't happened I should have doubtless plugged on dumbly in that office for the next three hundred years. Everything, it seems as I review my adventures, happens to my advantage in the end!

The imminent demise of Adonais[a] and the prospect of his tenderer successors in Nashville strike horror and amusement to my soul.[b] And you having joined them! Well, when you want another New York Letter let me know; I could discuss The Poetry Society of America and poetry societies in general; in fact, I could discuss anything. Hecuba, it is true, is nothing to me; but she's becoming something dangerous to you, and I could rant out the lines at a great rate, where the principals would remain dumb in the intimacy of the emotion. Really, this new turn of affairs seems to me to be the reductio ad absurdum of the whole Nashville scene. I think all of you are very strong men; it takes strength to react day in and day out to an artificial situation and not go mad: it is very much like "living a lie," the essential difference being that your way of living is approved by the majority and the result is not tragedy, *merely* sterility and decay. It is a sort of neurosis—I hate the word but I can think of no other at the moment—for you build up defenses for this artificial world in a desperate attempt to make it a reality, and all the time the real world not only passes you by but you automatically oppose it and contemn it a little. Ordinary life becomes

fantastic and abnormal. And I say these things because they are fundamental things, because they are at the basis of my own personal tendencies, of my determination not to be misled into an acceptance of
false issues in which life becomes dully insufferable to the participant
and a little ridiculous to the observer. I say them, moreover, because
you are one of the best friends I ever have had and because I am convinced that our roles are being interchanged by necessity, and I am
about to be Mentor. You are wiser in the expedient details of life: but
I'm damned if you're very farsighted.

Here is an interesting point, I think. You remember that certain
"critics" thought our poetry in the first issues of The Fugitive was very
much alike, perhaps written by one man? Well, it *was* much alike, in
spite of technical inequalities, for it was the expression of defeated
men. Mine was a little more ragged and violent, being produced by a
young man, than the other work; but it was in the same drift toward
defeatism. I am not writing any poetry now; and the reason is obvious:
I have no idiom for a Vita Nuova, for it will take a long time for me
even to understand it. For poetry is the triumph of life, not a commentary on its impossibility.

One of the attributes of poetry is its efficacy as a defense against
society particularly, as Shelley said, when society is most degraded.
Society is pretty degraded just now, and we need poetry badly. But if
poetry is *merely* a social defense it can hardly be serious, however interesting it may be; and it will not be profound even though it may
be subtly presented. Of course I am describing minor poetry; it is an
age of minor poetry of various kinds. I think a poet may be most honor-
ably minor these days by attempting some sort of assimilation of contemporary life and failing inevitably a complete assimilation; that will
come later if poetry survives at all, which isn't too certain in spite of
poetry societies and quantity production of verse. I remember John
once alluded to those persons who escaped common American life by
running off to Washington Square! Well, if John is living common
American life why is his subject-matter a melange of Church, State,
Kings, romantic maidens, all heaved up in an intellectual sigh!

I have got started, as usual, but it has been leading to something
all the time. Near the end of your letter you call yourself a "bright
young man." Now bright young men are wanted all over this common ordinary country of common ordinary American life, and they
are wanted outside Nashville. It happens that Columbia University
needs professors every year, and there is no reason under heaven why

you couldn't get a job there. In fact, I think I could have got one for next year, and if I can get an academic job anybody can. For the truth is, Columbia is perhaps the most liberal institution in this country; and they don't put a premium on dulness and inability to do anything but find out how many times Ben Jonson had measles. They actually want men who are capable of something outside the academic routine, and they have many of that sort. In short, if you are interested, I'll talk about it to certain acquaintances of mine; the first person I'll see will be Mark Van Doren, who already knows of you very pleasantly. New York isn't a paradise; but once you left your classroom, your life would be your own, whether for dipsomania or haircloth shirts and ashes. For I very much suspect that you would find character and not code to be the prevailing criterion. Write me your full mind in this if you are piqued at all.

Well, my review of the American Miscellany is being neglected for this letter; perhaps I want it to be, for I haven't an idea about that volume. It is certain there was no excuse for it except Untermeyer's whims and politics. John's sonnets and Eliot's three lyrics are good, but all the other stuff could have waited for appearance in private books or been discarded altogether; I must add Stevens to the list of exceptions.

I am thinking of moving to the country for the rest of the winter, but it's only a thought so far. Continue to address me here. I've never felt better in my life—and God! It's great to sit at home and write and read to your heart's content! My handsome daughter, by the way, is with her maternal grandmother, in Guthrie, for the winter; New York, you know, is hard on any young lady's morals, especially in winter when the age is tender.

I await the last Fugitive with much pleasure—not because it's the last—but because it's the Fugitive! Write soon.

Yrs. Allen

Your Conrad essay I have just read. Bias aside, I think it is the best of the lot. Scan the names carefully: Samuel Chew is "better known" than any of you in the contest; unless he had written perfect rot, it was unlikely he'd fail to get 1st Prize. What he wrote wasn't much. Of course I say this not having followed the Conrad story; but good criticism shines in its own light.

87 a. The *Fugitive*. b. Ransom and others were discussing the formation of the Nashville Poetry Society.

88/TLS

Nashville, Tenn.

29 November 1925

Dear Allen:

Your letter, just arriving, stirred me up considerably, so that I can't get mental relief until I answer. I'm quite willing for you to step into the role of Mentor. In fact, I accept as true and wise everything you say in that letter (N.B. This moment should be recorded as historically important). If you will advise me as to a way out of my present difficulties, I'll strike off a silver half-dollar to immortalize you when I become President.

The situation in Nashville *is* really horrifying. My position with reference to such a "society" as is being formed is naturally full of difficulties. I am one of those unfortunate people of whom things are "expected," and am all the more unfortunate because I am cursed with a conscience and a "tendre herte." I am the only one of The Fugitives who has protested against this society foolishness. Jesse, it is true, is suspicious, and so is Stevenson, but both have a considerable amount of curiosity. I argued violently, in fact heatedly, with John against the "society," but to little effect. Even so, I have not yet summoned up courage to oppose the thing before the organizers themselves, other than to declare positively and vehemently that I would accept no office, and to point out all the obstacles and objections that I could manage to conjure up. But as the time approaches when this thing is to be launched (Dec. 5), I get more and more angry and indignant. I really can't conceive of myself as going through the motions of belonging to a Poetry Society of this kind, especially when the damned thing will be associated (as it certainly will be) with the demise of The Fugitive. I'll worry through this thing for a few days and then decide something. My whole impulse is to cut loose from even an inactive relationship with the thing, even though I am the only one of The Fugitives who does so.

You can see that I have gradually gotten into the role of the Opposition among The Fugitives. Since you left, and since Stanley adopted the role of Ishmael and went to live on the Cumberland, there has been nobody to create a disturbance except me. And when it comes to an oral argument, I make a feeble showing; it's hard for me to make out a case.

The whole business is, as you say, reductio ad absurdum. I want to entreat you to keep the course of affairs under your hat at least until it is clear just what is going to happen here. I am disgusted with myself for getting upset over so small a matter, but it is annoying beyond words.

It isn't after all a minor matter. It's what it stands for that counts, and that, I dare say, is what led you into the discussion of poetry and society (in the large sense). I agree in the main with your estimate of poetry as a social defense, and with your determination of the elements of likeness in Fugitive poetry and the reason therefor. I would only supplement your remarks by saying that I do believe most of us really have approached poetry as a fine art and not in the spirit of dilettantes or moralists. That has been our great strength,—that and our serious-ness. But I will acknowledge that the defeatism crept in, some strain of it at least, in the bulk of Fugitive poetry; and so our "pure art" has here and there been touched with indignation or with wistfulness de-pending on the reaction of the writer to his confinements. It is possible, though, that what you term defeatism isn't a permanent quality; I hope it isn't. And I think, in your case as in mine and others, the surest way to pass beyond and out of defeatism is to acknowledge the thing for what it is in the hope that some sort of purgation may finally be accom-plished. Then may come the Vita Nuova and the triumphant idiom which you desire.

I pass on now to the more practical (or worldly) point of your letter. I was absolutely serious in indicating that I wanted to leave Nashville. Therefore I seize with all the eagerness of real hope on your suggestion. I should be glad if you had an opportunity to sound out any of your acquaintances, especially Mark Van Doren (I promised long ago to send him some poems, but have had none I thought worth sending). But first I had better explain my situation. I am forced to consider economics, you know; and you also know that here in Nashville both my wife and I have jobs. She gets a right good salary from the Law School (more than I was earning when I first came to Vanderbilt), and between that and my Tennessean job and my teaching plus occasional extras, we manage to live decently (though we are not yet able to afford a car, etc., etc.). Now if I make a move I will have to rake in as much money (at least as much) as I am making here, plus what my wife is making or we would have to be in a place where she could easily get a position. As a matter of fact, she, for her part, feels baffled in Nashville because she is worse than a 100 to 1 shot in trying to follow a legal ca-reer. Likewise, you know I can't show any array of Ph.D.'s and contri-butions to PMLA. My appeal to scholarly bugs is flabby; to literary bugs, however, it might be less motheaten (Blinkey Horn's[a] word). I do fear New York somewhat, and am not anxious to be swallowed; but I don't think the Battle of New York would be much more dreadful than the Battle of Nashville, 1925. Furthermore, since you asked me to let you have my full mind, here it is: I decided some time ago that the time had come for me to look around, and I am willing to cut loose, even from teaching if and whenever I find something that will pay me as much for the time required. I have also decided not to apply for a Guggenheim fellowship, not this year at least, but am keeping it in mind for the future. I am restless, and all the more because I feel that I'm caught in a blind alley. And this is true even though I should really prefer to stay in the South, if only I were financially independent.

At Vanderbilt things are going peculiarly. Dr. Mims nearly left us last year to go to Duke University. Curry and Ransom have had good offers but have passed them by. Yet here each of them is at present standing in the other's way. Confidentially, Ransom is figuring on making a getaway, eventually landing in the East (not Harvard or Yale), and I think he'll put his plans through. The scattering process goes on in spite of the fact that Vanderbilt is putting on a drive for $4,000,000 for the college of arts and science. Soon one won't be able to live here alone! Yes, even though a "younger generation" is really developing—Warren Taylor, Cannon Clark, Andrew Lytle,[b] etc.

I'm glad you liked my Conrad essay; it was too hastily done to be first-class. Chew took an unfair advantage in mentioning "when I last saw Conrad"; but I didn't mind. I can endure $50.

All this about myself! What about you? You mean to say that you can really make your way free-lancing? I didn't know that critics and poets could hope to be so independent, except after long experience. Well, I'm glad of it. I feel like chirping up with several heroic anthems but this letter is already too messy and too long. I'll quit with the brief observations that I have several literary projects germinating which I will later say something about; that I'm glad your handsome daughter's morals are being ably looked after this severe winter; and that your letter was immensely rejuvenating.

                                                    Faithfully, Don

I'll be your everlasting debtor for anything you may discover in my behalf!

We're expecting to see Red Warren this December. The rascal

hasn't written to us—I hear indirectly through Cannon Clark who is in my English 1 class. A great boy, that!

88   *a.* Pen name of an editorial writer on the *Nashville Banner.*   *b.* Taylor (Vanderbilt class of 1924), Clark (1929), Lytle (1925).

89/TLS

New York City
2 December 1925

Dear Don:

Your fine letter has arrived this moment, in the midst of our moving excitement and confusion. I am buried in packing; we go out to the country Friday. But there is always time for everything—I've learned that in New York; and everything somehow always gets done.

I can only touch on a few points of your letter; a fuller reply must await my settling in the hills. Your letter is the best, most satisfactory statement, the directest and most lucid, I have ever had from you. It shows that you at least, of those men in Nashville who are equally gifted, are not so utterly corrupted by compromise and expediency that you have forgotten how to give your energies to the only motives tolerable to civilized men.

Now, as to New York, I was already aware that you might find it difficult here even under the best circumstances. You have become accustomed to a fixed order of certainties, and I am certain that you could not thrive in such a chaos as I have had to live through, in the past five years, before I reached anything like a satisfying order of life. I am aware also that you have a conscience, but I must say that I have always hoped you might get some sort of work in which your satisfactions of conscience could be realized with an excess of energy left over for simpler activities. Conscience is surely the product of social and economic exigency—it has little to do with the essences, companionship and love—and where men are solely occupied with such an exigency life becomes hateful, at least to me; for all contacts are controlled by its considerations. Morality subserves ambition; but the secret of all morals, as Shelley (again) said, is love. I suspect I sound like a preacher: let it be—I *am*, for the sake of a life which always approaches the purity of art. . . .

However, I don't know just what can be done here. I will have to let you know later. I will investigate the Columbia matter when I return to New York for a few days two weeks from now. Don't build up too much hope; but for God's sake build up some, and continue to be restless. That's the only thing that will pull you out at all.

In the Nashville Poetry Society, who is going to write the poetry? More in a few days.

Yours always, Allen

II

Years between *The Fugitive* and *I'll Take My Stand:* 1926-1930

From the literary standpoint the most interesting passages in the letters of this period, 1926 to 1930, are those in which the correspondents exchange criticism of each other's poetry. They are both experimenting with new poetic forms, and their reactions are characteristically honest, at times sharply so. The Fugitives all differ markedly in the theory and practice of their art, which is probably the reason that they have been so stimulating to one another. The style of the criticism in these letters, especially in the case of Tate, has its historical significance. For some time in Tate's Spyglass *reviews, as the reader will have noticed, Davidson had encouraged his friend to try to develop a style similar to that of his letters. The advice, as Tate's superb later essays show, had its effect.*

As far as the general narrative of the Fugitives is concerned, the letters of this period are most remarkable for their treatment of events leading up to the publication of I'll Take My Stand: The South and the Agrarian Tradition *in the fall of 1930. To read the letters on the immense scheme out of which this agrarian symposium grew—and of which it was conceived to be only a small part—is to realize how little the general intent of the symposium was understood by the reading public when it was published. These letters emphasize the conviction of two prime movers of the Fugitive movement that real art is impossible without serious concern for the cultural soil from which it springs.*

The main events and decisions of the period are allied to this conviction. Tate says in 1927, "I've attacked the South for the last time." And after his return in 1930 from his Guggenheim fellowship in Europe, he leaves New York and moves to Benfolly in Clarksville, Tennessee, apparently planning to live there the rest of his life, although it did not turn out that way. Davidson had been speculating for some time on the possibility of leaving Nashville, even getting away from the South for good. He now decides, also in 1927, "My America is here or nowhere"—and it was.

90/TLS

Patterson, N.Y.

3 January 1926

Dear Don:

Your letter awaited me here last night when I got home from a four day trip, of which two days were spent in Washington with my mother, two in New York. I will do my best to answer all of your letter, though it contains so much of great interest that I may miss some of it. I may say that it is a fine satisfaction to me that, as the years pass, your letters continue to be one of my chief interests; and I always look forward to them for one of the few solid pleasures it is permitted me to enjoy.

First, since I have just come from the city, I must tell you that my plan to bring you before Mark Van Doren failed; he was out of town for the holidays. But I will be there again in two weeks, and will have a long talk with him. He is going to lend us some co-operation in a publishing venture which we have just about got through with the Adelphi Company, Laura's press.

By "us" I mean Wilson and myself. We are contemplating a series of new poets—whether they will come out as a series under a name, or separately, remains undecided—and they will include, roughly in the order of publication, the following: Laura (since she was being published anyhow and was eager to get in the series), Tate, Phelps Putnam (a fine poet, unknown), Malcolm Cowley, Hart Crane (withdrawn to our aegis from Liveright), Edmund Wilson, John Peale Bishop. These represent a good deal of fine poetry which, under the Untermeyer dictatorship, had little chance to appear: all have somehow failed to play politics in Mr. Untermeyer's way or have not seemed good material for Untermeyer to exploit. By the way, Wilson's attack in the N.R. is gospel; everybody knows it here, but Wilson alone had the nerve and the place to publish such an article. . . .

There is just one trouble with your plan for a small "Fugitive Press." We are thinking of one here, to be run in the country where all the printing can be done by ourselves (Brown is a good printer).

But seriously I think your scheme a fine one; and I would certainly be glad to give you any help I could, which more and more will be possible, I believe. The gravest difficulty of all would be the figure of an editor—whether he would be you or somebody else; for authors don't care much to turn over their work to an individual, whoever he may be. The great success of the erstwhile Egoist Press and later of The Hogarth is partly due to the casual circumstance in which the books are issued. And your greatest handicap, isolated in Nashville, would be inaccessibility to material. I bring up these points, not as objections, but as cautions. However, if you can swing it, let me know; and I will see if I can get you certain writers who have good stuff "unavailable" for the magazines, for your prospectus; that is, if you would care to have me do it. An impressive list could be drawn up, I think.

Now that this letter is already inexcusably long there is no time left for rhapsodies about my new life in the country. A few items: I saw wood an hour and a half every day; get up and make the fires; write all morning (eight to twelve); have lunch; go hunting in the afternoon, for partridge, pheasant, rabbits, squirrels, etc., or go skating on the lovely lake a mile away; come in to dinner (or supper, in the country); smoke happily for half an hour; then read 18th century novelists (Richardson at present) until nine-thirty when I go to bed. Result, in four weeks I have mounted up from one hundred and thirty to one hundred and forty-one; and sometimes I start to throw my forearm in the kitchen stove, thinking it is one of the hard hickory logs usually served up as fuel! Add to this visitors every week end, and life is complete; for they mean bringing the only good part of New York to your very door!

> How vainly men themselves amaze
> To win the palm, the oak, the bays.[a]

I forgot to say that Hart Crane is living with us—one of the finest men alive—if possible, finer than his poetry. You will surely meet some day; the few good men in the world deserve to meet.

Write me all about yourself. I am much encouraged about your mood and outlook recently; you seem much less depressed. Take heart! I want to see you get untangled from that mess as soon as possible. It may not be long.

Yours ever, Allen

P.S. Please don't tell anybody the details of our (Wilson's & mine) plan—that is, the name of the publisher.

90   a. Marvell's "The Garden," ll. 1-2.

91/TLS

Patterson, N.Y.
3 March 1926

Dear Don:

Your letter came to me in a time of considerable excitement. Not that anything has happened. Nothing ever happens in the country. Nothing could happen now that we are snowed in. I have simply been drunk with an idea! Happy state! One can be drunk in New York but not with an idea. For over a month I have been collecting notes for an essay.ᵃ The essay, I fear, will contain a discussion of Fundamentalism; not what the Methodist Bishops think it is, but what it really is. My purpose is to define the rights of both parties, science and religion, and I'm afraid I agree with Sanborn that science has very little to say for itself. I remember he used to emphasize that view, but I scoffed at it; I see he was right. The principle is, Science as we inherit it as Mechanism from the 17th century has nothing whatever to say about reality: if the Church or a fishmonger asserts that reality is fundamentally cheese or gold dust or Bishop Berkeley's tar water, Science has no right to deny it. On the other hand, the Church has no right to forestall *all* criticism by simply saying Science is wrong. The Church these days is of course decayed, but the attack on it should be ethical, not scientific. More abstractly, Science is, according to tradition, classification; religion, or more properly philosophy, is organization. As A. N. Whitehead puts it, philosophy is nature viewed as organism; science, as mechanism. Religio-philosophy is the organization of instinctive commonsense knowledge, by which we know ourselves to be organic and unmechanical; this organization is simply logic, which should be applied to science as its critic: philosophy the corrective of science. Etc., etc. This is certainly the principle. But to follow this idea out without criticism of the existing order, without investigating whether the existing body of religio-philosophic doctrine is capable of being an adequate critic of science, is to become a victim of worse than the infinitely multiplied entities of the schoolmen. It is simply the substitution of a wish for a fact: a wish that the Church were an integral body of doctrine, instead of finding out whether it is. To prove that science, on principle, is wrong, doesn't prove that the Church is right. Those who attack science from the rightness of the Church aren't likely to shake it; they should attack science from principle, philosophically. This is my thesis: it will be about five thousand words. I will be at it another month, at least.

. . . Being drunk with the idea, I have plunged into it, and perhaps smothered you, at the outset. Now to other things.

As to the New York matter, you will have some news within the next week. Despairing of getting to town to discuss the thing in person, I wrote day before yesterday to Van Doren (Mark). If anything can be done, he will put me onto it. . . .

For reading mss. for publishers there's no set price. I've done a little of it myself, and the pay varied. I think the average is somewhere between 15.00 and 20.00 for a novel; the work includes a full critical report, something like a review only much more candid; in New York you are supposed to tell the publisher whether the book would make money, but if not whether the merit of it might justify the loss. Poetry is much less: about five to ten dollars. There is no way of getting the average on other types of books. That ought to be a good arrangement for you; charge him the New York rate; it isn't too much.

Alas, our poetry series has evaporated. Our publisher got cold feet at the last minute. Everything is withdrawn except, tentatively, my volume. This survival of our great plans is due to Wilson's generosity solely. He may succeed in flattering my work so that it will get across; he was good enough to say that of the eight poets on our list I was the most deserving of publication. I would I were a better wish-thinker; I'd like to think so too! I'll let you know the outcome.

Your picture of Nashville is, as usual, my dear Don, depressing. Try to stick it out a little longer. And write up that essay: I'd like to see it as soon as it's done. And send the new poems too: I have my evenings for miscellaneous pursuits, and they couldn't be better spent than on your poems. Your report of literary activity there is funny—now that I'm out of it; but if I were there, I'm sure I'd get out on the street-corner and flout God, whence the good citizens would conclude with beautiful logic that I believed in free love. Such is the penalty for being a little impatient with dulness, for mildly objecting to stupidity. . . .

My life here is one of undisturbed peace and meditation. An occasional evening at the Browns' or an afternoon of skiing is all the diversion we need. I never hope to live in town again. I am buying three acres here this spring; a small house will follow next fall; I shall remain forever! I can do what I please, see only those few persons I please or correspond with them. I may then say with Yeats—

There is not a fool can call me friend.

Write again soon, and write me another fine letter like the one I am answering.

Yours ever, Allen

91   *a.* Although some of these ideas appear in his contribution to *I'll Take My Stand* and elsewhere, the essay referred to here was never published.

92/TLS

Patterson, N.Y.
24 March 1926

Dear Don:

I am extremely glad to get your note. I do hope my comments were really valuable; I was very busy at that time, and I feared afterwards that they might seem to you abrupt and arbitrary. But try to read that quality out of them, if you found it; it was the accident of haste.

I don't know what your reasons are for preferring The Saturday Review, but I hope they're good. That sheet seems to me to be the most contemptible and dull in this country. Mind you: I say this from an opinion utterly unbiased: for I suppose I should think highly of Canby. It happens that he wrote me a letter last fall, returning an essay much too long for him, that flattered my critical powers more than any other statement I have ever had made about them; I am saving it, whether for my biography or his it is impossible to say just now. But I hope he does take your paper; it ought to get conspicuously into print very soon. Let me know.

I'm glad you like the new poems; let me have a smashing criticism. By the way, Eliot had twelve poems of mine for some time, and today I heard from him to the effect that he will use some of them in The Criterion very soon. Moreover, he has invited me to contribute an essay on the writings of Paul Elmer More![a] This latter was prompted by a rather long digression I made on him in a paper about Marianne Moore, which Eliot sent back saying his audience knew nothing about her. Incidentally, you can't afford to miss the "Criterion" (I should have said this all along, even before Eliot's cordiality), for it's the finest journal of ideas in the language. I suppose I kept it out of the Vanderbilt Library two years ago: I recommended it to Will Ella Johnson,[b] and she demonstrated how superior she was by ignoring it. Please don't tell this Criterion matter of mine to any one, except Jesse, and swear him to secrecy. I trust few persons these days—after having had some defamatory letters written about me by well-known gents in Nashville. I suppose I've developed a sort of neurosis on this; I'm now very clandestine!

Write me the news; and send other works of yours for perusal.

As always, Allen

92 *a*. None of Tate's poetry was published in the *Criterion*, but this essay, "The Fallacy of Humanism," appeared there in July 1929. *b*. Mrs. Stanley Johnson, librarian at Vanderbilt.

93/TLS

Nashville, Tenn.
29 March 1926

Dear Allen:

At last here are your poems, with my very considerable admirations. But I hardly know what to say by way of criticism. One important point, however, occurs to me. Heretofore, in your poetry there has been so often a lack of elasticity that you left your reader in a state of defeat, unable to bridge the ellipses which your close crowding of images and ideas produced; there was (as I saw it) not enough play in your lines; your association of ideas was very rich, but it produced that "telescoping of imagery" to which I recall Curry objected. In these three new poems this defect does not appear, if defect it is. You retain a rich texture of associations, but they come consequentially and are not too tightly crowded. I think this is an evident and a very valuable development. Your style, always highly individual, is becoming more and more an adequate vehicle for your ideas. You seem to me to be approaching or even attaining perfection in the only kind of poetry which your artistic conscience will permit you to write. I may regret that your conscience has driven you into a narrow lane from which I can see no emerging; but I accept, since it is your choice, both the lane and you, and I do not know of any other poetry in this field which has such a cast of the inevitable in phrasing or which represents more adequately the artistic reactions of a thoroughly twentieth century mind, encircled by a complex whirl of influences, yet so far abstracted from them as to be sensitive (if remotely) to tradition. Furthermore, though Dr. Mims and even Ransom would think of your poetry as poetry of the head, I do not see it that way; it is intellectual poetry, to be sure, but intellectual poetry pouring a definite light (as Donne's did) on physical and emotional experience. So there!

I have no preference between the three poems; just about equal admiration. Yet "Causerie"[a] is the most astonishing. It really knocks me off the perch. Your selection from miscellaneity to get a sort of meditative unity produces a remarkable effect. You give a "catalogue," but not the Whitman type of catalogue, since each one of your items has its separate individual and emotional significance. The "Ditty"[b] is as clean and beautiful a pattern of comparative simplicity as the "Causerie" is a pattern of miscellanies. I like it, particularly the ending. I have a feeling that these two poems are more original pieces than the "Pastoral,"[c] which perhaps is more of a repetition of things you have done before. But I couldn't say for sure. I like it, as all the poems. I am seized with an immense desire to see a collection of your poems; it seems a shame not to have them together. If I did have a lot of them together, before me right now, I feel that I could execute more intelligent criticism. I see you as developing, and enthusiastically congratulate you on your distinct forward movement, but the lack of specimens leaves me vague as to the ultimate direction in which you may be going. I believe, though, that you are gradually working toward a very definite Tatian contribution to poetry.

Your own comments were mighty valuable, never fear! I'm downright grateful for your taking the time to look over my things. Especially cheering was your confirmation of my feeling that "The Long Street" was the best of the lot. I will not perhaps add to it, in the sense of prolonging it; but it is one of a closely related group or scheme of poems which I am gradually building up.[d] These will, in a roughly unified way, present what I intend to be a fairly complex portrait of a person (say myself) definitely located in Tennessee, sensitive to what is going on as well as what has gone on for some hundreds of years. "Fire on Belmont Street" is another one of this set of poems, and I have still others under way which I hope to make more successful even than these if I develop my symbols and medium as I want to.

My reason for sending the article to Canby was, in the first place, that it seemed entirely too long for The Nation.[e] In the second place, The Nation had already carried one article on this subject (yours) not long ago. In the third place, I was thinking of Southern readers whom The Nation would not reach or else would merely irritate (since Southerners think of The Nation as an enemy), and I am particularly anxious to reach as many Southern readers as possible, for reasons of my own. I agree with your opinion of The Saturday Review, however. I don't see why in the devil Sherman doesn't enlarge his sheet a little so as to permit publication of articles (not reviews) besides his own. It is a sad fact, but it seems that there is no first-class critical weekly or monthly in this country which gives anything like decent space to discussions other than reviews. I am not at all sure that Canby will take my article, however; and if he doesn't I think The Nation would certainly be my next best bet, though I don't see how it could publish the article without injurious cutting.

I'm heartily glad you are doing so well with Eliot. I have not seen The Criterion yet; but just the other day I got Mrs. Johnson to say she would subscribe to it. I'll check up on her; and if she doesn't get it I'll have to subscribe myself. Of course I'll respect your desire that these formidable operations of yours should remain "clandestine." Who were the persons writing "defamatory" letters? And what did they say?

Nobody around here (with the sole exception of Curry, strangely enough) seems to have any definite reaction, favorable or otherwise, toward what I'm trying to do. I meet absolute indifference, or polite toleration. Last night I showed "The Long Street" to John and one or two others without getting even a polite hearing. Of course Ransom is all wrapped up in his philosophical-literary studies and can think of not much else.*f*

I have a book (not of poems) in mind that I'll tell you about later. At last I am in a position, I believe, to make my Tennessean writing count in the direction of a volume.

Curry has been offered a big job at Iowa which he'll find it difficult to turn down. If he leaves next year, and John departs too, the complexion of the landscape will change considerably.

Thank you again many times, Allen, for looking over my stuff. I enjoyed your poems immensely as always. You are certainly moving ahead.

Faithfully, Don

93   *a. Calendar of Modern Letters* (October 1926); the title of this poem was later changed to "Retroduction to American History." *b. Nation* (July 23, 1926). *c.* Tate's poem "Light Interval" was published as "Pastoral" in *Mr. Pope and Other Poems* (1928) and in subsequent editions. *d.* He is writing the poems for *The Tall Men* (1927). *e.* "The Artist as Southerner," *Saturday Review of Literature* (May 15, 1926). *f.* Ransom is engaged in writing a book-length essay which he is calling "The Third Moment." It was never published.

94/TLS

Patterson, N.Y.
2 April 1926

Dear Don:

Your letter came this noon, was received by my hands from the hands of "Andy," the R.R. postman, who greets one daily with a gigantic Rabelaisian metaphor usually drawn from intestinal processes. Sometimes he varies it with an allusion to Venus, in which the goddess becomes brilliantly profane; but if the day is cloudy and the roads muddy he simply says Hell. He is the most important person in the mere mechanism of my life: I could cook my own meals, but I couldn't bring the mail—the stuff men live by.

Your satisfying compliments to my poems modestly put aside, I can say that your criticism is excellent. You picked out the flaws unerringly. And you are perfectly right about Pastoral; it *is* repetition. Malcolm Cowley meant the same thing in calling it "mannered." I'm wondering if I sent you, in a later mail, another poem called "Idiot"?[a] I hope I did; I'd like your opinion; it's the best of the recent output. There are no copies to hand at the moment, or I'd risk sending another. You are one of the few who can be depended on for a clean reaction; you have always given me your views forthright, from the time you didn't like my verse down to now, when you seem to be liking it better; and I must say that I value the old unfavorable opinion as highly as the new and supposedly more satisfactory one. It is the consistency of attitude—much more valuable than consistency of opinion—that I like. I can put it this way: you have not seen the necessity of fitting me or disposing of me in a fixed little cosmology of competitions and rivalries in which you make yourself safe for Donald Davidson. There are others whom I could not be so sure of; I could become another Donne, and they would remember that I didn't have the right "attitude" in college and knew my own mind (however gropingly) before it was convenient to them that I should know it. I despise their criteria of success, which are completely derived from the current social criteria; but even from their viewpoint I have already at twenty-five achieved more in literature than any of them had at my age. Such comparisons are odious to me; but when I was in Nashville I had constantly to meet those terms, for I was being measured by them. It was prophesied that I should never come to any good, would never do anything; and one reason why I wish my projects to remain secret until they are firmly realized is simply that some persons will go to any length to make their prophesies come true. The next time we are together it may be possible for me to be a little more explicit. In fact, I was almost explicit in this letter: I wrote it out, and then amputated it as this sheet shows, fearing after all to commit such matter to the postal service efficient as it is in this efficient nation. Suffice it here to quote a line of poetry from one of the great Elizabethans: it speaks for two villains:

> You have a pair of hearts are hollow graves.[b]

Let me know what luck you have this time with Canby. If you have to send it to The Nation, let me know that too; I would be glad to mention it to Van Doren—"I think Davidson is sending you a fine article on the South: I hope you like it—it supports parts of my recent thesis," etc.—not that suggestion of the sort is final, it is simply influential. But I agree with you that it would be a shame to cut the essay the least bit; *I* always feel as if I have been emasculated.

When you add more poems to the Long Street series, please let me see them. In a way I am not surprised that Curry is the only interested person there; he has his faults, which permit him to go so far and no further; but he is fundamentally honest and lacks corruption. I have several things to be grateful to him for, and I wish the gratitude were unmixed with a sense that he committed a useless breach of courtesy with me about two years ago; but that's very little to hold against any man. What is the prose book you allude to so mysteriously? Out with it!

My next prose is a rather long essay on Eliot's Collected Poems, for the New Republic.[c] It's ticklish business; I am not so concerned with making it "favorable," but the essay has simply got to be the best I can make it. Therefore, it goes slowly—fifty to a hundred words a day!

Write soon; and stay in the good mood you seem to be in now. What news from Erskine?[d]

As always, Allen

94 a. *Virginia Quarterly Review* (July 1927).   b. *The Duchess of Malfi*, IV, ii, 330. c. *Poems, 1909–1925*; reviewed in *New Republic* (June 30, 1926).   d. John Erskine, English department, Columbia University.

95/TLS

Patterson, N.Y.
14 May 1926

Dear Don:

It is fine to hear from you again, even though the letter be disappointingly brief, and to get the two long poems. I have read them through twice, and while there is much to say against them, there is certainly more to admire.

First, let me say a word about the plan of a Tennessee Faust. It looks very impressive; and I think you can make it work. Just reading these selections, I am reminded of the true definition of poetry with respect to time and place—that it must be local to be universal; while on the other hand, much poetry that deliberately sets out to be universal merely exposes its provincialism (Dubose Heyward). As to the possible success, however, of such a poem in the grand style, that of course I couldn't predict—any more than could you. But I'd like to see it tried out; and I can think of nobody else who could do it better than you. I couldn't even begin it; Ransom probably has too much of the same poison in his system as I have to do it.

Of the two pieces The Tall Men is by far, in my opinion, the best. I can't see the direction of The Sod of Battlefields—although it might acquire more meaning fitted into a larger scheme. Also, it seems rather unorganized. And your sudden shift to the modern scene (in both poems; but more so in The Sod) is rather jerkily done; the symbolism, moreover, is a bit too obvious and expected—typewriters, automobiles, asphalt. There are fine lines in these poems—so many that I couldn't record my pleasure in them here; but fine lines will not produce a poem of this order, will they?—however indispensable they may be.

You asked for my criticism. Criticism of these poems must certainly refer to your previous work in lyrical poetry, and I prefer the latter. I'm afraid Eliot is about right in saying there are no important themes for modern poets. Hence we all write lyrics; we must be subjective. I doubt if it was wholly due to a personal richness of mind—Milton's deliberate casting about for subjects; the English mind was more fertile then. I am convinced that Milton himself could not write a Paradise Lost now. Minds are less important for literature than cultures; our minds are as good as they ever were, but our culture is dissolving. Plotinus was as profound as Plato, but not so good a philosopher. Arnold was more intelligent than Shelley, but not so good a poet. Something happened to us in Arnold's time. You can't escape it even in Tennessee!

I think there is one fundamental law of poetry, and it is negative: you can't *create* a theme. Themes are or are not available. If you can name me a single great poem the theme of which the poet invented, I'll send you a case of beer for the Fourth of July. Remember—a *great* poem. You can't put your epic of Tennessee into the minds of Tennesseans; the pre-condition of your writing it is that it must (in an equivalent of spiritual intensity) be already there.

Questions on this head: 1. Why are Bridges' Hellenic poems such dull stuff? He is probably as great a master of English verse as Milton. 2. Why have we both liked Leonard's Two Lives? It lacks a cosmic myth and is subjective. These interests extenuate his "vicious style." 3. Why has Eliot's The Waste Land held people against their will? Because it exhibits the present state of European culture and tells us what we hate to believe—that our traditional forms are dead. It struck a spiritual accord in every sensitive mind; some minds gave in, others combatted it: the one attitude was as significant as the other. I remember Ransom fought it, and then went on proving its thesis in every poem he wrote: "All the wars have dwindled since Troy fell." They verily have. (See my review of Eliot in a forthcoming N.R.)[a]

I seem to have gone pretty far off the subject of this letter; but I believe I really haven't. The substance of your proposed epic is appealing. But account for two qualities which I think I already detect. (1) Thinness of effect; (2) Incoherence. The first, I suspect, is due to the fact that you are attempting to envisage an experience of the first order with a symbolism of a lower order: you are really trying to write a history of your mind, but this mind is not so simple as you think; it cannot be so homogeneously accounted for as your schematism would lead one to believe. At the present moment you represent the convergence of forces that will not be adequately represented by reference to a Tennessee history, and the result is thinness; the symbols seem trivial. This brings up the second quality—incoherence. The triviality of the symbol will not carry all the emotion you bring to bear on it (cf. paragraph 3, of this letter), and the disparity produces a jagged, incoherent pattern.

I hope you write this poem. Even if it shouldn't turn out to be a masterpiece, it will certainly interest those minds that are prepared to see an issue involved in it. When a man is a poet, as you are if any man is, poems fail for one reason: the theme is unsuitable. Why not test your capacity for this theme? If you fail it will not mean you have failed in *poetry*. . . .

Glad Canby took the essay: won't you send me a copy when it appears? I seldom see the S.R. Good for Van Doren!

Must go out now and plant a few rows of beans. My Garden is my Pride. Write soon.

Allen

On this point, see Paul Shorey's irascible and bombastic attack on a mythical modernism in his Vanderbilt address.[b] There's very little in it to *disagree* with, but consider the *attitude*. Even the defenders of the Humanities are becoming polemical & vulgar. Every professional Hellenist in America (Tolman was no exception, though it is significant that he wasn't mentioned *once* in the Semi-Cent. address) is full of the "Service" idea—an idea the Greeks never heard of.

95   *a.* Tate's marginalia here are given at the end of this letter.   *b.* The distinguished classicist, at this time a member of the faculty of the University of Chicago, addressed a session of Vanderbilt's semicentennial celebration. The paper was entitled "The Discipline of College Culture and the College Curriculum."

96/ALS

Nashville, Tenn.
14 June 1926

Dear Allen:

It's a long time between letters, but I can't help it that fate insists on being savage. After your letter came, there were examinations and pedagogical agonies, then a spell of illness (I skipped blood-poisoning by a slight but safe margin), and now I am involved in a series of family tribulations—daughter ill, and then wife. Still, I'm unconquered, and things are looking better at last. So I write.

First, as to "Idiot" and "Spring Poem."[a] By way of general criticism there's nothing I can add to what I've already said about your poetry. You have developed an idiom that satisfies your conscience and taste. My acceptance of it is assured, but toward any particular poem my experience is that I get aesthetic enjoyment only very gradually, after repeated readings. Then finally the thing sticks. I never get your full meaning, nor accept *all* your word-twists, but the pleasure I get from the thing as a whole is always distinct and recognizable. And so it is with these poems, which seem to be, if anything, better than the preceding batch. They seem on the positive side to have more intensity

—on the negative side, *Idiot* particularly resists interpretation. It produces an effect, but I as reader find my sensations, emotions, intellectual recognitions blurred and teased, in spite of the very exact language. You make great demands on the reader. You force me to pay terribly close attention. This is an exciting experience for one who usually takes in a page at a gulp. I swallow your poems like old wine, tasting slowly every separate drop, with strange stimulation. Is that what you are after?

When Untermeyer was here, I had the pleasure of engaging in a mild argument with him. To his criticism that you "tortured" words, I had to offer that your integrity permitted you to follow only the particular idiom you chose. As it was a rather rapid luncheon conversation, I didn't succeed in carrying my defense as far as I would have liked. I hope I did convey that you weren't a belligerent monster, but a young man of engaging presence and great penetration. Well, perhaps you'll laugh at such gestures. It was fun for me, too.

Untermeyer spent the better part of two days here. He was mostly all for J.C.R., and had very little ear for me (not one word of real interest or encouragement in fact). Nevertheless I rather enjoyed meeting him. He is very alert and apparently much in earnest, keen-minded, very positive, but polite and not snobbish. Not much high-hatting, either, though some egotism. We put on a real Fugitive meeting, which he seemed to enjoy greatly. I figure him as a very quick-witted, rather well-meaning fellow, with not too much real background and foundation, but with fairly good equipment and intention for his main function, which is to chart the course of modern poetry. *Chart*, not lead, or explain in very fundamental ways. His faults are those of training, I believe. His virtues come from natural sensitiveness and pretty good taste. Conclusion: partly I liked him, partly I didn't. Hard to say where the preponderance lies. About half and half.

John took his Guggenheim rejection very well.[b] He has a leave of absence for the fall term next year, to study & write. Knopf has accepted a MS of his poems for spring publication.[c]

Jesse caught the measles recently, and so had time to sit down and write a batch of good poems, the first he has done in a long time.

I'm selling my Spyglass column to a Miami paper now,[d] and hope to get other papers on my list before summer is over. Later I have some idea of broadening out some of my newspaper stuff into a book of critical essays. I'm making my stuff more solid and considered now.

As to the *Sat. Review* article, if it stirred a single ripple anywhere,

I don't know it. A few people liked it here, or said they did; some lady in Rhode Island wrote a letter; Cale Young Rice & Addison Hibbard gave me mild hell—in letters.

Now coming around to my poetical project. Your criticism is simply *remarkable*. There's no other word. You go right to the fundamental problem, which is what I want to get at. Your letter made me think hard, and is continuing to make me think hard.

I am much heartened that you concede, even with reservations, that my attempt is worth while. I was afraid you would put me in Purgatory, if not in Hell. What you say confirms my own feeling that I have at least a chance to struggle through to a possibly interesting result, whatever may be its ultimate merit. I certainly admit the main points of your unfavorable criticism. They indicate difficulties, perhaps minor, that can be ironed out. I admit also your point about themes. But I must refute other implications by declaring that I am not writing an epic (good lord, surely not an *epic*) for Tennesseans. I will merely use your phrase and say that I'm writing the history of a mind— my mind, to an extent—and therefore I come within your requirement of subjectivity for modern poetry. I conceive of the series of poems as essentially subjective, however much I may dramatize incidents or people here and there. The "thinness of effect" will have to be remedied. As for the "incoherence," I'm not so sure that I can get rid of all of it, or that I want to. At points I must be apparently inconsequential, and since I'm not writing a narrative poem, maybe I can do the thing without great violence to the general frame of the poem.

Whatever else may happen, I have already reaped $100 benefit from one of my attempts. The "Fire on Belmont Street" poem got the South Carolina ("Southern") Prize. Whether or not this is an honor depends on the other poems entered. So you don't need to bear down hard on the congratulations. . . .

What would you think of a sort of Fugitive yearbook, gotten up in respectable format and issued next fall?*e* We are contemplating such a move and may presently be seeking contributions.

What are you writing besides reviews and poems? Working on anything formidable? I'm looking forward to the time when all the wise boys will say—well, there's one real critic in the U.S., anyway,— Allen Tate.

I expect to be in Nashville most of the summer,—writing, if God is good and my domestic tribulations abate.

How are the *nine bean rows?* What'll you take for some fresh

beans? I get mine from Piggly-Wiggly and my exercise at dubious intervals on the Shelby golf course.

Faithfully, Don

I have no new poems in shape to send. Maybe later.

96   a. "Spring Poem" was not published.   b. Ransom applied again and received a
Guggenheim award in 1931.   c. Two Gentlemen in Bonds (1927).   d. This column
later appeared in the Memphis Commercial-Appeal and the Knoxville Journal,
as well as in the Nashville Tennessean and the Miami Herald.   e. This proposal
resulted in Fugitives: An Anthology of Verse (1928).

97/TLS

Patterson, N.Y.
19 June 1926

Dear Don:

. . . I have hoped for some time that I'd get around to a note about
your essay in the Saturday Review. I received it from you and also from
Lucille Fort, who follows Southern letters very closely. The changes
you made in it were slight but good. But I must say I can't get the intention of your blurb for Dr. Mims at the end. A mollification of disagreements, by means of hortatory inspiration, will not produce a literature. But your article is by far the best on the subject that has
appeared, I think perhaps mine was a little sounder because I stuck
pretty closely to negative statements and tried to find no solution at all.
One time, Don, when I was more cautious than you! But your chart of a
possible Southern literature may be argued about but not refuted. The
two gentlemen who gave you mild hell will never die of brain fever.

I'm glad you liked my criticism of the Big Poem, and I wish I could
have gone into such an interesting matter more deeply; perhaps you
will let me when more of the poem is available for inspection. Meanwhile I'm tickled to death that Fire on Belmont Street won the hundred
bones. It should have won it. I wish you'd supply me with a copy of
that poem; I believe it is one of your five or six best.

It is too bad, for my sake, that I know so much about Untermeyer,
from his enemies and friends alike, without knowing him personally at
all. I know I don't do him justice as a man. But at a distance I can
perhaps see his criticism all the better. I think he is a very clever and
ambitious journalist, who has a gift for the pat pseudo-critical phrase
by means of which he gives poetry a great news value publicly; but I

think persons like him and Harriet Monroe are menaces to the art, though I put him much above her in intelligence and below her in honesty. They create *interest* in poetry, but it is a false interest and will not outlast the period of their propaganda, which in effect is already beginning to wane; poetry is rapidly getting back to the state it was in before 1912. This interest has been simply a stirring of the bourgeoisie with the idea of "culture" and "self-expression" (two words that should be tarred and feathered), and poetry has thus become identified with the longings of misfits and weak sisters. This sort of interest is no substitute for ideas, which a genuine criticism should supply. There has been a great deal of fine poetry written here in the last ten years, but nobody knows just how much of it is fine, or why. Untermeyer, of all people, doesn't know; he thinks the office of criticism is to boost or condemn, never to analyze and compare. The truth is he couldn't analyze and compare; he is too ignorant, and while he is alert, he lacks intellect altogether. I can't agree with you that he has taste; that quality he lacks preeminently: see his own poems and his vulgarity of expression in his criticism—such phrases as "piquant accents," "the spiritual bucolics of Vergil and Wordsworth." I cull these from his latest book, The Forms of Poetry; they are vulgar simply because they pretend to a meaning which they could not have; they look good to a member of the Woman's Club, but they are meaningless vulgar pretensions only. Most of his criticism is composed of these pat phrases, which serve two purposes—to disguise his really muddled sensibility, and to avoid committing himself. But I burden you with some of the steam I am getting up to attack him and Miss Monroe this summer in the Herald Tribune.[a] The article is sold in advance; it will appear sometime in August—you know Sherman vacates his column for outsiders in the summer months. But keep this news to yourself, please.

This article and another on Oswald Spengler will take all my time until August. The Spengler essay will go to the New Republic—also sold in advance.[b] I've at last got to the point where I can describe my proposed essay to an editor and he will tell me whether he will take it. It's a great advantage; one doesn't waste time over essays that only serve to clutter one's desk. My article on Fundamentalism is almost complete, but I've had to put it aside for these others, which are assured of a market.

You mention a Fugitive yearbook. I think it's an excellent idea. Would you like for me to try to tempt some of the New York publishers with it? Or what plan had you in mind for publication?

Your criticism of my two poems pleases me enormously, but I hesitate to say that it is good because it contains such a large ingredient of compliment that I shouldn't know whether I was appreciating the criticism or the praise. If my poems really do give you a "total effect" which you can't rationalize, I am very happy indeed. For it is difficult to eliminate explicit "ideas" from poetry, and that is exactly what the best poetry does. The idea has got to be there, but it should never become explicit. If you can fully render the content of a poem into an exactly equivalent prose, then you may be sure that it was not a poem in the first place. This is a limited view of poetry, one that would have been impossible before the romantic movement; it would hardly include classical poetry at all. That's what bothers me about it. It doesn't include, among moderns, Ezra Pound, whom I enjoy immensely; his best work is pure classicism.

My line is run out; I must stop. Write me soon; send poems; send prose; send anything.

Yours always, Allen

P.S. Tell Jesse I hope he has leprosy next time.

97   *a.* Appeared August 1, 1926. *b.* Tate published an essay-review of Spengler's *Decline of the West* in *Nation* (May 12, 1926) and one of *The Hour of Decision* in the *American Review* (April 1934), but the proposed *New Republic* article did not appear.

98/ALS

Patterson, N.Y.
26 June 1926

Dear Don:
   ... The Criterion and The Calendar are the only *literary* journals in English worth the paper they are printed on. The Calendar, by the way, will use a series of Crane's poems shortly; they've been turned down as "incomprehensible" by all the leading American journals. If his work, *after careful reading*, the kind of reading we accord Keats, Shelley, Baudelaire [is incomprehensible]—and a contemporary artist has the right to demand such care—then poetry itself is incomprehensible in this age. The reason why we lack such a journal as The Criterion is that *ideas* have no meaning here; a man has no chance, if he wishes to publish a journal, unless he has a "cause." He has to be of *immediate* "service" to the social order; observe I underscore *im-*

mediate. You've got to be a messiah; you've got to have something "new to offer"; you've got, above all, to have superficial enthusiasm. The more covert enthusiasm of persistent attention to ideas is a scandal these days. You become a "mere aesthete." You are confronted with—"What are you *doing?*" You answer: "Ideas." Blankness. Perhaps hostility.

I notice that C. A. Beard, in the N.R., did Dr. Mims "proud." I'm glad of it. I decided finally not to do the book. He deserved the sort of review Beard gave him. Dr. Mims is unquestionably the best man in the South for that sort of thing; but I do think he refuses, in this book, to see the meaning of his own evidence. Dr. Mims' viewpoint is liberal and I like it; but his whole system of values gets me so irritable that I couldn't have reviewed the book so liberally as it deserved. For instance, he doesn't see that, although a body of liberal opinion is necessary, the first duty of a society is to produce first class minds, liberal or illiberal. The South since the Civil War has produced some liberal second rate minds, of whom Page, his hero, is one. Ad infinitum.

Write soon. Recover your health.

Yours, Allen

99/TLS

Patterson, N.Y.
29 July 1926

Dear Don:

I am very glad to have your letter. First, as to the Yearbook. I will have to go to town within the next ten days to escort my mother-in-law to the Pennsylvania Station, and I will take the opportunity to see a few publishers. I will talk to several persons about it—Van Doren and Wilson—to try to get their support. Meanwhile why not present the thing to Houghton Mifflin?

There is only one disadvantage in local publication for the book (by local I mean Nashville). There is the problem of legitimate self-interest to consider. Publication by a New York concern would remove this problem. But publication in Nashville would raise it; if the contributions will be worth printing at all they could be placed to conspicuous advantage elsewhere, and by conspicuous I partly mean financial advantage. It seems to me that if one of the conditions of eligibility to appearance in the Yearbook were freedom of selection from previously published material, this drawback would be overcome. Such freedom also would make the Yearbook much better; each contributor could resurrect his very best stuff; and in this plan the book would undoubtedly become one of the most formidable literary exhibits in many years. Instead of calling it a Yearbook, it could be called a summary of Fugitive activity to date—or some name containing that idea. It would be an anthology in one aspect, and doubtless those people who have published books could get permission from their publishers to use stuff from them. Please write me immediately whether you feel this idea could be fitted to the main plan of the book which you have outlined, so far as I'm concerned, to my complete satisfaction.

I have just finished the Introduction to Hart Crane's "White Buildings," which Liveright brings out in the fall. O'Neill was to write it, but after fumbling for eight months or so, gave it up. I believe it's the best piece of criticism I've done; I hope you like it. I'm adding about six hundred words to it, making it an essay for magazine publication in advance. If I don't place it here, I'll be sure of acceptance with The Calendar (London).[a] This journal has already used some of Crane's work; and it will use a long poem of mine in the October issue.

Eliot, after ten months of assurance that he would use my poems, finally sent them back with a long letter of the most penetrating criticism my humble production will doubtless ever receive. It was both flattering and discouraging; flattering because of his evident great interest, discouraging because he believes me to be a much better critic than poet. In fact, he has engaged me for another essay to follow the one he is publishing on Poetry and the Absolute.[b] Eliot is positively uncanny; he traced out my influences as unerringly as if I had confessed them; he put his finger precisely on my defects; he pointed out the valuable element in my work. Nevertheless I continue to be chiefly concerned with my poetry. . . .

I didn't feel your enthusiasm for the anonymous survey of current literature in the June 30th New Republic, and I registered my dissatisfaction in a reply, signed An Observer, in the issue of July 28th. But you're certainly right in saying it's the best thing we've had of its kind. Wilson, of course, wrote it—I say "of course" because I am mentioned.

My latest thing is a long essay for BOOKS.[c] I have the nerve to call it outright a Defense of Poetry! Look for it in the next week or so. Tell me, please, what you think of it. As the title implies, it is assertive rather than analytical; and my attack on Untermeyer and Harriet is relegated to a Postscript: I got far beyond them and they didn't, therefore, fit into the main body of the essay. The Postscript may not appear; it extended the article much beyond the allowed space.

Let me see the new parts of the Tennessee poem. I can always read 500 lines. Jesse sent me some new poems recently, those written under the auspices of the measles, and I must say the disease was not without its advantages. They were fine; Jesse has one of the finest talents I know of. Would to God we could make him do something with it, or at least something with what little he writes. The poem called Automobile Ride is a beautiful thing; and the sonnets were excellent.

I hope you and yours are at last entirely well. We get along as usual. Nancy is of course here, at least for the present. She is the most beautiful creature alive! I spend a great deal of the time recalling Mother Goose. Her favorite is the one of the barber who shaved a pig.

For the nonce, my dear Don. Allen

99   *a.* The only essay Tate published at this time on Crane appeared as the foreword to *White Buildings: Poems by Hart Crane* (1926).   *b.* The *Criterion* published "The Fallacy of Humanism" (July 1929); "Poetry and the Absolute" appeared in the *Sewanee Review* (January 1927).   *c.* Not published.

100/ANS

[Patterson, N.Y.]
12 August 1926

Dear Don:

How do you like this?[a] It's a sequel to the first *Causerie* I sent you; four more will probably follow. This one needs more detail work, but it contains what I have to say.

What do you think of the device of mentioning actual persons, on page 3? It's a device of ancient integrity, now in disuse. In case you like it, don't feel slighted at your absence from this list. You follow in the next poem!

You know my poetical theory used to keep me from approaching "life" directly. But I do it here—I fear, with a vengeance!

Hastily, Allen

P.S. *The Calendar* is printing Causerie I.

100   *a.* "Causerie," which here Tate calls "Causerie I," was printed in *Calendar of Modern Letters* (October 1926); the poem he refers to as "Causerie II" was also published as "Causerie" in *Transition* (June 1927).

101/ALS.

Nashville, Tenn.

15 August 1926

Dear Allen:

How you've startled me with Causerie II! I've just read it, and as yet hardly digested it, but I'm ready to say that it gets hold of me more immediately & deeply than any poetry of yours I've read in some time. I salute you! Passage after passage in Causerie II gives the satisfaction of finality—as if something had for a long time waited to be said, and now is said once and for all. The poem has movement and energy—not the stiffness of some of your writing—it flows. It has less, though perhaps still too much, of the superabundance of images which in your poetry often makes the brain go through a strenuous quick change procedure. The poem reads as if this were something that you had been holding back some time and now have let go resonantly, like a bowstring. I like the form you use (as in the Causerie I); it seems to give you a much-needed fluidity.

As I say, I haven't fully digested the poem, and so am not prepared to comment much on the substance. It seems to me an emotionalized intellectual statement of the modern mind in a characteristic mood of restless contemplation. I remember you've commented on the difficulty of attaining objectivity in modern poetry—I rather agree. Sardonic, ironically wistful (?) self-inspection, centered around striking but pertinent syntheses of ideas & associations, occasionally flashing up into a fiery-hard lyricism. This is one thing left to the modern poet to do, at this time, and you do it particularly well because of the vast number of correspondences you can command and the peculiar kind of rhetoric (I think it is that) which you have cultivated. Causerie II is one of your best exhibitions. I am not sure that I would put it higher (for out-&-out poetry) than, say, *The First Epilogue to Oenia*. But it is broader, deeper, surer, if not so tersely beautiful. And it continues a vein which I think you began in *The Screen*, and which I've always hoped you would continue.

I'll send a marginal criticism later. I want to ponder. Meanwhile, as to comment on living persons, it seems to me legitimate if you feel it belongs organically in the poem. I see no argument to make against it. It is startling to run across Ransom, Warren, & Wills in your poem. I don't know quite what to think of it. I'm inclined to believe that I'm a poor person to judge whether they or I should go in. *Ought* seems to me your prerogative. I'm a little puzzled about this—flattered, of course, that I should be conceived as an implication in one of your later strophes, wondering how it could be possible. Well, I defer to you, subduing my curiosity.

I'm not yet ready to send my own bulky verses. I'm a little fearful of submitting them to your piercing eye. But right here I must record a series of exclamation points (!!!!) and question marks (????) upon discovering, from your work and my own, that you & I are hitting some of the same spots. My recently written "Conversation in a Bed-Room" is somewhat reminiscent of your newly seen "Causerie II." How is this?

Recently I thought of the word that describes a good deal of your writing. *Astringent* is it. Your poems bite the reader like acid. They have sometimes less an expanding than a reducing influence: though (compensatingly) the aesthetic experience one has, in this astringent process, leaves him with a curiously provoking crystal residue from which he can't escape. Also in criticism—a writer doesn't bloom under your handling. He is exposed to a severe but just, white intellectual light that leaves no shadows or colors. But he cannot complain, for the detached judge reveals him in essentials, inexorably as mathematics, but purely and fairly. Your method is the precise opposite of Spingarn's "creative criticism" (which I can't endure). And nobody else that I know is doing what you are doing so well and so consistently. Still I would like to see you achieve in criticism a somewhat lighter touch. Your prose isn't yet as fluent & clear as I personally would prefer to see it—as it is, for example, in your critical letters to me. Nevertheless, so far as I see from this distance, you're filling a place in criticism that nobody else (or few) have the guts to try to fill. I certainly do rejoice in your Arrival (with a cap.). And this is a good place, too, to congratulate you on placing stuff with Eliot. I'd like to know what he said about your poetry, etc. I think publication in *The Criterion* is the greatest compliment that has come to you so far.

Yes, I saw your name with Hart Crane's in the Boni & Liveright catalogue. I wish it could be your name signed to a volume of your own poems or criticism instead of only an essay. But that will come. . . .

I agree with your disapproval of Braithwaite, though maybe there's no serious reason why you should refuse permission to use your poem. If one's poems are good, they are good anywhere—unless there's something disreputable involved. Such is almost the case in B's hold-up plan for a Who's Who of Poets. I dropped his letter on that matter into the wastebasket, unanswered. But he had previously requested permission for a poem of mine, and I haven't withdrawn that permission.

But what about the Fugitive volume? Have you had any encouragement from publishers? I have opened matters with Houghton Mifflin, but have no answer yet.

As soon as you have any definite news or any possible leads, I want to send around another bulletin to the brethren.

A word about my own work. When I finish, if I ever do, this long series of poems, I have two projects—one, a "war book" on a small scale; two, a book of critical essays following up the line begun in "The Artist as Southerner." I'm praying to my Lares & Penates for time. But the household gods aren't very kind these days.

Faithfully Don

Damn, what a monumental letter. . . .

102/TLS

Nashville, Tenn.
27 December 1926

Dear Allen:

At last I am able to send a copy of my MS.ª It is on the way under separate cover.

I don't live in any great hope that you will find all parts of the book up to your very strict standards. Indeed, I can well imagine what your reaction is going to be on some sections. But I do ask this: read it through consecutively from beginning to end and see how the thing strikes you as a whole; does it get over or doesn't it? I ask you to be charitable in the general view. In the particular parts I am sure you will discover weaknesses,—and on these, show me no mercy, but come down hard in the old Fugitive way. Thank God, I've been brought up (thanks also to you) in a hard school of criticism, and I can certainly stand a lot of pounding.

The Ms, by the way, has been sent to Houghton Mifflin. I have no great expectations of them, but I felt more or less obliged to give them at least the chance to reject the book.

I feel pretty good, having gotten it all out of my system at last. Whether the book is worth anything or not (and I flatter myself that some of it is the best stuff I have ever written), I have gotten it behind me, and can go on to something else.

Since you've probably already seen Mr. Valentine of the Oxford Press, you know what the "something else" is. A book on Southern literature, chiefly contemporary, but viewed against the background of the past,—that's my next project.[b] It is my intention to broaden considerably the thesis I evolved in my Saturday Review article, and to apply it in such a way that my study may prove to be of general critical value,—not a mere provincial business, not a compendium, not an opportunist survey, but an organic study which will involve historical and even social considerations. Does that look like a hopeless job to you? I don't believe it is, but there's no telling, of course, what turn I may find it necessary to take when I get under way.

I earnestly solicit suggestions and advice.

Returning again to the poetry MS,—I don't want to propose to you the onerous burden of a line-by-line criticism such as we have been in the habit of making for our shorter things. But I'm all humility and receptiveness. I'll appreciate the time you may be able to spend and the thought you may be able to give my work. Your opinion, you know, counts mighty high with me, even when I disagree with you.

And what about the Fugitive book? Have you been able to do any good with Liveright?

Ransom is expected back here this week. I am eager to see his new book.[c]

Old scout, hope you've had a merry Xmas, and here are my bountiful wishes for a great New Year.

Have you ever completed the Causeries? I have an idea that you and I have been working on parallel lines though in somewhat different manners. The Causeries still keep hanging in my head,—they stick, you bet.

Faithfully, Don

102   *a.* Of *The Tall Men*, published the next year by Houghton-Mifflin.   *b.* This
volume was never completed.   *c. Two Gentlemen in Bonds* (1927).

103/ALS

New York City
29 December 1926

Dear Don:

I have spent most of the day at your MS. and I am about to deliver judgement! I hope you'll be able to read it: the eminent Ford Madox Ford is using my typewriter for a day or two.

You have asked me to be charitable "in general view." *Without* your permission I shall not attempt a general view at all. In particular, your poem has for me three, the usual aspects—good, bad, indifferent. It is not necessary to account for the good: excellence is always unpredictable. The real criticism I think comes in with the bad and indifferent. These adjectives are by no means entities; they are convenient terms.

First, I think the bad verse in it may be due to a desire to round out the scheme of a vision when the vision isn't there; or, grant the presence of the vision *in a certain condition*, this condition is disordered, and the texture of every section of the book is disordered too, mixed, repetitive, and abounding in over-emphases. The most successful piece in the book is the Prologue. The indifferent verse may be distinguished as that which isn't bad.

To return to the good verse: the book is full of it, but you seem determined not to give it a chance. In fact, I do not believe it was your intention to write a poem; you wished to do something else. Had you done it outside of poetry it might well have succeeded; you decided to do it as poetry, and whether you have satisfied yourself or not, your intention, now exhibited, can be judged solely as poetry. I think the best comment I can produce on the mixture of your performance is that I should expect you to keep on writing the poem indefinitely: the solution of your poetical problem is no clearer on page 84 than on page 1; so why should you stop there? Of course, you offer a solution of another sort; I may call it a doctrine of love. You didn't need to write a poem to expound the doctrine. On the other hand, there is no reason why the exposition of a doctrine shouldn't be poetry. I simply believe that on the whole yours isn't.

We needn't argue it from an aesthetic, or a moralistic, or a metaphysical viewpoint. From any viewpoint the work represents a failure to reduce the material at hand to order—describe the order in whatever terms you choose. It isn't that I disagree with your "ideas"; I am personally inclined to believe that Southerners are better men than Yankees, that the fall of the South meant a State for the pig, and that some sort of love is the keynote of ethics. But if I *dis*believed these doctrines, I should feel as much interest in them, *as poetry*, as I do believing them.

This point, as follows, illustrates my objection: In *Geography of the Brain* and *Conversation in a Bedroom* you smother the *attitude* beneath the paraphernalia of the attitude. Read over the first page of the former.

In general, the *form* of the poem is still in your mind.

In particular, there are countless lines which betray the hurry of their writing.

For God's sake, Don, don't publish the poem in its present state. The material has great possibilities, but it is not yet mastered. If I had the time I should like to point out the fine lines and passages everywhere; they would leaven the severity of my criticism, which in all honesty I feel bound to make. . . .

In the faith, Allen

104/TLS

New York City
5 January 1927

Dear Don:

I am very much afraid I deserve some of the accusations you bring against me; my only dissent is on the theory you offer to explain my alleged mistakes. I haven't only not been drinking bad liquor; I have drunk no liquor whatever for a long time, of any sort.

I am not recanting; I am merely confessing to the lack of documentation which my remarks betrayed. I felt this, however: that you were familiar enough with my "aesthetic" to place the detached comment in a proper context. But it seems that you suspect me of springing a new doctrine on you. This is far from true. I did not for a moment use the term vision as a Victorian. If I may return upon you the retort courteous, I may say that the trouble with the vision of your poetry is that it is exhibited in something of the fashion of the Victorians! In short, as I said, the vision is dissociated and beyond your control.

What I said was not the product of abstract principles. I felt an immediate dissatisfaction with the volume, and I set about finding terms which might convey that dissatisfaction to you.

As for particular lines, please don't scorn their excellence. Not all of Milton's lines are marvellous, but there's not a positively bad line in Paradise Lost. But in general you are certainly right about the *pointilliste* brilliance of modern poetry choking the stream and largeness of presentation. There's a reason for this too. I doubt if the evil is to be remedied by simply deciding not to have pointilliste brilliance.

I agree with a comment of Mark Van Doren's on the two poems you sent him. He says that while you think the subject-matter is important for you, the failure of the poems *as poetry* proves that it is not; for if it were you would, on the certain evidence of your poetical powers in the past, have converted it into *poetry*. This is identical with something I wrote you long before I saw the poems, to the effect that our past is buried so deep that it is all but irrecoverable. The result of this remote stratification of the material is that you offer a product which is neither bird, nor beast, nor fowl: it is not poetry, it is not philosophy, it is not sociology: it is a little of all three, and none. I think you misinterpret my remarks on the "doctrine."

I am sending you two new ones which I rather hope will give you grist for the mill. Slaughter them!

Ever i' the faith, Allen

105/TLS

New York City
19 January 1927

Dear Don:

The ms. of the Fugitive Anthology has been returned to me. Liveright made no statement beyond the bare rejection. Poetry is anathema; and that ends it. But there are several hundred other publishers, and we might take them in rotation.

Before I take it to Guy Holt, where it is almost sure of a rejection, I'd like to remind you of the offer made us by The Adelphi Co. This firm has combined with Greenberg, and they may be more liberal now. However, I doubt if they would take it on full responsibility. We might have to put up something. Do you care to entertain such a proposition? It would settle the matter definitely. Of course, it would shrink our pocketbooks too, and I'm not sure I could stand that. But there may be some way out of it. . . .

In reading the ms. over I'm astonished all over again at how good we are. No other set of poets in the country could offer such an exhibit. The best of you, Don, is there, and the best of all of us except Ransom and Laura Gottschalk. No collection of Ransom, to date, can be best without History of Two Simple Lovers,^a his finest poem.

I observe the passage of time, in which no letter comes from you. If those damned poems of yours have caused any, even the slightest, disruption of good feeling I shall regret more than ever that you wrote them! At the same time I shall be sensible of regret for the hard-boiled reception I gave them—which reception, however, was perfectly regular and consistent. That doesn't keep me from regretting it in this instance. . . .

As always, Allen

105   *a.* "The Equilibrists."

106/TNS

New York City
20 January 1927

Dear Don:

A display of all the publicity which Fugitives and The Fugitive have received would be a great advantage in getting a publisher. Would it be possible for you to lend me the file of material you have on hand? I swear to return it later in perfect condition.

Mark Van Doren was in last night. I read him portions of the ms., particularly the poets unknown to him, like Merrill, Red, and Jesse. He said he knew that you, Laura, Ransom, and I were good; but he was astonished at the quality of the group as a whole. He was knocked cold by Red, and greatly diverted by Merrill. You know Red is pretty close to being the greatest Fugitive poet. There are certain obstructions to this realization, of course. He is the only one of us who has *power.* Letter of a Mother and To a Face in the Crowd are the only poems in the collection to which the description great can be applied—in spite of a few technical imperfections in both of them.

Let me know about the publicity stuff.

In haste, Allen

Have you received Crane's book? It's great! Tell me what you think of it.

107/ALS

Nashville, Tenn.
21 January 1927

Dear Allen:

Overwork and a slight indisposition are to blame for my not writing you. Besides, I have had to get ready to lecture at Lexington, Ky., tomorrow on Conrad—I *hate* lecturing, but I get well paid, you see.

I should have told you that Kronenberger (or something like that)
of B[oni]. & L[iveright] wrote a fairly decent letter—which I can't put
my hand on right now, but which I'll send later if you wish. It was
complimentary enough, I guess—but it was a rejection all right. I
haven't had time to make a canvass of opinion, but I think you can
be sure that none of us here will pay a damned cent to any publisher
for bringing out the book; for fear of government inspection I will not
quote a violently obscene expression dropped from the lips of one of
the austere Fugitive poets. I should say try Guy Holt of that new
company, if you like. But here's another thing: Saxton of Harper's
just wrote me asking to see that new MS of mine. I haven't answered
him yet, partly because I am waiting on a contract from Houghton
Mifflin who have accepted the book. If you like, I'll tell Saxton of the
Fugitive Anthology—think I'll tell him anyway, if you don't mind
holding the MS till you hear from me again. I'm glad to hear your impression of "how good we are"—I believe in *us*, you bet. Ransom's
exhibit probably can be improved somewhat, after his new book gets
under way.

As to your criticism, I'm going to have much to say later, and I'll
also go into your new poems thoroughly, for so they deserve. My present
feeling about reduces to this: it would be wrong no doubt for *you* to
write *The Long Street* as it has been written; but it isn't wrong for
me to do so. I'll explain later.

I veto any introduction by Pleasant Louis.[a] One can say this for
him, however; he pays without qualm for poems that have appeared
in volumes, unlike many of the rascally anthologists—damn them all.

There's no disruption because of your criticism—none whatever
—and why should there be—though your rejection, I must say, bothered
me more than twenty publishers' rejections could.

Until *after Lexington*, then,

As ever Don

107   *a.* Louis Untermeyer.

108/ALS

[Nashville, Tenn.]
15 February 1927

Dear Allen:

At last I have, because I am taking it, an hour to write, and I am
taking the hour because I have already kept your poems indecently

long and you may begin to think that I have not read them, or will not read them, or, having read them, am angry or petulant and will say nothing. I have really read the poems many times, and just as many times my vocabulary has failed me.

What can I say, after all, without repeating, *totidem verbis,*[a] the comments I have made on the poems you have sent me the last two years? Or I might, working in the spirit of honesty I hope I possess, write an extremely lengthy essay. I would have to, to be fair.

But I may say this thing, which perhaps has not yet been said. I admire, but am not deeply touched by your later poetry as I was by much of your earlier things, as you well know. Admire—I trust I can admire even where I do not approve your methods, for you have committed yourself to a poetic scheme, you have adopted a certain rhetoric, you have an invariable method of attack, and since I concede you the absolute right to use any style, I must say, from a critic's standpoint, you succeed—you succeed perfectly. I clap my hands just as I might for a difficult series of Liszt cadenzas, performed with great skill, but my enthusiasm has no passion in it.

I think the reason is this. Your poetry, like your criticism, is so astringent that it bites and dissolves what it touches. You have decided that the opposite sort of poetry (say, an *expansive* poetry) can no longer be written in an age where everything is in a terrible condition. But this attitude does not merely lie behind your poetry; it gets *into* it, not in the form of poetry but of aesthetics, so that poem after poem of yours becomes aesthetic dissertation as much as poetry. Wherever your poetry is out-and-out argumentative (as in your sonnet on Beauty) I follow you all the way and am nearly ready to say you are at your best; when you deal with *things themselves,* the things become a ruin and crackle like broken shards under your feet. The Confederate dead become a peg on which you hang an argument whose lines, however sonorous and beautiful in a strict proud way, leave me wondering why you wrote a poem on the subject at all, since in effect you say (and I suspect you are speaking partly to me) that no poem can be written on such a subject. Your *Elegy* is not for the Confederate dead, but for your own dead emotion, or mine (*you* think).

The poem is beautifully executed. I do not quibble over a single word. Its economy is striking; its tone is sustained; it has very fine individual passages and is this much beyond anything of yours I have recently seen, that it is coherent, structurally unimpugnable. But its beauty is a cold beauty. And where, O Allen Tate, are the dead? You have buried them completely out of sight—with them yourself and me. God help us, I must say. You keep on whittling your art to a finer point, but are you also not whittling yourself. What is going to happen if the only poetry you can allow your conscience to approve is a poetry of argument and despair. Fine as such poetry may be, is it not a Pyrrhic victory? MacLeish's poetry—the same!

You see I refuse to wield your own favorite word—*failure*. With the utmost assurance you say on every possible occasion: *The Pot of Earth* is a *failure*; my poems are a *failure*; so-and-so is a *failure*,—thereby assuming a remarkable critical responsibility.

Your poem, I say, is a success, and if you want that particular kind of success, nobody should say no.

I do not see how you think the battle between poetry and science can be won in such ways as you use, for do you not strive for and attain a rigidity as inflexible as the rigidity of science?

Well, these are terrible questions. I assure you I tremble before them, and I do not feel at all satisfied over the statements I have put forward in this helter-skelter discourse.

I've just seen *The Nation*'s prize poem, and again I am puzzled. I have no resentment at all over failing to win honors myself—one never expects anything and therefore cannot be disappointed. But if my poems were, as you and Mark Van Doren say or imply, *not good*, what is the *superior* goodness of the prize poem? I would like to see it defined.

Your article in the New Republic was splendid—better even than your preface to Hart Crane's book, for which I am just about ready to attempt a review—a very difficult task, because Crane's poetry hits me as yours does—I admire his ability, but I am uneasy before his methods.

Any news from Harper? And from yourself? I have nothing to say for myself except that I am working mighty hard.

Faithfully Don

108   *a.* "In just so many words."

109/TLS

New York City
20 February 1927

Dear Don:

Sunday it is, and time to write a reply, a rebuttal, a polemic (innoculated though with high gratitude for your attention), on your good criticism. If I were sure you had never fallen below the standard of this latest letter, and never would again, I should greet thee, O Don, as peer of the greatest critics. This does not mean, however, that I feel your comment to be without fault, even without excessive error; but error is the lot of all; comprehension is the main thing.

In the first place, you chide me for not having written your own poem; that's what it comes down to. And though you argue from this point of view with consuming conviction, I feel that since it was never my intention to write your poem, the criticism becomes equivocal.

1. I have by no means decided that an expansive poetry can't be written. I say that none is being written—successfully. Crane's is the most expansive poetry of the age; but for some reason it fails to expand, except line by line. Why didn't Keats finish Hyperion? It is idle to say because he got sick and love-sick, as Forman, and Houghton, and Rossetti, and the rest say. Keats had, I daresay, a finer talent than either you or I; but both Hyperions are failures, from the point of view of their intentions. And—here's the dogma—there has not been a successful expansive poetry in English since Keats. The Victorians fell on the rock of scientific doctrine—as if Keats, in giving up the second Hyperion, hadn't shown them the whole fallacy of injecting 18th century philosophy into poetry, to take the place of the myth. As for your poems, I don't mean that the material is irrecoverable in the spatio-temporal sense; but that it is epistemologically—if this gets it across.

2. One kind of criticism (the kind I try to write) should dissolve what it touches. But I think your application of the acidic metaphor, further, to my poetry leads you astray. At this point I begin to suspect that we are shouting to each other across immense voids. To many people my work seems quite emotional.

3. My treatment of *things themselves*. You say I destroy them; that, in the Confederate Dead, I use the deceased to hang my contradictory argument on. I feel that you took yourself unawares there. Was Keats' Nightingale Ode *about* Nightingales? And does he not, somewhere in the poem, assert his doubt of being able to utter all he feels about the nice bird? Didn't I express the same doubt about being able to sing out all the properties of the Con. Dead? Don't, please, begrudge me a little satire woven into the pattern. Satire, unless you dislike it, was the intention of the remarks about the impossibility of writing a poem on the theme; it is only a way of attacking those who, some years ago, removed the theme from the sphere of actuality. I take your remark about my dead emotion to be one thing or another. It is mostly

another; I answer it by referring to the poem itself: if I have a living emotion about a dead one (assuming it for the moment to be dead), isn't that enough for a poem? It has been enough for many poems. As for your metaphor about "whittling" down my art, and thus myself, I find it not intelligible, really; though it does almost mean something. It means that essentially you don't believe in accuracy of statement. I said all I had to say; you can take me to task in a moral sense for not having more to say; but not for refusing to exceed my material. That was my whole quarrel with your new poems: you exceeded your material.

A word about my accusation of failure on all sides. I do not mean that, within the contemporary aims and possibilities, all these failing poems are necessarily failures. I have in mind, when I approach any single modern poem which pretends to the scope and purpose of major poetry, all the poetry of the past which I have read. I haven't read all of it, but I have read as much as most persons my age, perhaps more. From the viewpoint of the past, most modern poetry is rot, or if not rot, blind, insipid, and tangential. Perhaps this will be an astonishing assertion in the light of my defense of modernism. I defend modernism just as I would defend legs and arms if somehow they came after abdomens and necks. They are all, arms and abdomens, part of the whole organism. I try to see all poetry as one living whole; and my charge of failure is only a device, a piece of shorthand, as if I cussed out an arm for not being a belly. In my doctrine as a whole, either when all my scattered things are collected or I do a book, this convention will be seen for what it is—I hope. Meanwhile I shall suffer its inadequacy simply because in limited spaces I can't expound my full creed every time. My attempt is to see the present from the past, yet remain immersed in the present and committed to it. I think it is suicide to do anything else. From the attitude of my own criticism (perhaps from that of others' too!) my own poems are "failures."

One more thing: you speak of the *battle* between poetry and science, and the limitations of poetry such as I write for the purposes of victory by the former. The term battle gets you into a metaphor which destroys you. There is no battle. As for the rigidity of science, and the participation of my poetry in that rigidity, this is another metaphor. Art is just as rigid as science. The implications of your remark might lead me to suspect that for you art is vague and science exact. Art, in a sense, is more "exact" than science, and in what sense it is clear; so I won't argue this point further.

And so on. We don't get anywhere, but I enjoy it. I hope you do. The Nation Prize Poem was terrific. Let's forget it. I hope the public forgets my honorable mention. One of the most dishonorable things one can imagine.

Please observe that I haven't argued for the excellence of my poem; I argue against the criticism you offer; which is another thing.

Please give me advice about the Fugitive garland.

Yours as always, Allen

110/TLS

Nashville, Tenn.
23 February 1927

Dear Allen:

The Harper rejection is grievous and makes me wonder whether there really is any balm in Gilead. I don't know what to do next. Perhaps you might like to wait until we can have a meeting of the Fugitives now hereabouts and talk matters over. I haven't rendered any report to them in some time. I'm afraid that what you say of log-rolling, novelty, etc., may be only too true. I do wish we could find some new publisher who would be willing to take a plunge. Meanwhile, what about such folks as Macmillan, who get out a generously large list of poetry?

Your letter—the second one—is here, and I am in a great mood to continue the debate, for I find all your points have so much strength that I am obliged to respect them even when I disagree. I like very much this interchange—it clears the air. I believe this is true: you and I agree in condemning a great deal if not most of modern poetry, one of the largest indictments being its triviality. Where we don't agree is in the matter of the routes the creative artist can or ought to take in meeting the situation. And whatever personal discoveries we make immediately come uppermost in the mind and serve, perhaps unfortunately, as the test or standard we apply to whatever productions come within range, even from friends. Yet I suppose it was always thus.

I'll write in a few days what reactions the bunch gives to these terrible rejections. One bad thing is this: it is hard to get much first-class pushing out of Ransom, partly because he is committed to that damned American Miscellany, and also he has been all along a little queasy about our own anthology. However, keep a stiff upper lip. Even if we don't get immediate publication, the time will come for us sooner or later.

I wish you'd tell me HOW the Nation's prize is chosen. Also what's behind this Literary Guild, presided over by that sweet-toothed Carl V. D.? As a Southerner, egad, and a gentleman (I hope) of independent mind, I hate these cliques and Star Chambers. So far as my critical word goes—and I have some faint hopes of sending it gradually further and further in the South as Dame Fortune smiles—I propose to fight 'em like hell.

Faithfully, Don

111/TLS

[New York City]
1 March 1927

Dear Don:

I hope you can give me some edifying and constructive advice about the Fugitive manuscript before long. My conscience gets uneasy, if only because I am at a loss to dispose of it in any likely quarter myself. It lies around here, a constant reminder of the futility of Art.

I wish you *had* replied to my onslaught. I'll look forward to a renewal of the fray at your leisure.

Did Ransom show you my review of Two Gents in Bonds? He seemed to like a great deal—said I got to the bottom of things, etc.— the two main ideas which according to my analysis lie back of his work. I'd be pleased to have your opinion. Particularly of the way in which I relate him to the Old South. And, by the way, I've attacked the South for the last time, except in so far as it may be necessary to point out that the chief defect the Old South had was that in it which produced, through whatever cause, the New South. I think the test of the True Southern Spirit would be something like this: whenever the demagogues cry "Nous allons!" if the reply is "Non! Nous retardons!" then you may be sure the reply indicates the right values. The symptom of advance must be seen as a symptom of decay. The decay is not wholly external blight; it is largely organic. That's why contemporary Southern poetry which contains any of the Pure Ingredient is incomprehensible in its milieu. The sham stuff, like Hervey Allen[a] and Dubose Heyward, is easy. They merely exhibit for a foreign audience; they employ the accidents and omit the essences. It is needless to say that the essences are not magnolias, niggers, and cotton fields.

And so on. But my supply of wisdom for the day is run out. What about the Fugitive business?

Yrs, etc., etc., Allen

111   *a.* "Allen, you know, is a Yankee anyhow; went to S.C. to hold down a job and made 'copy' out of his new environment. According to reports here, he conquered N.Y. as a 'Southern gentleman' with an accent that seemed convincing in these parts." [Tate's note.]

112/TLS

Nashville, Tenn.
4 March 1927

Dear Allen:

What a devil of a life I lead, that I can't find time to write even the letters I specially want to write. My day lasts from 7 a.m. to 11 p.m. and I can only carry on because I manage nearly always to get eight hours sleep. I haven't written sooner and more fully because I just couldn't. Even now, I must stick to business mostly.

We had a meeting Monday night. Opinion is like this on the Fugitive MSS. If you know any likely publishers, it is suggested that you try one or two more. If we are still rejected, we have two alternatives to fall back on: (1) we can raise some funds for guaranteeing cost of publication, perhaps resorting again to our old "patrons"; (2) we can "salvage" the whole project (in the army sense) and get up a volume of totally new or almost new material. The last is probably the best scheme of all, for we have already been much too slow in getting up our "anthology," and if we have a book composed of new stuff we can attract a publisher much more easily.

I suggest that you take one or two more shots where you think there is the best chance; or if you're tired of peddling the darn thing around (I wouldn't blame you for being), ship it back to me, and I'll let the U.S. Postal Service do the work. Meanwhile, let's have your opinion on the two alternative ideas. As I believe John has written you, The Old Fugitives are far from dead; we still have ideas and vim; and somehow we hang together. I am delighted at your own new annunciation of the True Southern Spirit, and though I haven't yet read your review of John, I do most heartily agree with your line of thought as John relayed it to me. I said recently in a little speech here that I thought

John's poetry was the poetry of a gentleman, and I must confess to you that I like it better than the bray of midwestern jackasses and the girlish hip-movements of the Yale-Harvard-Princeton pretty boys. I have serious objections to some of Hart Crane's methods, but by Gad, he is, in his best work, masculine. I guess you get what I'm driving at incoherently.

You know that I'm with you on the anti-New South stuff. Since I have become a member of the Old Oak club[a] here, I am more and more anti-New South. And I am disgusted with the sham stuff that you speak of. I feel so strongly on these points that I can hardly trust myself to write. I'll leave my thunderings to a later letter. But know this: though I trust my sense of humor and balance will save me from becoming a Bourbon in the extreme, I have fully decided that my America is here or nowhere. I am thinking that I may make that projected new book (for which I have been reading) not so much a "history" of Southern literature as a study of the Southern tradition—where it is, where it isn't, what and how and so on. And I have been going through a spiritual "Secession," in fact, ever since that Sat. Review article[b] which made me examine my own mind. As to the organic decay you speak of, I believe there's less of it in these parts (Nashville, especially) than elsewhere in the South. I wish I had time to discourse fully. I tell you I am very much stirred up.

It's a shame that I have to approach Sinclair Lewis with such aroused feelings, but I can't help it. I've just read his *Elmer Gantry*, which seems to me the Portrait of a Cad written by a Cad or at any rate a Jackass.

I've run on longer than I intended.

Allons, nous retardons donc, Don

112   *a*. A literary and historical club to which Davidson, Ransom, Jesse Wills, and other well-known Nashvillians belonged.   *b*. "The Artist as Southerner" (May 15, 1926).

113/TLS

New York City
7 March 1927

Dear Don:

I'll try some of the publishers you suggest, but I fear nothing can be done unless we get somebody behind it. It is almost impossible to do this. Once again I have the material of a moral reflection upon the Southern situation. There can be no true provincial art (which is, of course, quite different from local color) until we can write directly for home consumption. I'll try Macmillan and Viking, in the order named. Harcourt will mean Untermeyer; he reads the poetry for them. Did you realize this when you suggested that firm?

The Literary Guild I know very little about; what I know comes from their ads, which you have access to. I deplore the whole mass sales movement. I fear it will mean, in a few years, a large coalition, a publishing trust, which will mean death to everything but commercial publishing. There was never a more deep-dyed set of numbskulls collected than that editorial board.

The remarkable thing about the Fugitives, as you say, is their cohesive power. I have always thought of you, John, and myself as the Final Causes, as distinguished from the merely Efficient Cause (Dr. Mttron Hirsch), of The Fugitive. If there are any ideas to be formulated for the future, it lies with us to do it. What these ideas are I have yet to see—as you already know if John has passed on my statement recently made to him. The situation implies more than the purely literary question. As I somewhat fiercely told John, it seems to me that your willingness to oppose the New South carries with it a willingness to lose your jobs. I should like to be convinced that this is not true.

About the poetry of Gentlemen, there is one thing we must always keep in mind. Ford[a] told me before he left N.Y. that he couldn't help preferring that poetry which is written by English gentlemen, but that he realized that not all poetry was written by gents of that blood, or even by gents of any sort. We've got to observe some hard distinctions. Poetry by a great many gentlemen offends me utterly. The real point lies elsewhere.

At the same time I agree with all you say, and I agree with Henry James that the quality of the work of art is somehow commensurate with the moral quality, in a very high sense, of the artist's mind. Yet, by moral quality I do not mean what a great many perfectly good gentlemen mean by moral quality. Hard distinctions again. Henry James, from the viewpoint of his cousins in New England, was not precisely moral, correct as he was. "I believe," said Socrates, "not as the many believe." The moral quality is by no means confined to gentility, though it usually is and I should like to think it is always.

If you write a book on Southern traditions I should be dying of excitement till I see it. It comes over me that one good preliminary distinction would be that between the spirit of G. W. Cable and of J. B. Cabell. I am convinced that Cable was the superior in every respect, even style. Cabell, by the way, is a pretty good example of what a true gent isn't. You know a great deal has been made, in some quarters, of the attitude of Walter H. Page regarding the Reconstruction; perhaps another good distinction could be made there. Page was a fine man, and it was not so much corruption as lack of a strict intelligence that betrayed him.

If you have any idears (as they say hereabouts) on a programme (I don't mean a public policy), I'd be right proud to hear 'em.

As usual, more later.

Allen

113   *a*. Ford Madox Ford.

114/ALS

New York City
17 March 1927

Dear Don:

I was glad to get your note. Thanks for telling the Yaddo people about me: they already knew. I've had some correspondence with them, and their place seems to be a fine one, but for our purposes not so good as the one we already have at Patterson, whither we return in June for three months. I'm sorry you're not considering it. I should insist on your stopping at Patterson for a couple of weeks or a month. We have an enormous house there, five miles from any taint of urban life. If you feel justified in making so long a trip, please come up for a month with your family.

By this time you've probably seen my recent communication to John regarding a Southern symposium of prose.[a] (I'd write it again to you, but I do so damn much writing I can't face the repetition.) Tell me what you think of it. I asked John to pass it on to you.

We're having Fletcher in this evening. Met him last week. He's a fine man and about as uncorrupted as they come these days. Write when you can.

Yours, Allen

114   *a*. This is the first mention of the book that became *I'll Take My Stand* (1930).

115/ALS

Nashville, Tenn.
21 March [1927]

Dear Allen:

I'll write later about the Symposium on Southern matters, for I can't now write fully (damn these apologies I'm always having to make). Let me say hurriedly that I am out-and-out enthusiastic about the project. I'll join in and go the limit. Am willing to write on almost anything. The Colonial period will be the first thing I'll tackle in my projected study; but I can do the novelists, as you suggest, if that is preferable. I cannot, however, do any real writing for a month at least, on account of routine undertakings here. More of this in a day or so.

Meanwhile, here is a carbon of my review of Hart Crane.[a] I wish it could be more favorable, for I respect both your judgment and a great deal of his poetry. Nevertheless, I cannot get around an unpleasant effect that I constantly get from his poetry, and I do not believe poetry should leave an unpleasant effect. *Unpleasant* is an equivocal term, I know; but I can't quite analyze my own reaction, and take refuge in a vague adjective. Part of the unpleasantness comes, no doubt, from elements mentioned in the review; but there's something else I can't define. I just give up, gasping like a fish.

Remember, too, that this review was written for The Tennessean, not the New Republic, etc., and forgive commonplaces. My congratulations to Crane on the fine press he is getting,—so far as I have seen.

I have been attempting to revise my book,[b] and am now inclined to sing the Cowboy's Lament.

O-o-o-o-, bury me not—on the lone prairie
Where the wild coyotes will howl over me
In a narrow grave—etc.

Yours as ever hurrahing Don

115   a. *White Buildings: Poems by Hart Crane, Nashville Tennessean* (April 3, 1927).
b. *The Tall Men.*

116/ALS

New York City
24 March 1927

Dear Don:

I'm forwarding your fine review of Crane to the author, who is snowed in up at Patterson. The review is in many ways the best he has received; and I'm sure he'll be grateful for it. I prefer it greatly to Frank's belligerent and, in places, nonsensical apocalypse.

I don't think the lines you quoted about the "gunman" are so difficult as you suppose.[a] My interpretation (for what it's worth) follows: The "religious gunman" is the symbol of the present-day American conquest of space, conducted in anarchy and with a sort of mystical ferocity. He is the "arbiter of beauty" because he represents a new scheme of values (good or bad, is indifferent), and his "street," his world, opens up a future, "a motor dawn," of formidable and perhaps inhumanly beautiful machines. Beyond this he is the "ambassador" of a new spirit, arising in triumph above the steel and stone of the age. I don't subscribe to the prophecy, but there it is, I believe, as Crane intended it. We now know that Blake's lines prefatory to his *Milton* were false prophecy; but they remain great poetry to this day. Crane is a sort of Blake, but not nearly so solipsistic and eccentric. He will appeal only to those persons who can read Blake with pleasure and understanding; those persons are few. I confess that only an edge of my system of responses overlaps Crane's; but in the bare intellectual sense I think I "get" him. This is all a critic can be expected to do, but he *must* do this at least.

Your review (I repeat) is excellent. More power to you! The Southern symposium could be put off until next fall. I should have to postpone my part in it; I'm swamped now with other things. But it's not too early to plan it. Fletcher wants to contribute; and Foster Damon,[b] though not of the South would write beautifully of Chivers, a fine and neglected poet. Let's hear more from *you* about it.

Yrs, i' the faith, Allen

116 *a.* Davidson's quotation in his review and part of his comment follow:

> Capped arbiter of beauty in this street
> That narrows darkly into motor dawn,
> You, here beside me, delicate ambassador
> Of intricate slain numbers that arise
> In whispers, naked of steel; religious gunman!

"The meaning even with the context to help, eludes one in spite of the extraordinary definiteness of the language. 'Narrows darkly' is perfectly comprehensible; 'motor dawn' is more difficult, but one can propose meanings; 'intricate slain numbers' and 'whispers naked of steel' are next to insoluble and is a gunman 'religious' "? (*Tennessean*, April 3, 1927). *b.* At this time an assistant professor of English at Brown University; author of *Thomas Holly Chivers, Friend of Poe* (1930).

117/ALS

New York City
28 April 1927

Dear Don:

I'm glad to have your silence broken, but now it is my turn to plead guilty to rush and business. I am writing a book which must be finished by January 1st. My reading in the last two years has led me into ante-bellum Southern history; and since I must make my pleasures pay, I have determined to write the book. The immediate subject is a biography of the late Lieu.-Gen. Thomas Jonathan Jackson, 1824–1863. My contract is signed with Minton, Balch & Co., and my first royalties are in hand in advance. Farewell to mere literature for 8 months at least![a]

I will send the ms. of the Fugitive garland to Harcourt. Macmillan wouldn't look at it, and my preoccupations prevented further canvassing of the field. We should have news soon; they do quick work at Harcourt, Brace.

I'm reading nine hours a day and doing, at present, 3 hours' work at night. The latter will cease in ten days; so let me continue this then. But meanwhile write me the news. The promised clippings didn't come.

Yrs. e'er, Allen

P.S. Since I'm convinced that the South would have won had Jackson not been killed, I'm doing a stirring partisan account of the Revolution. The Stars & Bars forever!

117   a. *Stonewall Jackson, the Good Soldier: A Narrative* (1928).

118/ALS

Nashville, Tenn.
3 May 1927

Dear Allen:

The news of your biography is so exciting that I feel like rushing out and lighting a firecracker under Chancellor K's nose—about the most joyously insalubrious gesture I can imagine. Well, I applaud with both hands and feet, and furthermore I congratulate you on your good sense, and I trust that you will surpass even the famous Henderson,[a] whose biography of Stonewall I read last spring while I was (without knowing it) in danger of my life from a tedious infection. Go to it with all vim and let me hear, when you have time & get well under way what you propose to do with Old Stonewall.

This is all strange, for as I was lying a-bed last night, just before dropping off to sleep, I was thinking what a novel I would like to write around Old Stonewall—only I would make this novel speak as if from Stonewall's view—he would be the whole thing. We have had enough of nincompoop heroes, and that explains why Boyd has failed in his new Civil War novel *Marching On*.

Enclosed is that cursed clipping. I *know* I mailed the book page. And I am glad you're sending the Fugitive garland ("garland" is good!) to Harcourt.

Do you know Morris Markey—author of "The Band Plays Dixie" —he must have some promise—that's a queer, almost first-rate performance, I think—somewhat with reservations.

Yes, I'm all for you. We'll whup the Yankees yet.

Faithfully Don

118   *a.* George Francis Robert Henderson, *Stonewall Jackson and the American Civil War.*

119/ALS

New York City
5 May 1927

Dear Don:

I'm greatly stimulated by your congratulations on my coming book. I am buried in a great heap of war memoirs, campaign histories, official records—so much of it that I am quite bewildered. But I hope to bring a little order into it as times goes on. Jackson's character lies hidden in it all. Meanwhile I am not too eager to come directly to him: The Civil War in all its vast detail is so interesting that I could easily let myself be tempted into the by-paths, and remain there for years. I excuse this dereliction by saying that I must know the whole war before I can know Jackson; but the soundness of that view I could carry to specious extremes. I am already convinced that had Jackson been in chief command from the beginning we should now be a separate nation, and much better off than we are now; and that, if Jackson hadn't been killed in 1863 the battle at Gettysburg would have been won. I think these things because I want to; yet I have a surprising weight of expert opinion, political and military, to support my prejudice. The general plan of my book easily follows: nowhere will I look beyond the evening of the great flank attack on the Federal army at Chancellorsville. The bright hopes of the Confederacy will therefore support the mystical sort of optimism which Jackson held; and thus I hope to give the character of Jackson a great deal of drama and the narrative as a whole an atmosphere of suspense. It may prove to be too much for me, but I am trying to project the story from the contemporary point of view. I intend to issue a little doctrine in the book, but I don't want it to be obvious enough for the reader to be able to put his finger on it. My greatest difficulty is the military business, of which I know nothing, not having ever seen a battle-field. I intend to go to Virginia in June, to Manassas, Fredericksburg, Chancellorsville. Manassas has been a romantic spot to me since childhood. My grandfather fought there; and my great-grandfather was four miles away, on his farm, an old man, listening to the roar of the battle. There is a wonderful story of General Jeb Stuart's raid in Fairfax County in 1862: he came to the house of my great aunt, who had sheltered two wounded stragglers, one a Yankee, the other a Confederate, and seeing them there he praised my aunt for her mercy on friend and enemy alike; and he is said to have given her good Federal currency to buy the necessities of life for herself and her cares, the farm having been pillaged by Heintzleman's German mercenaries a few months before! You may remember that this raid of Stuart's was the occasion of one of the most entertaining episodes of the war. Stuart took Burke's Station, the telegraph communication of the Federal Army: he wired General Meigs in Washington to improve the quality of his mules, or hereafter they wouldn't be worth capturing!

There is only one clause in your congratulatory message which I question. I doubt the good sense of my choice of subject. It unfits one for the present world. But I shall have to run the risk, now that I've begun.

Some time I'll have to get you to tell me about the War in the West. I've never known much about it. I was brought up to think that all of it happened in Virginia, most of it in the county where my people lived.

The ms. of the Fugitive is now at Harcourt. I'll have news in a few days. . . .

Yours ever, Allen

120/TLS

Nashville, Tenn.
9 May 1927

Dear Allen:

I am still more and more vastly excited over your new undertaking. And so excited am I that I hasten to offer some notes which you may want to use. For a Yankee version of the battle of Chancellorsville, see Carl Schurz's Reminiscences.[a] Perhaps you have already looked it up. Schurz was more interested in justifying himself and his command than in glorifying Stonewall, especially since his division was one of those rolled up in the flank attack; but that makes his dread of Stonewall, as expressed in his account, all the more striking a tribute. Remembering what Henderson said of Stonewall's large plans I quite agree with you in your ideas as to the outcome of the Civil War had Jackson not been killed; and it is interesting to speculate on what would have happened if Jackson, not Lee, had been supreme head. Also, I agree that we might have been a damn sight better off if Stonewall had lived to realize his ideas. Nevertheless, don't you have to take Lee into consideration as the directing, co-ordinating military mind, and deal very carefully with the relations between Jackson and Lee? Maurice, in *Lee, the Soldier*, tends to magnify Lee, and I am tremendously interested in what you're going to say about this matter, which so far as I remember has not yet been handled with full convincingness. Another thing: Jackson's death at the hands of his own men is symbolic of what happened to the Confederacy through and through. We killed ourselves more than once and in more than one way, as Owsley's book on State Rights in the Confederacy shows clearly, and we are continuing to do the same thing today, through the "scalawags" whom you mention in the letter to Jesse—I thank thee for the word, O righteous judge.

What you say about the project of a magazine is probably only too true, but if any attempt in that line can be made, I have an idea it is worth making, no matter how desperate the affair might seem. When I see that so-called magazine, The New South, published at Chattanooga, with a reputed circulation of 80,000 (padded, no doubt), I get sick with the black vomit and malignant agues; when I read Bruce Bliven in the New Republic, I am willing to take to my bed and turn up my heels,—except that I am too mad to die just yet, and itchin for a fight, if I could only find some way to fight effectively. If genuine sectional feeling could be aroused there might be some hope; I do not yet venture to say whether that is possible. John Ransom and I are greatly riled; Jesse is less combative but sympathetic. Let us keep thinking about this.

I'll add one to your list of "carpet-baggers." I fear very much that our friend Addison Hibbard (no doubt a good fellow in some respects, perhaps many) must go in this class. He is not originally from the South, and his mid-west origin shows.

There are so many things that make me mad. Good God, what is a man to do to remain decent. Look at Lowes' book on Coleridge, and remember that Harvard ideals of "scholarship" are the dominant force in this country among the profs. I have read 100 pages of this book and as yet Lowes has proved nothing except the obvious facts that Coleridge was a poet and read widely.

Glad you sent the MS to Harcourt. If they don't take it, I suppose we must give up. My idea always was that the publication of our "garland" would give a certain solid recognition and furnish a point of vantage for future operations which would take the form either of successive "garlands," or, still better, the volumes by individuals. I hope you carry out your project of publishing Jesse. For God's sake keep on prodding him, for there's no unpublished poet more deserving unless it is yourself, and I desire book publication for you just as ardently as for Jesse.

I must stop this palaver, but it will indicate the agonized state of my mind. Don't let my letter or letters interfere with the progress of your work. If I can help in any way, don't hesitate to ask me. I have followed some of the military phases fairly closely,—in fact they once composed a great part of my reading. If you carry out your projected tour of the battlefields, and I trust you will, why not yield to the temptation to run further on into Tennessee, and I will offer the services (if my good wife will consent) of my newly bought Essex coach for traipsing around the battlefields hereabouts. Besides, there would be the prospect for a reunion glorious!

Faithfully, Don

120   a. *The Reminiscences of Carl Schurz*, 3 vols. (1907–8).

121/ALS

[New York City]

13 May 1927

Dear Don:

Yours of the 9*th* rec'd. I fear this can be only a note, as I must get my correspondence in in the few moments between breakfast and nine o'clock.

I can only say that I share all your exasperations and belligerences, but we are so reduced that we can't even fight it out on paper, except in the secrecy of letters. But these, it would seem, are contraband of war.

I know the sources you refer me to. Schurz was a rather interesting man, and I will use his memoirs. If I were intending to write a literal, technical account of Jackson's career, I wouldn't write it! Henderson has done that to perfection. The question of Jackson's relation to Lee is a difficult one, and with you I feel that Maurice doesn't give Jackson his due. But I may not get to go into the matter; the kind of book I plan will probably compel me to avoid it. Still I intend to come to some conclusion about it before I write, and it will be implied in the narrative. I am putting powder, blood, dirt, stink and sweat in the story; and I am going to try to give it the unity of a novel by passing it through Jackson's own mind. So far as I know the Army of Northern Virginia shed a great deal of blood without anybody even having seen it.

Will you do something for me in your leisure? You see I am taking advantage of your offered kindness. Describe for me the atmosphere and feeling of a battle. (I think you were in several in France.) I've got to put something of that in the book—in fact, a great deal of it, and I have no experience of my own.

I should like nothing better than to come over to Tennessee, but I fear it is out of the question. I can only go to Virginia because my mother expects me to visit her at Fairfax Court House, and I can work in the research on the side. It is only ten hours from N.Y. to Washington; it is twenty-four from Washington to Nashville. But I verily hope to see you soon. Why not drive East in the Essex?

There is no word yet from Harcourt. The project of the poetry series advances, but I still refuse to believe in it until the first book appears. What is your plan for a Southern magazine? My scepticism is hardly disinterested.

Write when you can.

Yours ever, Allen

122/ALS

New York City
8 October 1927

Dear Don:

"The Tall Men" is here and I am all gratitude for it. I haven't yet had a chance to go through it again with care, but the fine passages I missed in the ms. stand out, and I shall probably have to retract most of what I wrote you last fall.

By this time you have the page proofs.^{a} Unfortunately they will not give you much of an idea how the book will be. I think it will be an attractive volume. Smith insisted on calling the book "Fugitives: An Anthology of Verse," for commercial reasons. I preferred "A *Collection* of Verse"; he thought it ambiguous. We'll probably have advance copies about Nov. 15th. Quotations from Fletcher's essay will appear in the jacket blurb.

Red is now in New Haven, 48 Lake Place. Professor Tucker Brooke told him on sight: "Now, young man, you must forget your own writing; you can't serve two masters." Red is determined to stick it out and get his union-card emblazoned *Ph.D.* I feel like writing an essay on this subject, showing how a worthless idea dressed up with pious research can produce a monstrosity like Lowes' *Xanadu.* These fellows are ingenious enough at working out evidence, but they haven't the slightest notion where they get their dogma. They don't even know where they get the dogma because they aren't aware of using one. Lowes' worthless dogma is that the mind is an efficient instrument, and when you once restore the stuffs, the quantities, that this instrument acted upon, you restore the mind. Why such nonsense should be respected because it is garbed in learning is beyond me. Hinc illae lacrimae.

What's the news? There's none here. Jackson goes on day by day, but I am sure he is scoffing at the slowness of the march.

As ever, Allen

122   *a.* After being rejected by Houghton-Mifflin, Liveright, and Harpers, *Fugitives: An Anthology of Verse* was accepted by Harcourt, Brace, and Co. and appeared in 1928.

123/ALS

[New York City]
19 January 1928
Dear Don:

Again I should like to answer you decently but again your letter finds me snowed in. But I did 2400 revised words today, and at that rate I will be through in ten days.

I have passed the addresses on to Smith. Much obliged. I think he will send copies to our friends and former patrons, but I have told him, in case he finds the list excessive, to charge them to us, as you suggest.

I am sorry not to be able to say a word for Merrill. I have no acquaintance at Simon & Schuster at present; I used to have, but the man is gone. I hope Merrill gets published. You will be astonished, I suspect, to learn that, in spite of four years here, I have yet to hear of one volume of poems accepted on its merits. Your first book is the last of that miraculous order to come to my notice. It is all politics. In the case of the ladies, who get more books of verse published than the men, it is something else.

If you haven't received a copy of Fugitives by the time you get this letter, write me or wire me. I will prod H–B to action.

Who *can* review Fugitives for your page? It would be nice, I should think, to get some one sympathetic with our doctrines, who at the same time is intelligent enough to understand our work *as poetry*. Where is such a man to be found? I suppose the local people will think at last that we are pretty good because we bear the mark of a New York publisher. Sometimes I don't know whom I hate more—the local people or the Yankees who battered them into what they are. Pity is in particular; beyond that it is too abstract to believe in.

Who will review the book? The review should be an event. As things are, it is likely to be an occurrence.

I hope you like my Jackson as much as I dislike it. It seems awfully tame. There is one little trick of nomenclature that I think will amuse you. I withhold it, so that it will take you by surprise.

Yours ever, Allen

P.S. Please send me a clipping of the Tennessean review, whoever does it.

Are you subscribing to a clipping bureau for Fugitives?

124/TLS

Nashville, Tenn.

27 January 1928

Dear Allen:

The Fugitive anthology is here at last, and we are all greatly re-joiced. Harcourt has certainly done well with the printing arrange-ments. I don't remember any book they have put out that is better looking, and all of the group that I have seen are very much gratified with its appearance. Will you pass the word along to the head gentle-man at Harcourt—I forget his name—that we are immensely well pleased and thank the firm for their pains and attention. Later, if you think proper, I will be glad to write him a more official sort of letter.

The bird on the dust-cover and title-page was a happy and a beau-tiful idea. From whom, I wonder, did it emanate? The Phoenix-Fugitive, arising from the ashes of the Old Regime, I suppose is what it may signify. Remember also Jesse's sonnet, "Riddle," and his line, "My figure for It's bird because It flies."

My impression of the poems is still about as it was. I get more real satisfaction out of reading the Fugitive poetry than most that is pub-lished nowadays. And I want to say here that I got the profoundest impression from my re-reading of your "Ode on the Confederate Dead." I am convinced now that it stands at the very top of your work. My pre-vious strictures on it were decidedly overdone and may, I suspect, have proceeded partly from unconscious wrath following your deunuciatory remarks on my own book. I don't remember what unfavorable things I said, exactly, but let it be said here that I retract all the most consider-able indictments. I still have not fully digested Causerie; it takes pull-ing. But your whole showing is extremely powerful, not to say stunning.

As for my own offerings, I am disgusted with them. They don't jibe at all, but fall into two crazy divisions, the Belmont Street thing war-ring against all the rest. Perhaps they are more indicative than I realize of my own confusion.

We are having a jubilation meeting Saturday night. I wish you could be here.

Yes, I have subscribed to Romeike's clipping bureau, ordering clippings in duplicate, so that we will have two sets to pass around. After this I propose that all of us forswear the reading of reviews of our own work. To do so is certainly bewildering, and I am convinced harm-ful in many ways, however much it may satisfy curiosity and tickle vanity. You'll agree with me after you have gone through the experi-

ence. I assure you that there are more sapheads in the U.S.A. than you
ever dreamed, and all of them think they can write reviews. . . .

By the way, Simon and Shuster did this for Merrill's MS. Although
they swore it was against their policy to publish poetry, they kept the
book a long time. It was, their Mr. Fadiman said, the first manuscript
to cause them to reconsider their policy, which, however, they finally
decided not to change. But so great was their enthusiasm over Merrill's
work that they propose to help him get his book published and to that
end asked Merrill if they might offer the book to their friends, the
Viking Press, who now have it. Can you do any good there, if perchance
you have any sort of a drag? I am writing a letter to Fadiman, descriptive of the general personality of Merrill, his claims to the quality of
genius, if it can be called that, etc., and asking that he pass it on to the
Vikings. . . .

Faithfully, Don

125/TLS

New York City
26 February 1928

Dear Don:

Please forgive me the neglect your recent good letter has suffered.
I am out of the turmoil at last. General Jackson died on Thursday: 300
ms. pages, 90,000 words. And I hope now to resume, for a while, the
normal routine of life.

You are one of the few people whose opinion of the book will interest me, and for that reason I am sorry it isn't better than it is. I think
if you will not look at it as biography, but as a narrative of which Jackson is the central figure, you will at once get my intention and like it
better. I tried to get the publishers to entitle it: Stonewall Jackson, A
Narrative of the Civil War. But the word "biography" is commercial
magic these days, and they wouldn't sacrifice it to accuracy.

I am thinking seriously of plunging right away into a book about
Jefferson Davis—before my Civil War fever cools; in a year or two it
may never rise again. I don't contemplate a full biography; only a study
beginning with 1860 and ending with his arrest in 1865. It would be a
sort of psychological history. These years could be made dramatic. Davis
is the only material for real tragedy I know of, in American history.[a]

I have not seen a single review of Fugitives, but then I have been closeted for weeks. Wilson's review will be out next week, and Mark Van Doren is doing one. How do they sound, those you've seen? Is there to be a regular review in addition to the notices the book has already received?

I have eight or ten other letters to write; but I'll do better next time. Write me the news.

As ever, Allen

P.S. The brief review of your book in the N.R. was by Malcolm Cowley. Have you seen any of Red's efforts in that sheet? They are models of critical reviewing. Red's a great fellow!

125   *a. Jefferson Davis, His Rise and Fall: A Biographical Narrative* (1929).

126/ALS

New York City
16 March 1928

Dear Don:

The publishers have asked me to cooperate with them in getting review copies of Jackson circulated, and I have accordingly advised them to send you a page proof right away. You ought to receive it any day. The point is, if you intend to review it or have it reviewed on your Page, we should naturally like to see the review as early as possible. In fact, I should be highly grateful for a carbon of the review as soon as it is written. A regular copy, duly inscribed, will arrive in a couple of weeks.[a]

My head, Don, is verily anointed, and my cup runneth over. It all happened in one day—not only the Guggenheim, but Balch's acceptance of my poems for publication this fall.[b] Old Jack did it all. Before even a copy is in circulation, he has paid for himself. The advance sale is most promising....

That's all at present!

Yours ever, Allen

126   *a.* Davidson's review appeared in the *Tennessean* (April 29, 1928).   *b. Mr. Pope and Other Poems*; Tate received a Guggenheim award in 1928 and spent from September 1928 to January 1930 in Europe.

127/ALS

Nashville, Tenn.
21 March 1928

Dear Allen:

Returning from the Smoky Mountains, whither I fled to salve my wounds, I found your two letters, the proofs of your book, and all sorts of tremendous good news about you. For all this I am exceedingly rejoiced, and I congratulate you with all my heart. This success and recognition and help are, however, no more than is your due; and so I turn around and congratulate the folks who have had the wisdom to see your virtues and give you the opportunity you deserve and need. I am very happy over it all, especially the Guggenheim fellowship, as it will give you such wonderful chances to develop the projects you have under way. I have had no time to speak to other folks around here, but I know they will be gratified. I enclose a clipping which you should carefully paste in your album, as it has served, I'm sure, to give the old doubters and scorners hereabouts something to think about. Those who formerly underestimated you will now have a very proper chance to revise their estimates, while your friends, who have believed in you all along, will wag their chins in cheerful I-told-you-so's.

This would be a good place for a long sermon. But knowing your dislike for preaching, I won't indulge the natural inclination that I have for telling people what they ought to do. Before you go abroad, however, I should like to write an elaborate critique of your poetry— not that my criticism would amount to much or be any particular help. But I have always wanted to write the critique anyhow.

Now about Stonewall. I have just glanced at the proofsheets so far. Within a few days I will have read him, and I am sure I can immediately write the review, of which I'll certainly send a carbon copy if you want it. I'm amused at your word "co-operate," which I recognize as a publisher's euphemism. To tell you the truth, I am not on the best terms with your publishers. They are nasty fellows who don't ordinarily send me any review copies without much hard squeezing. Also, I have formed the bad, contrary habit of taking pains to see that no review I write, no matter how favorable, contains any easily quotable tag—which perhaps is one reason why some publishers ignore this book page. But your book makes everything different—I cheerfully set aside my natural hostility to Minton, Balch & devote myself to Tate & Stonewall.

There's another development, however, which may affect my reviewing. Recently I quit the Tennessean, having suffered long enough under the indignity of a pitiful wage. They countered by putting me, technically, "on leave of absence," while they stirred up Colonel Lea. The Colonel,[a] after some prodding by Nye and Finney, evidently decided he wasn't going to let me go. He came forward with a staggering financial proposition, and plans to syndicate my page in the three Tennessee papers he owns—the Memphis Commercial-Appeal, the Tennessean, the Knoxville *Journal*. If the project goes through, it will mean that the character of the page will be considerably modified. I should try to give it, within limits, the character of being the most substantial and distinctive thing of its kind in the South, and in the U.S. if possible, & should hope to do so in large part by attracting the right sort of reviewers—more and better people than we now have on our list. If the syndication should begin at once, my review of Stonewall would thus appear in three papers. But I know not what will happen—I don't want to keep your book back too long. And so I'll write the review as soon as I can, and let other matters take care of themselves, although I should like to have your book as a feature of the proposed new page.

I am tempted still to say nay to the Tennessean and so keep my independence, but the financial pressure on me now is terrific.

All this about the book page is highly confidential.

And now about your poems. I am greatly pleased that you have placed a volume. I very much hope that you won't be too strict with yourself in selecting poems for inclusion. Look twice and thrice at some of the early stuff before you leave it out.

Lord, you certainly are getting into a lot of things at once. More than I can write about. Even good old Jeff Davis—in which project you are wise. He is a most tremendous figure. . . .

I know what you say is true about Wilson, & I can understand the printer's error, which isn't unusual. You know, I respect and admire Wilson & think his review a very considerable and valuable thing. But whenever he reviews poetry, he absolutely flabbergasts me. I am astonished that a man so remarkably discerning and able in all other respects should make the most singular criticisms when he comes to poetry. I'm glad Wilson has read my poor books—it relieves my apprehension that he was giving me a good Princetonian snub[b]—but I can't believe he approves of me very highly. That's all right, though. I know Wilson is a good fellow—and generously inclined. His review helps a lot. Be sure to thank him for all of us.

Mark Van Doren's review was excellent, I thought. He put the case, so far as our project is concerned just right, although he, very much like Wilson, wrote a notice rather than a critical review.

We are all duly inflated by the praises of these gentlemen.

You ask for news, but *you are* the news. There's none here. We are to meet Saturday night.

I wish you would help me find a publisher for Merrill.

It is barely possible, but not very probable, that I might meet you in Virginia. I wish I could, for I'd do almost anything to see you.

That's all—and now for Jackson. I salute you, with all my heart.

Faithfully, Don

127   *a.* Luke Lea, owner of the *Tennessean.*   *b.* Wilson's review of the Fugitive anthology mentioned erroneously Donaldson's poetry instead of Davidson's.

128/ALS

New York City
2 April 1928

Dear Don:

I am glad to hear from you on Jackson, and very, very glad you like it. I am afraid I can't agree that, in style, I held myself back. It is the best I could do; though in fairness to myself I should point out that all told I could spend only about six or seven months at the job—reading & writing. I *might* have made it better with more time, but I couldn't afford the time for such a piece of work. However, I am by no means ashamed of it.

Jesse, in a recent letter, reported one of your comments, and I found it most just: that the background is a little thin. There are various reasons for this—shortness of time, etc. But I believe the chief reason is lack of practice in narration. I didn't know how to enrich the story without losing the story itself in a welter of detail: I know three times as much about Jackson as I put in the book. But the main object was a swiftly moving narrative, which I was willing to sacrifice everything else for. I have learned a little from this job, and I hope the Davis will be better.

I am naturally looking forward to your review.

The prospect for publishing poetry is looking up. I am therefore prepared to suggest that you or Merrill send his ms. to Coward-

McCann, Inc., 425 Fourth Ave., New York City, with a note saying that is one of the mss. I am proposing for their poetry list. It may be some time before Merrill gets a decision, but there is at least an equal chance that it will be favorable. I'll explain later. Politics again. There's never anything else.

Don, shall I attempt to thank you?

Yours ever, Allen

129/ALS

[New York City]
[12 April 1928]

Dear Don:

The review is here. It is great. I shall not attempt to thank you. The heartiest thanks would look feeble.

You not only let me off light; you let me off *too* light. There are all sorts of imperfections that you have surely seen. I feel just a little uncomfortable about this, a little responsible for it.

Your general discussion is most interesting and important, and justifies the length of it—which the book doesn't. Your conjecture as to the origin of the book seems right. The Confederate poem, specifically the passage you quote, is its germ.ᵃ That passage came out of God-knows-where (as most poems do); and after it was on paper it served to bring up a whole stream of associations and memories, suppressed, at least on the emotional plane, since my childhood. This quest of the past is something we all share, but it is most acute in me—more so than in you, I suspect. You, for example, have never changed your scene; your sense of temporal and spatial continuity is probably more regular than mine; for since the Civil War my family has scattered to the four winds, and no longer exists as a social unit. Such isolation is ordinarily a pit-fall at the bottom of which lies eccentricity (some of which I probably have) and sentimental extravagance of the most appalling kind. In this situation I can only thank God for scepticism, which, like formalde-hyde, is a great preservative of all sorts of things—of a sense of how things really *were* and of resistance against things as they are. To lack the one, I believe, is to lack the other.

I have been greatly impressed of late by a book called "The American Heresy," by Christopher Hollis. He is an English Catholic, and the ablest defender the South has had since Dew, Harper, and Calhoun. He points out that to all appearances, because of post-bellum Northern propaganda, there was never civilization, character, or intelligence in the South. If I have written a line that refutes the Northern legend, I shall feel pleased. (I'll send my copy of this book. It was published in England; it's hard to get in America.)

I think you have something of Jackson's contempt for public opinion. Without it you couldn't have written such a review. You are the man to be saluted, and I salute you!

Yours ever, Allen

129   *a.* In his review Davidson had quoted from the first version of "Ode to the Confederate Dead":

> Turn your eyes into the immoderate past,
> Find there the inscrutable infantry rising,
> The demons out of the earth—they will not last.
> Stonewall, Stonewall, and the sunken field of hemp,
> Shiloh, Antietam, Malvern Hill, Bull Run. . . .

130/ALS

[New York City]
25 April 1928

Dear Don:

Your letter, fine as usual, is here. I am sending the reviews to Red. They are stupider even than the first lot. Miss Pinckney does pretty well.

Your page looks fine, and I have read your Almanac*a* with great interest. It is sound stuff. There is just one specific question which I feel you don't face. The exact relation between style in poetry and the background. You seem to say that there is some inevitable correspondence between the style of, say, Father Tabb and old-fashioned provincialism. Now I deny this. His style was not derived from his background, but from 18th century English poetry, and is not necessarily closer to the Southern soil than your style, or Ransom's, or mine. Now as a matter of fact, such a style, used today, is much farther from the Southern tradition than yours or mine, for it thus becomes merely a literary property lacking roots in any soil; while we, affected by the contemporary problem—which you aptly put as uniformity versus unity—try to recover the lost ground by sudden reversions to it through contrasts, etc. In other words, the degree of a man's provincialism is not to be calculated by the period of his style, but by the moral outlook of the poetry whatever the manner may be. For example, Ransom is far more sectional and provincial than his contemporary, W. A. Percy, who is more old-fashioned than he. This is because John's sense of the provincial values is stronger and truer, and because this sense gives him a sharper issue for his poetry. I think it is almost a truism—the history of English poetry bears this out—that the so-called radicals are the true guardians of tradition, and are fundamentally arch-conservatives. (Radicalism is really quite rare in our time: for example, the free-verse people were really anti-radical, fashionable, decadent.)

We are still uncertain about the Southern trip. The problem is, can our daughter, aged 2½, stand the trip? Or can we park her with a trusty person long enough to justify coming? We shall see. If we go to the Lytle farm in Alabama, we'll be nearer you in Tuscaloosa. The reunion would almost justify anything.

I look forward to seeing the Jackson review in print. The publishers say there is a one percent return on publicity; 250,000 readers ought, ergo, to sell 2500 copies!

I am honored to be a contributor to such a page! I herewith make my first offerings: three poems. The *Epistle* is brand new;[b] it was taken by the *Nation*, but I withdrew it for the American Caravan, but I withdrew it again because the Amer. Car. wanted 6 mos. serial rights, and I want it in my book in Sept. If you want it, take it, but use it before August 15th. The two other poems are vastly rewritten old ones, and they should never have appeared until they were as good as they are now. In offering rewritten poems for second publication, I have recent precedents: Poe did it; Yeats does it; now Tate, in his small way.

I am now reading galleys of the book of poems, which will be entitled, "Mr. Pope and Other Poems."

Until later

                                                  Yrs. ever, Allen

130   *a.* Davidson's feature column in the *Tennessean* was called "The Spyglass" from 1924 to 1928, after which he changed its name to "The Critic's Almanac." His first essay in the newly-named column was entitled "Provincialism." *b.* First published in *Mr. Pope and Other Poems* (1928).

131/TLS

New York City
3 May 1928

Dear Don:

I went by an "out of town" newspaper stand today and got a Sunday's Tennessean. Your review is even better than I thought it was in manuscript. Please accept my thanks again. Curiously enough the review of the Boston Transcript, out of the heart of Abolitionism, was more laudatory. But it was not so penetrating. You are the only person so far who has got the underlying intention of the book, and this is doubtless due to the fact that you accurately divined my motives in writing it. I was fascinated with the subject, but I had to write the book hurriedly and give it to Balch in much doubt; yet here comes a letter from Dodd,[a] following his review, asking me to contribute a 200 page book on some Southern figure of the Civil War period to a series now being planned by the University of Chicago History Department. This academic reverberation both amuses and pleases me. Unfortunately I am having to turn down the offer: Davis is sold to Balch, and unless Dodd can wait about five years I'll not be able to face another biography. I am not a biographer. The Jackson is due to a reversion to the romantic feelings of childhood. Who can be romantic about a politician? A dead soldier may be a hero, but a dead politician is a dead politician. Even the best.

The new Weekly Review looks fine. You can easily make it the best one page review in this country, and I am sure you will. I imagine your policy will be to gather up the best talent in that region—a policy that I ardently sympathize with—but should you wish to extend your staff, you might easily get hold of the best reviewers up here, provided, of course, you could pay at least a cent a word; if you paid two cents, you could take your pick of the country.

Did Merrill ever send his ms. to Coward-McCann? I'd like to know, so that I can make my next move at the right time.

Yrs. till later, Allen

131   a. W. E. Dodd's review appeared in New York Herald-Tribune Books (April 27, 1928).

132/ALS

[Nashville, Tenn.]
21 August 1928

Dear Allen:

Your book just came in, also your letter and copy of review of *The Lyric South.ª* As I'm just getting off to Beersheba for a bit of mountain seclusion, I'm in a furore of preparation, and can write just a brief note, which I'll supplement later.

I'm delighted with the general get-up of your book & much pleased & flattered by the personal inscription. So far I have been able to look through it only hastily—but my first impression is that you have made a mighty powerful selection from your work, and this book is going to establish all the more firmly your already decidedly firm standing. You are more conservative than I thought you might be in your choice of poems; I was very happy to see some of my old favorites, "The Screen" & the "Oenia" poems. Among these latter the famous "Epilogue" is *you,* genuinely *you,* at your most characteristic & enjoyable, if not your loftiest.

I shall write you more in detail later. Now—I congratulate you, for the second time in a few months, but this time with a peculiar pleasure that I don't think anybody except Jesse and I (and a few as close to you as we seem to be) could have. I rejoice exceedingly in the book— I wouldn't take anything for my copy! And Sir, here's wishing, the sure mark of immortality to your verses.

As for Hibbard, you did him up properly, though not so savagely as John, and you were especially gentlemanly in your treatment, considering *his* treatment of you.

I'll certainly hope to see Fletcher if he comes South. If you leave a note for him, *stress* the fact that he has an urgent invitation to stop off here. (We'll keep the literary ladies away from him, too!)

I shall read your poems over and over and roll the taste of them on my tongue.

It was a grand pleasure to have you around for the few short days. It was good to see that you were still essentially yourself, unchanged by these adventurings afar. I shall expect to see Allen Tate in the same identity on your return from England, France, or wherever it is you sojourn. So *Bon Voyage,* cheery and indomitable Tate (now I include Carolyn, for now I can with the pleasure of acquaintance, visualize her), and on to the conquest of Europe.

Faithfully, Don

P.S. I'll write that criticism within a week, I hope. My regards to Carolyn and Nancy.

132 *a.* Addison Hibbard's anthology.

133/ALS

London
24 October 1928

Dear Don:

I had barely recovered from the effects of our stormy passage when the treacherous British climate betrayed me, and I came down with the "flu." I am up today for the first time since last Friday. I have seen very little—Westminster Abbey, St. Magnus the Martyr, the Temple. We have been to Oxford; it is far beyond expectations. I shall not write you my impressions of it; suffice it that we are going there to stay for six weeks. I believe I can work there. Red is curious but not yet happy;ª I think he may be. On the whole none of us seems to like England. The men seldom speak, and when they do, they usually say something unpleasant. The women are appalling. Great God! What feet and ankles! And their eyes look like fishes'. I begin to see the use of British Imperialism. It is something for the men to be so devoted to that they are willing even to mate with the awful women, in order to give sons to the Empire. I have conceived a respectful sympathy for Oscar Wilde.

Well, my impressions, are, as you see, frivolous and muddled; yet if I were not done in by the flu I should certainly be having a good time. You don't need to like a place to enjoy it. In fact, I feel about Europe as most Americans, if they are honest, must feel—erroneously or not: I can't help feeling quite superior to most of the people I meet. I don't mean in any personal sense. I can explain it only in this way: the English seem to be living against a background that is much too large for them. I am sure that no one who is not a confirmed democrat could make this observation. You can not tell immediately whether an Englishman's integrity is his own or the common integrity. This has its advantages; but it is perplexing. There is the curious impression that I get from the intelligent Englishmen I have met, that they feel a certain remoteness from their own past almost as deep as the breach that we feel as transplanted Europeans. This is true beyond question. The inference to be drawn is vast; so I leave it to you.

I have met most of the people who are behind the Criterion, and

I like them all. Herbert Read is the best mind in England. (Remember ten years from now that I said this.) Eliot, of course, was due to be the most interesting, but he is a Sphinx and you can't tell much about him: not that his mystery is a pose. He can't help it. He is really a nice man, and most amiable. I expected to see a small man with an extremely intellectual face, yet lacking those features which signify Will. As a matter of face, put into 17*th* century clothes, he would look like a New England Divine—which he really is. I should say that his character, far from being weak, is almost overdeveloped. It is both amusing and impressive to observe the attitude of the English towards him. It is almost worship, and it contains no reservation. I witnessed a curious scene. The other day at lunch he had to leave early; the moment he left, the others burst into spontaneous tribute to him. It was ludicrous and it was affecting. There is something very American about Eliot's whole procedure, and I like it. He came here unknown and without influence. In fifteen years he has become the undisputed literary dictator of London. What I like is that he doesn't seem to feel the role.

I am written out for the moment. Please write me when you can. You can't imagine how welcome messages from America are just now. I am by no means so diverted that I can do without them. I may add that I shall never be. Carolyn joins me in best regards. Remember me to Jesse and John.

Yours always, Allen

133   *a.* Warren has received his Rhodes scholarship and is already at Oxford when Tate arrives there.

134/TLS

Nashville, Tenn.
5 February 1929

Dear Allen:

I have been a long time writing you, and I'm grieved—have long been grieved—at my absurd delay. It is absurd because my life has become quite absurd. It is without pith. It is given up altogether to mercenary pursuits. I teach classes and I edit a book page, both things being done in order to live and to support a family; and, completing the circle, apparently I live and support a family in order to teach classes and to edit a book page. In such a scheme of things there has been no room for letters (other than strictly business), for poetry, for thought, for decency. I suppose I am as near as I ever was to being a lost soul. For all reasonable and intelligent purposes, I am now no more than that—just a lost soul. The only thing that makes me think I am not quite altogether a lost soul is that I recognize the absurdity of my condition and am dissatisfied with it. And out of this discontent I ask your pardon for a long wait in writing. I assure you that all the time I have thought of you with the semi-buried part of my mind—which is to say that you have never been out of the part of my thought that is really vital.

Another reason why I didn't write you is that I have been ashamed. I have waited so long to review your book. I didn't have the face to write to you until it was reviewed. My review is enclosed.[a] It will appear next Sunday, in a slightly modified form. In partial excuse I may say that first I had thought to get Red to review your poems; but he proved to be inaccessible. Then I solicited Jesse; and he was chary of attempting the task; perhaps he didn't feel himself equal to it. Next I asked Ransom, and he at first consented. But on further thought, and after studying your book, he decided he wouldn't. I think he felt that if he reviewed it, he would, despite sundry positive admirations for your writing, have to take strong issue with you, and in such a case, it seemed to him that it ill befitted good friends to show their differences in public. Well, then, there was no one else. I had to do it—and though I would have preferred to have passed the task to somebody else, especially because of our close relation and because I reviewed your Stonewall so favorably, nevertheless I took a real pleasure in turning my energies, such as they are, to the difficult business. But I wanted to do it when I felt at my best—weak as that is. I was surprised to find myself defending your poetry in a large measure; I don't know whether you will be surprised or not. You will see that I did you the courtesy to avoid a great many of the ordinary clichés of reviewing. Instead of comparing you to Hart Crane or Louis Untermeyer, I chose to compare you with Milton and Tennyson, partly because I thought they represented a standard by which you would prefer to be measured. Also, I found I had no space for reference to particular poems and phases of your style. I had to discuss you altogether in order to say anything very effective. Thus it happened that many things I might have said could not go in. Yet, though my review is vastly insufficient to the book itself, as I well recognize, I am foolish enough to believe it is a juster review than Winters' in the N.R.[b] Why in God's name does he give himself such authoritarian airs: The solemn ponderosity of his utterances is worthy of a Methodist bishop. I hope you'll tell him I said so.

Your letter from London gave me an excellent foretaste of what I'm hoping to hear from you, when you have gotten entirely over the Flu and are quite well acclimated. I enjoyed all you had to say, especially your impressions of (1) Englishwomen; (2) Eliot; (3) Read—two of whose books have just come into my hands. I don't deserve long talkative letters, sinner that I am; but with a sinner's faith I hope you'll write them, in order that I may know just how Europe strikes you and how the magnum opus moves along. Merrill has given me your Paris address, and so I suppose that you are staying in Paris awhile to get the pulse of the literary world there, as well as to soak up Paris. Will you be moving on soon, to South France, where the weather is more benign (I know what French winters are like), or to some provincial city (like Dijon) where one can live unmolested, or even to Germany?

All of us have read with extraordinary interest your article in The Bookman[c] (Is this a descent for you, or an ascent for The BkMan). My reaction is briefly: all your generalizations are very good indeed, but most of your particularities are dangerous, reflecting your aversions and obsessions too closely. So, while nobody has written so well about poetry in many years, you are open to attack in your references to poets. All the same, it is a relief to have your courageous frontal approach rather than the devious effusions and politenesses so common nowadays.

There is little news to give, but such as there is I will try to sum it up. Ransom's book on aesthetics is taking a final shape;[d] it will not be, however, a thorough and definitive work, but a looser, less formal study than he had at first planned. Last Saturday night at Fugitive meeting, he read a very brilliant paper—about an hour long—in which he gives an exciting new turn to his familiar dualism. Now he is dallying with a masculine-feminine principle in literature, and, if I am any judge, with great conviction and force. Nobody else among the Fugitives is doing anything worth note, except Merrill, who is still trying to find a publisher, and Mr. Frank, who suddenly burst out with several poems, better than anything he has yet done. I am doing no writing except hack writing, but I am now definitely committed to plans for a complete summer to do with as I please. I shall go away somewhere, leaving the book page to hired help. The end of it, if all results well, will be some sort of a book. One can't resist the publishers. They have hungry scouts in the field, looking for Southern authors. At least three publishers have been after me—well, mildly after me. Marshall Best, of the Viking Press, seems extra anxious.

I wish you would write to Jesse in your very best vein. The good old boy, I greatly fear, is much besieged with family troubles. I know nothing definite, but I have the constant feeling that Jesse lives under domestic pressure which we can hardly imagine. If his situation were not as it is, I feel that he might energetically have taken hold of the Fugitive Press idea, about which we have talked at some length this fall and winter. As things stand now, I believe it is not practicable, for the simple reason that there is nobody who is free to devote himself to it with all his heart. But it is an idea that I favor very much. Only, I should go much further. I favor a fully financed Southern magazine, openly provincial; associated with this magazine, a publishing house of a distinct sort; and associated with the whole enterprise, a chain of bookstores, to serve as a distributing medium. Such an enterprise, of course, calls for millions—plenty of which are in the U.S. But how to get hold of them, that's the thing. I am an impossible visionary, but I should dearly like to get embarked on some grand enterprise that had only a fighting chance of success.

This leads me to speak of what is to be done in the South, anyway? My impression is that the people who are of your opinion and mine and John's about things Southern are few and far between, and furthermore of little influence. If there were a Southern magazine, intelligently conducted and aimed specifically, under the doctrine of provincialism, at renewing a certain sort of sectional consciousness and drawing separate groups of Southern thought together, something might be done to save the South from civilization. The great trouble is that there is no such magazine in sight, and, still worse, there is no real issue strong enough to renew or create the conception of Southern life for which I think we could argue. Economics, government, politics, machinery—all such forces are against us. With the issue of prosperity before everybody's eyes, Southerners get excited about nothing else— except religion; it was religion and prosperity that beat Al Smith and broke the Solid South. Where can we join up, with our mysterious doctrine of provincialism? Still, I believe in agitating. The losing cause is not always the better one, but it is in this case.

Ransom, Wade, and I have been trying to get up a symposium on Southern matters, but without success so far. Of the people we approached, only one, Gerald Johnson,[e] answered, and his answer showed that he didn't understand what we were talking about. You were on our list of prospective contributors. Will you come across with something, if we revive the project?

No doubt, at a great Trans-Atlantic distance, you are getting an entirely new perspective (dear word, beloved of liberals). You are finding out what is American as well as what's European. Well, let's have the straight stuff, old-timer. Best wishes, as always, in all things, and regards and cheers to all members of the Tatian Expeditionary Force, who I trust are all well and happy.

Faithfully, Don

134 *a.* Davidson's review of *Mr. Pope and Other Poems* appeared February 10, 1929. *b. New Republic* (October 17, 1928). *c.* Tate's essay "American Poetry Since 1920" appeared in *Bookman* (January 1929). *d.* Another reference to Ransom's "The Third Moment." *e.* Gerald White Johnson, Southern journalist and historian; at this time he was on the staff of the Baltimore *Evening Sun*.

135/TLS

Paris
18 February 1929

Dear Don:

Your excellent letter of the 5th and the super-excellent review came today to raise my spirits, which have been uncommonly low. We have been through a dreadful siege of the flu, from which I alone came off well, and the cold weather (around zero Fahrenheit) takes all the Europe out of our lives because it keeps us bound to the grate fire. I am afraid you see me having a great time absorbing French life and learning much from the French writers. I see but little of the French, writers or citizens; though warm weather may give me some social impulses. We came from Oxford on Thanksgiving Day. Except for Warwick Castle and Stratford we saw in England only Oxford and London; in France only Paris. I have been so swamped with illness and the desire to get some work done that I haven't felt like seeing any one or anything.

First, your review is the most intelligent I have yet had, and provided that it isn't keyed up too high (both in praise and censure) it analyzes my virtues and defects as they have never been analyzed before. The charge of Expressionism is a most acute thrust. I think there is a reason why most of us are Expressionists (you are one) against our will, and this reason is the proper subject of modern critical speculation; though of course it has no place in a review. All the Fugitives are unwilling Expressonists simply because to write poetry at all these days we must violate the current meanings of words with our own personalities; the current meanings of words are President Coolidge's, as you imply, and they are debased. When we use a word we use it two ways; for the sake of communication we take hold of it first in the current sense, then recharge it with the value that it ought to have. This describes your method as well as mine, and it describes Ransom's better than either. I think John is quite right about not wishing to air the differences we must all feel; the public never understands the philosophical intention of such disagreements, and takes it to mean that we think our colleagues are no good. For this reason, when I reviewed John's Two Gentlemen in Bonds, I suppressed the abstract reservations I feel about his poetry, and issued a public statement; more and more I believe that this is the correct procedure for reviewing. Reviewing is propaganda for the best current production, and it can never be more than that unless the public is better educated. I am not prepared to say when that will be. In the present state of things, if I reviewed you and John in a high way, showing perhaps that you both fall short of Dante, the public, fed by Louis Untermeyer, would suppose that I meant you were inferior to Elinor Wylie. Therefore, reviewing John, I pointed out that his distinction is not surpassed by any contemporary poet in America; which is perfectly true.

Your recent depression is not the peculiar property of your environment, as I see it; though it may be due to your special reaction to that special environment. All places are equally the wrong places. We are all at present doomed to live a harrowing life, and it may or may not be more harrowing than the lives of all men everywhere who have tried to find some ultimate discipline of the soul. It was just as hard to attain to salvation in the 13th century as it is now (perhaps harder), although the results of the quest in literature were grander and more coherent. That was largely because salvation was common, not personal. I would like some time to talk to you at length about this— it is not the kind of thing you can talk about in short visits. I am more and more heading towards Catholicism. We have reached a condition of the spirit where no further compromise is possible. That is the lesson taught us by the Victorians who failed to unite naturalism and the religious spirit; we've got to do away with the one or the other; and I can never capitulate to naturalism. What Babbitt and More and, recently, Foerster call humanism is impossible; for humanism at any time is simply a derivative of the main faith of the age; and our main faith being naturalism, humanism must be naturalistic also. The humanism of the Renaissance was better because it was still energized by the Church. (I am at present writing, at Eliot's solicitation, an essay on modern humanists from this point of view.)[a] In other words, the modern humanists, however they try, cannot, without religion, get rid of the monistic assumptions of naturalism; without a clean break between the natural and the supernatural humanism commits suicide. It can't be both monistic and dualistic, and unless it espouses religion (which it refuses to do) it must cling to science which is monistic. There is no dualism without religion, and there is no religion without a Church; nor can there be a Church without dogma. Protestanism is virtually naturalism; when morality lacks the authority of dogma, it becomes private and irresponsible, and from this it is only a step to naturalism. Even two generations ago this was not as clear as it is now. The forms of impersonal and authoritative conduct remained in the characters of Protestants, but without the external authority good conduct cannot last; it becomes, as it did in Henry James, merely "gentlemanly feeling" which is not enough to keep in control those who lack it. So on and so on.

I am sorry to hear that Jesse is feeling low. I wrote to him from Oxford, but I have not received a reply. It would probably take more money than Jesse could afford to put all your schemes on foot; but a little would be better than nothing. At the outset, of course, the question of "lost causes" would come up. There is no such thing as a lost cause. There are permanent forms of truth which, under the varying conditions of time and place, may be made pertinent. Our time and place would require the adjustment of these truths to our provincial history. The trouble is that Americans are afraid of any idea of which the immediate fruition in action is not clear. Any coherent point of view, whether it have any chance of practical success or not, becomes a valuable instrument of criticism. The chief virtue of such a stand is to make contemporary abuses stand forth for what they are. By finding good in a little of everything, as the modern liberal does, you find no good in anything. No cause is lost so long as it can sustain a few people in the formulation of truths.

To return to your review—which I like without reservation. One of your best points concerns the quality of traditional poetry. The people who opposed the Fugitives as radicals would oppose, certainly, such a poem as Lycidas if it appeared in a modern journal. Tradition is the intensest expression, or communication, the past has reached. This is always difficult. What most people mean by tradition is the debased and diluted version of the great masters which the second rate poets have passed on. Like Tennyson. It is worthy of remark that the only Victorian poet who is in the great tradition (Arnold) is put aside for Browning and Tennyson. These latter give the reader all the illusion of reading poetry, without forcing him to extend himself to the great effort of reading poetry itself. It is almost as difficult to read poetry as it is to write it. I find it so, and so should the reader, I believe, who is a little less practiced at it than I am. I need only to add that my poetry is not necessarily in the great tradition because it is found difficult. I have played the sedulous ape to certain masters, but I hope not merely to dilute what they say. As to Lycidas again, it is certainly one of the most difficult poems ever written; I read it first when I was about fourteen years old, and in certain ways I understand it as little as I did then; and I must have read it three or four hundred times.

I am glad to hear that you are going to have the summer free. What will you do next? Are you continuing your studies of the Southern tradition? May I suggest that you apply for a Guggenheim Fellowship? I think you would be almost certain to get it. You would only have to tell them that you wanted to write a book, without going into detail or making the project seem too original—this was what kept John from getting his. The selection committee didn't understand what John was talking about. No matter what book you are writing it would profit by European research. The Guggenheim people really want to help all kinds of scholars, and the European end of it exists only to give them publicity, although they have a high-sounding interpretation of it. Moe,[b] the secretary, a very intelligent man, has a most flexible interpretation of his programme. I talked to him about you, and he is extremely interested. I could almost swear to your success. Coming to Europe is not an unmixed blessing, but it gives you leisure. I don't particularly require leisure; but perhaps you do.

I have written some new poems, and written about seven hundred lines on the long poem. The latter isn't much good, though parts of it are. Jeff Davis was put aside in the fall; he has been resumed; but he will not be out this spring. Eliot has tempted me into a by-path wherein I am committed to give him the essay on the Humanists by April first; he asked me to apply to them the ideas in my essay on Emily Dickinson —which in a longer and more closely argued version he is printing in June.[c] I wish John would send him some chapters of his book;[d] John's thought and Eliot's run along the same line; in fact, if John's book is what I think it is, it leads right up to religion, whither Eliot has been bound all the time. Ransom and Eliot are more alike than any other two people alive; I have always suspected this, now I am convinced. It is very hard for me to distinguish the influences they have had on me; they merge. It is quite proper, and quite amusing, that John from the beginning seems to have had an instinctive dislike of Eliot. The poetry of both is highly original; it is very much alike.

I am afraid I have got no new perspective on anything. I have probably reached the limits of my power to learn; the rest of my life will be devoted to strengthening the conclusions I have already come to. In fact, this is the genuine attitude for learning: an "open mind" never learns anything because it can't contain anything. This is the trouble with our liberal friends like Dr. Mims. Of course, I have got some "new ideas," but they are extensions of what I already thought. I will spare you these until my next—which will come closely upon the heels of your next. I miss you a great deal over here, Don, and I hope we meet shortly after I come back. But perhaps you will be a Guggenheim Fellow yourself, and come here to see me. Best regards to you and family, and remember me to the Fugitives.

Yours ever, Allen

P.S. I read Winters a lecture on his review. If you have any extra pages containing yours, I would appreciate receiving them—2 or 3.

135   *a.* "The Fallacy of Humanism," *Criterion* (July 1929).   *b.* Henry Allen Moe, from 1925 to 1967 president of the Guggenheim Memorial Fund.   *c.* This version was first published in *Symposium* (April 1932).   *d. God Without Thunder* (1930).

136/ALS

Saratoga Springs, N.Y.
29 July 1929

Dear Allen:

A note from Merrill Moore reminds me—as I have long been reminding myself, without effect—that I haven't written you in a long time. I have had your letter of the winter past on my desk for months: it is on my table now, for I brought it with me here. I never could seem to get time to write the answer it deserved. Besides, I am always ashamed when I write to you and, in less degree, to other old friends, because I have been doing so little to justify my existence and you have been doing so much.

I especially wanted to say to you, after I got your letter, that you simply *must not* be as gloomy as your letter seemed to indicate you might be. Surely you must not, like Eliot, give up the ghost in favor of a combination of classic-Anglo-Catholic-Conservative, principally because that combination (good as it may be) isn't good enough for you, however much its elements may attract you, or even serve your poetical purposes now and then. I, too, am attracted somewhat toward Catholicism, as toward High Church Episcopalianism. But I like better to be tied up with no church at all. I find myself more repelled than attracted by all clergymen and priests. If it were not for them, possibly I could become something-or-other in a religious way. As matters stand, I seem to be bothered less by religious matters than by anything else. Maybe I'm just an animal after all. At any rate, I do agree that Babbitt's "humanism" is very weakish in omitting religion—but that's purely an intellectual statement of the matter to me.

I hope very much that you will soon complete your labors and return to the States—incidentally and (for selfish reasons) principally, to visit Nashville also. God knows (I say it with all the piety I can manage) I need the conversations with you that you mentioned in your letter as wished-for. More especially, your services are badly needed in a big fight which I foresee in the immediate future.

It is this. For several months, with the partial and somewhat hesitating encouragement of Ransom, I have been agitating the project of a collection of views on the South, not a general symposium, but a group of openly partisan documents, centralizing closely around the ideas that you, Ransom, & I all seem to have in common. It would deal with phases of the situation such as the Southern tradition, politics, religion, art, etc., but always with a strong bias toward the self-determinative principle. It would be written by native Southerners of our mind—a small, coherent, highly selected group, and would be intended to come upon the scene with as much vigor as is possible—would even, maybe, call for *action* as well as ideas.

I enclose a prospectus of this scheme, very tentative, and also enclose a comment by Gorham Munson, whom I found here at Yaddo, and who now has a connection with Doubleday-Doran and is holding out very strong lures of publication. (Macmillan & Scribner are prospects, too.)

But I also enclose a copy of a letter from Howard Mumford Jones[a] which just reached me and is self-explanatory. It upset me!

You will see, after reading it, what is before us. If Jones, whom I like and respect in many ways, put his scheme on foot, the "progressive" note will be accented very much, I greatly fear. You can imagine, for instance, what a man like Odum[b] would have to say about the Negro question. For us, the issue is: Will we let the Progressives (some of whom are "immigrant" Southerners) capture the field and walk off with public opinion. But they have great strength on their side—prestige, resources, etc. They can get eminent contributors. They may even cut the ground out from under us.

I was astounded at Jones' letter and gave him, for the time being, a non-committal answer, inquiring from what point of view the symposium was to be prepared. I secretly (but maybe unjustly) suspect that he is taking this method of letting me know that he has found out our scheme and is forestalling us—perhaps being a little put out that he himself had not been consulted or asked to enter, as he would not have been. But this is pure speculation.

I'm therefore asking you (keeping Jones' letter confidential) to write me your opinion and to indicate whether, if we should launch our own ship of ideas, you would contribute and what you would propose, in special and in general. I am much hampered by the uncertainty of my own mind, by lack of knowledge of possible contributors, and by a certain hesitancy on the part of Ransom, which, I fear, might be duplicated in others. If within the next three months, there doesn't develop a clear possibility of getting the project under way, I'll prefer to drop it, for the time being. But I'd like to make a fight, and I'd like to have your advice & help. In fact, if you were on the ground, I'd propose that you should be editor of the project. I would have written you before if things had not been nebulous in the extreme.

Yaddo is a good place. I've enjoyed it thoroughly, but have not done much effective work. It is a better place—indeed a delightful place—to recuperate and to finish up work; not so good to begin it, for one tends to relax in these wholly ideal surroundings. For the first time in two years I have written some poems & hope to write more,[c] which I'll send you when they are in shape. I have nibbled at a book (prose) on Tennessee. . . .

Your reviews, by the way, have delighted me greatly as I've seen them here & there. You and I (I strongly believe) wrote better reviews of Phillips'[d] book than the coterie of New Yorkers because we were not totally ignorant of his materials. I have corresponded with Phillips; asked him about the symposium, but he could only offer good will and suggestions for contributors, as he is about to go abroad.

Tell me of yourself & your fortunes. I've heard from various sources that you've had much illness and I'm dreadfully sorry for it. I've had, personally, the most difficult year of my life, but we won't go into that. Regards to Carolyn.

Faithfully, Don

136   *a.* At this time a professor of English at the University of North Carolina. *b.* Howard Odum, sociologist at the University of North Carolina and author of *Southern Regions* (1936). *c.* These are the poems in the collection *Lee in the Mountains and Other Poems* (1938). *d.* U. B. Phillips, *Life and Labor in the Old South* (1929).

137/ALS

Concarneau, Finistere, France
10 August 1929

Dear Don:

Yours of the 29th is just here. My delight is best witnessed by the speed of my taking up pen and ink.

I have recently had news of your activities in behalf of a Southern movement. Ransom sent me a letter of yours to him and enclosed Munson's very acute remarks on his essay. All this is in full agreement with my own views.

The other day I wrote to Warren, and suggested the following tactical program:

1. The formation of a society, or an academy of Southern *positive* reactionaries made up at first of people of our own group.

2. The expansion in a year or two of this academy to this size: fifteen active members—poets, critics, historians, economists—and ten inactive members—lawyers, politicians, private citizens—who might be active enough without being committed at first to direct agitation.

3. The drawing up of a philosophical constitution, to be issued and signed by the academy, as the groundwork of the movement. It should be ambitious to the last degree; it should set forth, under our leading idea, a complete social, philosophical, literary, economic, and religious system. This will inevitably draw upon our

heritage, but this heritage should be valued, not in what it actually performed, but in its possible perfection. Philosophically we must go the whole hog of reaction, and base our movement less upon the actual old South than upon its prototype—the historical social and religious scheme of Europe. We must be the last Europeans—there being no Europeans in Europe at present.

4. The academy will not be a secret order: all the cards will be on the table. We should be *secretive*, however, in our tactics, and plan the campaign for the maximum of effect. All our writings should be signed "John Doe, of the ———— ————," or whatever we call it.

5. Organized publication should be looked to. A newspaper, perhaps, to argue our principles on the lower plane; then a weekly, to press philosophy upon the passing show; and, third, a quarterly devoted wholly to principles. This is a large scheme, but it must be held up constantly. We must do our best with what we can get.

The advantages of this program are the advantages of all extreme positions. It would immediately define the muddling and *unorganized* opposition (*intellectually* unorganized) of the Progressives: they have no *philosophical* program, only an emotional acquiescence to the drift of the age, and we should force them to rationalize into absurdity an intellectually untenable position. Secondly, it would crystallize into opposition or complete allegiance the vaguely pro-Southern opinions of the time. These two advantages of my proposed academy seem to me decisive. Without the academy we shall perish in two ways: (1) under the superior weight of metal (not superior strategy) of the enemy (Progressives); and (2) our own doctrine will be diluted with too many shades of opinion.

In short, this program would *create an intellectual situation interior to the South*. I underscore it because, to me, it contains the heart of the matter.

For the great ends in view—the end may be only an assertion of principle, but that in itself is great—for this end we must have a certain discipline; we must crush minor differences of doctrine under a single idea. I suggest a repudiation of Jefferson and a revised re-statement of the South Carolina idea. We shall never refute Progress with the doctrine of a man whose negative side made Progress possible. Jefferson's system (!) was made to oppose an illusory monarchy in the U.S. In short we cannot merely fight centralization; we must envisage a centralization of a different and better kind. In fact, we must here oppose one of the ideas of the Southern tradition. Emotionally this does me considerable violence because I am, emotionally, a Jeffersonian. This is what I mean by discipline.

Another and greater Southern movement foundered on indiscipline of ideas. I refer to the Montgomery Convention of February, 1861. Study it and take warning. Those men *felt*, but they would not *think* through habits and political inertia. The Montgomery Convention lost us the war. There was no one to tell them the logical consequences of their position. We must take logic to the most extreme ends, and then perform what we can.

Jones' proposal is amusing and a little annoying. It demonstrates the need of our academy. If it existed now, one of two things or both would happen: his symposium would be largely written with our announced program as a background; we should be able to pigeon-hole it and effectively neutralize its influence by a fusillade of *academy* reviews. *Organization and discipline are indispensable.*

By this time you've seen my essay on the Humanists. We shall have to refer to these fellows pretty often. Their difficulty is that they are trying to refute Progress merely with anti-Progress—or Naturalism with mere anti-Naturalism. Munson puts his finger precisely on our advantage over him.

The publication of a manifesto would relieve any one person of the responsibility for what his colleagues say, but it would not keep the natural leader as leaders of the movement from winning their just laurels. These would follow merit, industry, etc.

The symposium would do better *after* the formation of the academy, but that will take time. Therefore it must precede organization. However, no one should contribute to it whom we aren't sure of. Our ultimate purpose should be hinted at in an anonymous Preface, or a Preface signed by all the contributors.

Jones (a Yankee like Knickerbocker and Hibbard who take to Southernism as a means to academic preferment)—Jones will not hurt us if we are quick. I have just signed a contract with Harpers for my third prose book (on a Southern subject) and it is more than probable that they will grab our symposium without delay. I plan now to return in September, or by Oct. 12th at the latest: I will see Saxton and Wells immediately. My contract with Harpers is mentioned in absolute confidence: I haven't yet disposed of Balch to my satisfaction. (*Davis* will be out Sept. 20th—a better book than Jackson.)

I enclose a slightly revised table of contents and contributors. It may give you some new hints. I also enclose a letter from Fletcher written after I had outlined my idea of an academy. He is with us—a powerful acquisition. (Can't find it. Will send it in a few days.)

There are other details, but I will wait till I hear from you.

We are all well again, but on the 17th of July my mother died at Monteagle, and I have felt very low because I could not be there. Her death was sudden; she took pneumonia and died in three days. There was no use coming home; I should have been too late to be of any help to my family. Carolyn's mother died in January, and it has been rather hard on us that both calamities should come while we were abroad.

Please let me hear from you immediately. I am getting really excited.

Yours ever, Allen

Contributors and Subjects

1. The Philosophy of Provincialism—Ransom.

2. The Southern Way of Life—*Perhaps* Stark Young, if he can be prevented from including anecdotes of his grandmother. I suggest Red Warren.

3. Contemporary Southern Literature—Davidson, because he knows and understands it better than any of us.

4. Humanism and the Southern Tradition. (This is the title I would give to your Numbers 4 and 5—the Philosophy of South. Hist. and the Historically Minded South.) I would like to do this.

5. Religion and Aristocracy in the South. (Your Number 6—"Protestantism in the South".) The problem here would be: Was Southern religion in accord with social and political tendencies? I can't suggest a writer for this, unless Warren does it, leaving No. 2 to Young.

6. Harper and Dew:[a] Philosophers of the Old South. (We must revive these men. I know a good deal about them, but we should get some one else to do them up.) This essay should lead off or at least come second.

7. Politics—The article should be as you describe it. But where is the writer? W. Y. Elliot knows all about it, but he is not a separatist, and he aspires to be Jesus Christ. Very important subject.

8. Economic Issues—The contributor here stumps me too. *We need a most efficient economist on our side.*

9. Education. John Gould Fletcher. He is just the man. He already knows the subject.

10. Literature in the Old South. Who could do this to our satisfaction? I think the subject must be discussed.[b]
Note: A man like Phillips, good as he is in his line, must be used only as a document: he is limited to facts, while we wish to rise upon facts to salvation. He is a fine example of the *dilution* we shall suffer without a definite program. The academy could use him; he would dissipate us otherwise.

The symposium should be heavily cross-referenced by footnote.

137   *a.* Thomas R. Dew and William Harper, two of the most provocative of the proslavery writers.   *b.* See Appendix A for the final list of contributors.

138/ALS

[Nashville, Tenn.]
20 August 1929

Dear Allen:

Just returned from a long motor trip through Pennsylvania, Virginia, East Tennessee, etc., and found your letter awaiting me. I hope very much that my letter (with various enclosures) written from Yaddo & mailed to your Paris address, reached you. It contained information about the Southern project & explained (though inadequately) my long silence.

I hope very much that we can get into more immediate communication soon, for I am all excited over various things and long very much for an exchange of ideas with you. I agree that the New York influence is very dangerous. We must not be swallowed or exploited or corrupted. But how shall we avoid it? I tell you, it will take some clever fighting, some terrific blows intelligently delivered and backed by sound information as well as theory, to put over any program such as we are talking about. The forces against us are colossal, and we shall have to work with swift subtle strategy to overcome the lead they already have.

The topics I want to discuss with you, as soon as I get time and space, center around such items as these:

1. The Southern book—as a heading-up of ideas and as the basis of a program.

2. The reformation of my Book Page, especially with relation to the program under discussion.

3. The possible establishment of a magazine *or* the capture, as you suggest, of the Sewanee Review.

4. Ways of getting in touch with the young people, especially young literary groups at colleges, & heading them in the right direction.

5. Ways of interesting & influencing Southern Newspapers, by a studiously organized system of letters, clip-sheets, etc. (*Vide*: the established technique of propaganda—fight fire with fire.)

6. In general, to get down to the practical plane—to act as well as speculate & talk. There is no telling what a few determined souls may accomplish!

I'm very eager to see your Criterion essay, of which John has just told me. Will have a look at it this week, as soon as I see John. How is your work coming, and when are you coming back?

A letter from Robt. Graves informs me that Laura R. has been seriously injured by a fall, but will recover. Merrill Moore's book of poems is coming out soon—I hope. You can help him, if you feel that conscience will allow! I believe you formerly did not always think highly of Merrill's sonnets, but I recall, too, that, at the time of publication of the Fugitive Anthology you thought much better of his work. There are material reasons, as much as aesthetic, why Merrill hopes anxiously (almost too anxiously) for the book to succeed; every penny Merrill makes is a help, for the family, since Trotwood's death, is not in a flourishing financial condition. I shouldn't be surprised if the good old man left heavy debts!

Am very anxious to hear from you fully. Best regards, salutations, good luck.

Faithfully, Don

139/TLS

Nashville, Tenn.
26 October 1929

Dear Allen:

As I explained in a note just sent as forerunner, I have been under all the usual pressures for the past six weeks or more and have not been able to sit down and compose an intelligent letter to you. I sent the cable, with the other friends, to let you know you were by no means forgotten.

I had looked forward to seeing you this fall, for your letters had indicated a hope that you would be in the States in September or October, and that was another reason—until your later note came— why I did not write at once. I'm really disappointed, for selfish reasons, that the Guggenheim people decided you should stay abroad for another six months. Doubtless this is in the best interests of literature, etc., but it doesn't conduce to my happiness, for, things being what they are, I feel an extraordinary need for talking things over.

As to the projected symposium, I do not think it can really develop until you get back to the States, for I cannot swing it by myself, busy and distracted as I am now, and I sadly need advice, comfort, and the aid of a strong right arm. There is nobody around here who has either sufficient zeal or vision to pitch into the business wholeheartedly. Ransom, you know, never was a man to push anything. He will give moral support, he will write, he will be a strong man in conference, but he does not energize. Andrew Lytle is terrifically interested, but he has to get his Forrest out of the way before all else.[a] I simply cannot fit the project into my routine until things loosen up a bit, but I am ready to do all that I can do under the circumstances. I lead an incredible life, hardly ever relaxing from the round of hard driving work. In a month or two, however, I may be better organized. I have about reached the conclusion that I'm going to have to neglect a lot of routine things, or do them superficially, or delegate them, in order to get down to the important things that must be done if I am ever to pull out of the hole I'm in.

All this is to say that I have gone no further with the symposium idea than when I wrote you this past summer. Events and further rumination indicate that it has been just as well to wait. The terrific industrial "crises" now occurring almost daily in North Carolina give present point to all the line of thinking and argument that we propose to do. I don't know whether you have read of these or not. It is enough to say that hell has pretty well broken loose, and the old story of labor fights is being repeated. It all means more ammunition for us.

Now let me make some remarks on the revised scheme of the symposium that you sent me. Three points are now definitely taken care of between you and Ransom and me: Ransom, the Philosophy of Provincialism; you, Humanism and the Southern Tradition; me, the Literature, especially the new. As for Stark Young, I think it would be extremely wise to have such a man as he is, if we can be sure he understands the full import of the affair and does not treat it simply as a literary or sentimental excursion. These points are in his favor: he knows the tone of Southern life at its best and writes extremely well; he comes from Mississippi originally, but has wandered widely enough not to be accused of narrow parochialism; we need at least one such eminent Southern writer, outside of our own circle, to strengthen our array, and he would put us in no danger, I think, of being swallowed up by New York. I happen to know also that he is very bitter against Howard Mumford Jones, who represents the "enlightened" N. Carolina school. I have been in correspondence with Young recently and intend to feel him out gradually and see just exactly how the land lies. With him, four of our topics will be taken care of.

As for Education, I am quite opposed to Fletcher (of course, I respect and admire him completely) no matter how great his knowledge of the subject. He is too far away from the scene. I don't see how he could help us. As I see this array, it must be composed of people who are *in the melee.*

I am not sure that we should try to discuss literature in the Old South at all, but am open to conviction. I know of no one who could handle this topic. Neither can I suggest anybody to discuss Religion and Aristocracy.

What we *must* find is an Economist and a Political thinker. Bill Elliott won't do, no matter what his ability, for we can't entertain Caesars in this scheme. If we could find these two contributors, we could really enter the fray, for at a pinch Religion could be covered by either you or Ransom, and we would not absolutely be compelled to resurrect Harper and Dew.

We have either got to find the right men for the various subjects, or write the entire book ourselves. I don't know how to find the men except by a process of watchful waiting and slow inquiry. We run up against, here, the lack of knowledge of our own people that is a handicap to promoting anything in the South. I know all the people we ought *not* to ask, but I don't know who our friends are, for they are heretics and must keep quiet, or they are sentimentalists and have been squelched. What can be done but study the situation and chew the rag cautiously until we get the right line-up? I wish you would rack your brain for suggestions. I'm willing to take almost any line-up of topics if we can only get the right people.

One thing I intend to do at once. I am going to try to find that Economist. The North Carolina situation is sure to bring him out, somewhere.

The rest of your scheme—what you propose as really overshadowing the symposium—I am ready to support for all I'm worth. I believe in practically everything you suggest. I would differ with you only on points of strategy. I believe also that the scheme, ambitious as it is, is not too large for realization, or at least not too impractical to work for and to bring into something like realization. A small group could do it, if they had the proper weapons,—that is, money, literary power, access to the public mind. One man couldn't do it unless he were Jesus Christ.

It isn't the sort of thing one rushes into overnight. We can take our time. To you goes the credit for defining sharply and ambitiously the loose aspirations that have been rattling around in our heads. It's a tremendous stimulus just to have your letter with its grand outline of activities, and though I've been a long time in answering, I want you to know that your letter shook me up from top to toe and filled me with a new fire. Ransom and I talked it over at great length, and Andrew Lytle was with us, too, I believe. You put us all in a stound, but not the kind of stound that lays people flat. Rather we were raised up—but all we seem to be able to do for the time being is talk.

I don't know how I'm going to talk about this sort of thing in letters. There is simply too much to say. I'll just repeat my hope that you won't be any later than is necessary in coming back, and when you come back, let's get together at once. Lytle has been urging Ransom and me to take a week-end off, with him, to discuss the whole project more fully.

All that I see that I can do for the present is to talk, sow seed, accumulate data.

One weakness in your program I should like to point out. The Southern people are not actually united on anything these days—except the Negro question, and they do not know each other as well as they used to. How are they going to be attracted to a Cause unless it is linked up to something very concrete and of an importance that overwhelms all else—it can't be a mere intellectual issue or pure sentiment. It must be as important as Food, Money, Sex, before real work can be done. Too bad that the second Ku Klux Klan came along when it did. We shall have to be careful not to fall into that slough.

I want to know where the money for newspaper, weekly, quarterly, etc., is going to come from, too. That's something to think about.

Your *Jefferson Davis* is, as I told you, magnificent. You are sweeping to a real triumph with it. Owsley told me that he was simply amazed.

He knew you had not done the long meticulous reading that "trained" historians usually do; how then had you, almost by intuition, seized just the right things, seen through problems, struck just the right answer? I told him that was the effect of real critical intelligence plus poetic sense at work; you simply didn't have to be as dull as the regular historians in order to be as right as they—in fact, you could beat them any time, because you didn't have your nose in the molehills, yet didn't overlook the molehills, either. Owsley thought there was really no unfavorable criticism to make of the book. Only on certain points where you couldn't have had access to information (in some cases, things that only Owsley has worked out), did he disagree with you.

What I liked best about the book was its underlying meaning or drift, which might not easily be perceptible to readers who don't know what you are finally after. To be sure, you express yourself openly in such passages as those Owsley quoted; but that there's more yet, I think I can see. It fortifies the Southern position immensely to clear up certain old issues and also to throw overboard certain debris—you do that. The style of the J. D. is a great advance over Stonewall. It's written with great effectiveness. If Bowers's book[b] hadn't unfortunately preceded yours just a little, I should think you would have had a very wide sale, and you may yet. You are moving right on the crest of a wave of popular interest, and yet you are not merely exploiting that popular interest,—you are shrewdly informing it and teaching it something worth learning.

I should have liked to review your book myself, but I thought it would mean more to you locally to have Owsley do it.

As for news: John Bell Keeble[c] died suddenly, about two weeks ago. Dr. Mims's new book, "Adventurous America" is out (Dr. M is quite humble & apprehensive about his book), and of course we are all talking about it—it has some very bad chapters, but all in all is a better written book than the previous one. Merrill's book of verse is just out—it is fine in all except this, that the advice of Untermeyer spoiled the arrangement of the lines in M's sonnets. They are made to look like E. E. Cummings. The situation in the English Dept. is getting serious: we are overcrowded with students and over worked and all (Curry, Ransom, Wade, and I) inclined to be greatly dissatisfied. Something has got to be done about Vanderbilt. In effect, the situation is that the Chancellor and his small circle of advisers (Glenn, Mims, Reinke, Sarratt)[d] have created an organization that is becoming unmanageable from sheer size and utter lack of policy. The faculty is weaker than ever: constantly we have new infiltrations of Northern and Mid-western Ph.D. non-entities. But the medical school seems to flourish. Dr. Fleming,[e] you know, is out of the running—a terrible loss—he is almost a complete invalid.

Nashville is smoky as ever, but autumn in Tennessee is still wonderful. My wife, Mary, and I spent almost the entire Sunday at Glendale, reading and studying quietly in the open air and looking at trees and animals. There was a small Fugitive meeting last night, and things go on but the years go by, too,—and you must come on and freshen us up.

I hope very much that this finds you and your family in good health and as happy as devoted Southerners can be in Europe. Keep away from the "flu."

Faithfully, Don

139 a. *Bedford Forrest and His Critter Company* (1931). b. Claude Bowers, *The Tragic Era.* c. Dean of the Vanderbilt Law School. d. All members of the Vanderbilt faculty. e. Walter L. Fleming.

Post Scripta:

(1) Such books as Borsodi's *This Ugly Civilization* & Jas. Truslow Adams' *Our Business Civilization* indicate a drift of opinion that is very much in our favor. I'm reading these now, & commend them to you.

(2) We might seriously consider doing the "Symposium" between us—you, Ransom, possibly Red Warren & Lytle, possibly S. Young. Maybe you and Ransom & I could do it. There is nothing to keep us from plunging into economics & politics as we have already plunged into religion & history. If we, by ourselves, published such a book, we would then be able to find our real friends. They would surely make themselves known. And it is our great weakness now not to know *who* is on our side.

140/TLS

Paris
9 November 1929

Dear Don:

Your note enclosing Owsley's review came in the same mail with your fine long letter of October 26th. They catch me at a bad time for correspondence: I have just got up from the flu, I am undergoing a course of treatment for my nose and throat, and I am on a diet. The easy life in France has not offset the effects of the vicious climate. I was riding for a fall anyhow; too much work and hard living in the past five years had prepared me for it. I can only be thankful that it did not come when I was living on my own money.

I will answer your note first, because it contained the letter you wrote me in August. The six points you outline there meet with my entire approval. The first two—the symposium and the possible use of your Book Page as an organ—are the only ones that do not require money. Big money is needed for a magazine, for "ways of getting in touch with young people," for "ways of influencing newspapers and magazines," and for "getting down to the practical plane." It costs nothing but room and board to think; a good deal more to act.

I will not go into detail this time on matters of policy. It seems to me that the two great things we must have are these: Money and an issue to the people. The two things are closely united. To make a popular issue effective money is required; and no matter how appealing the issue may be, money will give it power. Where will it come from? The two or three friends who are well off are not well enough off to support such an undertaking. . . . Andrew informs me that he wishes to buy a county newspaper: who will edit it? I doubt if Andrew could do it. He is *too* able. It would be pretty feeble too without other kinds of support. But the idea is right: it would begin from the ground up.

As to the symposium. I am stumped to find any contributors. . . . Why won't Owsley write an essay in politics and economy? We should probably have to rewrite it to make it readable, but that makes small difference. He evidently knows a lot about it: I suppose it all depends on his conception of his job as a historian. I didn't mean to vote against Stark Young. I was only not certain that you were aware of a sentimental leaning in his writing. As soon as I get to New York I will talk to him. He is sensitive, but the problem is to make him see that a certain amount of abstraction is necessary to connect up his feelings with a large program of ideas. He is an intelligent and highly cultivated fellow, and we mustn't lose him.

I heard from Lyle Lanier the other day. Do you ever talk to him? He said some things that indicated that he is moving in our direction, and though I don't know what he could be used for, he might do something. Strangely enough, he said precisely the same things about the University as you say. That it is going to hell.

I have the man to write on religion. He is a Rhodes Scholar from Texas—Dixon Wecter, a very good friend to both Red and me. He is about the most learned man I ever saw—though he is only 24—and he understands and shares our views on all points. I recommend him without reservation. He is one friend discovered among divers enemies.

We are perfectly at liberty to plunge into politics, religion, literature, history. Departmental learning is by no means a product of the scholars; it is part of a larger movement towards the repudiation of responsibility. Scholars are no longer compelled to think about anything; they merely keep scholarship going without knowing why; so the politician with the state. If we are mere researchers, say, in literature, we don't care what the researcher in history does. But the same values are involved in all kinds of intellectual work, and part of our job is to show the relations of value.

There is one feature of our movement that calls for comment. We are not in the least divided, but we exhibit two sorts of minds. You and Andrew seem to constitute one sort—the belief in the eventual success, in the practical sense, of the movement. The other mind is that of Ransom and Warren and myself. I gather that Ransom agrees with me that the issue on the plane of action is uncertain. At least I am wholly sceptical on that point; but the scepticism is one of hoping to be convinced, not by standing aside to watch the spectacle, but by exerting myself. In other words, I believe that there is enough value to satisfy me in the affirmation, in all its consequences, including action, of value. If other goods proceed from that, all the better. My position is that since I see the value, I am morally obligated to affirm it. That sounds pretty grand, but I can think of no other phrase. . . .

Your column about Bowers, Schlesinger, and the others is very good indeed. Keep it up.

I must close now. This is a scattered letter because my wits are still a little scattered from the flu. I will do better next time. I hope you can come up to New York in the next six months. It isn't likely that I shall be able to come down there for some time: it is a matter of money. Balch is making a failure out of a book that should sell very well. My biography business has to date left me with a deficit of about $400.00. I mean I've made less than I spent in writing the books. I'm just where I was before. So it goes.

Best regards and wishes to you all. Write very soon.

Allen

141/TLS

Paris
11 December 1929

Dear Don:

Yours of Nov. 26th this moment arrived. I can't answer it in full, as I am finishing up several articles and reviews: we are sailing on the George Washington, Dec. 28th, and unless the boat sinks, as seems likely from the recent storms, we will land on Jan. 5th.

As to details you bring up: Dixon Wecter is a Catholic, but also a philosopher, with a philosophic view of religion very much resembling our view. In fact, I have discussed the whole issue with him, and feel sure he is on the right track. In the end of course, we don't have to print his essay if we don't like it: it must not contain a special plea. This is your point and mine.

Ransom's man Nixon[a] sounds good—a student of agrarianism. Or is it Dozier[b] who is Ransom's man? I don't know anything about these people. As to Stringfellow Barr,[c] he is just our man; I can't imagine why I didn't think of him. He is, in the first place, a historian, and in the second an extremely good writer; and in the third he is absolutely on our side. I have seen a good many essays and reviews by him recently, and they all bear this out. Why not get him to write on the educational matter, not merely reminiscently, but to propose some *practical* end from our general point of view.

The other day I received a long letter from Lyle Lanier about our discussion. He is with us to the limit. (Observe how a little activity brings out support.) Now, he is one of our most valuable men: he is a technically trained scientist who intends to acquire more scientific technique, largely to philosophical ends—i.e., in order to criticize the abuses of science. He made a most interesting point: he argues that industrial society, being a product of the mind running on one of its functions, is a close parallel to "dissociation" in the individual. His remedy of course is ours—to restore the latent and suppressed values of the South. We *must* get him to contribute an essay to the Symposium along that line. The effect of a scientist pointing out the abuses of applied science would have a much greater tactical effect than what we say from the outside. Besides, Lyle has an extremely efficient and canny intelligence; he will know where to argue his points. I don't know anything about Mitchell and Anderson.[d] I am suspicious of Johnson[e]—not of his character but of his head, which is not of the best quality. He writes adequately enough.

People like Owsley, who may not enter the immediate arena, have an immense value; we need more of them. . . .

Best regards from us all, Allen

141   *a.* Clarence Nixon, until 1928 in the Vanderbilt history department.   *b.* Howard Douglas Dozier, professor of economics at Dartmouth College and author of *A History of the Atlantic Coastline Railroad* (1920).   *c.* Although Stringfellow Barr was considered as a contributor to the symposium, he and Howard Mumford Jones became outspoken critics of its principles. Barr debated Ransom in Richmond on a program chaired by Sherwood Anderson and attended by 3500 people.   *d.* Broadus Mitchell, political economist on the faculty of Johns Hopkins and author of the *Rise of the Cotton Mills in the South* (1921). Sherwood Anderson at this time was the editor of two Marion, Virginia, newspapers.   *e.* Gerald W. Johnson.

142/TLS

Paris
12 December 1929

Dear Don:

When I wrote to you yesterday, I hadn't had time to read the issue of your Page that you so thoughtfully sent me.

Your discussion of the Southern issue around such people as Young and myself as against Stribling is very good indeed. It is more than merely good, it is downright daring. The few issues of the Page that I have seen in the last year or so have all contained very pertinent discussions of the two general divisions of Southern writers. There is certainly place for a revaluation by you of our leading novelists, particularly those who have great reputations in New York—Ellen Glasgow, for example. I am of the opinion that she writes an abominable prose style, and that she is one of the worst novelists in the world; it is about time that we repudiated people like her and Cabell. These two writers are fine examples of running with the hare and hunting with the hounds. Miss Glasgow has everything that I have learned to detest in the transformation of the Virginian character—the feeble and offensive assumption of past superiority along with casting a vote for Hoover: she exhibits the "aristocratic" manners of the South and shows how ridiculous they are: she is an incredible old snob who would not receive in her house a "man of the people" (as she would put it) and yet she wrote a novel proving the sterling worth of a man born in a circus tent, the whole atmosphere of the novel being that of sniffing and calculating condescension. The people like Miss Glasgow and Cabell convince outsiders that all Southerners are snobs and pretenders, wherefore their books sell by the hundred thousand. Our job is to point out that Mr. Cabell and Miss Glasgow simply happen to be two snobs who took to writing—there being in any society a few snobs if you look hard enough. The Isabel Patersons[a] get their version of the South from Cabell and Glasgow; so when Stark Young gives a different version, i.e., one in which the characters are not snobs, he is made out to be one himself. I am enclosing a carbon of a long review and a somewhat general discussion at the same time, of Cabell's new novel;[b] the review will come out in the N.R., but I wanted to be sure you saw it, as it falls right into line with your discussions. This much can be said for the N.R. They are bewildered, but thoroughly honest and without a special plea on the issues that concern us. It is my hope (confidentially) to capture the New Republic to a certain extent for our views. Young's position on the staff is a great help in that direction.

An incidental point in your discussion brings up an issue that I'd like to get your views of. There is a particular way in which we can overstate our case and do it harm where we might as well do it good. Take Hemingway, for example. You speak of his writing as "scientific ministration." Please, for my sake and for the sake of English prose, look at Hemingway again. I hereby accuse you of taking a thesis to Hemingway and coming away with it proved. There is nothing scientific about Hemingway. And if you think he is a realist, then realism must be redefined. He is unquestionably one of the great stylists of English prose, and it is not his fault if a horde of damn fools have taken him up: in reading Hemingway it is hard to get rid of the nonsense that has been written about him, and see his work in itself. All of which leads to this: we must not get so lost in our vision of what novelists should do to the Southern scene that we reject the version of "reality" given us by writers who are not Southern. In short, to do that is to commit provincialism at its least attractive level. In short, again, we cannot afford to commit the converse of the Stribling[c] fallacy: when we look at literature we have got first to decide that it is literature, or that it is not, and make our thesis secondary. We cannot afford to admire only those writers who explicitly support our thesis. Now, as a matter of fact, if you look closely enough, Hemingway really supports it: in other words he is a Yankee writer whom we would do well to capture. You must remember that Hemingway's characters come to him through observation, and that his sole scene of observation for ten years has been, due to certain accidents, which he did not choose, the European milieu of mixed Europeans and Americans. Whether or not you like the kind of people he has had to observe, the very fact that he sticks to concrete experience, to a sense of the *pure present*, is of immense significance for us. Hemingway, in fact, has that sense of a stable world, of a total sufficiency of character, which we miss in modern life. He is one of the most irreconcilable reactionaries I have ever met; he hates everything that we hate, although of course he has no historical scene to fall back on; and, amusingly enough, he told me recently that when the South lost the Civil War it was a great calamity for all men, for it made the ordinary pleasures of life cost money! The man has an astonishing, if untutored, insight into all these things. Now the point I am after is this: if Hemingway were a Southerner he would be just the novelist we are looking for—he would present us without any thesis at all. In other words, the ideal Southern novelist is the ideal novelist anywhere—I don't mean that Hemingway is the ideal novelist, only that he is nigh perfect in his own job—and ultimately there is no difference, for literature, between one thesis and another, in the sociological sense. That is the trouble with Cabell and Glasgow—a sociological thesis underlies their work. Our true Southern novelist at present is Elizabeth Roberts, who does not write as a Southerner or as anything else. I agree, therefore, with your position as I see it, only in so far as our thesis is as good for literature as that of the opposition. I agree with it wholly in so far as it is better for society, for the kind of society that we want. I don't think we can afford to give the opposition the slightest chance to say that we aren't as disinterested as to literature as any critics can possibly be. Shouldn't we keep the two things distinct? Otherwise logic brings us back to Thomas Nelson Page.

I've had this on my chest for some time: it seems to me that we should watch out for this point in the Symposium, for if we don't the enemy will beat us over the heads with it in his counter attack.

Caetera desunt.[d] More later. Hail without farewell.

Allen

Isn't the point about Cabell and Glasgow this: that *because* they have a mixed thesis—i.e., mixed of old Southism and Progress—*because* their intelligences are split into contradictory values, they are bad novelists. This would be *literary* criticism using the social material to explain the literary deficiency. That is to say, we must attack them first as artists, and then show that their social attitude, because it is muddled, distracts the creative mind into mere propaganda and ruins the work of art. This could almost be made into a principle—that all great, or really good writers, must have a simple homogeneous sense of values, which incidentally are the kind of values we wish to restore.

142   *a.* Writer of the column "Turns with a Bookworm" in the *New York Herald-Tribune.*   *b. The Way of Ecben;* reviewed in *New Republic* (January 8, 1930). *c.* T. S. Stribling.   *d.* "The rest is wanting."

143/TLS

Nashville, Tenn.
29 December 1929

Dear Allen:

This will be an All Hail and Welcome letter to greet you on arrival, and to answer in all haste your two letters that have just reached me—the one announcing your imminent return, the other about Glasgow, Cabell, etc.

You could hardly imagine how overjoyed I am that you are back. Good God, what a relief it will be to have you near at hand again and not to have to write across the water, with time all against one as well as space. Furthermore, the pot is a-bilin'. You are arriving just at the crucial moment and can do the pushing and shaping that has gone a little slowly and lamely with you in France. I see my metaphors have got mixed, but lay that to enthusiasm.

Ransom, Lytle, and I have been having a series of earnest conferences in the past two weeks, and we have decided to push things to a rapid conclusion, if you will help us as I know you will. It seems, with matters as they now stand, that we should be able to have the articles all written and ready by early spring—say April at the latest—and, if we then submit the book to a publisher and place it, we ought to get it out by next fall. The time is ripe. We mustn't wait too long, even if the book doesn't have the full-rounded perfection we should desire.

The lay-out is about as it was, with the addition of Nixon. I enclose two letters from him (please return them) that indicate, surely, that he is our man—even if he may need a little coaching. He has not yet been definitely solicited. I am to describe the project to him this week, when he returns from the historical convention at Durham; and I shall sound him out thoroughly before a final committance; it need not be final, anyhow, as, in the case of your man Wecter, we don't need to take his article if it isn't what we want. I shall also write Stringfellow Barr a "feeler" this week. He might possibly have been solicited for H. M. Jones's book; but that should make no difference. We still need to find a man for politics, though I don't consider that an absolute essential, as politics is involved, and can be implied or explicitly defined, in our various articles.

I think you should see Stark Young as soon as possible. I am not sure, though I have corresponded with him considerably, that he thoroughly understands what we are up to. Can you take the job of explaining matters to him more fully than I have, in my hurry, as yet been able to do?

To the end of clarifying "objectives" (great word!) Ransom, Lytle, and I are working on a sort of Credo or Manifesto, which will serve to acquaint contributors with our aims and to furnish a definite line for articles to follow. We'll send this to you as soon as it is ready in its tentative form, and you, no doubt, will either want to compose one of your own for comparative study or to make amendments and suggestions in extenso, or both. This Credo, in its final form, can be used as a foreword to the volume; and I have suggested that we also have a final summary, at the end of the book, in which the various articles are reviewed and applied to the general purpose—this will be a wonderful help to future reviewers, of course!

The discussions with Ransom and Lytle have given the book (in our minds, at least) a slightly different turn, but I think that it will harmonize, rather than otherwise, with what you have probably been thinking. What you say about Hemingway and our critical attitude towards literature, leads me to guess that you may have had some of the same thoughts we have had.

Our movement (if it can be called that) more and more takes a broad range. In recent talks we have got the idea that perhaps we ought not to limit our consideration to the South, as sectionalists endeavoring to reconstruct our home section and therefore addressing ourselves mainly to the South. Perhaps we ought to leave the gate open for an appeal to any of the parts of the country that may be suffering from the invasion of the metropolitan, industrial, business mind and that may be restive under the yoke of progress. Perhaps our program develops into a program of provincialism in general, not only Southern provincialism, and with it all the values (to be defined and announced) that belong to a country life, decentralized, stable, local, self-sufficient, etc., as opposed to the other thing now rampant but already attacked from various quarters. In that view, the South would be the most obvious historical and contemporary example available, and the most exciting example; but we would thus be able to make it clear that we are not proposing simply a romantic recession, but a straightforward set of doctrines for the day, opening a fertile field of general interest anywhere, but especially to Southerners, our immediate concern. It would amount to this: that we would go beyond the scientific meliorists (the New Repub. thinkers belong to this group, don't they?), beyond the humanists, who after all are vague, and entirely away from the Mencken-Lewis trend (I should say theirs is a criticism of manners only), and diametrically opposite to the socialistic radicals (who have a megalopolitan proposition to urge), and we should offer a doctrine full of rich particularity and immense appeal. Turn this over in your mind. It will come up in clearer form in the Credo.

I see from your letters that you didn't receive my hasty scribble about Howard Mumford Jones's solicitation of me for his symposium, now definitely under way. I enclose the letter I wrote him, and again ask for your advice. The main question to settle is: will I do the cause good by appearing in two places, or not? And second, can I write two pieces on Southern literature, both different? I think I can do two different things, especially as Jones wants a "report" rather than a program. But I want to do nothing to injure our own case in any way. Hurry up your reply on this as much as you can, for I must give Jones a final answer. His lay-out of contributors, as given to me, now includes Broadus Mitchell on Industry, Knight on education, Lathan on politics, W. W. Alexander on the white view of the negro, Moton of Tuskegee on the negro view of the negro, Archer Bass on religion. About as I suspected; it will be mainly a progressive line-up.

Returning to your letter,—behind my phrase "scientific ministration," as applied to Hemingway, lies the story of a review I wrote of his book,[a] which I will send you if I can find it. In this I discussed his book very harshly, I fear, as a misguided application of science (in this case, it seemed to be behavioristic psychology) to literature. Perhaps I was wrong, and if so, I'll be glad to be proved in error, for I never really made up my mind about his book. I said to myself that I might just as easily have written a thoroughly favorable review, following another line of discussion. And I must confess that I extended myself at Hemingway's expense partly for a local purpose. I am simply compelled to do something strenuous in order to get the public ear. I can't go along mildly in a sweet Harry Hansen[b] manner. And one of the best ways to get people to listen is to devote all possible power to a surprising angle (not otherwhere discussed) of the work of an author much in the public eye. I am afraid that I sacrificed Hemingway (to some extent) in order to make a point against science. But I should add that I did this the more readily because I felt that he was exposed to criticism, at least to debate, on this particular point. I certainly respect him, and I'm glad to have your opinion of him to take to heart. And with what you say about literary judgments in general, as not to be made from a sectional basis, but on the higher level, I'm in perfect agreement. I've felt for quite a while that I was in danger of losing balance and becoming merely a cantankerous localist, and your admonishment warms my conscience to its task.

I won't have time to discuss your Cabell review at length. It is one of the best reviews you've written. You say what I think, exactly, though I wouldn't have hit on the very precise and applicable terms you have used. But why has nobody seen this? Simply because Cabell has not been approached with the point of view that throws him in a proper light—five years ago your point of view would have been simply literary, wouldn't it? What a difference it makes to see him in a total perspective. Here, I should say, sectionalism has been decidedly to your advantage. Edmund Wilson, for example, could never have made such an approach. I think it very important that Cabell should be handled just as you have handled him. You've given me much food for thought, —of which more later. This helps me in a book I'm thinking of—informal probably—essays on Southern writers of the last ten years.

I hope when this reaches you, it will find a happy traveler completing a happy voyage. Now you know more or less how I felt when I came back, under different conditions, in 1919! Write me as soon as possible. Your letters have made great good cheer! And in the very near future, somehow, somewhere, we must get together. Nothing will fix things up like several good talks—and besides there are the old reasons of friendship, more important than all. *Regards to your wife and daughter.*

Faithfully, Don

143   a. This review appeared in the *Tennessean* (November 3, 1929). b. Former literary editor of the *Chicago Daily News,* at this time Hansen was writing "The First Reader" column in the *New York World.*

144/TLS

Nashville, **Tenn.**
21 July 1930

Dear Allen:

I was relieved to get your note and shall look forward buoyantly to the arrival of your essay tomorrow morning (Tuesday). The word from you lifted me somewhat out of the slough of depression I have been laboring in for the past week or ten days—what with the heat, with grubbing in libraries after biographical data, and this and that worry. I know you must have had a struggle; I'm sure I could never have finished up a weighty essay in temperatures that run to 100 degrees and above. I have thought about you and your labors almost constantly but did not want to bother you with inquiries.

Harper's Southern agent, young Mr. Rose, an intelligent and likable man, passed through here last week. Owsley, Lanier, Alice Stockell, Mrs. D. and I met with him at my apt., and we talked matters over at considerable length. He showed us a dummy of the book, and we were all very greatly impressed with the looks of it. It is quite dignified and attractive. I think that Lanier and Owsley were very much inclined to withdraw and put to rest any qualms they may have had about the title, after seeing how it "sets up." And I should feel pretty well satisfied to let 'er go as she stands, if others are. The Harper people, it seems, are quite taken with the present title: and Miss Stockell, as bookseller, thinks it would be fatal to change. The Harper people have got it in their catalogue, and are taking orders now: so it seems that unless we can propose something mighty good,—definitely better and more advisable in every way—and propose it quickly, there will not be much reason for revising the title and not much chance to do so unless somebody gets busy and pushes matters. With Saxton in Europe, and the book being set (dated for Oct. 15), and in view of the difficulty (already experienced) of getting agreement among our group of essayists on such matters as titles, I am inclined to say: let's go on, as we are. But I'm ready, also, to chime in with any better plan than can be put through, even at this late date. I don't think any of us will regret the present title, in the end. There is certainly as much to say for it as against it, and to see it in print, especially with the present subtitle, makes it look quite different.

I'm sending you herewith—as I should have done before this—Red's essay. Will you read it and give your frank opinion of it? At first, after reading it hastily, I had thought it would be quite all right, though not a very strong essay. Since reading it this morning again, very carefully, and after having gone through Lanier's and Lytle's fine pieces, I was rather shocked with Red's essay. It hardly seems worthy of Red, or worthy of the subject. And it certainly is not very closely related to the main theme of our book. It goes off at a tangent to discuss the negro problem in general (which, I take it, is not our main concern in the book), and it makes only two or three points that bear on our principles at all. Furthermore, the ideas advanced about the negro don't seem to chime with our ideas as I understand them. Behind the essay, too, are implications which I am sure we don't accept—they are "progressive" implications, with a pretty strong smack of latter-day sociology. Furthermore, I think there are some things that would irritate and dismay the very Southern people to whom we are appealing. (Have made certain changes in Red's wording here and there.)

I simply can't understand what Red is after here. It doesn't sound like Red at all—at least not the Red Warren I know. The very language, the catchwords, somehow don't fit. I am almost inclined to doubt whether RED ACTUALLY WROTE THIS ESSAY! . . .

Whatever has happened, I have begun to be quite doubtful in my mind whether this essay, dealing as it does with a matter of such grave importance, ought to go into the book. If Red were here, we could talk to him, draw him out, get him to make changes and enlargements, perhaps. Since he isn't here, we'll simply have to face up to editorial responsibility. True, we invited him to come in and ought to consider that we are in a sense bound to take what he writes. But Red being quite inaccessible and time being short, ought we, nevertheless, to publish an essay which is far from being closely tied up with the project and which might actually hurt us with the public.

Owsley has read the essay, and thinks about as I do. Will you read it and return it, with your opinion, by Friday? Ransom will be back then, and we can thus obtain a fair consensus of opinion. I'll get Lyle to look at it, too. (Andy has not seen it: I think he would blow up if he should read it.)

I'll send in your essay at once, with Lanier's and Lytle's that are now in hand, and we'll hold Red's till the last.

Thanks for sending me the proof from Louis U. I read it with great interest, though with hardly so much excitement as I would have experienced five or six years ago. It is interesting to see that Louis still stands strongly by the Fugitives and, in special, has come around strongly to you and others. Time works wonders. What a difference a few years make.

I wish I could see you! I wish you were here in Nashville (despite the God-awful heat). I wish that you and John would just take over all this stuff I've been attempting so lamely to do and let me collapse and that the Lord's business could be attended to far better than I have attended to it.

Regards of the heartiest to Carolyn. Hope you are standing the heat.

Faithfully, Don

145/ANS

Clarksville, Tenn.
3 September 1930

Dear Don:

Don't faint! Just read the enclosed letter. Red and I are holding the original until we hear from you, John, and Lyle.

What we want to get you all to do is to take a vote. Andrew votes with us, making three in favor of sending the letter to Saxton.[a] If you three vote nay, it is a tie, and I don't know what to suggest, unless Owsley is around to make a seventh vote.

The point is, that we need a categorical answer by return mail. You will see that I am doubtful if there is enough time; but we can leave that to Saxton.

On the way up here, we were suddenly seized by the horror of I'll Take My Stand, and rushed to the typewriter. Like most horrors we don't think about it all the time; it just comes over us occasionally!

We had a fine time—come up here as soon as you can.

Yrs. ever, Allen

145   *a.* A copy of the letter to Eugene F. Saxton, a Harpers editor, is in the Joint University Library; for other letters on the subject see Appendix B.

146/TLS

Nashville, Tenn.
5 September 1930

Dear Allen:

I would like for you to consider this letter as private and personal. But the enclosed signed statement, which is the expression of Ransom's and my views on the question you raise, is of course for any of the group who may be concerned. We could not locate either Lanier or Owsley, by the way.

You urged me—I take it, quite humorously and a little teasingly—not to faint on reading the proposed letter to Saxton. You must surely have anticipated, then, the astonishment that I naturally felt. I was quite taken aback; and so was Ransom.

I must beseech you, good friend Allen, for God's sake to stick your head under the pump; or take calomel and castor oil and go to bed to ponder on your immortal soul; or do something else to revive your practical sense, which seems to be getting clogged up with foreign vapors.

It is just about six weeks until the book is scheduled to appear, and there is some excitement already in the air. George Fort Milton, in the Chattanooga News, just wrote an editorial on our book—a leader, a column and a half long; and you may be sure this editorial, with T. H. Alexander's widely distributed comment, will be extensively noted. Yet at this moment, you three stalwarts suddenly get the horrors and again propose drastic measures about the title.

This is like stopping to polish your shoes in the midst of a headlong charge, just before you reach the enemy's breastworks; or like pausing to argue about the wording of the motto on the flag—"Are we right sure, Soldiers and Comrades, that it should be 'Sic semper tyrannis?' Would not 'Lux et veritas' better describe our dignified array?"

I do not understand how you can help seeing that fastidiousness is nothing short of fatal, at such a time.

We had discussed this whole matter before, and I had gained the impression that you were reconciled, or if not reconciled, you at least were conscious of the difficulties of opening a matter which was at the very least a debatable one.

Another point. You and John and I signed the contract for this book. We are the responsible parties. John and I feel that you are taking our responsibilities a little lightly. We are unwilling to see the matter go to a vote, because it is not the title that is being decided but, in substance, the question of whether or not the book will appear at the time scheduled—which happens to be a singularly propitious time. You spoke of having the horrors. Well, after sweating over this book for the past six months, I am exposed to nothing short of delirium tremens when faced with the prospect of a democratic majority coolly voting, at the last moment, to argue with the publisher about a change of title—as if that were quite easily done. Good lord, have ye no bowels? And Red and Andy, with those ballots of theirs so gaily cast,—are they whetting their beaks on the old man's gizzard, clack-clack? Do *they* propose to sign that letter? Or are you going to do it, yourself?

Faithfully, Don

147/TLS

Clarksville, Tenn.
7 September 1930

Dear Don:

You will get this with our Official Reply, but it is written twenty-four hours later, and the smoke of battle has cleared away.

I was very much astonished at the high seriousness of your reply. We didn't take the matter half so seriously, and we were amazed that you all should enlist the cosmos behind you, making the proposed letter to the publisher an affair of good and evil, honor and dishonor. It was, of course, nothing of the sort, and I am afraid, my dear Don, that in your anxiety you all put the issue in a category where it didn't belong, and punched us most grievously below the belt.

I say we didn't take it seriously, but of course we did—only in another way. Your Official Letter brought up a very good point—that as historians we know that movements have failed because their groups couldn't work together. It is obvious, of course, that we haven't worked together, and it is also obvious that my protests, and Red's too, have been efforts to work together. For the title was never submitted to a formal vote, and the two attempts that I have made to get the group to work together on the title have been blocked.

It seems that you and John have been the defenders of the title, Red and I the opponents. Your position was not backed by a formal decision of the group, or by a quorum of the group, and in the face of this, since we stood two against two, we felt that it was our privilege to test your position in the hope that we might vindicate our own. In either case, we should have been eager to stand by the results of the vote. . . .

There is no personal issue involved here whatever. It is simply a situation arising from the practical exigencies of action, and it has nothing at all to do with the friendly relations of the group. To assume that we can't face an issue of this kind on the ground of personal friendship is a perfectly suicidal position. I hold no such position.

It is over now. Your title triumphs. And I observe that Alexander today on the basis of the title defines our aims as an "agrarian revival," and reduces our real aims to nonsense. These are, of course, an agrarian revival in the full sense, but by not making our appeal through the title to ideas, we are at the mercy of all the Alexanders—for they need only to draw portraits of us plowing or cleaning a spring to make hash of us before we get a hearing.

My melancholy is profound.

Yours ever, Allen

III

From *I'll Take My Stand* to the End
of the Agrarian Movement: 1931-1942

The publication of I'll Take My Stand *seems to have been felt by the chief members of the Fugitive group as only the beginning of their Agrarian phase. In one sense it was. Though they were unable to establish a magazine of their own—which was a part of the Agrarian plan—they were able to utilize the* American Review *as an organ for their views from 1933 to 1936. In 1935 the* Southern Review *began publication with Robert Penn Warren and Cleanth Brooks as associate editors, and many Agrarian articles, particularly those dealing with literary aspects of the movement, began to appear in its pages. In 1936 the second Agrarian symposium,* Who Owns America?, *was published. But in another sense* I'll Take My Stand *was the beginning of the end of the movement. Tate's letter of October 29, 1932, from Europe deplores Ransom's backsliding from "true agrarianism." In the same letter he says, "I came back to live in the South, and I've been let down." It was hoped that* Who Owns America? *itself would be a new beginning. When Davidson sends in his contribution to that volume, Tate writes him, "Agar says that you've laid down the program that we shall be working upon for the rest of our lives. And I agree with him." But as the correspondence will show, the volume becomes instead a cause for dissension and bickering; and the close personal contact which movements seem to require becomes less possible. In 1937 Ransom leaves Vanderbilt and goes to Kenyon, and thereafter he clearly indicates in his writing that his interests have changed. In 1938 Tate leaves Clarksville and goes to the Woman's College of North Carolina for a year and from there moves to Princeton University. Though Davidson and Tate*

always remained Agrarians in the broadest and best sense, it now seems clear that by 1942 Agrarianism as a fighting cause was dead. This section of the correspondence ends with a letter of that year which deals with the sending of "relics" to the Princeton library for a historical display of the Fugitive movement and, by implication, of the Agrarian movement also.

148/ALS

Nashville, Tenn.
14 January 1931

Dear Allen:

Thanks very much, Allen, for your note which so kindly expressed your sympathy in the matter of my father's illness. I greatly appreciate your writing me in this understanding way.

My father's condition and concurrent distressing problems of all sorts have very much upset me during the past few weeks. I have hardly been able to do or say or write anything intelligent. But I'm happy to say that things look much better now. My father is vastly improved, and we hope that he will be able to make a fairly good recovery, though it will be slow.

I haven't any other news, but have much to talk over with you when you come this way again—among other things a project of my own, long contemplated, that I am now planning to get under way.

You will want to see the new batches of clippings that are coming in, some of them much more favorable than the earlier reviews we had. And did you see Henry Hazlitt's outburst in the latest *Nation*—the leading review, about two columns, nearly all falsification and bitter attack. Now we can *know* we are right, having got such savage treatment at the hands of the most South-hating of all the magazines.

I salute you and hope your writing goes well.

Faithfully, Don

The debate at Chattanooga, John says, was well-attended, but instead of being a hot debate, it was only mildly warm, because Barr was not so pugnacious as at Richmond.[a] He is almost won over to our view,

John thinks,—at least he is inclined to be conciliatory. They had a grand time with Milton,[b] Barr, and Hesseltine[c] the next day—had long discussions, in which Andrew captured the crowd.

I was unable to go down.

148   a. Ransom debated Barr in Richmond on November 14, 1930, and in Chattanooga on January 9, 1931.   b. George Fort Milton, publisher of the *Chattanooga News*.   c. William B. Hesseltine, southern historian at the University of Wisconsin.

149/TLS

Nashville, Tenn.
14 April 1931

Dear Allen:

. . . John told you, I suppose, that I am to debate Knickerbocker in Columbia in May. The date is still to be finally fixed. I dislike to appear against Knickerbocker, because I don't think there's any debating with him. But I look on this as a chance to make a stand among our own folks. And so I expect to make a more or less local speech, hitting just as hard as I can, making as strong an emotional appeal as I can, because I believe that line—rather than the coolly logical one John took—is the right one for me. I shall hope to make it appear by implication that Knickerbocker is the academic person, and I shall talk about perfectly familiar and immediate things that folks can take to heart.

Finney[a] is very keen on the debate, and will push it in the Columbia Herald, which is already carrying the banner high. I shouldn't be at all surprised to see him burst into oratory himself—(he is going to introduce me, and an Episcopal clergyman will introduce Knickerbocker), and I shouldn't be surprised, either, to see him turn out a brass band, or something of the sort, and make a real hoorah. You are coming, I hope, to brandish a towel in the agrarian corner; but before that, give me all the advice you can think of. I will do my utmost to be worthy of the occasion, but my utmost certainly needs considerable reinforcement.

About the Southern literature—I have ditched the whole project. I came to this resolution after great travail of spirit. But with the prospect before me of having to teach full time, indefinitely, I don't see how I can commit myself to critical grubbing for two or three years. I would end up by being even more mentally exhausted than I am at present. I feel that if I can write something else first—something that is myself, and not just myself analyzing other persons in the thankless process of literary-historical-social criticism—I had better do it. Also, all my other projects have collapsed, it seems. My article on the book page business has been twice rejected already, and I'm just about to give up and send it to the Bookman in despair.[b] (Mencken wrote me a cheerful long letter, but turned it down.) Furthermore I find no welcomers for a book I had tentatively designed which would collate some of the best bits out of the old book page. And as for the contemporary Southern writers, I have dropped them too, along with the rest. I believe the time is bad for a book on the subject. A little more water needs to run over the dam, first. Besides, I dislike, more and more, the awkward positions one gets into by being honest and blunt with one's contemporaries. I am not cut out for a critic, anyway. I feel so down-in-the-mouth myself that I am beginning to shrink from the inevitable butchering that has to enter into a piece of criticism, especially when one is to take up the "new" Southern writers. I am satisfied to let the whole thing soak awhile.

You will perceive that I am at a pretty low ebb. I am, and I don't know what to do about it. Somewhere along the line I have had my fighting spirit and vitality knocked out of me. I have not told anybody else what my state of feeling is, but I am telling you because I think you will understand.

However, though I seem to feel myself slipping—slipping—slipping—I'm still clawing a bit, and trying to get toeholds here and there. I have returned to the old project of tinkering with Tennessee history and traditions, and am daily reading and thinking in the field. This, too, may turn out to be nothing, but I somehow feel that the right word hasn't been said yet—though I am shocked and intimidated by the number of enormous books already published. Also, I have been reading the Odyssey, and contemplating the astounding episode of the return of Odysseus, who went first to the home of Eumaeus the swineherd, a trusty man, and then with the help of the gods slew the suitors, not neglecting also to slay the housemaids who lay with those riotous men. That was a good king! I recommend him to you, in Palmer's translation, as a real comfort to one's sore spirit.

Mr. Frank is trying to get up a Fugitive meeting for Saturday night. Are you coming? I shall probably have to go to it late, after the Old

Oak Club meeting. It is now getting on to ten years since we began that old adventure.

I do hope I can see you soon.

Faithfully, Don

149   a. Editor of the Columbia *Daily Herald*, sponsor of the debate.   b. "Criticism Outside New York" was published in *Bookman* (May 1931).

150/TLS

Nashville, Tenn.
11 May 1931

Dear Allen:

I like the poems you sent me very much. They stir me with very grave and deep emotions. This is the kind of poetry I should like to write, myself, if I could get back to poetry, for the things you write about are on my mind, all the time. I don't think much about other things—only the things that are all bound up with this whole deep thread of life and experience.

May I keep the poems a little, to show them to John, and to study them a little more? I'll then return them, with comments, as of old.

I like to see you writing in this somewhat more declarative style. It's directer, simpler, and I think more powerful than your earlier vein.

I saw, read, and admired greatly your N.R. review of Millay.[a]

I am hard at work on my speech against Knickerbocker, just about in act of reaching my peroration, in which I propose to emphasize the historic politics of the South. Mine is a more "political'" speech than John's.

Faithfully, Donald Davidson

150.   a. "Fatal Interview," *New Republic* (May 6, 1931).

151/ALS

Bread Loaf, Vt.[a]
29 July 1931

Dear Allen:

For four or five days (ever since getting your fine sonnets, in fact) I have been pushing myself toward this pen and paper; but it's a slow process to get around to letter-writing again. Take it as a compliment, young man, that I'm writing to you the first *considerable* letter (barring one to my sister) that I've written since coming to Bread Loaf. To keep up with my course in the Romantic poets I have to do some hours of reading every day (it's not irksome, it's something I've always wanted to do), and then, for the rest of the time, I just get lazy and stay lazy. I eat (too much), walk, talk, play tennis, swim, and sleep. Somehow it has been hard to turn a hand to letters.

I admire and like your "Sonnets of the Blood" [b]—better than anything else of yours I've seen in these latter days, though in the batch of poems you read to Ransom & me, and which I never got to study closely, there may or may not be better poems, as I said of the two or three short poems you sent me not long ago. I like most of all the turn your style has taken in the direction of a more forthright diction, less complication of metaphor, less of hiatus; and in turning this way you seem to me to be coming back to a real self which was long obscured by your experiments in one direction or another and by your New York & European excursions. The newer verse is quiet, & not always so exciting verbally as the earlier; but it gains in strength by being less daring and wasteful of poetic energy.

I am fumbling for words, am a little out of breath indeed,—it has been so long since I tried to frame a critical impression of a brother-Fugitive's verses, after our old fashion—but you will understand that I emphatically applaud your sonnet group! And how I do envy you that you can still turn to poetry, again and again, and let all your feelings out; while I remain stopped-up, raging speechlessly when I should be raging in verse.

I gather that these sonnets tie up somehow with the genealogical matter you showed me some weeks ago. There are personal and perhaps mystical issues involved that are a little obscure to me after two or three readings. But I think I share the feelings that animate you in these sonnets and follow the general line of thought fairly well. I think you ought to try to correct any unnecessary obscurities and perhaps tone up the rhetoric just a little here and there—I'd like to see the lines have a little more of the declamatory ring which comes in very nobly in the best of the sonnets.

In general, as to the subject and its possibilities, I am again struck by the comparison between the modern poet's predicament & that of the 19th Century Romantics. Here, I have just finished Shelley, who had fine doctrines that he took occasion to set forth; but he was always driven, at last, to thinking about himself and to writing about himself.

SONNETS OF THE BLOOD

I

What is this flesh and blood compounded of
But water and salt, potash and quick-lime?
That prowling strife of cells that men call love
Is the long claw of flesh-devouring time:
We who have seen the makers of our bone
Confused a little while, then make more dust,
Easy forever with, over their dust, a stone, --
We know the chastened look of men who must
Confess the canker gnawing the fresh flower
And are made brothers by mortality:
Lest we think sin's cleaved by the murderous hour,
To think of us brothers, that identity
Not made of salt and slime by time undone
Nor poured out quite when the life-blood has run.

This is one treason to the murderous hour —

A magnificent sonnet, but the "salt-lime" part (put that well) echoes in my mind of Masefield, or somebody. Could you change your terms?

Need this line be so rough?

IX

Not power of wealth nor even faith in God
Shall keep us whole in this dissevering air,
Which is a stench upon our pleasant sod
So foul the very buzzard sees it fair;
Therefore I ask you: Will it end tonight,
And the moth tense again the brittle flame?
Or spiders, eating their loves, cease the delight
Of self-devouring cruelty and shame?
This is the house of Atreus where we live;
Which one of us the Greek perplexed with crime
Questions the future that with a lucid sieve
Strains off the imponderable wrecks of time:
Do not, my brother, do not say it's so
If I am chosen, being less strong, to go.

ALLEN TATE.

Good

Obscure, & "brittle flame" is one of your old phrases remember you once told me not to parody myself & I feel somehow this isn't up to the other sonnets especially VII & VIII

But — in general — wonderful stuff. Your best, probably, since The Ode in The Confederate Dead!

Typescript of "Sonnets of the Blood," I and IX,
with Davidson's comments.

It was inevitable with him, and it is just as inevitable with us—the world being arranged as it is. But there's this difference in the South, or should be; we have a not altogether dislocated society to fall back on, we have family and friends—and Shelley was pitched out altogether, though perhaps as Santayana intimates, it was partly his fault—since revolutionary poets "always want to be more disinherited than they already are." Also, we've gone beyond Shelley's perfectionism, which has now been taken over, almost intact, with belated folly, by the vulgar humanitarian crowd—Rotarians, Scientists, Communist Messiahs; and we in the South don't expect, from experience, to win, anyhow—at least not completely. So there's every reason for us to talk to our brothers, who understand such matters. I hope this doesn't sound too muddled; it bears somehow on your poems. . . .

Perhaps I am a little of a curiosity among these folks, to whom the South is really *very* remote; and I may be all the more so because I'm unlike James Southall Wilson, who was here the last three years in the Southern niche of the faculty. But I'm having a *good* time. We all are—Theresa & Mary have gained in strength & spirits—even in weight, though all of us have been doing strenuous mountain climbing. All in all, I'll be quite content, I think, to accept the invitation to come back here another time—it's an ideal summer school, I should say.

I am doing no writing—can't get it in. But I won't hear to your letting-up on Lee; no matter what torture, you must do that book. I'm bound to have your biography of Lee. (Incidentally, H. Allen[c] told me he has designs on Lee, some time—Allen is the grandson of a Union Colonel, & from what he says can be counted on to give quite a strong Yankee treatment!)

I saw Wilson's piece on the Tennessee Agrarians.[d] It is—I take it —Wilson's way of being handsome toward people (especially you) whom he respects and likes but who have gone off on an "impossible" line. His piece is full of holes, of course. He leaves out economics and history (all but slavery) and politics and religion—he leaves out pretty well everything but a slightly revised picture of the old Southern mansion & the "younger sons." Also, he has a beautiful faith in engineers. All we can say in reply is, I suppose, "May the Lord have mercy on your soul!" and nominate him for the editorship of some such comic periodical as "Social Forces" or "The World Tomorrow." Wilson's view of the world—politico-economically—is that of well-bred Princeton plus a very ill-bred & swanky Y.M.C.A.-ism. In *this field* (not in his own field of criticism) he is first cousin to Sherwood Eddy and John R. Mott.[e]

That's all! Write and tell me all about Stark Young's visit, the local news, your own progress, Carolyn's, etc., etc. Also give me the low-down on Andrew's Monteagle project. I am supposed to lecture there on the Agrarian program, Aug. 28th.

We expect to be here until the 17th of August, or thereabouts, and should be back in Tennessee about the 22d or 23d.

Faithfully, Don

151   a. This is the first of thirty-odd summers that Davidson taught at Bread Loaf. b. First published in *Poetry* (November 1931). c. Hervey Allen. d. Edmund Wilson, "Tennessee Agrarians," *New Republic* (July 29 1931). e. Eddy was a publicist and crusader who later started a cooperative farm in Mississippi; Mott was president of the Institute of Social and Religious Research.

152/ALS

Bread Loaf, Vt.
6 August 1931

Dear Allen:

Things are getting congested here toward the end of the session, and so I won't have time to do more than scribble a note in answer to your letter, which put me in some excitement. I do hope you march right on with Lee;[a] there are most important things for you to say & you should proceed with utmost confidence. I rejoice in the news of your volume of poetry[b] and of Caroline's novel; I shall keep my appetite whetted for the grand treat of reading them in the coming months.

As to answering Wilson's piece, I would like to see it answered, but I have not much faith in the effectiveness of a reply in the N.R. itself. How I do wish we had a place to give them the really formidable public pounding they deserve.[c] In the wind-up of the session here, I am much too hurried to give proper thought to the composition of a reply, such as you suggest, and am not sure that we will gain anything by answering. However, if you and John feel the emergency justifies my writing a piece, I will do what I can to point out the misdeeds of the N.R. God knows I feel hot enough to write in the proper cold-heat! I wish that you, John, Red, & Andy had some other place to publish your poems, reviews, articles, etc., for the N.R., in its various

jocose references, has acted toward you all with the worst possible
manners. I detest their sneers & wisecracks; but I console myself by
remembering that nothing the N.R. has said or can say can have any
appreciable effect on the settlement of the issues we are interested in.
They might as well be writing from China, for all the bad or good
they do to the country at large. And I think that John is throwing his
economic articles away, if he succeeds in selling them to the N.R. He
might as well bury them; I have the most disrespectful views of the
influence, information, editorial acumen of the N.R. crowd, though I
will agree with you that they may be, in a blind way, honest in their
delusions. It is only in a literary way that I can keep my respect for
them. I say this after following the N.R. closely ever since 1920.

Enough of this tirade. I must study some Romanticism. We leave
here about Aug. 17, motoring back via Ohio, & expect to be in Nashville
about Aug. 24. See you all soon, then.

Faithfully, Don

152   *a.* Tate's proposed biography, which was never finished.   *b. Poems: 1928–
1931* (1932).   *c.* Later the Agrarians were able to give them some of this public
pounding in the *American Review* and the *Southern Review.*

153/ANS

[Clarksville, Tenn.]
15 January 1932

Dear Don:

In great haste—Aunt Harriet has asked me to edit a Southern number of *Poetry!* I have accepted. Besides the good general effect such a
number will have, it means that she has capitulated, and where she had
the S.C. group in '22, she must come to us or no one. Now, doggone it,
have you any poems? You've simply got to have some. Write that ballad
you and Caroline were talking about. And please give me suggestions.
Won't you make me a list of the people who ought to be represented?
Make it inclusive, with a question mark after doubtful ones. Of the
S.C. group I'm asking DuBose H. & J. P.[a] only. And give me any general
or particular advice you can think of.

Yrs. Allen

Is Conrad Aiken a Southern poet?

153   *a.* Dubose Heyward and Josephine Pinckney.

154/TLS

Nashville, Tenn.
21 January 1932

Dear Allen:

I hope this letter finds you in better health, flu conquered and biliousness dispersed. You didn't write, though, like a man with flu, but in spirits more ardent than I can ever muster in such spells. I wish I could get such vitality.

And I wish I had kept on writing poetry, as you have done. I am finding it very hard to get back to my lost poetic self (if ever indeed I had such a self; I am almost beginning to suspect what I had was an imitation). I have many "poetic thoughts," but somehow lack the particular magic that used to make them move around on the page. I have either lost the ritual, or it doesn't work any more.[a] I will have to get a new magic or discover the missing links in the older one. That means I don't know whether I will have a new poem or not. It will take time, unless a miracle happens, and you didn't tell me how much time I have.

Just to show you how bad a poet I am, I am sending crude copies of the only poems I have completed in the past few years. I think they won't do, but you can look at them and try to figure out what has happened to me.

I think your list of poets is better by far than the one I suggested, if you can only get the stuff from the poets named. You should by all means put in something of your own. The showing would be painfully incomplete otherwise.

I mentioned on my list several names that I know aren't first class; but you may be driven to solicit some of them, from paucity of material. I think Wade writes *good* verse, but of course he does only a little of it. As to Mr. Frank, I have no recommendation to make. I simply remember that a group of poems he read to some of us, a year or so ago, were really not bad. I will sound Wade out, if you wish, but Lord knows I won't undertake to raise any delicate problems with our friends, the Prophets. My feeling is about like yours as to Vestal and Virginia Moore.

I agree fully with your general discussion of Aunt Harriet's capitulation. It is just as you say.

I feel cheerful, but am in a sort of numb placidity. The concentrated indignation and turmoil of the past two years have apparently left me, for the time being at least, all washed out of any creative spirit.

I suppose one gets over such spells, but I certainly stand in need of prayer.

Faithfully, Don

154   *a.* During the next year Davidson wrote "Lee in the Mountains," his best-known poem.

155/TLS

[Nashville, Tenn.]
11 February 1932

Dear Allen:

Enclosed is a draft of a poem I have been working on.*a* I wish very much you would look over it and see whether you think it is worth lavishing any further effort on. I am afraid that it will seem very pedestrian, likewise too repetitious, too full of echoes. It is the only thing, however, that I have come at all near to finishing recently. I have begun two or three other poems, in rhyme, but they refuse to march and I fear are going to perish unless I have some sudden afflatus. It is terribly hard for me to get back to poetry. I am like a man learning to walk after a long illness, and I am trying, feebly enough, to imitate the old motions in the hope that energy really will return. If it doesn't, I'm afraid I'm not going to be a contributor to your Southern number.

I wish you would return the two bad poems I sent you.

I enclose a note from Best, of the Viking Press, who wrote to me Christmas, asking whether I had anything in the way of a MS. He has been after me for two or three years. I had nothing much to say for myself, but mentioned Ransom's book in passing. If it is not being scrutinized and considered anywhere, what about trying it with the Viking Press?

Munson has written me, asking me to contribute to The Bear Garden, a controversial department of the *Sun* literary page. He wants a piece on regionalism, or something like that, and I think I will write it.

I have not seen the New Republic this week, but Wade tells me that Edmund Wilson has written a terrific Communistic outburst in it, and furthermore, that Wilson is now in Kentucky, right in the midst of the Harlan fracas. Do you have any news?

Untermeyer was here Tuesday, and we had a very good talk during the afternoon.

Theresa and I want you and Caroline to come and stay a week-end with us sometime soon. I am very anxious to have a talk—such a talk as can't be had in gatherings. Shall I set a date?

Faithfully, Don

155   *a.* "Aunt Maria and the Gourds," *Poetry* (May 1932).

156/ALS

[Clarksville, Tenn.]
12 February 1932

Dear Don:

. . . Your poem is extremely good, Don, so don't make any more excuses! The last page works up a fine climax. Perhaps the first section, or paragraph, should be shorter—Aunt Maria herself should be more vivid there, rather than the ravages of time. I mean that the reader's interest should be fixed on her as a character at the start, so that the symbolism and reflections that follow will have some concrete anchorage. But, as it stands, it is a good poem, and a splendid come back after so long a neglect of the muse. By all means finish those other pieces you're working on. If I can find copies of the two poems here, before mail time, I'll enclose them; if not, in a day or two.

I wish we could promise a visit soon; but all that is vague now.

Yrs. Allen

It goes without saying that I want the new poem for the S.N. unless you finish the others and would rather have me use them.

157/TLS

Clarksville, Tenn.
10 March 1932

Dear Don:

Aunt Maria is indeed greatly improved, and in spite of your modesty and your long absence from the Muse I think it is one of your best poems. There is a quality to the rhythm that you may not recognize—it is more supple and stronger, without being forced, than your rhythms of old. I devoutly hope that you will follow this poem up, and let the mood seize you long enough to do twenty-five or thirty poems. The first section of the poem is a fine piece of rewriting; I doubt if you were capable of such skillful revision six or seven years ago. I suggest one change. In the line beginning, "And no faith even to die." why not substitute *will* for *faith*. Brittle is my word, and I fear that faith is yours. I can't tell you how much the writing and the completion of the poem delights me; it is like meeting a friend long absent.

Stuart[a] shows some good qualities, but I don't see how I can use any of this stuff in this number. In the longer pieces there are flashes, but the short ones lack the headlong freshness of some lines in the long, and are merely clumsy. (It is a minor point: but the boy should learn that *lie* is not a transitive verb.) But he does have a genuine flair, and being near him you have a good chance to give him pointers. It seems to me that he lacks the sense of form; and by that I mean that he doesn't know what emotions and images belong together, and he has no sense of the leading image of the poem. His composition, to put it another way, is bad. Yet it is obvious that this fellow has some experience that he is trying to understand—a genuine problem; don't you think that this kind of integrity is a fine basis to work from?

Your essay on the Liberals is a *fine start* for a fine essay. It is not as closely written as your best prose, and I believe the relation of liberalism to money and politics could be pinned down more luminously. Why don't you work it up? You could surely place it. Your analysis of the situation is absolutely new and just. You mustn't let it drop.

I will be in town next Friday, and meanwhile I hope your regionalism piece gets here. How are you all? We are both better.

Yrs. Allen

157   *a.* Jesse Stuart, who at this time was a graduate student at Vanderbilt.

158/TLS

[Clarksville, Tenn.]
22 March 1932

Dear Don:

Well, General, you've done me wrong again. You're always doing it. You are constantly saying that it won't be any good, and that you don't know about it. And here is your article proving that you misled me. It is a very good article indeed. I hereby entreat, implore, conjure, and enjoin you not to fool me again. I can't tell you how much I appreciate the special effort it took to get the piece done. It has saved my life.[a]

I've been thinking over our conversation and the plans you outlined, and I have come to some drastic conclusions about them, the plans particularly. I can reduce my conclusions to a very brief expression: you will be an unmitigated and immitigable damned fool if you don't seize the opportunity to get away this next year. There it is, General; put it in your pipe and smoke it, or if you chew, chew it, or dip, dip it. Thar it be. I know that "circumstances" must be considered, but—drawing on my long and, if I may say it, affectionate knowledge of your character—I think you are a little inclined to use circumstance as an excuse for inaction. I am well acquainted with this vice, having so large a share of it myself; but I think it is more deadly in your case just because on the whole circumstance for you is more complicated. I can't tell you, Don, how anxious I am about this matter, and though this expression of anxiety is impertinent, silence in these matters is often very much like indifference. I feel that you may give up the project at the very end on the ground that it is too hazardous, or you will find new complications; but remember that the field of real complication must be reasonably limited, otherwise there is no end to it, and all action is throttled. I feel as if I were looking at the wrestling match, in which the slightest pressure on the one side or the other may decide it. This is the decisive moment in the contest. And it is all up to you.

I will be in town again this week, about Friday. I have to come in to get the tenant's family whom we took to town last week for a visit. I don't believe I told you that your article will of course be paid for.

Yrs ever, Allen

158   a. Tate had asked Davidson on a week's notice to give him an editorial for the southern number of *Poetry,* and Davidson had responded with "The Southern Poet and His Tradition," *Poetry* (May 1932).

159/TLS

Marshallville, Ga.
29 October 1932

Dear Allen:

I had been wondering when I was going to hear from you and had been thinking I would write you and get Lyle Lanier or somebody else at Nashville to send the letter to your French address, which I had not learned.[a] Then came your letter, to my great satisfaction—though I wish it had been a much longer letter. I have waited to answer it only long enough to collect my thoughts after a five-day trip to Charleston and Savannah—attending the Southern writers meeting in process of the jaunt.

It's good to hear of the happy progress of your writing. I am keen to know more about it. If the book has turned out to be more general than you had anticipated, that's all the better. It will have the more force and application, perhaps, as it is less strictly personalized. And what of the essays and the story?[b] If these are to appear anywhere, let me know. I am not taking any magazines as yet, but will want to look your things up.

I saw the Chapman[c] reply to Knickerbocker,[d] and I don't think it was collusion. At the Charleston meeting I talked at some length with the Chapmans, Mary and Stan. They—and particularly she, who is the more articulate of the two—seem to be very ardent Agrarians and anxious to forward our cause. She, in fact, queried me almost impatiently as to what we—"we" including herself—must do next, for something concrete and active must be done, she thinks. I agree with you that her reply to Knickerbocker was milder than it needed to be. But I intend to keep in touch with her. She—or I should say the two—seem to me genuine recruits for the cause, and people who may in time help considerably in their own way.

The Charleston meeting was delightful on the entertainment side, but in other respects completely uneventful. There was no fighting at all; there was almost no discussion. My impression was that the Charleston committee, or Heyward at least, had judiciously oiled the wheels and arranged that there be no discussion of the sort that arose last year. At the first session Heyward called on Laurence Stallings,[e] who harangued us very amusingly on the relation of literature to the movies. A few questions passed back and forth: one as to whether book publishing was possible in the South. There was a little light chatter, and then we went to lunch. There was only one more talk meeting. It consumed about fifteen minutes at the end of the second day, and it consisted only of announcements by Heyward as to the future course of procedure. Vice-Chancellor Finney of the University of the South has invited the Southern writers to meet at Sewanee next year. This invitation and other matters are to be turned over to a committee, Heyward said, and the committee will decide. The committee was not named in the meeting. I suppose it will consist of Heyward and some of the Virginia and North Carolina people who seem to be acting as managers. Nothing was proposed and nothing was voted on in the meeting except thanks to our hosts. Between times we went about the city and enjoyed ourselves, and were lunched, dined, cocktailed, etc. The best feature of the entertainment was a negro sermon in Gullah by Sam Stoney (coauthor of "Black Genesis"). It was about the best I ever heard. And this Sam Stoney ͫ is really somebody, I tell you—a Tory and not ashamed of it, a vigorous antiquarian with something of Andrew Lytle's spirit, and a man who likes his liquor. I would like to see Stoney and Andrew together.

In another envelope I'm sending some clippings which tell the story of the meeting in more detail. I think it is enough to say of it that it was thoroughly enjoyable and perfectly innocuous. I hardly opened my mouth in public. There was nothing to discuss, nothing to fight about with that group of pleasant souls, who for the most part are simply successful authors or want to be, and therefore do not worry about what perplexes us. Cabell wouldn't come this time; Ellen Glasgow was ill and couldn't; Paul Green and Faulkner are both in Hollywood; Jas. Boyd and various others sent regrets. Those who were present seemed to me to be about one-half Northerners or emigré Southerners. The presence of Donald Adams of the N.Y. Times, Irita Van Doren of "Books," and Fanny Butcher of the Chicago Tribune means whatever it means—perhaps that the invitation-managerial committee has at least half an eye for literary politics. I understand that Canby and maybe other editors were invited.

I must say that I felt rather alone at the Charleston gathering. There was nobody there of my persuasion unless it was the Chapmans and William E. Dodd. I had a very fine talk with Dodd, mainly along political lines. He is very close to Roosevelt, it seems. Dodd believes fundamentally as we do about the economic situation. Nothing can be done to set the country right until the farmers get back on their feet, he says. There will undoubtedly be a movement back from the cities to the farms; for the moment this will depress the farmer still more, since his urban market will diminish. But in the end, if things work out as they should, we will be in tremendously better shape. This is what he believes must happen. And Roosevelt's job, if he is elected (as seems almost certain now) will be to hold his contingency in line while the slow rebuilding is going on which cannot be completed within a mere four-year period.

As to that invitation from Sewanee, of course Knickerbocker is behind it. I said nothing about it, pro or con, except to Mrs. Chapman, who said, if the meeting should be held at Sewanee, I would have to be on the arrangements committee. I certainly will not do any such thing.

In fact, I don't think I particularly care to go to another Southern writers meeting. It is interesting to meet the people one would like to meet, but the chatter of teas, luncheons, dinners, and cocktail parties is not conducive to the kind of acquaintance I would wish. And with discussion cut out, there seems to be no particular object in going, for me at least.

I suspect that the Sewanee invitation will be declined by the "Committee." Perhaps they will fancy that the theological surroundings of Sewanee will not permit a free flow of cocktails; perhaps they'll be afraid of Knickerbocker; perhaps they just won't want to go. I have a notion, too, that a strong effort will be made to bring the writers to Chapel Hill, N.C., or back to Virginia.

At various times, you'll recall, we had talked of the possibility of getting Vanderbilt to invite the writers for a Nashville meeting. This fall, Wade told me, Dr. Mims was again at the point of "taking the matter up with the Chancellor," and he was supposed to wire me if any invitation was forthcoming. He didn't wire me.

Somehow I don't think that a meeting under Vanderbilt's sponsorship would impart a desirable tone to the proceedings. Furthermore, I have long since passed the point of wishing to ask anything whatsoever, in the way of promoting the welfare of Southern life and art, at the knees of the present Vanderbilt administration. They seem to me hostile to all I believe in. Besides the general reasons, there are personal reasons why I don't want to ask for anything. These personal reasons have become very strong of late—my blood pressure goes up as I think about them, and I had better pass on quickly.

What I am leading up to is this: Why not, either next fall or the following spring, sponsor a genuine dyed-in-the-wool True Rebel Southerners Convention of our own. Let the Agrarians lead and manage their own assemblage, not hang on the outskirts of a miscellaneous social body that calls itself Southern. It seems to me entirely feasible; it connects, too, with your idea of an Academy. Maybe we could even organize such an Academy. It could have its private meetings, and there could be public meetings, too, for everybody in general. The Southern writers meetings at Virginia and Charleston had somehow a strangely exclusive air, as if we were all bankers and directors whose deliberations had to be guarded from public violation; and yet we had no deliberations, after all. I must admit that wild notions race through my head whenever I think of the hush-hush arrangements for a group of people who really live on "publicity" and many of whom are avid for it.

Enough of this. I can give you none of the news of the brethren that you ask for. I don't know what they are up to. I saw Ransom, but only very briefly, when we came through Nashville in mid-September, and said how-de-do to Owsley. I have heard tell of Andrew through Wade, whom of course I have seen both in September and more recently. Andrew is very angry, I hear, because Couch of the Univ. of N.C. Press has turned down the article Andrew wrote for him on The Southern Backwoods.[g] Apparently Andrew put in too much argument and not enough statistics to suit Couch.

Ransom and I had only one or two brief talks while he and I were flitting busily about Nashville. If he has written anything since he has been in England,[h] he won't tell what it is, and I didn't push him to tell. Of course there are the things we know about—the economics book, the articles, etc. Ransom says his economics book is already stale stuff. He is going to let it drop. He has passed beyond that point. I get an impression that residence in England has caused him to change some of his views a little. Some American practices that look bad in America look very good when one gets abroad; one finds oneself defending what one formerly attacked. Is that the effect of Europe on you, too? Owsley says the temptation came upon him to find good in what he had deplored in American life; he had never felt so patriotic as when he was in Europe. Your homesickness perhaps is of somewhat the same order. I know just how you feel. I felt much the same way, after the Armistice, in France.

You wonder "why we got so weak last year." Private exigencies, as you say, undoubtedly played a large role. People who are ill, poor, hard-worked, troubled with family responsibilities, deaths, fires, the woes of relatives, are not in a position to give a great deal of time to civic agitation. Not indeed, unless they are really crusaders who will risk all in the fight. Andrew is about the only one of us who has had the crusading spirit. Andrew is not married; the rest of us *are* married, and we are timid about losing the humble security against disaster that we now possess. Isn't that so? And isn't it true that not a one of our wives (who are all paragons, the Lord knows,—the top of excellence among womankind) would say to her warrior: Go forth with this spear and shield against industrialism, and return with your shield or upon it. That is, take that $500 out of the savings bank and use it to organize a political party among the farmers and small merchants of Alabama.

That sort of thing simply doesn't happen among us; it will only happen if times get much worse, and we get much more passionate in our seriousness.

Nevertheless we have never quite made up our minds whether we are crusaders or not. We like to think of ourselves as crusaders; in our minds' eye, we can see ourselves doing a kind of Pickett's charge against industrial breastworks, only a *successful* charge this time. But we don't actually do the crusading. We merely trifle with the idea a little. And while we trifle with it, we neglect the other role in which we really can accomplish something, though results will be very slow. We are, after all, writers before everything else—and only secondarily, if at all, cavalry commanders, orators, lobbyists, and ward-heelers. We ought to write, then, and keep writing. And we should organize our effort around our writing, as we have done in the past, with the sure conviction that if our ideas are right, we shall in the end reach the people who can do the other needful things; and if our ideas are not right, then they deserve to fail. I believe our ideas are right. I believe we would be fools to give ground now, when the times are still malleable and can be swayed, and will be swayed, for better or worse within the next decade. I favor therefore the following measures:

1. Another symposium, to be published in 1933 or 34. This should be a simpler, more compact book than the first. The Statement of Principles should be republished and revised. The book should make full use of the present new trends toward the farm and small town; of regionalism in art and economics; of what is best in the Humanist and other anti-liberal movements. We should be careful to present ourselves as the advance-guard of the new dispensation, not—as our critics tiresomely say—"reactionaries." We ought to have definitions, instances, illustrations—all much more concrete than in the first book.

2. An agrarian meeting, at Nashville or Clarksville.

3. A definite plan for the establishment of a weekly.

4. We should somewhat more closely organize the efforts of those interested in our program. Our own writing and all that we can solicit should be less desultory. We may not be able to organize political clubs, etc., but we should be able to get a good-sized number of people to aim their writing in certain specific directions.

But above all, if we are not to be actual political crusaders and revolutionaries, like Gandhi or Mussolini in their domains, then we must have a care to the books and articles we write. These must be made better and more attractive; and we must keep on and not weary in well-doing, for, as the apostle said, In due time ye shall reap, *if ye faint not.* We must also be careful about our contracts with publishers. We must have the right sort of contracts and the right sort of publishers. It is strange to see how even those who denounce you most fiercely are finally influenced by your ideas. Presently they are speaking your vocabulary and applying your principles, as their own. Note the speech of Gerald Johnson that I am sending you. A few years ago he would not have consented to make this speech, and if he had agreed to speak, he would never have talked like this. Perhaps we are among the folks who have made it possible for him not to be ashamed to make this speech.

At times I get very much discouraged, but when I think of such matters as I have related, I feel better. We are still not old. We have ten, twenty, maybe thirty years of activity ahead of us. When we have written our score or more of volumes apiece, it will be time enough to say whether we have been on a losing side.

I am well located at Marshallville. While you are studying the agrarianism of Provence (I have only been on the railroad, from Paris to Marseilles to Nice, and don't know Provence), I am studying the agrarianism of Middle Georgia and other parts. This country is really Old South, and very fine; but is crumbling because the planters have been too reckless with their money. They reaped enormous gains from peaches ($50,000 a year profit from one crop seems to have been common), but lost it all when peaches failed, or else tossed it away in Florida, or got eaten up by boll weevils, taxes, and mortgages. They still live in pretty grand style, though, for folks as poor as they claim to be. They don't seem to worry. There are more negroes here than I've seen in years, and blacker ones, who say "Ole Miss" and "Little Miss"; more horses, mules, wagons, buggies, turnip-greens, collards, sweet potatoes, cotton, pecans, corn, scuppernongs, peppers, asparagus, sugar cane, sorghum, ground-peas, and God knows what else. The land produces so freely, it has almost spoiled the people. We are enjoying ourselves very quietly and modestly. I have planted a winter garden and am cultivating it. Mary is in the town high school and likes it. Theresa, now that the first agony of settling down is past, is getting back to Roman law and that sort of thing. We are mighty well pleased, and anticipate a pleasant winter here. We expect to drive to Florida during Thanksgiving week, possibly to New Orleans Christmas. That will be about the extent of our travels.

As yet I haven't got down to writing. I expect to do so this week—in fact I have already made a small start. Incidentally, I am reviewing Virginius Dabney's *Liberalism in the South*, U. of N.C. Press, for the Saturday Review. I am planning an essay on Vermont and Georgia.[i] I have other things in mind that I hope to fit into a book. I hope, too, to do some poetry, but can't predict what the muse will offer.

Hound and Horn have treated me peculiarly, not to say badly. About the first week in August, Bandler wrote me, asking whether I could have the article on Sectionalism in America ready by September first.[j] I told him I didn't know, but would try. I did try, and finished it and sent it in on time, spoiling my vacation somewhat to do so and working under a good deal of a handicap. Bandler's secretary then wrote, saying that Bandler had gone to Europe and that the article was too late for the fall issue anyway, and that Bandler would write me about the middle of September when he returned. That's the last I have heard from Hound and Horn. Not a line from Bandler. Complete silence. My article may not be the best I could possibly do; nevertheless it has some good stuff in it. If he doesn't want it, I want to go over it again and submit it elsewhere. I consider that Hound and Horn is acting a little shabbily; but this may be their way of rejecting an article that they are sorry to have ordered.

This has been too long a letter. You don't have to read it all, or to answer it all. I have taken the better part of a morning to write it because I wanted to get down some of the things that have been tumbling confusedly about in my mind and had to remain unsaid because there was no one to say them to. I wish you were here. So far I feel—though my location is pleasant enough—about as much on exile as on leave. I fear I must join you in being somewhat homesick. But never mind. We'll soon all be back at the old rendezvous, with new books written and much more to write—and talk about. All of us send affectionate regards to Caroline and Nancy and you.

Faithfully, Don

You'll have to take a day off to read this!

159   *a.* On leave from Vanderbilt, Davidson spent the academic year of 1932–33 in Marshallville, Georgia, at the home of John Donald Wade. Caroline Gordon received a Guggenheim award in 1932, and the Tates spent the year in Europe. *b.* During this period Tate is working on two prose manuscripts, a biography of Robert E. Lee and a novel tentatively called "Ancestors of Exile." Neither was published but some of the novel was used in *The Fathers* (1938). *c.* Mariston Chapman was the pen name of the husband and wife team of novelists

composed of John Stanton Higham Chapman and Mary Isley Chapman. They lived for a time in Sewanee, Tennessee. *d.* W. S. Knickerbocker, at this time editor of the *Sewanee Review.* *e.* Georgia-born novelist and playwright; best known for *What Price Glory?*, written with Maxwell Anderson. *f.* Samuel Gaillard Stoney, author of *Plantations of the Carolina Low Country* (1939), and other works. *g.* For *Culture in the South* (1934). *h.* Ransom spent 1931–32 in England on a Guggenheim grant. *i.* "Still Rebels, Still Yankees," *American Review* (December 1933). *j.* "Sectionalism in the United States," *Hound and Horn* (July–September 1933).

160/TL

Paris
10 December 1932

Dear Don:

Your letter came a few days before we left Toulon, and at present I cannot hope to answer it as it deserves. We left suddenly but reluctantly, after I finally faced the fact that I couldn't get books there for the completion of my opus. Paris is horrible this time of year; I have a cold; but still I feel that I can at least get something done between sniffles. I can't tell you how much I appreciated your letter; it was long and full—full of much that I wanted to hear. It was far more hopeful than anything I've had recently from Nashville, where gloom can actually be measured by the irrelevance of the hopes and fears that reach me. Andrew alone seems to be wrestling with something comprehensible to my (now) antique ears. It seems that John has found the virtues always latent in the Tariff; I'm sure it is a great triumph of John's dialectic even though it may be the death-knell of true agrarianism. But what of that? Not long ago John wrote me that he was glad that I had found something good in this wicked country France; it may be wicked, but so far it has not turned this fellow's (Me) brains to buttered toast. The more I see some kinds of Englishmen the better I like them and the more I detest the "English tradition." Looking back on our Symposium I am increasingly convinced that it was sacrificed to the English tradition; whereas any school-boy who has read his Jefferson knows that as early as 1770 we had something very different. Our program stood or fell by virtue of its standing-on-its-own-feet-ness. There was too much Anglo-nostalgia in it to achieve that.

But there I go off on diatribes. My only excuse is that I foresaw it, and tried to talk the Anglophiles out of it. I am beginning to think now that the very word tradition in our campaign was a tactical mistake, due to our academic minds; we should have stood flatly on the immediately possible in the South.

Let us forget these Southern Writers' Conferences. What you say makes me even gladder than before that we missed it. This disgusting parade of successful authorship should be ignored if possible—if not possible, then attacked. You know in my long desultory correspondence with Ellen Glasgow I have referred to this defect of Southern writers time and again, but never got any response from her. I admire her new book very much, but I can't see how she managed to write it.

I make haste slowly with my book, and I'm not sure that I shall be satisfied with it. But who can be sure of that? I have written some poems—and a short story, my very first one—and the poems seem better than any prose that I do. I'm sending them along for your comment.

The trouble with our agrarianism is not that we don't believe in it enough to make sacrifices; it is rather that we don't believe in it in the way that demands sacrifice. In other words not one of us has a religion that any of the others can understand. That sort of understanding is necessary to fire the enthusiasm of a group; it is reciprocal in its action. *Vide* my Remarks on the Southern Religion.

What I hear from Nashville seems to prove that the Agrarian Movement has degenerated into pleasant poker games on Saturday night. Not that I object to the best agrarian game in the world; I object to the kind of pleasure they seem to be getting out of it. Of course from the ashes the Phoenix rises in new strength, but after his second appearance we had better name him a Buzzard.

I get a little bitter about all this. I came back to live in the South, and I've been let down. There are curious ways in which this comes over me. For example, the apparently irrelevant behavior in France last summer of our confreres who accompanied us for the first six weeks. They behaved as if the whole country were a criticism of them; that didn't seem to me to be good agrarian courtesy and urbanity. . . . There is something wrong with us. All these things are connected. It is a bad sign when our folks can't take Europe simply and naturally, and not like a crowd of self-improving Yankees.

I must quit this before I proceed from indignation to violence. Let me hear from you soon, and keep a stiff upper lip. I know you can't help doing that. Caroline joins me in love to Theresa and Mary, and yourself,

Yrs ever, [Allen]

161/TLS

Marshallville, Ga.,
23 January 1933

Dear Allen:

I have a pile of letters on my desk that have come since Christmas: relatives, Ransom, Wade, yours. I am going to answer yours first, because you are two letters ahead of me, and you are farthest off, and the things that you and I have particularly at heart are pushing very hard in my mind right now.

Your first letter came on Christmas day. If it hadn't been for the bright Georgia weather, the camelias blooming and narcissi popping out, your letter might have made me rather gloomy. I'm glad now that I waited awhile to answer, for your next letter indicates that you are feeling better about the world, and so I don't have to plunge in and get up some encouragement for you.

The poems you sent are, I feel sure, among the very finest you ever wrote. I put them at the tiptop. Europe is certainly doing your poetry no harm whatever. I like Picnic at Cassis^a above the other two, perhaps because it lifts me more; but only a little above them. Aeneas at Washington is a stronger poem, a really tremendous one; it drags me to the deeps, but also stirs me with some of the profound fury that must have stirred the Stonewall Brigade in its bloodiest hardest moments. I think you are doing in it just what the poets ought to do: keep thundering away at the defilers of the altar, and reminding people of the thirsty grandeur of the tradition they are neglecting. Yet my comments seem quite inadequate, beside your poem. It is all really grand stuff. The Meaning of Life is in the vein of The Cross and The Twelve, in your last book. I like it, too, except for the conclusion, which jars me, I must argue, unnecessarily. Yet there's not a change I would honestly advise. The poems seem to me *final;* you write that way, always, now that you've fully got your style in hand. I certainly don't know anybody else, writing now, that has your touch of finality. Which is to say, you have come to what poetry ought to be.

I am going to pass by your diatribes on the iniquities of the brethren (though I'll say, in passing, that I quite agree with you about the fault of too slavish a devotion to the English tradition), and go on to other matters.

Instead of sending you my poems, which are not in a shape to go out, I am sending a carbon copy of the revised version of my Section-

alism essay, which has just gone forward to Kirstein.[b] Also I'm enclosing a carbon of my letter to him, which will divert you somewhat, perhaps, with his extraordinary criticisms and my answers. The style of my
essay has suffered through revision, I fear. The other version was freer
and more easygoing. But the substance of this is better.

In a former letter you said that in I'll Take My Stand we ought to
have stood on what the South offered us, and let the Anglo-nostalgia
go. You will see from the essay how my thoughts have been running on
precisely the same line. I think we did poorly to try for a too general
appeal in our book, and I think we could have developed a far more
reasonable position by studying more carefully the nature of sectionalism itself. I believe the argument of my essay gives a stronger approach
to the questions we are interested in than an out-and-out attack on industrialism as *the American* thing, which was, I seem to recall, John's
way of putting the matter. Ought he not to have said the East, where he
said America? It would have given us better touch with the West, which
seems to be growing more anti-Eastern, and it would be historically correct. By the way, did you hear of the new secession doctrine in the Middle West? One of the state senators got up in the Dakota legislature (I
forget which Dakota) and proposed resolutions for the journal to the
general effect that the South and West ought to withdraw together, or
at least ought to kick the East out of the Union. No secession resolution
per se was passed. But the resolutions giving the sense of the house went
through with a whoop and were written in the journal while the gal-
leries applauded. The western farmers are, in fact, almost at the point
of concerted violence. They are stopping foreclosures and raising the
devil generally. The movement seems to be even more angry and determined than the farmers' "strike" last fall.

I am thinking of eventually expanding my essay into a monograph.
As it stands it is incomplete and defective, both because of the limitations of space and my inability to refer to a library. I left out of this
version something I referred to in my first version: the relation of the
frontier to sectionalism. That phase of the subject needs a lot of
working up.[c]

I am coming last to the matter that most excited me in your recent
letter. By all means let us follow up Virginia Moore's suggestion and
see what there is in it. I am all for the idea. I think the historic title
would be a great help itself. One thing I think we should keep firmly in
mind: anything worth doing at all is worth doing in a thorough and
ambitious way. Let us avoid anything that smacks of The Reviewer

slant or even the Hound and Horn idea, for neither of these types would reach the people we must at all odds attract. We must be able to reach a public of about Atlantic Monthly quality. I would prefer an even more popular appeal, but I am not sure, from past performances, that we could manage it. I favor also, as I've told you before, a business-like proposition; we must plan to make a commercial success. To prepare the way for rounding up the capital we need: a prospectus showing our aims; lists and sketches showing the contributors and kinds of material we would publish; an estimate of circulation, etc.; a description of business arrangements. In all this, we will need substantial business advice. It will take work and time. The magazine should be gotten out by a stock company. The stockholders should put up enough money to run the magazine for a definite period; but this would not be "endowment." They should expect returns on their money if the magazine succeeded, and losses if it failed, just as in any other business. No "angels." I do not see that we can do much about it until you and I get back to Nashville, other than correspond and work out what it is in our own minds. But we ought to get the magazine going in 1933. And the magazine should lead to other things. For instance, a publishing house. But I won't discuss that now.

As to our present vindication, and getting in effective blows, and so on, I don't think we can do other than write books and hope for eventual results *unless* we develop a more effective organization. Our present group is too small—and maybe too lazy or too preoccupied. That matter of writing letters to newspapers, for instance. It does no good unless it amounts to a bombardment. I think the people to organize are the young folks, first of all. I refer you to Lucius Burch's[d] letter to the Vanderbilt Hustler, herewith enclosed. I don't know whether it was ever answered. You are in a good position to answer it—better than any of us who are on the faculty. Why don't you do it? I would certainly do it if I were not on leave of absence. I may do it yet, if you don't, or I may do it anyway.

Another item. I recently received a letter from the Night Editor of the United Press at Atlanta; he says he is a great friend of Ralph McGill[e] and gave a Rebel Yell for us when our book came out. Now he wants to get up a story giving the reactions of the twelve agrarians on the Southern situation after two years of depression. I wrote him a statement, and gave him the addresses of the rest of the crowd. He may decide that you and Fletcher are too far off to write to, but Lord, I do hope the rest respond and the story goes through. . . .

I had an extremely good letter from John just after Christmas. He told me of increasing support for I'll Take My Stand in high quarters in Tennessee, and for certain ideas he has developed and tried out on groups of people—national self-sufficiency, etc. Also of his and Red's project for a series of critical monographs, giving some true-gospel in that field. It was a regular Ransom letter, meaty and flavorsome. Wade writes me news of messy affairs in the university which I won't go into. It is Mary's bedtime, and I must stop typing. Salutations and regards to you and Caroline.

Faithfully, Don

161   *a.* Later called "The Mediterranean."   *b.* Lincoln Kirstein, one of the editors of *Hound and Horn*, which was published from 1927 to 1934.   *c.* Davidson is writing some of the essays included in *Attack on Leviathan* (1938).   *d.* Vanderbilt class of 1934; his letter to the *Hustler*, the undergraduate newspaper, calls for a continuation of the Agrarian ideals.   *e.* Vanderbilt class of 1923.

162/ALS

Marshallville, Ga.
6 February 1933

Dear Allen:

Your curiosity about the Secession movement in the West will probably already have been satisfied before this reaches you. I enclose a few clippings (please return those marked—I want them for my sectionalism file). Beyond these, I have no information, and comparatively few reflections to offer. The Secession resolutions were certainly a very spirited gesture. They came out of genuine anger and reflect a real antagonism of West for East. But it will all come to nothing if the East is able to continue its old policy, which can be summed up in one word: bribery. The right sort of political plums will be distributed. More money will be handed out. And all the riotous spirit will presently subside. The difference between the South in 1860 and the West now is right there. The West can be satisfied, or at least calmed, with money, because it has no leaders capable of thinking-through the situation. In 1860 and the years preceding, the South did have such leaders.

Nevertheless, the crisis obviously has its very serious side. For instance, the money may not be available this time, as it was when Mark Hanna put the kibosh on Bryan. The mortgage-holders of the East are meeting the situation by postponing foreclosures for a year. Several important insurance companies have already done so. But that, of course, is no solution unless prosperity returns pretty soon, and there seems not a glimmer of a prospect of its early return. The likelihood is, I think, that the clippers of interest-coupons will next make themselves heard. The East will see itself in process of being ruined by the Western flouting of contract obligations. At that point the conflict will really start in earnest. It may be a furious conflict, but nobody can tell now, because the whole country is waiting in a sort of hopeful panic to see what the Roosevelt administration will do.

My doubts as to the Roosevelt administration have been awakened by recent grandiose announcements (maybe "trial balloons") sent out from his Georgia "White House" at Warm Springs. He is talking about a grand "development" at Muscle Shoals and like places, with the idea of combining cheap power, industrial decentralization, forest conservation, and a back to the land movement. I don't know quite what to think of all this. Maybe Roosevelt is really going to bring about his "new deal"; maybe his smile is going to come off quick when he gets Congress on his hands.

The present Congress—a lame duck one, to be sure—presents a really ghastly spectacle. The Congress is not only impotent and unable to make any use of the ability that is really there; it is also scared, very noticeably scared.

I can't say that things look any better here than when you left, except that business seems calmer. There has been a new outbreak of bank failures. Scandalous things are being said about the Reconstruction Finance Corporation. "Technology"—another phenomenon of panic—has blurted out its fatal message and blown up. It has done some good, I think, in putting a healthy suspicion abroad that too much machinery is bad medicine—or too much science is.

Nothing of importance seems to be happening in the South, so far as my information goes. Some of the regular sort of outcry about the Georgia chain-gangs—anxiety about taxes and cotton—a pretty steady complaint about spending too much public money on luxuries like public education—etc. etc. In the crisis, the South seems to me passive and fairly helpless—divided against itself, too. That is, as far as "public opinion" is an indication. We show the bad effects of 20–30 years of liberalism.

If there is any drift, it is not, I think, in the direction of the liberalism and progressivism of the 30 years past. I think the Virginia-Carolina element is still pulling somewhat toward the East. But the rest of the South inclines more to the West. This is something we have talked about.

By the way, I saw no Southern comments on the sectionalism-secession theme. Of course, I see only the Atlanta Journal and occasionally the Macon Telegraph or Chattanooga News, among Southern papers. . . .

My writing goes very feebly, I fear. Theresa has been ill. I have been much held back by this-and-that. However, I have done some poetry. One "big" poem is about two-thirds finished.[a] I will send a copy as soon as I feel satisfied with it. It has to do with the battle of Franklin and is in a way an answer, or a comparison piece, to your Ode to the Confederate Dead. I can't rival the finish of your poem, but I do have some sentiments along the memorial and heroic line, to record. I also have some other war poems planned. And I wish I could do several "Georgia Pastorals" like the one I enclose.[b] Ordinarily, I wouldn't attempt dialect in a serious poem. But I couldn't see how to avoid it here. Besides these, I have some satirical poetry in view. I think that we who write poetry (I say *we*, boldly included myself) would be fools to neglect the strongest weapon in our armory. A book like I'll Take My Stand has to be "proved." Poetry doesn't. We should do our damnations in satirical verse, our heroics in heroic verse. They would stick longer. No Barrs, Knickerbockers, etc. could argue them down. Of course, we can do the logical, prose thing, too—but not neglect poetry.

I have about run out of talk, at least for this rather cold February evening. One cannot think very mighty thoughts in a room hardly warmed by a meagre little oil stove.

This is wonderful weather, though. Flowers blooming, my garden growing, a fine sky most of the time. If we all become real agrarians, we'd better come down here to grow our food. But then I don't know how we'd manage to live with these Georgians *permanently.* They are a grand race, or rather they *have been* a grand race; but now I fear greatly that they have lost the fighting spirit that we retain in Tennessee. (But don't ever tell John Wade I said so.) I enjoy the Georgians but could never copy them without making some awful compromises, abhorrent to the shades of my ancestors.

Faithfully, Don

162 *a.* See Appendix D for this heretofore unpublished poem. *b.* "Old Black Joe Comes Home," *The Yearbook of the Poetry Society of Georgia* (1934).

163/TLS

[Clarksville, Tenn.]
9 January 1934

Dear Don:

I think your letter to Macmillan is just right, and it ought to get results. We can't do anything until next fall anyhow—which seems to me all the better, since we will have the opportunity to digest thoroughly the stuff in the N.C. book.

There are some very able articles on special subjects, but there is no trace of a comprehensive program, or any program at all but drifting except in Poe's article,[a] which on the whole is the best on the socio-economic subjects. I've finished the book, and will have to begin writing the review tomorrow in order to get it in on time.[b] For sheer fatuity the Introduction seems to me to be particularly distinguished.

If you have read the book, please forward me any notes that occur to you. I want to make this a review from the whole group as much as possible, though naturally it will be personal. But I don't want to miss any points.

I was simply overwhelmed at the end by the truth of our own position. The reduction to absurdity of the whole liberal-industrial outlook is in Broadus Mitchell's article: the South is still three-fourths agricultural, but in order to catch up with the world and have enlightened labor problems to solve, we must have more industrialism in order to solve them. Good God! That is actually his reasoning! Outside the economic and purely descriptive pieces, you and Wade alone are thoroughly sound, though Wesley Hatcher is mighty good.

And by the way you haven't sent me anything for this A.R. poetry issue.[c] Please send it along right away. As you know, he has cut us down, so that there will be about three pages, or 75 lines, available to each contributor.

We were mighty sorry you all couldn't come to the party. We will hope to see you when we come to town next time.

Yrs ever, Allen

163   a. Clarence Poe's contribution to *Culture in the South*, "The Farmer and His Future." Other articles in the book mentioned in this letter are Broadus Mitchell's "Survey of Industry," J. Wesley Hatcher's "Appalachian America," John Donald Wade's "Southern Humor," and Davidson's "The Trend of Literature." b. Tate's review appeared in the *American Review* (February 1934). c. *American Review* is planning a poetry issue with Tate and Warren as guest editors, and they had asked him for a new poem. He finished "Lee in the Mountains" and sent it to them.

164/ALS

[Nashville, Tenn.]

12 January 1934

Dear Allen:

Your view of *Culture in the South* seems to me about right. I read most of the book before it was sent to you. Most of it, I should say, I read with satisfaction, and some of it with real admiration. And then there was some simply awful stuff, like B. Mitchell's piece that you refer to (he is lecturing in Nashville tonight, by the way, at the "Y," under the auspices of the "League for Industrial Democracy"). Mitchell is the perfect example of the Scalawag, 1934. Older liberals, like Page, Aycock, & Co. appear like angels of enlightenment and good breeding, in comparison. I hope you damn him thoroughly. Did you ever read Mitchell's insulting references to the Confederate Veterans—something about their linens being habitually soiled, etc. etc.?

The weak essays, in addition to Mitchell's, seemed to me to be: Gregory on The Fine Arts; Poteat on religion; Milton on politics. Perhaps there were others I can't recall.

The excellent ones: Ramsdell on The Southern Heritage (except for its weak conclusion); Pinckney on Manners; the Dutchman (I forget his name) on Poor Whites;[a] Wade on Humor; Nixon on Colleges and Universities—it is sound, as far as it goes; I don't think I read Hatcher. Vance is good—his piece is more or less lifted from his "Human Geography of the South." I can't remember any others of the first order. The rest seemed average, though Couch's piece on the Negro, while I didn't agree with his conclusions, seemed in its detail more discriminating and exact than anything of the kind I have yet seen.

The book is an encyclopedic affair, a kind of source-book rather than a really critical study. Its value—and perhaps it is a considerable value—is in the authoritative information it disseminates. Anyone who reads the book carefully (especially a non-Southerner) will *not* be moved to repeat the old shibboleths about Southern civilization but must see the South as a very diverse, wholly alive section, which is still separate from the American turmoil, more or less.

Of course there is no program at all. Our opponents—so far as they are opponents—are revealed as thoroughly muddled people. I agree with you entirely—our position, by contrast, becomes convincing and very clear. I think Couch's introduction is an inept and vain attempt to make the book appear like an answer to *I'll Take My Stand.* Of course it answers nothing. But I hardly think it worth while to argue much with Couch. It is obvious that the majority of his contributors agree with *us* rather than with *him*. Did you notice that about half of the essays make positive and favorable references to *I'll Take My Stand?* Our policy should be calculated to enlarge this circle of supporters. We can win them over, all except people like Broadus Mitchell, for whom nothing short of hanging will ever serve as an answer, or Yankees like Parkins, who will continue to be remote and academic.

I wrote Couch, heartily congratulating him on finishing a big job. I said, though our opinions differed, I had a great deal of admiration for the book in its informative and diverse aspects and that, if the Confederate Congress were in Session (as it ought to be) he would be made a Major General at once; but the only trouble would be in assigning him to duty; if he were put with troops of the line, he might order the rebels to shoot the Pennsylvania industrialists and not the Pennsylvania farmers! Then I argued with him a little about his foolish industrialism vs agrarianism talk.

But you don't need any palaver from me, Allen. Go to it and write a big review. You know where we all stand. Smite the wicked and reward the faithful. And let's have a carbon copy down here so that we can all enjoy this day of judgement upon the sheep and the goats.

About the poetry, I didn't know we were going to press quite so soon. I'll rummage through my thin sheaf at once and see what's what. The 75 line limit may knock out my best stuff—I tend to be prolix, these days.

What about my suggested essay on Frost, Lindsay, Masters, etc.? What length, when due.

My piece, "The Dilemma of the Southern Liberal," appears presently, in the February *Mercury*. I had to boil it down and leave out a few salty references to protect Hazlitt, who, I gather, is not without qualms—I think he fears some back-kick from his radical readers. But I don't mind; the main argument is in itself hot stuff and is inescapable, I firmly believe. If any further proof was needed, here comes "Culture in the South" to supply it.

Faithfully, Don

164 *a.* "Note that the poor whites come off mighty well in the book—better than I should have prophesied." [Davidson's note.] A.M.J. Den Hollander is the author referred to.

165/TLS

Clarksville, Tenn.

19 January 1934

Dear Don:

I hope to see you tomorrow soon after you get this. Early in the week I kept thinking Saturday would be the 19th, so it is too late to get to Nashville to hear you read and Andrew speak.

Your Lee poem is the finest you have ever written. I say this deliberately after much meditation and study of it. I thought your other recent poems, in the last couple of years, too argumentative and documentary. This new one is about Lee and about a great deal more than Lee. It is a very fine poem. If you lose what you've got here and relapse into documentation, I shall come over and cut your ears off!

At first I thought (not wishing to give you the benefit of any doubt whatever) that I might be moved too much by the subject as such. But that was not the case. It will be the chief ornament of our A.R. exhibit.

Of course, I must carp a little over details; I have questioned a few places. Whether you think my suggested emendations right or not, I believe the places require retouching. It seems to me that the opening lines are far too pat and abrupt. A more halting introduction to the theme, as if from the scattered images of a moment a line of meditation suddenly took hold and went through to its end, is what you want. At present the opening is oratorical, almost set; but you want to make it dramatic. What I offer here is not a suggestion for you to adopt literally, far from it; I mean it as an illustration of what the dramatic effect might be:

> Walking in the shadows, walking alone . . .
> The sun falls through the ruined boughs of locusts,
> Walk to the president's office . . .
> The president!
> A boy mumbles *Hush it is General Lee!*
> The soldiers' faces under the tossing flags
> etc., etc.,

I think that is the idea. And at the end of the passage why not interpolate a line or two or three of perfectly inconsequential observation on Lee's part. Make him see for a second a pile of rocks by the path, or a bush, on the fringe of his gathering meditation; even make the statement of this bald and flat. You have no idea what dramatic effect, what context it would give the whole poem. Powerful as the conclusion is, it would be twice again as powerful. You have let Lee speak, but you have not let us see him. Just make him say: I must have those rocks moved; or that spirea will bloom in two weeks, it should have been trimmed; or anything like that.

It is a magnificent poem!

Yrs ever, Allen

P.S. Caroline thinks this dramatic effect might be achieved by having him address the casual remark to some boys standing by. I might add that while such an interpolation would be outside your "form," it would really by its slight violence establish the form. The interpolated passage might even be put into parenthesis.[a]

165   *a*. For an analysis of this and other points connected with the poem, see *Donald Davidson: An Essay and a Bibliography*, T. D. Young and M. T. Inge (1965).

166/ALS

Nashville, Tenn.
15 February 1934

Dear Allen:

Here is my revision of *Lee in the Mountains*. In the first part I have attempted, so far as I could, to follow your suggestions—or at least the spirit of your suggestions, which I thought were excellent. I am not sure that the revision is a success. If you don't think it good, I can only offer the original version, for I feel that I can't do very much more to this poem until it has lain awhile in psychological storage!

Elsewhere in the poem I have touched up words and passages, I believe with fairly good results.

I'm giving you this poem for The American Review, somewhat against my sentimental inclination and in spite of the South Carolina possibilities (which are, after all, only possibilities). But the old Fugitive loyalty is the strongest pull of all, you see—the principle of let *us* stand together, wherever others may stand. Lee goes with the Fugitive Army —with the Agrarians.

Please don't forget to send me a paragraph description of your symposium article. I am anxious to get that Table of Contents in the mail.

I have seen two reviews of *Culture in the South* besides yours: Constance Rourke in *Books,* rather silly in places, but fairly decent on the whole; Jonathan Daniels in the Sat. Review, altogether silly, inadequate, and inaccurate besides. I have read yours again with increasing admiration and rejoicing. Whatever Collins' defects, we owe him endless gratitude for giving us a place to fight from;[a] without him, we would be doomed to much greater silence.

Faithfully, Don

166   *a.* Seward Collins, editor and publisher of the *American Review,* in which the Agrarians were publishing many of their polemical essays.

167/ALS

Memphis, Tenn.
24 September 1935

Dear Don:

I've been waiting for the chance to write a long letter, but it doesn't come. I should have made it plain that Agar and I went ahead on our own[a] because (1) we were the only people at hand and (2) Agar could come down only at that time. To wait till we could have a big meeting would have postponed action till Christmas—too late for spring publication and effectiveness in the campaign.

Agar took nothing upon himself. I wasn't sure of support, but I risked that in the interest of speed.

We started out with the idea of a book, and outlined as comprehensive a performance as we could. We then selected—subject to consent and ratification—the contributors. That seemed the only possible way to organize the book. If we had started with the notion of a group and then found subjects for them, we should have ended with a very scattered exhibit. In our group the technical economists are few, and while the other phases are still there for us to handle, we assumed that all would agree that we must employ the allies drawn to us since 1930. They are a kind of ally that is now indispensable.

As I say, I plunged, and prayed for support. I do think that we have a rounded prospectus that ought to win everybody. That is what we tried to make it. Of course, there are names that I would like to see—Wade, for example. But where could we use him? Nixon is a fine fellow too; but hasn't he waxed a little cooperative and pink in the last year?[b]

I'm going to try to come to Nashville this week-end if I can. Till we can talk it over,

Yrs. ever, Allen

167 *a.* On *Who Owns America?* (1936). *b.* Nixon did not contribute to *Who Owns America?;* Wade's essay in that symposium is "Of the Mean and Sure Estate." See Appendix A for other contributors.

168/TLS

Memphis, Tenn.
28 September 1935

Dear Don:

I am extremely glad to get your letter. I had no idea that all these reservations filled your mind. Agar wrote me early in the week that you were enthusiastic. I think there is general misunderstanding of the purposes that Agar and I had when we got up the outline.

These purposes I have explained to you. It astonishes me that you see your part in the book as a minor one. Isn't regionalism a vital thing in the whole program? And as for sectionalism, I assure you that Agar is as much a Southern sectionalist as any of us. There are more ways than one of skinning a cat. Our purpose is to be heard, and we can't be heard now if our program is set forth as primarily sectional. That is all there is to it. Our choice lies between a temporary disguise for our ultimate objective, in which case we can get attention, and writing avowedly sectional articles to be read chiefly by ourselves. It is my impression that this has been our conduct since 1931. If you don't think your subject is important, what subject, pray tell me, is? It is so important that if you don't write it up, the book will be wrecked.

Are you and Frank really upset because you were not "consulted"? I wish to God someone had organized the book without consulting me. The whole point about that is simply this. If Agar and I hadn't got the outline together, it would not have been got together at all.*a* As God is your witness, you know that that is so. We've vaguely consulted off and on for five years, and I am damned to hell if we have accomplished anything as a group. You know that that is so too.

Frank writes me as if he thought that vaulting ambition were back of our conduct. He urges Agar and me to be not only editors in fact but editors in name. We've all been friends too long to get insulted. If anybody, you or Frank or for that matter the ghost of Huey Long, wants the honor of editing, he is damn welcome to it.

You and Frank are in a position to ruin the book. Are you going to do it or are you not going to do it?

Or if you have another kind of book that you prefer, send me an outline of it, and I'll support you. But I warn you that I will not consult with you about the outline for five minutes because the five minutes would lengthen out to five years.

Here is a book that we can gather around. It is not the book suited to what small talent I may possess. In fact there is no real place for me in it. My assignment to Article One was strictly tentative. I've been trying desperately to get John or some one else to take it. I was assigned to it because there seemed to be no one else to whom it could be given. I am simply ready to take what is left over, and if nothing is left over I will have the satisfaction of seeing the book published, and of working to get it published.

If this sounds a little noble, I can only say that I expect you to be equally noble. I expect this most emphatically when you are assigned to a vital subject in which you are a recognized authority. It wasn't necessary to find employment for you; the job drew you to it. In my case it is the exact opposite. Why am I not sulking in my tent? Is it because my vanity was appeased by the extremely unpleasant labor of helping with the outline?

I feel like giving you the poet's curse, damned if I don't!

But I want to repeat again that Agar must not be held responsible for our proceedings. He foresaw that he might be accused of presumption. I foresaw that I would be accused of presumption, but to be perfectly frank I didn't give a damn. For this reason: we've got to put up or shut up. We can't go on writing our pleasant little laments for our own consumption. We've got to get into action or admit that we are licked. The whole agrarian movement has become a reproach. Of course we can say privately that we don't care, but if we don't care what public opinion makes of us, why do we write for public opinion?

To go back to the kind of book we've outlined. Doubtless other possible kinds were open to us. If we had consulted, we should have been consulting at this time next year as to the kind of book we wanted. We've done that for five years.

It seems to me that Agar is a gift from the Gods. He is a born public figure; he is intelligent; and he is with us to the hilt. He is just what we needed. He is a leader, and not one of us is a leader that anybody will follow. We are an army made up of generals. I will be in Nashville next Friday evening. I expect Andrew to meet us there, and

I hope we can get together and talk. But for God's sake don't let's consult. Let's talk and put our decisions into action.

Yrs ever, Allen

168   *a.* See Appendix C.

169/TLS

Memphis, Tenn.
18 January 1936

Dear Don:

Agar has sent me your essay, and I've just finished reading it.[a] I've got to read it several times again to get it all. I am convinced that it is the most statesmanlike paper I've seen anywhere, and it is not sufficient praise to say that it will be the best article in the book. And it is beautifully written—clear, orderly, and precise. I wish I could print a hundred thousand copies for public distribution. General, you've outgeneralled yourself, and done a magnificent piece of work.

Agar says that you've laid down the program that we shall be working upon the rest of our lives. And I agree with him.

I wish the whole book were one-half so good. Till recently I've felt good about the book, but now, chiefly due to my own article and others—two or three of inferior quality, my fears begin to mount, and I expect only a fraction of the effectiveness that we might have achieved.

I have no alibi for my article. It is simply that the technical subject of property was beyond me, and I ought to have had sense enough not to take it on. I took it because no one else seemed to want it. And it was made worse by the other jobs I had to do—the secretarial work, teaching (an excuse you won't take seriously), and correcting the proofs of my essays.[b] But nothing short of knowledge would have made the article good.

We shall be in Nashville again when the proof is ready. Don't you think it would be a good idea for as many of us as possible to get together on the proofs? We can do a big job of final editing, and remove many defects at the last moment.

Herbert says that James'[c] article is good, but badly written and organized. I meant to suggest to you that you help him, but I forgot it. That can be a job for the proof.

Congratulations again!

Yrs ever, Allen

P.S. I greatly appreciated your word about Greenslet's mistake over the editorship. I wish I could hear as pleasantly from Frank about it, for until I do I will feel very uneasy.

169   *a.* Davidson's essay is "That This Nation May Endure, The Need for Political Regionalism"; Tate's is "Notes on Liberty and Property." *b. Reactionary Essays on Poetry and Ideas (1936).* *c.* James Waller.

170/TLS

Memphis, Tenn.
23 February 1936

Dear Don:

The proofs have begun to arrive—the duplicates—and I suppose that means that some of the contributors are getting their sheets. I hope we may have the conference this coming week-end, but it may be the next.

The enclosures will put before you a matter of great interest and importance. I think Agar is right—we've got to do something about Collins. I am sure that Miss Lumpkin[a] misrepresented him in so far as he appears the fool, but he certainly must have said most of the things attributed to him. However valiant he has been in the cause, we can't let him make us Fascists when the big plank in our platform is that we are offering the sole alternative to Fascism.

Please mail Agar's letter when you've read it and shown it around. I hope you will call a meeting and discuss what should be done. I think we ought to draw up a statement of fundamental principles, pointing out our opposition to Fascism and our indifference to the restoration of the Middle Ages, monarchy, etc., and send it to Collins for publication without pay. If he published it, we could refer to the statement and prove that he doesn't represent us; if he refuses to publish it, that would signify a definite break, and we could print the statement elsewhere as a matter of record.

We've got to seize this occasion to clear up all the nonsense that has been said about us. I hope you all can have a meeting and have a draft of some kind of manifesto ready to submit to the conference. I'm afraid if we wait till we're together over the proofs there won't be time to go into it.

Of course, if we break with Collins we've lost his magazine,—and so has he, because he can't run it long without us. I don't know how this will strike the group. The American Review is a mighty convenient place to publish things. But if we're to have everything we write discredited with charges of mediaevalism and Fascism, all we shall get out of it is the check, and I imagine we might make more money in some other business.

I've written Miss Lumpkin a letter pointing out to her that we don't subscribe to all of Collins' views, and that we'd rather have our real views attacked—unless she is merely trying to make out a bad case and feels that any tactics are fair.

I also enclose a copy of a remarkable monthly paper, The Catholic Worker. The editor, Dorothy Day, has been here, and is greatly excited by our whole program. Just three months ago she discovered I'll Take My Stand, and has been commenting on it editorially. She is ready to hammer away in behalf of the new book. Listen to this: The Catholic Worker now has a paid circulation of 100,000! (She founded it three years ago with a capital of exactly $50.00.) She offers her entire mailing list to Houghton-Mifflin; I've just written to Linscott about it. Miss Day may come by Nashville with us if the conference falls next weekend. She has been speaking all over the country in Catholic schools and colleges. A very remarkable woman. Terrific energy, much practical sense, and a fanatical devotion to the cause of the land!

I'll write or wire you all a couple of days before the conference will begin, so that you can get John Wade up. Or I'll wire him myself.

Yrs ever, Allen

170 *a.* Grace Lumpkin, a southern novelist and contributor to *New Masses*, published an interview with Seward Collins entitled "I Want a King" in *Fight Against War and Fascism* (1936); the Agrarians answered in an open letter to Miss Lumpkin, "Fascism and the Southern Agrarians," published in the *New Republic* later in the same year.

171/TLS

Memphis, Tenn.
27 March 1936

Dear Don:

Here is the carbon of your letter to Miss Morton,*a* and a carbon of one I wrote her after I had read yours.

I wish I had been able to get a letter to you before you wrote to her. My telegram must have been misleading. It is true that my understanding of her intentions was the same as yours—she was to study the material but not to copy it. But I am convinced that I failed to make this perfectly clear. So the responsibility is chiefly if not all mine, and your reference to legal action is a little too drastic for the occasion. But I feel that I am responsible, to her, for that also; hence this second letter that I've written her.

I join you in being willing for her to use the Corymba ms. But I am telling her that she must ask John if she may use my mss with his comment.

I can see how you feel about it, and I think your objections are in every case good ones. But, Don, I do feel that your letter is hard on the girl. She is of very limited capacity, but she is a nice, honest girl, painstakingly conscientious. She hasn't the slightest suspicion that she has exceeded her rights, and I imagine she will be horrified when she gets your letter. . . .

We hope to be in Nashville for a day around Easter. The final proof of the table of contents arrived today; so the symposium is at last complete.

Yrs. ever, Allen

P.S. I've just read again your special delivery letter. I add this personal note. Don, I do hope that you don't feel I've ever had anything but the warmest feelings for you: the phrase is hardly adequate to convey all the sentiments that have accumulated in my mind in the course of fifteen years. What I have felt at times is this: some mild resentment for your withdrawing from us, for your difficulty of access, for your refusal to take any part in the simple social pleasures that not only give us relaxation from the difficulties of a special kind of life, but actually strengthen the more serious ties that hold us together. As an example of your remoteness, I would cite the fact that both Caroline and I have always found Theresa extremely charming and interesting, and felt that she would be a great addition to our social life; but, Don, you have put such a dense barrier between your friends and your private life that we cannot penetrate it. All efforts that we have made have met with no encouragement from you. You have left us only the high intellectual plane of ideas and of the cause upon which to communicate with you; but that isn't good enough for the human sensibility, and in fact it dries up in the end from lack of sustenance from the lower and more human plane of intercourse. I cite all this to explain my own behavior in the last few years—behavior that can best be described as motivated by a feeling that it is futile to seek you out and attempt to continue our social life with you. This is the way it seems to us. What effect your attitude has upon you I do not know, and it would be presumptuous for me to form a definite opinion. We've got to live our own lives. The way you live is very probably the best way for you. I can only wish, if this is so, that it weren't. I do happen to believe that your very health is affected by your social habits and all that those habits imply—your introspection, your mounting anxieties, your excessive seriousness. But whatever truth these intuitions about you may contain, and they may contain none, I feel most strongly the force of the social privation that your attitude makes for us.

171   a. A graduate student at New York University who had requested permission to use quotations from the Davidson-Tate correspondence in her master's thesis.

172/ANS

Nashville, Tenn.
9 April 1936

Dear Allen:

I have been intending for a week to write you, but could not do so on account of trouble, distress, & confusion. Miss Morton sent back the letters and wrote pleasantly, being it seems not very much taken aback, yet was apologetic, too. Apparently she did not take my letter hard. I have been very much bothered in my mind over the postscript of your letter. I would like to talk to you about this when you come, although in truth I do not know how to describe my situation, which I feel you ought to understand. You mistake disability for something else. I hope you will never have to go through what I have had to go through during the past five years and am not done with yet. When I say *I*, I should add my wife, daughter, family.

Come to see us when you come to Nashville.

Faithfully, Don

173/ALS

Nashville, Tenn.

31 March 1937

Dear Allen:

This correspondence is developing,[a] and I am glad to see it develop. For I have had a lot on my mind for a long time—really, ever since the year when I was in Georgia. But I have never had the opportunity to get it off my mind. If you, Allen, "know me like a book," as you say, you should remind yourself that you have not opened that book for about five years. You should change the tense of the verb *know*.

You have been consistently wrong in your estimate of my views of Agar. I have never had any spleen toward him except in one matter, which, it happened, was a rather important thing, at least to me personally. I felt that he took for granted, far too often, that *his* views must also be *my* views and *your* views and *our* views; in short, that, although he always disclaimed any intention to presume, he did in fact presume, by general advertisement and continual vocalization, to be spokesman, with or without consultation. And in this way, consciously or unconsciously, he used us as it suited him to use us. I could not help objecting to that, because I was always finding myself committed to positions I did not want to occupy; and I felt the more uncomfortable because I never had a fair chance to state the ground of my objection, and, to my great disgust and chagrin, had continually to appear in the light of a silly impractical sorehead. It is on that ground, I suppose, that John has been led to think me—I quote his polite euphemism—"a perfectionist." And, for all I know, worse terms, not euphemistic, have been used on occasion.

But I don't really want to go into all that. It is all past, so far as I am concerned. I have not, so far as I can see, had any direct quarrel with Agar. And though I don't consider that he has behaved very well, I have not been thinking of him as an opponent (though I suppose he is, in a way); but I don't propose to wage any feud with him; I shall preserve an amiable countenance at Chicago and pray that the talk does not get around to issues on which I, like you, disagree with Agar.

I have not seen John's essay, though he said he would show it to me. He seemed to me (when I talked with him) definitely to be giving the signal for a crossroads at which he takes a turn to the left. Perhaps I am mistaken in this; I can easily be wrong, for John is sometimes hard to follow. But I felt last fall that John was giving a signal of some change when he said in public, after Couch's address, that "Mr. Davidson had always taken a more *Southern view*, etc., etc. than the rest of us." Somehow that seemed to set either John or me to one side, though he may not have meant it that way. John's view of American affairs, I believe, is economic & aesthetic, not political-historical; he doesn't read history —I really wonder if he has ever read much American history. And so, he is psychologically prepared for New Dealism when other things seem hopeless. I don't reproach him for this. I am merely trying to fathom a mystery—a kind of cycle of mystery, for these changes come over John at intervals. I don't think it would make any real difference to him what my notion of the matter would be; but if he does haul down the old flag, or, so to speak, alter its design, I'll have very queer feelings —especially when I'm called in to say whether those are my views—and Couch can add another to his list of contradictions. I suppose this is the disadvantage of being, or having been, a well-defined "group." There is nothing to do about it. I feel exactly as you do. I wish to stick to the literary side now, or return to it. I am tired of argument and hope I can stay out of it.

As to the book[b] these are the circumstances. Some years ago, when Couch first visited Nashville, he asked me to give him a chance at the book on sectionalism-regionalism which I was projecting. I made a kind of informal commitment to him at that time, but made it clear that I might want to try a commercial publisher first. I have discussed the project at various times with Houghton Mifflin, McGraw-Hill, Little, Brown (through Everitt), and (a little) with Doubleday, Doran, but without really encouraging results. I finally decided that there wasn't much hope of placing the book in New York or Boston and that, even if it were placed there, the publisher would probably take no real interest in it. And why not publish in the South, anyhow? So I returned to my old half-commitment with Couch. We exchanged letters last fall and discussed the matter a day or two before that historical meeting. I have since signed a contract with him, and, if I can complete my revision in time, the book will appear next fall. However, the contract has not been finally approved by his Board. If there should be any hitch, I'll certainly be glad to take advantage of your good offices with Perkins.

Of course I have felt a little awkward about signing up with Couch. His conduct—you know my opinion of it; though I might add, I don't think his case is at all like Milton's, for Couch has at least an intellectual respect for our position—he knows that we *have* a position, as Milton does not. His trouble is probably that he doesn't understand how to carry on an argument in the right terms; he inhabits a quite different atmosphere from ours. Yet, though I don't excuse him in the least for his errors, I don't really see why I should withhold the book simply because he has irritated me. The U. of N.C. Press is a good press, and he manages it well. I feel he is interested in my book and wants it to have a good chance. My relations with him are strictly business. I asked John, Lyle, and Frank whether they would think ill of me for publishing with Couch despite all that has happened. And they said they thought it all right. I would prefer a true Confederate to do the job, but, lacking such an angel, I turn to what is, after all is said, the nearest thing to a Southern publishing house that we have.

I am now at work revising. The opening essay, which is an expansion of the first essay I wrote on the subject (the Hound & Horn piece), is the only one which will give me any real trouble. Most of the others will be put together practically as they have been published. I may add an essay on National & Sectional Songs.

The pieces on sociology seem to me to constitute a separate work. If I could find a publisher, I'd be glad to put them together in a single volume. But I will consider the matter carefully. It may be that they can go into the sectional-regional book as a kind of separate division.

If I can keep my health, and find the time for uninterrupted work, I shall finish the book speedily, and you will have no reason at all to invoke the poet's curse on me.

When I get this out of the way, I say farewell to polemics and return to poetry & other matters. Couch has asked me for a book of poems —a collected edition, of a sort. But I am not committed on that as yet.

Don't let all this gabble interrupt the steady progress of your novel. I fear that I have talked too much of myself, but you called forth this outburst.

Faithfully, Don

173 *a.* The letters referred to are not in the file. *b. Attack on Leviathan* (1938).

174/ALS

Nashville, Tenn.
26 May 1937

Dear Allen:

I don't need to tell you how glad I am that you wrote that open letter to the Chancellor.ª You've struck a blow that needed to be struck, the Lord knows how much—and you're one of the few people, I think about the only one, really, who could have done it, because you have both an independent position, an understanding of the situation, and the ability to say the thing as it should be said. Also, you have the *right* to say it, as an alumnus, a Southerner, and a friend of John's. I felt like throwing up my hat and giving the rebel yell as soon as Lyle showed me your letter, at noon yesterday. Immediately after, I met Jack Nye of the Tennessean on the street uptown. He stopped me and assured me that few things in life ever had given him more pleasure than to publish the letter. He told me, that, the night before, one of their reporters had called up the Chancellor to ask the extent of Rockefeller's gifts to Vanderbilt, and the Chancellor told the reporter it was *none of his business!* Jack Nye's remarks to me were, you may be sure, properly seasoned with language suitable to the occasion.

Now I don't know how much effect your letter will have—that is, whether it, or anything, under the circumstances, can save John for Vanderbilt, or rather, I ought to say, save Vanderbilt from the disgrace of having him go to this little college, after his long years with us. Still, it may turn the tables, especially if it calls forth other letters and drags the whole thing into the light. (My metaphors are mixed. I am too agitated to unscramble them!) What we have been needing, not only for John's case, but for the whole situation is some sort of public attention. But it was impossible to get public attention for the involved and subtle issues of the fight that has been going on. Even if some of us on the faculty had risked our official necks by breaking into print, we would have been represented as "faculty politicians" and wouldn't have got a decent hearing. But your letter opens the thing up on a very particular & important issue, that is also dramatic. There may be, of course, plenty of people hereabouts (no doubt a large number of Vanderbilt alumni) who think John a negligible person in comparison with, say, the football coach; but even these dunderheads may begin to take notice if the outside world is heard from, and there may be alumni, especially of the younger generation, who will see what it is about and act accordingly. I hope that there will be results. I can still see a chance that John may be kept, though I should not in the least blame him for accepting the offer. I understand he is not going to decide until after he visits Kenyon.

Your letter of course produced a very marked effect upon Dr. Mims. He came immediately to me, and we had about a half hour of the warmest conversation we have ever had. He said, oh, if Allen had only waited—if he had only talked to me (Dr. M.) first!—but this letter now makes it almost impossible to do anything! I told him, with all the brusqueness that I could command, that he ought to be glad the letter appeared *before* and not *after* the case was closed; it, or an even stronger letter or other publicity would have appeared anyhow; its early appearance gave him and the Chancellor time and occasion for acting. He complained that the university could not possibly meet the offer; that even he, if he were Chancellor could not (granted that the money should be available) give John a salary beyond the scale even of dept. heads. I told him that the extra money was no more than John deserved, especially in view of the past—that I thought the salary system prevalent at Vanderbilt ridiculous—that distinction ought to be rewarded, regardless of rank, regardless of whose feelings were hurt—that a university couldn't flourish on any other basis. Also I told him I considered Vanderbilt would be disgraced if John was let go. Also that I was glad of your letter, even though I might have advised you to word it differently at some points, if I had known about it; that I thought it was high time some public interest was being shown in Vanderbilt internal affairs; that I thought the university could turn your letter to great good if it seized the occasion to make plain the needs of the institution, which, if not better supported from the South, must inevitably run the risk of seeing its best men picked off. In general, I tried to indicate my feeling that he wouldn't hear the last of it very soon and that there was need of *action* at once. All this was maybe a little incoherent; I am naturally incoherent at such moments, anyhow, and God knows Dr. M. is a hard man to talk to, especially in something that involves him deeply as a person. But I managed, I think, to get a good deal said. I have been raging helplessly for days and weeks, and have just about reached the point where I am ready and willing to revive the vocabulary of profanity that I acquired in the U.S. army, and use it without much consideration of persons.

I don't know what the result, if any, of my conversation will be. I have never seen the Dr. in such a state as he has been lately. He has not taken a single decisive step toward filling the vacancy left by Stewart's resignation, except to indicate that I'm slated to go up—he has got Beatty, Bond, Drennon,[b] and several others dangling in the air; and now, with John threatening to leave, he has stopped all negotiations for the moment. He has consulted the department again and again, but without doing anything. I can only conclude that he is completely disorganized—just "in a state"!

By the way, he was dallying with the idea of asking you to come down two or three times a week to take over some of John's work, if John should leave. When he mentioned that to me, I told him that I should certainly have urged you for the place, if he had asked my opinion (he volunteered the plan—you must give him credit for that), as you were the only person who could possibly handle with distinction the kind of thing John has been doing; but that I was not at all sure you would be attracted to the idea—I would like very much to see you come, but didn't know whether you would. But now, he undoubtedly feels that your letter kills that plan.

And so it has gone—on and on. I have never been so angry, disgusted, and sad in my life, and all the more because of my own feeling of impotence—of not knowing how to tackle the monstrous & incredible situation.

I'll be much interested to know what, if anything, you may hear in answer from the Chancellor. Probably he will ignore your letter, but he may write sharply. I have warned Dr. M. that it will be a great mistake to try *that* line with you.

The general public, probably, will miss some of the irony in your letter, but everybody who knows the situation will get it and rejoice in it. As for the unrighteous, I hope they have sense enough to catch the meaning and *squirm!*

When are you coming to Nashville again? I am anxious to see you, and I can't get away until after exams, if then.

Faithfully, Don

174 *a.* See Appendix E for this letter. Ransom had been offered a position at Kenyon College, and some of the Fugitives believed that Vanderbilt was not making sufficient efforts to keep him. *b.* Richmond Croom Beatty was later employed to replace Randall Stewart when he went to Brown University. Stewart returned to Vanderbilt as chairman when Walter Clyde Curry retired in 1955. The other men mentioned here are Richmond P. Bond and Herbert Drennon, two other Vanderbilt graduates who were being considered for positions in the English department.

175/TLS

Clarksville, Tenn.
7 October 1937

Dear Don:

I have been hoping for some word from you. We must get together soon. Frank Owsley told me the other day that your book was nearing publication. Has it gone to press?

We wish you and Theresa would drive up to see us. But I've been wishing that for a good many years. We're only forty-three miles now. Please choose your own time. We have a telephone; so you could call us. Number: Clarksville 833.

I'm still at my novel. Some of it is fair, but on the whole I'm convinced that fiction was not meant for me. The inventions of poetry are credible, but the inventions of fiction seem to me to be monstrous and unbelievable. You can believe in a figure of speech, but how can you believe in circumstances of your own invention? But I plough right along anyhow.

Let me hear from you. I will be in town next week end. Caroline joins me in best regards to you and Theresa.

Yrs. Allen

176/ALS

Nashville, Tenn.
7 October 1937

Dear Allen:

I am just catching my first breath of semi-freedom since we returned to Nashville a month ago. The time has been full up (1) with getting my book ready for the press and (2) getting organized again at Vanderbilt. I hardly know which has been the greater agony, but at last both are done. I sent the book off Sunday night. It had to be delayed because I could not finish it by Aug. 15 (the date when Couch wanted it for *autumn* publication). It is to come out early in '38. It is 110,000 words, as it stands—17 essays; about $\frac{1}{3}$ of the book is new stuff. It may have to be reduced, but I don't know what to leave out. I have no great hope of success for it; it is for the record.

Getting reorganized at Vanderbilt has been very bad. I am taking over John's old contemporary literary course and, for one term only, his advanced composition. Those two new things burden me heavily this term. Later it will not be so bad. Also I had to get about 340 fresh-men divided into 13 sections of Eng. 1 and get the teaching staff at work—another annoying job.

Despite all this, I'm in good health, if only fair spirits. Much is changed at Vanderbilt, and I think much more will change, and that rapidly. I naturally feel lonely, but it is a comfort to see Owsley & Lyle Lanier occasionally, and to begin to have a few words now & then with Beatty. O'Donnell[a] is here this week, and he cheers things up.

What are you doing, I have heard rumors of your going to football games here, in the rain! Theresa and I all but got on the road to Clarks-ville—all but. The *but* that intervened is like Hardy's crass casualty, a large fumbling monster that I can do nothing effective about, most of the time. I hope to improve. And won't you, for your part, at least look in, some Saturday before the kickoff or after the last whistle?

Your fine *Selected Poems* came, to my great delight & admiration, some time ago—in the midst of my worst flurry, when I could hardly even stop to eat. If you don't receive the Pulitzer prize for this book, it will be only for the same reason that an Agrarian Law could not pass the Supreme Court. Only a few collections of single poets' work published since 1920 can match yours, if any can—I should say only Eliot's, Hopkins', Frost's (you won't like that idea), and *maybe* one or two more; and the excellence of yours is quite different from that of these much be-laurelled persons. It is the peculiar excellence that comes of your being your own severest critic—which is at once your burden & your crown. When I think back over old Fugitive days I can see that you have been writing, as you say, always one book. It was all predicted, & it has come to plan. You have excelled & outdistanced us all. John has not kept up. I am far, far behind. Red has diffused himself in many directions. And where are the rest? I prize the book too highly to note cursory opinions here. I will say only that I am full of much to say, and cannot say it. This one thing only: your later style, as in the Mediterranean poems, is better than your earlier—which gives me leave to anticipate more poems, and more, and more. Give our love to Caroline.

Faithfully, Don

176   *a.* George Marion O'Donnell.

177/TLS

Nashville, Tenn.
3 January 1938

Dear Allen:

After talking with Tom Walsh at Chicago, I acquired the notion that the best first step in the poetry book matter was for me to write to Wheelock. That is what Walsh advised. And so I've done it. If you want to add a note to Perkins or Wheelock, that'll be fine, and I'll greatly appreciate it. No hurry, I suppose. I am just making a general statement concerning the plan of my book and am offering to submit the tentative MS, now about ready, if Scribners wants to see it.[a]

At the Chicago meeting of the MLA I saw Mark Van Doren, but only very briefly. He was on the program (a fine paper, too!) for which I was group chairman. He asked about you and sent his regards. I saw Zabel,[b] just for a handshake. He said he was invited to visit you some time and thought of coming this winter or spring. I told him that I thought you might be going to N. Carolina before so very long. Is that right?

I was so busy in attending to the management of the affairs of the Contemporary Literature group that I didn't get as much time with our literary friends as I had wanted to; and I also got involved in two other academic (more or less) groups. My impression is that this was a far better meeting than the Richmond one; the younger element in the MLA are making the thing move very much more in a literary-critical direction. I had supper with John and we talked for about three hours —more about things here than about things there; and about our various projects. John was looking very well and seemingly was in good spirits. He also sent regards and best wishes. I will tell you of our talk when I see you.

Unofficially, I hear that you and Caroline—or is it Caroline and you?—are going to convert North Carolina, for an honorarium, a handsome proposition.[c] Though this subtraction makes addition to my loneliness here, I think it is a fine triumph for you, and am ready to shout my hurrahs. I'll forgive you for going if you'll promise not to stay too long. The heathen need you, but so do the redeemed. Lordy, if you all keep piling out, what will become of me? Yet I think the South is improving if, even in N. Carolina, you can be set up with a handsome what-do-you-call-it,—literary fellowship? Vanderbilt ought to have retained you.

Happy New Year!

Faithfully, Don

I have galley proofs of the regional essays,[d] if you want to see them.

177   a. *Lee in the Mountains and Other Poems Including the Tall Men* (1938). The other men mentioned were at this time editors at Scribners. *b.* Morton D. Zabel of the University of Chicago. *c.* Tate had accepted a position at the Woman's College of the University of North Carolina. *d.* *The Attack on Leviathan.*

178/ALS

Nashville, Tenn.
2 March 1938

Dear Allen:

I was just about to write when your letter came. My book is out, and I have mailed you a copy. Whatever you may say about Couch, I think you'll have to concede that he has done a very handsome job in the designing and printing of the book. To me it seems exceptionally good as a technical job of publishing, and I feel rather fortunate in that respect. I hope you'll like the design and the contents too. Looking over it for what probably constitutes my last survey for long while (since I propose to put it on the shelf & forget about it), I am impressed by the terrific inconsistency of style in the essays. Some have a little style, some are nondescript, some are just badly written. But at any rate my duty's done, as far as I can do it in my present circumstances. Such reviewers as notice it will probably make mincemeat of me, but I shan't know about their antics, for I am putting my mind on other things.

About the poetry, now. I appreciate very much your solicitude. The Scribner rebuff was probably to be expected, and I didn't mind it. I took the matter up with Houghton Mifflin. Greenslet wrote me a surprisingly friendly letter, and he is now considering the tentative MS. If he accepts it, well and good. If he doesn't, I think I'll follow your advice & try Holt. To fortify myself with H–M, I got Jane Fleming here and Alice Stockell in Chattanooga to write their estimates of sales in Tennessee, since there are a few special reasons why a collection including *The Tall Men* could expect sales in this state.

I broached the matter with Scribner, rather than H–M Co. in the first place, partly because of your recommendation, but also because I was at the time negotiating, through Tom Walsh, for a contract for a textbook to be published by Scribner. After some discussion, including a little haggling over contract terms, I have signed the contract, and it is a pretty good one, I think. What I am to do, alas, is a Freshman Rhetoric.[a] I hate the labor of it, but if I can do a successful one, it will relieve me for a while of the hard necessity of doing pot-boilers of other sorts. I have started on that job and will do little else, other than revision work on the poems, between now & next fall.

That is all the personal news I have. Your news of your occupations, or non-occupations, is mighty pleasant & reassuring, and means, I hope, that your writing projects and Caroline's are going to move along splendidly. We miss you both. There is an awful gap. I am beginning to feel as I did in army days when my closest associates began to be transferred from the old company & regiment to go into the Army of Occupation, or to go home to be discharged. Though Andrew & Frank are left, and Lyle is still here as yet, I don't see much of them. Andrew I see at Kissam occasionally; Frank & Lyle only when passing to and fro on the campus. It is an uncomfortable let-down after the stirring battles of the past 12 or 15 years. I am beginning to see myself as Ransom's Captain Carpenter, I am beginning to roll & stick like any tub. When straightening up in my office not long ago, I had to unbox and reorganize a lot of old papers, dealing with Fugitive & Agrarian activities, and in my sadness wished I had an Irish exile to sing me "The Harp That Once in Terra's Halls." Yet I tell myself that the long years of fellowship that have tied us all together have made the alliance something that cannot be casually broken. It is unthinkable that the communion should cease, and it won't. As long as any of us are living, some of us, whether of the older generation that we are becoming, or of the younger generation that succeeds us, will be hereabouts to keep the sacred vows, to keep the flag flying, and we'll all gather from time to time, I hope, as long as we can get about. I think, by all means, we ought to plan some reunion in June—why not send 'round the fiery cross and get all the wanderers back for hullabalooing and conspiracy against the Philistines? The political situation, by the way, is shaping more & more into our hands. Roosevelt is all but done for? Even Frank Owsley has given him up! The anti-lynch bill finished Frank! Now what next?

Frank (did you know?) is expecting Heir #2 at any moment; and *he* or *she* may have arrived already. Dick Beatty has finished his Macaulay book. I don't know any other news.

I'm glad you had the chance to make the Harvard lecture. Congratulations! It is good to have your message from Morrison & Spencer.[b] I like Ted Morrison very much personally. I know Spencer's work, but met him for the first time only last December at the MLA meeting.

This has been a long letter. I will conclude it by saying that I have been re-reading your poems. They help me keep my courage up—which may seem a strange thing to say, but their reassurance, though stern, is a reassurance. I think I can see things in your poems that your critics (that awful Belitt fool, for instance)[c] miss altogether, though perhaps the poems may not mean to me quite what you, in every case, would have intended. Your poems are also an implicit rebuke to me as an artist; they make me realize that I do not take enough pains. We have all lived so intensely, however, within such a complex set of circumstances, that our poetry—yours & John's & Red's at the more or less symbolist extreme and mine more or less at the explicit other end—is out of range of those who live less intensely & complexly, or else do not realize that their life is of that order at all.

Best regards to Professor Caroline! Theresa sends regards to you both.

Faithfully, Don

Write more, when you can, of your doings in N.C. And yes, of course, I'm always interested in the possibility you mentioned.[d]

178   a. *American Composition and Rhetoric* (1939).   b. Theodore Spencer.   c. Ben Belitt's review of *Selected Poems* appeared in the *Nation* (January 29, 1938). d. Tate wanted Davidson to apply for the headship of the English department at Greensboro, but Davidson decided not to.

179/ALS

Nashville, Tenn.
10 March 1938

Dear Allen:

Your letter sets my head to boiling on many topics. But first I'll say that you're mighty kind to offer to spend your hard-earned shekels on the distribution of my book. I wish I could give you a bale of copies, or get Couch to give them. Since I can't do that, I'll certainly arrange to get the discount for you if you're sure you want to make the purchase. Couch gives me a third off. I can get the books for $2.00 apiece. Shall I write him to send you the six copies, on my account? I will ask him also about Dorothy Thompson. She wasn't on the reviewers' list that he sent me. I should like for her to read the book, you bet, but of course she probably wouldn't review it, or even mention it; she would more likely just use the ideas, if she cared for them, as she has done in other instances.

If you do come to Connecticut, I hope we can get together during the summer, either in Vermont or elsewhere. We'll be in Vermont from late June to mid-August, anyhow. Nothing would please me better than to show you the wonders of Vermont. It is probably a quieter place than Connecticut, if you could only find the right retreat.

You are certainly right in your observations about John. I was amazed,—yet not so much, either, at the Shakespeare essay.[a] John returned in it to some notions he had when I first knew him, as to the weakness of the sonnets. But what was new was his application of the metaphysical canon. If John had analyzed the sonnets in isolation, just as poetry, as he so often does in his criticism, there would have been less to worry about. But he used Donne to whip Shakespeare with and hence inevitably raised a historical issue. If any comparison should be made, it should be done in reverse order—i.e., Donne is to be viewed in comparison with Shakespeare. The sonnet fashion prepared the way for metaphysical poetry; it set up an "analytic" method; and some of Shakespeare is of a "metaphysical" cast. But Shakespeare wasn't trying to do with sonnets, in general, what Donne did with his lyrics. The technical problem is different entirely. The sequence is a *sequence;* and individual sonnets are, almost like Spenserian stanzas, instruments for working out a situation & a complex of feelings & ideas; it won't do to try to take this or that sonnet apart, in John's way, any more than one can take apart a stanza in the *Faerie Queene.* I think a defect in John's general critical method shows up here. He is always building his argument on too narrow a basis—he looks at details & forgets other things. Also, he won't permit himself a catholic view. Of course I'm overstating the matter a good deal. What I say applies, as you suggest, to John only when he is on one of his tremendous excursions that end, almost, in fantasy, for all their logical brilliance. That is what makes Davis's[b] notion of John as a "balance wheel" ludicrous. John isn't a balance wheel, he is a mystery, as all who have known him as we have, recognize, but a mystery so friendly & homely & cheerful that you are always forgetting his capacity for turning up with an entirely new perspective. When I think of people like Lambert Davis, I know why men of letters are moved, often to their own hurt, to write their reminiscences. Men are made desperate by the prospect of misunderstanding becoming permanent. But I believe, of all the literary groups that ever existed, the Fugitive-Agrarians have done the least reminiscing, thus far—have disclosed least of their own relationships & mutual obligations. Nobody really knows how we have worked & lived & been friends together, except ourselves. We haven't been selfconscious in that way; we haven't mined out & exploited each other; we have escaped advertisement, and probably that has been in many ways a good thing.

I am supposed to be working hard at my freshman textbook, but I don't make much headway. Nevertheless, I must stick to it, and so for the moment can't yield to the temptation to project another symposium,—and it is a real temptation. Can't we let the idea lie fallow for a little while?

I look forward with eagerness to seeing *your* review (most of the others, I won't want to see). You are right as to the repetitiousness of the three essays you mentioned. My only justification is that they tie up with three different parts of the book. I knew there was too much repetition, even so, but simply did not have the physical strength to go through more agony of revision.

Faithfully, Don

¹⁷⁹   *a.* Shakespeare at Sonnets" was first published in *Southern Review* (Winter 1938) and was reprinted in *The World's Body* (1938).   *b.* Lambert Davis, managing editor of the *Virginia Quarterly Review*.

180/ALS

Nashville, Tenn.
16 March 1938

Dear Allen:

Thank you for your review.ᵃ It is masterly; and it is balm to an old soldier's wounds for me to think that you could get *that* review published in *Carolina Irredenta*. I can't tell you how I rejoice in it, not only for the good it does me, to have such a perfectly clear & sharp exposition made (you have stated the book's main purpose far better than I could ever have done it myself), but also for the sake of having it all said in N. Carolina. It couldn't have happened, but for your presence there. I am all hallelujahs. I have never had, anywhere before, a review as fine as yours, and doubt whether I'll ever have another such anywhere again. When the massacre starts, as it will start pretty soon, I'll get your review out and read it again to keep up my courage.

I have written Couch about getting copies for you and will handle the matter as you suggest, when you are ready. I also passed on to him your suggestion about Dorothy Thompson.

What you say about Couch wanting to conciliate interests me very much. I would like to see as much conciliation as the traffic will bear— at the very least, a *modus vivendi;* and I don't think we need to give up anything to achieve it. We can never be bosom comrades with the N.C. school; but I am inclined to think that the course of events is forcing them to make some choices they hadn't anticipated: for example, the Roosevelt administration is collapsing, hard times are looming up again, Europe offers no comfort, and even Communism has become disreputable in a sense it didn't have before, among people of the "left" in this country. They *ought* to be chastened by such things, and in a mood to listen to their former critics; and we, for our part, while not yielding one inch on principles, and pointing the moral all along the line, can certainly grant the need of dealing somehow or other with the pragmatic immediacies of the situation. As to Couch in particular, though I thought he behaved very badly a year or two ago, I am inclined to think his was an error of enthusiasm, with no doubt some vanity in it, rather than of malevolence & maleficence, such as we have encountered in some quarters. Somehow I have never been able to put Couch in the same category with Gerald Johnson, for instance; and I should guess he has far more knowledge of the Southern situation, & more feeling for it, than Lambert Davis. Also, I suspect that his troubles arise out of some psychological "trauma" far back in his personal history—the sort of thing you can suspect & see in a very malignant form in Stribling & Caldwell. But these are just speculations. I'll be much interested to know how the olive branch conversations proceed. You have a grand opportunity there in N. Carolina. More power to you in the good work. Convert the heathen, all you can; but in no case let them get you into any cannibal pot!

I'm still studying about your symposium idea. I believe it could be done, if we could work it out on limited & largely factual lines. But this time I would want it to be contrived somehow to reach the people immediately, rather than take the long chance of filtering down from the top—some inexpensive form of publication, like the pamphlets that Vance & others have been writing.

More of this later, when I have had time to reflect. For a while I shall be very busy not only with the composition book but with poems. Houghton Mifflin have accepted my book (I don't recall whether I wrote you this), and want a final MS April 1, to consist of the "Lee in the

Mountains" group and "The Tall Men,"—the miscellaneous poems, of the "Outland Piper" vintage, being omitted.

I took care to bring in Agar, where a reference naturally came into the pattern of discussion, in the "Leviathan"—all I could do without seeming to be just log-rolling. Perhaps I should have done more, but I felt that my subject didn't call for an expounding of specific agrarian and distributist tenets. I had a copy of the book sent to him. Have had no news of him since December (was it?) or early January. The news of Collins sounds ominous. Let me know anything more you hear.

The agrarian ranks have been increased here lately by the addition of Margaret Owsley, born last Saturday, to the pride & delight of the rebel parents & friends! Vital statistics is the best news I know, these days. Hurrah!

Faithfully, Don

180   *a.* This review appeared in the *Raleigh News and Observer* (March 13, 1938).

181/TLS

Greensboro, N.C.
26 April 1938

Dear Don:

The new poem is surely one of the best you've *ever* written.[a] Include it by all means. I have no criticisms to make. Put it in as it stands.

Surely Linscott[b] must be out of his mind to suggest that you lop off most of The Tall Men. Apart from the fact that the poem is a unit, and is familiar to many readers as a unit, you would sacrifice some of the finest individual pieces you've written. I think particularly of Fire on Belmont Street, which stands with Lee in the Mountains at the top of your work.

I know you want to get this book off your hands; but I do believe I would balk if Linscott really insists upon his idea.

In what way would the later poems in The Tall Men ruin the unity of the book? That seems to be Linscott's idea. It would rather be strengthened by their inclusion. You would bring the unity of material up to date. I wonder if Linscott's position isn't a regular Yankee wish to cut off your connection of past and present, and to limit the South to the "romantic" Old South?

Can I be of any help in persuading him? I saw him in New York two weeks ago; I wish I had known his plan then. Could I with propriety write to him? Let me know about this.

I've been so busy with my novel[c] that I haven't been to Chapel Hill recently. The other day Couch asked me for my opinion of a manuscript by Grant C. Knight called ON CONTEMPORARY LITERATURE. I told Couch it was one of the worst books I had ever read, but I gather that he is going to publish it anyhow.

You didn't say that I must return the copy of Sanctuary, so I'm keeping it.

There's a lot more to say, but I'm rushing this off.

Yrs. Allen

181   *a.* "Sanctuary," *Lee in the Mountains* (1938).   *b.* An editor for Houghton-Mifflin.   *c. The Fathers* (1938).

182/TLS

Nashville, Tenn.
1 May 1938

Dear Allen:

I am running short of writing paper this evening, and so, with apologies, must write you on a bedraggled-looking sheet.

I am delighted that you liked "Sanctuary" so well; indeed, I'm elated—this is about the first time since "Corymba" that I've got by without a criticism. "Sanctuary" is the only one of various fragments that I brought to completion in the last burst of poetry-writing before the book went to press. I began it several years ago, but couldn't finish. Suddenly, it finished itself, almost without effort. It came so easy that I was almost afraid of it. But I had put it in the book at the end of the section of new poems. (Keep the copy I sent—it's yours.)

Thanks very much for the offer to write Linscott. I wired you, as I felt the case was urgent, and an opinion from you might do something to correct his extraordinary misapprehension. I am glad you stand behind me in my first position, which is that The Tall Men should stand as a whole; then Linscott wrote again, and I was much bothered, because I feared that if I insisted Houghton Mifflin would of course keep their contract, but keep it tepidly, unenthusiastically. That was when I wrote you. I also wrote Red, but haven't heard anything definite from him yet. After your letter came, I studied the thing over once more and composed a pretty strong letter to Linscott, repeating my earlier arguments for the unity of the *T.M.* and adding some remarks about to this effect: that to cut the poem in half would seem to put me on record as standing by the pioneer–Civil War parts but repudiating the rest—and I didn't want to appear before the public in that light; that the parts he wanted to retain are not merely narrative (as he seems to want to argue) but are also subjective, reflective, personal, lyrical, etc.; that the new poems are not strictly narrative either; but that, nevertheless, there's nothing to prevent him from emphasizing the narrative element all he wants to in his announcements and publicity. As a concession, I offered to omit entirely the section entitled "Resurrection," which isn't very good (I had already considered dropping it) and to pare off the minor & non-essential parts & passages only of the three preceding sections; but I certainly intend to keep "Fire on Belmont Street" intact.

The clue to Linscott's position, I think, is this: poetry is hard to sell, and he believes he can sell the book if he can present it as being largely historical narrative. He spoke in his letter of being able to reach readers who don't generally take to books of poetry. I am inclined to think that they *may* be deciding to push the book a little. Their copyright man has been after me hard to check up on all previously copyrighted material. He has asked me to get assignments of copyright from Poetry and from The Southern Review and to check other items— there are only a few. I am having to go to considerable trouble to get all this ironed out. The thing has proved an unexpected worry. I have been a little upset, too, by Linscott's surprising letters. There may have been some disagreement in the Houghton Mifflin office, since Greenslet's letters to me, earlier, carried no hint of the view Linscott takes. . . .

Faithfully, Don

183/ALS

Nashville, Tenn.
3 October 1938

Dear Allen:

I finished reading your novel a few days after you left. It kept me fascinated, from beginning to end. It still has me fascinated. I want now to go back and read it over, at once—a desire I seldom have for novels, in these days. I ought to have known that you would be a good novel writer. Your biographies foreshadowed a gift for narrative; and

I knew the subtlety of your mind in the creative act and had acquaintance with your conscience & sure grasp of form. I ought to have known! Yet I was afraid (between us two) that to read your novel would be a kind of a struggle. I was afraid you would be a more intense Henry James, or something of the sort. Maybe I had this apprehension because of your *Hound & Horn* story some years ago, which I didn't really like very much.*a* But my fears were nonsensical. You are simply yourself in this novel. I think you are in some ways more completely yourself (and yet more detached, artistically) than in any other writing you have done. I admire the book intensely. It is a real triumph for you. And I think it means you must write some more novels.

Until I have had a chance to read the book again I won't be able to offer any of the criticism you solicited. You don't need any criticism, though, from me. You have mastered this fiction business. It is wonderfully well written! Not a weak page, or sentence! I see many things in the novel that delight me greatly, especially the possible several meanings more or less pointed up in the Golden Fleece myth. Among these meanings I seem clearly to detect that you are talking just as much of 1938–Virginia as of 1858–Virginia. You have, in short, by implication shown of what seed the Virginius Dabney—Lambert Davis complex is sprung. Am I right?

I was troubled somewhat by the final incident of Yellow Jim's doings, & what immediately followed. I shall have to read it again to check this. But you seem here to play into the hands of our Yankee torturers just a little. I don't so much mind Susan's monstrous connivance. I do mind the (to me) unnecessary blood-kinship of Yellow Jim & his own white folks. And certain other things, possibly—because they will be misunderstood. By the way, O'Donnell assures me that Yellow Jim did *not* rape the girl. I got the impression he did. Maybe you have been a little too subtle there for me to follow you.

This is not, however, a very strong demurrer. The book is remarkable. Nothing else like it has been written in *our* day—probably nothing else before our day.

One thing it proves to me. All of us will do better in the arts if we can find ways of casting off or of at least out-channeling the subjectivity that has hung over "Fugitive" verse. That's why I think you ought to go on writing more fiction. Incidentally, I want to try it myself—some day, some time. I have always wanted to. . . .

Faithfully, Don

183   *a.* "The Immortal Woman" appeared in the July–September issue, 1933.

184/ALS

Greensboro, N.C.
6 October 1938

Dear Don:

... This, then, is to thank you for the fine letter about *The Fathers*. I knew that you would question at least the Yellow Jim aspect, and I feared you might not like any of the book. Of course, I am delighted. As to Yellow Jim, I was perhaps led too far by certain actual circumstances pertaining to a negro in my grandfather's family. After the war he killed another negro, and was sent to the Maryland state prison. My grandfather got him paroled and took him into the family. He tried to assault one of the ladies after he had heard her say she was afraid of him. I followed that tale pretty literally because I knew that it contained a profound truth of the relation of the races. I wouldn't have felt so secure with an invented incident. The actual negro was not so closely related as half-brother, but he was at least a first cousin of the lady he attacked—on the other hand Coriolanus seems to me to strike the balance—the best effects of slavery, Yellow Jim the worst, Blind Joe the average.

But that you like the book as a whole counts a great deal. I must go and lie down now. The arm is painful. Our regards to you & Theresa.

Yrs, Allen

185/ALS

Greensboro, N.C.
12 May 1939

Dear Don:

Alas, it is not rumor, it is fact that I have accepted the Princeton offer.ᵃ As I told Frank Grahamᵇ the other day, if a Southern institution ever makes me a similar proposition, even with less money, I will take the first train South. I decided on this basis: I am a special man in the academic system, and I've got to take every concession of the system to my special status. Writers have been hired by universities before, for two reasons, both of which are unsound: (1) to teach something besides writing; (2) to teach nothing at all. The latter is our situation here; it amounts to a subsidy from the state of N.C., but in return we were supposed to be travelling salesmen for the college. Both (1) and (2) are forms of publicity, the former somewhat disguised. The Princeton offer is the first, so far as I know, ever made to a writer as writer; I will be *used* in my special capacity, and not as a publicized idler, or a dray-horse advertized as a race-horse. Dean Jackson here paid us a compliment in saying that our teaching was never meant to be the first consideration. What was, then? Publicity. He couldn't use us, but he could advertise us. Unfortunately, people really want to earn what they get in a very direct way.

As I say, I will take the first train back. I surmise that I will not have to do it. There will be too many people who will be pleased that I have joined Lyle[c] & John. I can hear the gossip: Tate sold out to Yankee money. I can at least refute that for you. It is $200.00 more than we get here. House-rent is exactly double; Nancy's school is $400.00—here it is free; living costs are generally higher. We about broke even here; at Princeton we shall lose money.

I would rather be at Chapel Hill than at Princeton; but there's a rule about transferring people from one unit to another. I tried, but nothing could be done. The sojourn at Princeton may make it possible for me to go to Chapel Hill in a year or two.

I will take another look at McGehee's poems, and return them with comment.

I can't imagine where Herbert heard that I was going to Bread Loaf. I haven't heard it. If I do hear it, the money will have to be big. I plan to write all summer at Monteagle.

Your Rhetoric came the other day. It looks fine; but I haven't had a moment to go into it fully.

We expect to reach Monteagle on June 7*th*, maybe the 6*th*. When do you all leave for Vermont?

Yrs. Allen

185   *a.* From 1939 to 1942 Tate was a resident fellow in the Creative Arts Program at Princeton. *b.* President of the University of North Carolina. *c.* Lyle Lanier has just left Vanderbilt to go to Vassar College as head of its psychology department.

186/ALS

Nashville, Tenn.
23 February 1940

Dear Allen:

. . . What you say of your prospects at Princeton and at the Library of Congress naturally excites me very much, but I don't presume to offer any advice. I will say that I, for one, rebel a little at seeing you take a place offered by *MacLeish*. But that arises only out of my personal feeling toward him. I cannot believe he is a disinterested person. He seems to me brazenly calculating. If you take his offer, be sure to look that gift horse in the mouth. I cannot help wondering about him. Two summers ago I heard him give a thoroughly Communist harangue at Bread Loaf (before the school there); and now he is trying to wiggle out of the hot spot. See the statement that he got the *Sat. Eve. Post* to print, in last week's issue, I think.

But either way, I know you are assured a very fine position, and I wish you all luck. No Southern institution can offer you $6000—or no Southern institution would offer that much, or even $5000, to you or any other Southern poet or man of letters.

The Washington position would of course put you near to Virginia (what's left of it). You can live in Alexandria with John Lewis and Mordecai Ezekiel.[a] You will be at the place, at any rate, from which the controlling of the U.S. is done. I hope you don't get so interested in those prospects that you stop writing—as JCR has seemingly stopped.

I would of course rather see you in the South. Right here, in fact. But how to achieve that, I simply don't know. I feel, however, that there will be some Southern opportunities for you and that they may come soon—they will not be magnificent, but they will be Southern. I will do all I can to see that they come to you. But maybe my *all* is not a very big lever.

About the *Southern Review*, which we were discussing. I had it in mind to reproach Cleanth but have never got up courage to write in stronger terms than I have already used, in discussing individual items, like Mildred Haun's stories (which by the way have been accepted by Bobbs Merrill). So I have let the thing go. Besides Cleanth is always so extremely nice to me, and always so completely explanatory.

I don't believe it's true, though, that they can't always get the pieces they want. The agrarians have been pretty heavy contributors—the old agrarians. The people they have failed to find out are the younger ones. What bothered me most in the last issue was the *principle* of getting Zabel to discuss all the poetry of the past two years—a bad editorial principle, that!

About Schwartz's essay on your poetry.[b] I don't for one moment mean to imply that it isn't a good essay, or that Schwartz shouldn't write it, or that Cleanth shouldn't publish it. I mean simply that *conceivably* somebody might have been found to do an essay on Tate who would be nearer to the corpus and spiritus of your poetry than Schwartz can ever be.

What you write of my poetry, while it may be plausible on the external critical side, is as far off from the essential truth as Schwartz's essay about your poetry. You say I conceive myself as the "spokesman" for a culture & a people! What foolishness! You talk like a New York *Times* reviewer, not like yourself. I believe in the "third revolution" that you talk about, in so far as it supplies a kind of a rationale for your poetry (some of it), some of Red's, and, decidedly, the worser part of John's. But you know we were all started, poetically, on our various lines *before*, long before, all the talk of the third revolution was hatched up. The third revolution is a critic's explanation, not a poet's. If I accused you of writing to uphold the third revolution, the charge would be as shallow as the "spokesman" phrase you apply to me. We would have to say, if that line of talk is to be followed, that you and John & Red are trying as hard to be "not-spokesmen" as I am trying to be "spokesman"—which is ridiculous.

I would not mind your calling my poetry "romantic" if you did not also imply that yours is not. And knowing how the word "romantic" has been used in your critical essays and John's, I know that you mean to say (though not quite, I hope, with John's cruelly polite snobbishness) that the non-romantic is of the superior, the winning order, and mine is (with exceptions) of the inferior and losing order. I have never understood why you think that your poetry is not romantic—or why John's, or Red's or T.S. Eliot's is not in the "stream of the romantic movement" while mine is, all wet, right in that stream.

I will not defend my poetry against the charge of inferiority, but I do rebel against the charge that it is inferior because it is romantic. Shelley is your type example of the romantic; and Donne of the non-romantic. But why do you let Donne escape? Romanticism in poetry (in *your* strict sense, not in the general sense) begins with the Renaissance, and Donne is just as much a Romantic, in my opinion, as Shakespeare—or Shelley.

We are too far apart on these matters. We have not understood each other. Let me remind you that in the past four or five years we have hardly had a serious conversation on such topics. What makes you think you know my purposes and beliefs when you have never—or rarely—asked me what they are? I don't like to be dismissed by a friend with a speculative generality. It isn't fair. I know that I am very far indeed from realizing, in poetry, the thing I have aimed at; and that, by comparison with your poetry, John's, and Red's, mine looks diffuse, fragmented, uncertain. Its failure & incompleteness are due to my own natural defects, no doubt—and yet in part to the fact that I have had to work very hard at other things. But I can perceive no defect in my purpose—which is simply to deal with certain subjects that interest me; and to find, if I may use the word, another kind of "objectivity" than the third revolution provides. The third revolution proposes that poems can be only short poems, pseudo-lyrics—the "rounded separate poem" that JCR so mistakenly accuses Shakespeare of attempting to write in his sonnet-sequence; and that "subjectivity" can be escaped & "objectivity" attained by the complicated fictions, the "meant metaphors," etc. described in various essays; and thus the poem becomes a specialized art-work, standing up quite independently and bravely. All right, I grant that it can be done, and is done, well. But does that mean we are forever excluded from narrative & dramatic poetry, in which the prized "objectivity" and all that goes with it comes much more easily and naturally? It is something to have a subject to write about that is not merely an ego but something outside, for the ego to look at. Other things being equal, the *subject* seems to me an important thing—the source of objectivity. I want to find a method that will render a *subject* in a narrative or dramatic form acceptable to the modern reader.

You have used the word *isolation*. Well, I certainly am isolated. No doubt of that. I do not grieve, however, over the kind of isolation that may occur from the disregard of Mr. Zabel or of the Communist reviewers of New York. I do not respect them; they can all go to hell. But I am decidedly grieved by being isolated from my friends. I don't mean physical isolation, deplorable though that is. I mean that I find myself suddenly at a disagreeable intellectual distance, for reasons that I do not in the least understand. You put me there, in your recent letter, by accusing me of being "contemptuous of art"—a hard saying, but not the only hard saying in your letter. I think your allying me with Keats, yourself with Donne, is worse even, from my standpoint. I *detest* Keats, on the whole, if I consult my personal taste. I have to teach him; I never read him when I'm not teaching him. I don't know why my remarks about *The Southern Review* brought forth in your letter such a hauling-over-the-coals for my poor case. Wherefore all this critical battering? Please explain!

It is this intellectual isolation, this lack of communion, which I feel the most. And it began before any of you left these parts. Why, is a mystery I can't solve. What fault was I guilty of? Did I just fail to keep up with the pattern of your thinking, and, though once worthy, thus become unworthy? I felt, more than once, that there was a cloud between me on one side and you, J.C.R., Andrew and perhaps more, on the other side. We were all apparently as good friends as ever, yet there was this cloud. I am not speaking, of course, of mere differences of personal opinion about this or that, at any given time, but of something more impalpable. But since I can't solve the mystery, I am going to stop thinking about it, and don't propose to return to the subject.

And of course it is also true that I have been publicly passed by, to a certain extent. John, as I am sure you recognize, has given me a practically direct snub; but I knew it was coming—it had been coming for a long time. By building up instances, I could, if it came to that, make out that I have been almost *forced* into isolation by my own friends. This "passing by" business may have actually hurt me, or at least not helped me; and yet I have no stomach for making out the case that could be made. The thought of it makes me feel foolish and irritated, and leads me to all sorts of self-doubts. But again, it's only when I get stirred up, and fall into black Scots moodiness, that I think much about it. I propose to go on, regardless.

Yet such meditations do make me hesitant about attempting, at this time at least, such a "Fugitive history" as you suggest. Hadn't I better let that wait?

Faithfully yours, Don

186   *a.* At this time Ezekiel was an economic adviser to the secretary of agriculture; Lewis was president of the United Mine Workers of America. *b.* "The Poetry of Allen Tate," *Southern Review* (Winter 1940).

187/ANS

[Princeton, N.J.]
12 July 1940

Dear Don:

We are coming up to Bread Loaf around August 1st, and although I don't know how long we can stay, I want very much to have a long talk with you. Andrew & Edna are here for the summer and will probably come with us; and Andrew wants very much to see you too. Since John is there, we can have a real reunion which ought to do all of us a great deal of good. Separation and isolation breed misunderstanding.

Yrs. Allen

188/ALS

Nashville, Tenn.
9 April 1942

Dear Allen:

I read your letter with considerable emotion—which was not mitigated by my recent delving among the old Fugitive relics.

Today I sent Mr. Boyd[a] a package containing what I was able to get together hastily. I am sorry all this has to be done in such a hurry. I might do better, with more time. But some of the items are interesting, nevertheless—and perhaps you will be a little surprised to see some of them: you may not have known they were in existence; I hardly did, either, till I looked. Among the notable are: 1) a holograph MS of Tate's "Nuptials" and a carbon copy of "Wm. Blake," signed "Feathertop"; 2) an "early" version of John's "Survey of Literature"; 3) the MS, in part, of one of the early issues of *The Fugitive*; 4) a pencilled notation showing the vote taken on poems at the meeting when we decided what would go in the first issue. This is a really precious bit. It shows the number of votes the poems got and (so I suppose) the number of lines in each; and there is something to show what poem, out of the group submitted by each, was chosen; I can't quite be sure what it all means. And all that notation is made on the back of a letter to me (a young, impoverished instructor, 3 years out of the army) from Chancellor Kirkland, concerning my application for an apartment made vacant for the coming year by Max Souby's[b] death. It was Dr. Mims, I suspect, who urged me to apply for this apartment, and you see how cruel and nasty the answer was! The old skunk went out of his way to be mean. The conjunction of the Fugitive ballot and the old Chance's letter simply appalled me—I had forgotten all about it. 5) Some Fugitive circulars, and a memorandum book, obtained free from Cullom & Ghertner, containing some records of subscriptions and of stamp expenditures! It is a pathetic little book. It also contains, under the mysterious heading, "VLB," the expense account of the "Vanderbilt Lecture Bureau," an enterprise ambitiously launched, which failed because the prospective audiences thought ill of us and of Vanderbilt because we asked a fee (never over $25.00).

There are quite a number of MSS, some unpublished ones, chiefly poems read at meetings, but all, I believe, of some slight interest. I tried to find something of everybody's, but could not locate with certainty anything by Frierson or Elliott. I think everybody else is there, at least once, including Sidney Hirsch, Mr. Jim Frank, and Laura R.

I could *not* find—much to my disgust—any of my MSS containing your critical remarks; or at least nothing prior to the "Lee," which isn't a particularly good example for exhibit. I know I have some, but I could not spend any more time looking, as other matters are pressing me hard. I will look further, this week-end, if I have a chance. . . .

It would seem to me better for *us* to provide the Princeton people with MSS from all the group. What they want to select is their affair. But you can guide them. I repeat, I think it should be a representative exhibit, not a specialized one. But that is just my opinion, given at a distance.

The only book MS I have that is interesting is the MS of *The Tall Men.* I don't believe I want to lend this, for various reasons. The MS of *I'll Take My Stand is* at the Tenn. State Library. We *gave* it to that library, don't you remember, when Mrs. [Trotwood] Moore pleaded with us to let her have *something* for their collection of original MSS.ᶜ Somewhere I know I have our *plans* for the Fugitive anthology (it didn't turn up, on this search), but I doubt whether I have that MS.

I did not find my copy of *The Golden Mean.*ᵈ If it didn't burn up in the Wesley Hall fire, it is in some one of my various boxes of stuff. Mrs. Moore might have it at the State Library. Merrill almost certainly has a copy. I envy him his filing system.

Do the Princeton people have *individual* copies (not bound copies) of *The Fugitive?* I have some, a few, that I can lend—including, I think, the first issue. Do they have a copy of the Poetry Society of S. Carolina pamphlet containing John's "Armageddon" and my "Avalon"? Do they have any issues of *The Double Dealer?* I have quite a number of the various "little magazines."

I noticed some sort of subscription, or mailing list in the file—not, I think, the original one. Would they want it?

As ever, Don

188   *a.* Julian Boyd, head librarian at Princeton, is putting on a display of Fugitive materials. *b.* Alumni secretary at Vanderbilt. *c.* Now in the Joint University Libraries, Nashville, Tennessee. *d.* Tate and Ridley Wills had produced a small volume burlesquing modern poets and Fugitive poets in particular, including themselves. It was privately printed in Nashville (1923).

IV

Later Years: 1942-1966

The letters from 1942 to the end of the file are not as closely sequential as in the first three periods. The correspondents were not following any program together, so there was not as much urgency to write frequently. There are also several breaks in this section of the text that do not occur in the file. For instance there is a whole sequence of letters in the early forties concerning the proposed establishment of a Fugitive collection in the Vanderbilt library. Totally frustrated in his efforts to give his letters and papers to Vanderbilt under suitable circumstances, Tate deposited them in the Princeton library. During the 1950s many omitted letters deal with the details of Louise Cowan's book on the Fugitives, plans for her visits to the Fugitives for interviews, what kinds of material she is to be allowed to see, and related matters. The general content of these omitted sequences can be followed in the register. Other breaks in the file are real ones, for often in this section Davidson will begin letters by wondering where Tate is. Tate's letters would not be expected to contain such internal evidence of real breaks rather than lost letters, since Davidson did not move around so much and could always be reached if letters were addressed to Nashville. Although sometimes the letters are far between, from a strictly literary standpoint there are several sequences that rival in fervor and acuteness the letters of the twenties. And since during the later years both men were producing some of their best work, their mutual criticism in these later letters has as great intrinsic interest as anything in the complete file.

189/ALS

Monteagle, Tenn.

4 December 1942

Dear Don:

Your final version of the article is much better, and I certainly see no reason to withdraw it.ª I still think that there are two points that could be questioned. First, I feel that although you are right about J.C.R., the Saturday Review is not the place to make the point. Second, I am not sure that the record will support your views on *Who Owns America?* Just recently, I went over the enormous correspondence of that period, and it is plain that our deliberations from 1933 to the fall of 1935 came to nothing, and although W.O.A. was not the symposium any of us preferred, I took the view that it was either that or nothing, and everybody but you and perhaps Frank took the same view. *All through that period you simply would not act.* And likewise the records show *conclusively* that even *I'll Take My Stand* would have been postponed for a year or indefinitely had I not taken it upon myself to *act* decisively in my high-handed fashion.

I don't like to talk this way; I am only moved to do it because you feel that you have been left alone to "carry the ball," and that belief puts me and others, as well as John, in a poor light. I don't deserve it. Don, you have a gift for persecution and martyrdom, and although the practical results of agrarianism have been slight, I don't see how, in your chosen sphere, you can feel any personal frustration. Frankly I was amazed when, early this fall, you told me your troubles, and expatiated on your anxieties, yet you could not give a moment's attention to the situation of an old friend, but returned me a blank look when I mildly alluded to my predicament. You have always had a steady job and security, and of late a considerable royalty income; I have had temporary jobs and insecurity, and right now I face great difficulties. So far as I can see you have not made any material sacrifices for agrarianism, while others certainly have. You, like the rest of us, have alienated the good will of our opponents, but that is all in the game, and nobody can claim credit for that kind of courage, even though it may have kept us from getting into the high places of the dominant groups. I, for one, never wanted to be there. I believe we must take things as they come. You evidently believe that agrarianism was a failure; I think it was and *is* a very great success; but then I never expected it to have any political influence. It is a reaffirmation of the humane tradition, and to reaffirm that is an end in itself. Never fear:

we shall be remembered when our snipers are forgotten. I have had a certain disagreement with you from the beginning; you have always seemed to me to hold to a kind of mystical secularism, which has made you impatient and angry at the lack of results. We live in a bad age in which we cannot give our best; but no age is good.

Your letter to Julian Boyd is excellent. I too had set January 1st as a tentative dead-line, after which, if Kuhlman does not act, I will.[b]

Yrs. Allen

189 *a.* "The 'Mystery' of the Agrarians: Facts and Illusions about Some Southern Writers," *Saturday Review of Literature* (January 23, 1943). *b.* Frederick A. Kuhlman at this time was director of the Joint University Libraries, Nashville, Tennessee.

190/ALS

Nashville, Tenn.
2 January 1943

Dear Allen:

Kuhlman told me, a day or two ago, that his plan is almost ready to present; that he has sent it to the heads of the three institutions (who constitute his Executive Committee for the Joint Univ. Library) and expects early approval; and that another meeting with us might be desirable. I will let you know as soon as developments occur. It seems to me that we should have his plan to study *before* we meet with him, if possible.

Your last letter about my *Sat. Review* article left me feeling very reproachful toward you, and I wrote you a letter which I did not finish and which I later destroyed. I don't feel that anything is gained by exchanging reproaches. We are both in a low state of mind, and it would be better to see what we can do toward cheering each other up.

However, I think I ought to reply to one or two points in your letter, but by way of information, not in argument.

I referred to *Who Owns America?* as I did because I wanted to get Agar out of the center of the picture; to dissociate him as far as I could from our own activities, which seem to me more important. Maybe I used too strong a word in saying that *Who Owns America?* "displaced" a sequel to *I'll Take My Stand.* But I had to write briefly. The brevity of statement does you some injustice, perhaps, but that couldn't be helped, under the circumstances. That book itself did some injustices and created some misunderstandings. I believe you receive full justice elsewhere in my article; and I have also indicated that we worked and wrote as individuals, most of the time. That is true, I'm sure. I had no opportunity in this article to give any detailed history.

You reproach me with "not acting" during the years from 1933 to 1935. You forget what a difficult position I was in during that time: burned-out of Wesley Hall, broke and in debt, ill with overwork and serious dental troubles, and my family ill too; my wife, in those years, had to undergo a serious operation which incapacitated her for a long period: we had to manage alone, unaided, without cheer or support from any quarter. I believe you should do me this much justice—to erase from your mind any reproachfulness you may have concerning my "not acting." It is my opinion, nevertheless, that if we had not got involved with Agar, we would have brought out another symposium and perhaps would have done other things still more important. But that's just an opinion. You are certainly right, on the other hand, in saying that it was your action with Harper's that resulted in the immediate production of *I'll Take My Stand.*

Now as to my remarks about my having to "carry the ball." I referred merely to this fact, which no one can gainsay: from 1936 to 1940 I published 17 articles and several reviews which bear rather specifically upon agrarian matters, as I understand them. In the same years I published *The Attack on Leviathan.* During this same period nearly everybody else in the group turned to purely literary articles or historical specialties. Thorp's bibliography of your writing will show that this is true, in general, for you. Ransom's desertion of this field is too obvious. The same goes for most of the others. Owsley made occasional small contributions, through his excellent reviews, but most of the time has been engaged in a big job of historical research; it is of great ultimate importance, but it has had no bearing on immediate problems. I might add, also, that I made certain public appearances during these years, at Chicago, at Notre Dame, at Atlanta, and elsewhere, and did what I could on agrarian and allied issues. Also, I have steadily taught in my classes at Vanderbilt the works of Tate, Ransom, Warren, Owsley, Caroline Gordon, and others; Beatty and Fidler's *Contemporary Southern Prose* has been my advanced composition textbook ever since it was issued; and I devote a special period of my course in modern literature to the works of the same group. Also, I took care that, in my *American Comp. & Rhetoric,* the same people should be fairly & favorably represented, and did so, as I am sure you will understand, with the certain knowledge that this editorial fairness would be called a bias, and would injure sales, as it did, especially in the South. You might be interested sometime, in seeing some of the low-down comments made by Southern teachers concerning this book, and in knowing how it happened to be excluded from use at the University of Georgia, L.S.U., and other places.

Now I don't believe there is anything about these actions to suggest a "persecution complex." I have simply gone ahead in the direction where my inclinations & convictions led me. That is all there is to it. I would have forgotten most of this if the reference by that idiot, John Rice, to "John Ransom's Agrarians" had not stirred me up to think about it all again, and suggested a peg on which I might hang that unfortunate *Sat. Review* article. I would never have remembered what articles I wrote, or how many, if Vanderbilt University had not published a little booklet (which I just consulted) showing the publications of its faculty, from 1936 to 1940; and I don't deserve any special credit for doing what I wanted to do anyhow; and furthermore, I don't seem to have accomplished very much by my efforts. So there is nothing, really, to argue about between you and me. I merely want you to recall the facts, as facts, and reflect that they are the background for my irritation at your suggestion, which I still do not understand, that I omit the reference to John Ransom in my article.

On the other side of the discussion, I do not in any way intend depreciation of your choice to devote yourself mainly to poetry and literary criticism or fiction. I think, as I know you do, that that kind of writing is of utmost importance, more important in the long run than the topical variety that I have been engaging in to some extent. You know my admiration for your work. I don't think I need say any more. I tried to indicate, in that brief article, that it is all one body of writing, in a way. But I could have excepted some of John Ransom's most recent essays in refined aesthetics, which I hold to be a misuse of his great gifts, and which I suspect of being in conflict with what I had once supposed to be his basic principles. Again, my "frustration" to which you refer arises not at all out of any notion that the agrarian principles are being made invalid or are being ultimately defeated, but from the immediately painful *fact* that, since John has not publicly disavowed his old principles, our interpreters will suppose, and sometimes say, that John's narrow aesthetics are my aesthetics and yours and are "agrarian" aesthetics, when nothing could be further from the truth. I simply do not want to enlist, or to be thought to be enlisted, under the particular flag which John has been waving, and, frankly, I would like for my unwillingness to be clearly understood by anybody that wants to know.

You make some reference in your letter to my personal affairs. Don't you think it would be better not to bring up such matters at all? After all, you are hardly in a good position to judge my situation, for you know practically nothing about it except a few obvious externals. And since you are not well informed, I don't believe you ought to think of my situation in comparison with yours. It is of course always a human temptation to do just that. For my part, I will say in regard to your situation that I have always admired the independence and courage with which you and Caroline have gone ahead on your chosen ways despite all difficulties and discouragements. You will have a credit that can be given to few in these times, for almost nobody has had the will or the courage to keep steadily on the line you have followed. I am very sorry if by my manner or words I seemed not to sympathize with you in present difficulties. I did not mean that at all, of course; and what you refer to as a "blank stare" was simply the inexpressiveness that, I am afraid, is a family failing—a Davidson muteness which you would recognize if you knew many of my people. You certainly know that I not only sympathize but stand ready to help you in any way that is within my power, as I always have stood ready, though so often unfortunately powerless and ineffective at times when I would most wish to be helpful.

Faithfully, Don

P.S. Eleanor Ross says you are translating the Pervigilium. I hope you will let Theresa & me see your translation. We were delighted to have the New Year's greeting and have spent some time discussing the translation of the Latin. The last lines of the poem seem even more applicable to this age.

191/TLS

Monteagle, Tenn.
5 January 1943

Dear Don:

I thought you and Theresa would be interested in the Pervigilium; and I agree that the last stanza would have been a more appropriate New Year's card; but I feared it might sound like a complaint of my own muse. I can't really complain of it, or at any rate not on the ground of silence. I have been busy as a bee for two months at verse, letting the novel go to hell. I am sending you the Pervigilium[a] and some other selected efforts of these two months.

The refrain of the Pervigilium is the tough nut to crack. Better than what I have, for meaning, would be: "Tomorrow may loveless, may lover tomorrow love." But I added *make* in order to continue the anapestic movement and to make the meaning immediately clear at the expense of complete accuracy. You will see that I am fairly literal in some places and very free in others. The poem is by no means uniformly rich and excellent; there are very thin places from the viewpoint of literal translation, that have to be filled in to make any show at all in English. I have wanted to translate this poem for twenty years, but could never get a satisfactory refrain. I am not wholly pleased with the refrain that I have, but it at least seemed adequate. I believe there is no way to translate the two occurrences of *amavit* as verbs; they are weaker as nouns, but as verbs in English they would be very awkward. I would like very much to have your and Theresa's criticism. I believe I have done better with the two last stanzas than with any others; but of course they are the best in the Latin.

I am convinced that we are not in as much disagreement as we may imagine. I think we ought to let this part of the discussion languish. I am very much interested in what you have to say about the boycott of your texts in Southern colleges. I don't pretend to understand it; that sort of thing has baffled me for many years. Now take Sewanee. I actually do stand for the things that they only pretend to stand for, and the result is that I am hated there by people with whom I have never exchanged a word and who have never read a line of my writings. Why is this? There's some kind of conventional view of us that has got mysteriously into circulation over many years. I am certain that the trouble with the South is that it doesn't want to be Southern, and when we offer the genuine thing it stirs a ferocity of resentment that wholly baffles us. There's another element too. When people have betrayed their own heritage, it is natural for them to hate anybody who reminds them of the betrayal. The other day I was talking to Alex Guerry,[b] who I am convinced is a very honest and sincere, if completely muddle-headed man. He was lamenting the collapse of the liberal arts under impact of the war, and seemed to think that the war alone is responsible. His own policies here and at Chattanooga were progressive and liberal, and now that the liberal chickens have come home to roost, he is bewildered. I said that I had forseen the collapse of the liberal arts in the next war, along with many other people. Then for malice I added that that was what agrarianism was all about—a redefinition of the humane tradition of the South which once had its education based upon the liberal arts. He said naively: "I didn't know that." In fact I have been told that he has never read any of us; and yet last summer when he was "considering" me for the Review, his one objection to me was that I represented agrarianism. He didn't know what it was, and he didn't know that it was a defense of what he thinks he believes in. This situation is almost symbolic of this mysterious dislike of us all over the South. Think it over. . . .

                                                          Yrs. ever Allen

P.S. Again as to the Pervigilium: I worked out the rhythm of the refrain as follows: It is completely anapestic except for the first foot. The movement of the rest of the translation is mainly iambic, with many anapests, and even whole lines that are anapestic. I wanted to keep the tendency towards an anapestic movement latent, never fully realized, in order to get a rising and falling effect, as of revery or dream. I am sure that the original convention of which the poem is an example included a public reading or celebration; but this poem is obviously a personal lyric based upon that convention at a far remove. It is very modern. Think of the personal turn at the end. I shuffled Mackail's order of the stanzas for better continuity. I don't know why he didn't do it. I should think that my arrangement ought to convince the textual critic that *all* the poem is there if you know what ought to follow what.

191   a. *The Vigil of Venus: Pervigilium Veneris* (1943).   b. Vice-chancellor of the University of the South.

192/ALS

                                                          Monteagle, Tenn.
                                                          29 January 1943
Dear Don:
    I am flooding you with letters. —*Refugees* is splendid.[a] Why don't you republish it in the *Sewanee Review?* Besides "agreeing" with the critics, I like it better than your Va. Quarterly poem (which by the way Andrew has not returned).[b] The latter had some beautiful passages, but I could never tell what you were saying exactly, and it seemed

necessary to find out, because, unlike much modern poetry, it seemed to depend on an "argument" about the pioneer. I know your ideas on that subject, and conjecture your thesis, but I felt it wasn't distinct enough in the poem.

If you would only turn yourself loose! And let your *theme* take you in any direction. You seem bound by *subject*. You are one of the best poets living, but you've roped and tied yourself.

I've been turning off one poem after another. I enclose the latest —that is the latest finished poems. Tell me what you think of them. I've projected three more (half through the second) in the same stanza (my own) as the *Dejected Lines* is in, one for each season, all the same length. I'm inclined to *hope* that *Jubilo*ᶜ is almost as good as *The Mediterranean*; but you set me right.

Yrs. Allen

192   *a.* A poem published in the *Bread Loaf Anthology* (1939).   *b.* "Hermitage" appeared in the *Virginia Quarterly Review* (Winter 1943).   *c. Kenyon Review* (Spring 1943).

193/ALS

Nashville, Tenn.
31 January 1943

Dear Allen:

I wish I could emulate you in your present outburst of fine poems. I feel the urge to try, all right, but to accomplish anything I would require what I don't have now—some degree of seclusion, for at least a part of my time, and a little relief now and then from pressures which I can't just at this moment escape. The "Refugees" poem was written a good many years ago—I don't remember just when. But when the Bread Loaf people decided to publish an anthology, three or four years ago, and almost demanded something from me, I dug that poem up from my MS book, changed it a little, and gave it to them, since it was all I had. I had intended to call it "Fugitives," but changed to "Refugees" to suit the times. I am glad that you like it. You are the first person ever to express liking for it. It has passed quite unnoticed. If Andrew wants to republish it, that is all right with me, but he will have to communicate with The Middlebury College Press, which published the *Bread Loaf Anthology.* I can't imagine, really, that Andrew would want to print a poem that has already been published, and has had some circulation. That B–L Anthology, I think, sold out its first edition and perhaps printed another—at least I recall their saying that the book sold very well. I think it is a fairly good poem, but I myself prefer the other one, "Hermitage," which contains more of what I feel bound to say. But of course "Hermitage" is very imperfect. I could not "improve" it beyond a certain point without feeling that I was losing it. There is no special "argument" or "thesis" implied in it that you are not perfectly acquainted with. I don't think of it as argumentative; rather it is personal. It is my way of tackling the theme you have in "The Mediterranean," but I see it in terms of certain persons & places. I am afraid that its fault is that it merely repeats what I have been saying or trying to say since about 1927.

Both of your new poems are fine! There is nothing about them I would criticize except that your "Dejected Lines"[a] are too evidently in Yeats' idiom, and that makes the poem a rather special thing. You accept this, and more or less explicitly acknowledge it and guard it in the poem itself by speaking of *"my master Yeats,"* but I don't think that Yeats really is your "master," though you have learned from him. I think it would be more in character for you to say *The Irishman* Yeats, or something like that, which is more after your usual mode of reference to literary persons. The Yeats idiom comes out most strongly in the latter part of Stanza I, the first part of Stanza II, the first part of Stanza IV. But the last part of Stanza II is definitely *Tate*. So is all of Stanza III, and so are lines elsewhere. You might, however, lose the power now in the poem if by a great deal of revising you attempted to take out the Yeats idiom, which, after all, you probably intend to be there.

The "Jubilo" poem appeals to me enormously. It rests entirely, of course, on the reader's capacity to digest the two conceptions you have woven into it: (1) The Civil War song, supposed to have been "composed" by Work (afterwards connected with Fisk Univ., I think), and the difficulties of Coleridge's Ancient Mariner. People like Donald Stauffer & Elizabeth Drew,[b] who were so busily "analyzing" your poems and others at Bread Loaf last summer, will *apprehend* those concepts, but won't *comprehend* them at all. Therefore the poem will not "bite" for them as it bites for me. I think it is a stroke of genius to unite the two. But they (the Drews & Stauffers) won't know that your poem not only bites but smites. And we have no chance of saying to them, as Jack said to the Giant (when the Giant said "Oh, you missed me!"), "Shake yourself and see." This is the difficulty that high satire encounters in our day. It's an inevitable difficulty, but it doesn't impair my personal satisfaction in the poem. I would like to see copies of the

poem in the hands of the people who would really comprehend it,—
and who need it, for solace & encouragement. I can think of several
such—all young people, in their early twenties, some of them now in
the army. (John Wade, also, would have a special enjoyment of it; it
is the kind of irony which he works into his own prose.)

For a footnote, I might add that Dr. Jackson[c] has discovered the
source of the tune which Work used for the "Jubilo" song. In his new
book, just out, he derives it from "The Boatie Rows," a Scottish song,
which was current in the South and in blackface minstrel shows before
it was "captured." I have Work's original if you ever want to see it. It
appeared in Root's book of songs for Union soldiers, etc., "The Bugle
Call" (about 1862 or 3). I bought a copy of this book at Tuttle's store
in Vermont. . . .

Faithfully, Don

193   a. An early version of the "Winter" section of "Seasons of the Soul."   b. Stauffer was a member of the English department at Princeton, and Elizabeth Drew,
a critic and author.   c. George Pullen Jackson was head of the German department at Vanderbilt and author of White Spirituals in the Southern Uplands.

194/TLS

Monteagle, Tenn.
3 February 1943
Dear Don:

. . . I am sending you another poem. It goes with the Dejected
Stanzas, and is in fact the second of a series of four which will all be
written in that stanza (my invention) and will all have six stanzas. The
Dejected Stanzas will be called Winter, and the two yet unwritten will
be Summer and Fall. A new title will cover all four, something like
"Seasonal Meditations, To the Memory of W.B. Yeats." You spotted
unerringly the Yeatsisms in the first poem. I deliberately used them
for a purpose something like this: I wanted to acknowledge Yeats as a
great poet, and at the same time ask a question which he never fairly
faced (the question of the last stanza); so the "my master Yeats" is partly
ironic; as if to say, through the imitation of his style, "You are a great
stylist, and in that a master, but there's something you evaded." Maybe
that's all too subtle. Only in that poem will the Yeatsisms appear. I
think you will find none in the new one.

If you want to show the Jubilo poem to some young men, do so.
I've sent it to the Kenyon Review, but I strongly suspect that John will

not like it. I predict his line: that the metre is eccentric. John has become a perfect neo-classicist and will have nothing to do with accentual versification: you've got to count your syllables to please him. I will not please him from here on out; for I see myself as more and more committed to accentual verse, with very little metre in it. . . .

Yrs. Allen

195/ALS

Nashville, Tenn.
21 March 1943

Dear Allen:

This is the first Sunday—indeed, the first *day*—in some months when I have not had a batch of student papers and similar things to worry over. So I have spent a while, quite a long while, in rereading and studying your "Seasonal Confessions."

It's a superbly written poem—one of your best, though I don't know whether it's in your best vein. That is, I like better those gloomy poems of yours (and this is a gloomy one) which have a somewhat defiant ring, along with the prophetic strain. This one is more inconclusive than most of yours, since you intimate that there's a point where your vision can't penetrate—you can't see, for sure, what is coming. I almost prefer you when you are categorically announcing destruction. However, you will say it is conclusive enough—as conclusively as it can honestly be.

I like the general symbolic organization of the poem—which comes nearer to "allegory" than you yourself will admit, having once condemned allegory. I like the technical organization, too: the modified refrain, varying in the four parts and within the parts; the hard, simplified diction, which still is smooth, and is heavily charged by its inherent ideas; and the meter; and the style in general.

For specific criticism of little things, I don't have much to offer. I tend to object to the prescript from Dante (is it?)—on the ground that such things have become a modern affectation; Eliot is a vicious offender in this respect; we have all been guilty, though; nevertheless, I have acquired a distaste for such things, which may be personal & invalid. I concede that the prescript does help one in the exegesis of the poem; I can see no other excuse for it. There are a few Tate-isms—words you are too fond of, have repeated here & there in your poems: "heart escheat"; "rind" (remember Oenia?); and the informal contraction in the next to the last line, "whether *you're* kind, mother." The game of taws in stanza 3 is, I submit, pure Yeatsism, since in this country we never speak of a *game* of taws, but "come to taw" (i.e., stand behind the line), or sometimes use taw for a specific marble, maybe, not for the game. I rather object to "refuelling juice" (Part IV, stanza 1), since it makes me think of gasoline—perhaps you want that, but it seems out of tone. Also, I don't get and don't much like "Jack-and-Jilling seas" (4th stanza from end).

But these things don't really matter much. I don't know whether they are worth changing. The poem is fine as it stands, and you may weaken the poem as a whole by making what looks like a technical improvement at a minor point. You *have* done that, in the past.

The poem is too heavily charged with meaning for me to be able to absorb it all, even after several careful readings. You have made the modern device of "inferential writing" (that's what I call it) carry a heavier charge than usual, despite the outward appearance of ease & simplicity. It seems to me that you have come to this poem, probably through the "Pervigilium Veneris"—both the poem (slightly) and the theme (clearly, though ironically) are echoed & used. That seems to me the basic pattern. Into it you have woven a great deal more. It is not merely a spring poem. It is a poem of all the seasons, which tend under the modern regime to blend into one abstract procession. In the blazing summer, with its sky grown infinitely tall (Seversky's[a] "ocean of air"—*air* is the thematic element in this section) we raise our tired eyes, not in praise of summer, but, in weariness, to read the common clause (i.e., the general & common fate, the "decree") that takes us all, both the prophet and his miraculous ass. We are impotent as the dead. And all are refugees, like the French, when they were beset—eaten up, even as the weevils eat the boll before it is a boll. But in this war summer we only inherit the evil we begot, and in our agony we dispense with our natural human emotions, lest the reasonable mind (which we really fear) engage & instrument them. The soul, too, must shut out summer—deathly summer—lest it be blinded, as the eye is blinded by sun. "Brothers in arms" is partly ironic, partly serious & direct. I don't quite understand the next stanza ("When was it that the summer") but in the last you call up Dante & Vergil, two men of the "summer world" that was better than *this* summer world,—who were "saved" for the unwell Renaissance world (ours, now ending maybe). I don't understand the "beast," or the centaur, though I suppose I ought to know the latter reference. It does make an effective ending of the section.

Your autumn vision is no less terrifying than the summer one. In the fashion of Dante—and Tate—you pursue a dream which deals with the horror of abstractions. A well that is a hall with false doors, where shades can slip in and out; but you in your dream cannot; it is a vision of the dead whom you cannot reach; and you cannot question them and get an answer, as both Vergil & Dante were able to. And your vision freezes you in the empty hall. This is all very powerful. I won't say, however, that I can get all the implications—the inferences that are there if I had only the context to make them. (*Earth* is the dominant element in Part II.)

In part III, turning from the autumnal vision of the dead, you pass to a treatment of Venus, seen in a wintry context. Here *Water* becomes your thematic element. "Eddying twilight" gathers upon the devotees of Venus—the lovers. Let Venus, now being contracepted out of existence, return to her element; the religion of love is now meaningless; the sea-gods are dead. But even the element of Venus is now hostile & sterile, where guerrilla sharks have become her doves (submarines?); and even the sea-conceited scop of the A–S "Seafarer" would find nothing to lure him back from the land to the sea, fouled with modern droppings; and then "the ingenious animal" (man, abstractly inventive) appears possessively, a veritable sadist & paranoiac, to wreak his ruin under the sea. (The "madrepore," I suspect, echoes an almost long-lost phrase of Alec Stevenson's!) You pluck a bough of the undersea grove, and the blood speaks as it did to Aeneas, and tells how man came to undergo the singular transformation you have been previously describing—wherein, really, intellect has ousted (dried up) desire—or so I suppose.

Part IV is "spring" (element, fire). You have arranged the poem so as to end with spring because you want to bring up that old matter of being reborn. Venus now seems to merge into "alma mater," the Virgin. And we are back, probably, at about the 5th century, B.C., or we are asking whether we are about to repeat the events of that time. I find this very hard reading. Are we to return to the Platonic cave and then re-issue—or not? Your prayer, which is quite pagan, is addressed to the "mother of silences," whom I cannot surely identify, but she must be, somehow, both Venus and the Virgin Mary. Monica was the mother of St. Augustine, was she? You are asking whether the mother of silences would have a vision like the mother of St. Augustine?

Are you? But there is no answer. You don't know. Will the mother be "kind" & let us be reborn; or be mother of silences (please explain)?

I've done my best at paraphrase—an art I don't often practice, before you, & about one of your poems. But perhaps it may be a kind of criticism to show you just what I do and what I don't quite get after the first readings (plural). At any rate you can see that I have read religiously.

At some later time I'd like to discuss with you the technique of inference, of which both modern poetry & modern prose have made so much in our time.

Well, congratulations on your fine poem, to which I will return later, probably many times. You need have no fear. It is an excellent fruit to come from the labor you have been spending on it. And you must have been, as I said, in a perfect fury of composition. It has been long since you have written such a sustained & fully rounded piece. The other long ones have sometimes been discursive.

That's all for tonight. Tomorrow I go to walk in the Academic procession for the first Vanderbilt Commencement ever held prior to June, and to witness the reception by my son-in-law of his M.D. degree. Time passes—how it gets along.

Yrs. Don

195   a. Alexander P. de Seversky, author of *Victory Through Air Power* (1942).

196/TLS

Monteagle, Tenn.
23 March 1943

Dear Don:

Only one thing could please me more than your magnificent letter about my poem, and that is a long poem of your own.

You put your finger on all the weak spots. Some of them I had already begun to deal with, but the others I was lazy about; you have made me face them.

Your paraphrase is wonderfully exact. I can't see that you missed anything important. You saw exactly what I was trying to say. Even when you confess that you don't understand the Mother of Silences, the *way* in which you state your failure to understand is exactly the way in which I wanted the figure to be understood. She is all the things you attribute to her, and not any one of them. More than almost anything else your exact and subtle grasp of my use of Venus pleases me. Several people who have read the poem failed to see the four elements and their relation to the seasons; I am simply tickled pink that you saw this.

Well, Don, such understanding ought to be enough for any poet. And it is.

I have not exhausted your letter. I will have to study it very closely as I begin a new period of revision.

Is there any news down there?

Yrs. Allen

P.S. Yes, Steve's "Only the ghostly madrepores" gave me the image. When I think the poem is really finished, I will send him a copy.

197/ANS

Nashville, Tenn.
10 April 1945

Dear Allen:

Your article is extraordinarily fine.ᵃ It is definitive and true, and it abounds with insight into both the modern disease and the nature of the wholesome opposite. Nobody has ever said more clearly what is wrong with the course of things modern. It is all, really, in your antithesis between "Is it right?" and "Will it work?", and in your just observation that we have abstracted a part of the Greek heritage, & junked the rest. I would disagree with you only, perhaps, in your estimate of Ellen Glasgow's *Barren Ground,* which I think is wrong in its basic conception, shoddy in its lack of knowledge, and shabby in its artifice. (Have you read it recently? I have! I teach it!) I hate the Va. Q. Review for their smirking retraction in the Notes on Contributors. I wonder who was responsible for that folly. What a hell of a world this is!

Yrs. as ever Don

197 a. "The New Provincialism, with an Epilogue on the Southern Novel," *Virginia Quarterly Review* (Spring 1945).

198/ALS

Nashville, Tenn.
2 October 1945

Dear Allen:

... It was too bad that our only possible vacation time had to fall at the time when you were away. We missed you. But we owe you many thanks for making the Monteagle arrangements for us. They were very pleasant and satisfactory.

The Autumn number of The *Review*[a] has just come, and I have been glancing through it. I can't follow Wyndham Lewis here or elsewhere with much satisfaction, but I do admire Caroline's story and other things. I was a little surprised at the Aragon poems; I didn't think he wrote so well formerly. Kirstein's stuff, on the other hand, seems to me trashy. If I were a Frenchman I shouldn't like to be represented by such scraps. Louis Wright's article is fine. He doesn't write particularly well, and much of what he says has been said before, but at this particular moment it is indeed helpful to have this particular man on this particular subject.

Your editorial is strong & right, and at many points is masterful in expression. I agree with you everywhere practically, but I think, if you had to differ with me on my points made in my article (as you readily might) you should have been careful not to misrepresent me as you have done—possibly because you were too conscious, at the moment, of the charges contained in those letters. Of course I do *not* believe that segregation was instituted for the protection of negroes. I did *not* say that in my article;[b] I said the opposite! But I added that the segregation arrangements imply a strong *secondary* concern for negroes. And I did *not* say that we "may nullify at will" the 14th & 15th amendments. I pointed out that we *have been* doing so and are doing so. It is matter of fact, not potentiality! What is the complaint against us if not that the South *does* deny the citizenship & due process of law supposedly provided by the 14th amendment, and that the South *does* abridge the right of suffrage supposedly provided negroes in the 15th amendment? I am not bothered particularly by your error of reference; there's no particular point in laboring the matter further; but some of your close readers may be puzzled. All I will say is that I just can't imagine what you were intending to accomplish in the sentence in question. ...

Faithfully, Don

198   *a.* The *Sewanee Review*.   *b.* "Preface to Decision," *Sewanee Review* (Summer 1945).

199/ALS

Nashville, Tenn.

3 October 1945

Dear Allen:

I just received, supposedly from John Ransom, a copy of the Autumn *Kenyon Review*—the only copy I have ever received from John since he began editing it, except for one copy I earned for my one and only review contributed. I wondered why he sent me this large new number. Then I looked through it and found out. It contains John's first open & public recantation of his agrarian principles.[a] I suppose by this time you have read it—his remarks (almost *obiter dicta*) by way of discussion of one Southard's earnest but labored discussion of Red's poems. I write you for the obvious reason: I want to give vent to my feelings, and to learn what your notions about John's performance are if you feel like writing me.

It is all right for John to change his mind, of course. Who could prevent him? And to change it in public if he chooses. Already by his silence on anything but purely aesthetic issues he had in effect severed his connection with his old friends, all but officially, and had implicitly chosen a new alignment. I deplore that, and have long since grieved over it much, but John is and has been his own master; and furthermore there have been other occasions when he swung an axe wildly, not much regarding his friends.

But what a shame that, in recanting from his agrarian principles, John accepts as a valid interpretation of our principles the silliest and meanest version of our ideas that our critics gave. And not only accepts it but restates it, and lets the world know that this is the sum and substance of the childish & unworthy belief which he once held and now has put aside. He even accepts the "nostalgia" part as authentic. And then he makes his apologia. J.C.R.'s nostalgia for the simple agrarian community was justified because it produced certain valuable works of repentance—the art works, including his own poems. I can only say, what devil has got into John Ransom?

It is a nasty sort of injury to his old friends, or so I judge it, since in a way it renders authentic the Geo. Fort Milton, H. L. Mencken, & Chamber of Commerce view of agrarianism; or it gives that view seemingly authoritative support, from within the old group. Of course we were not proposing to create any utopian & simple agrarian community; we were defending the one that existed in the South, such as it was, and were conducting an argument in the hope of directing attention to various important issues, still as pressing now as they were in 1930. We lost the immediate experiment; that is, we converted no large body of opinion, high or low, received no subsidies from foundations, formed no bloc of voters. Though John's now open defection exposes us, probably, to taunts and embarrassments, even to a kind of injury, it need not & should not affect the ultimate argument, which is still in process, and may or may not have its effect—who can tell?

But as for John—it seems too bad. Anybody can now observe that Ransom of the North talks differently, if not oppositely from Ransom of the South; and can also see that Ransom of the North has put himself on the side of the strongest battalions. What next?

Somebody ought, of course, to write the *Kenyon Review* a sharp letter and correct John's really awful misstatements. I hope somebody will, somebody with bristly & uncompromising words, but also somebody who is *outside the group connections altogether.*

I don't feel inclined to write John at all, even a personal letter. I wonder if I ever shall be able to again. (I wrote him, weeks ago, a letter about his book of poems—which of course he didn't answer.) What, in general & particular, do you think? My belief is that it would be best for all of us to ignore this outbreak of John's entirely—to give him no answer but silence.

Faithfully Don

199   a. "Art and the Human Economy."

200/ALS

Nashville, Tenn.
1 February 1948

Dear Allen:

Thank you exceedingly for the signed copy of your *Poems, 1922–1947*, which just reached me. The book tells me, once more, that the poems are as alive as ever, and also reassures me that the author still lives, a matter I had begun to wonder about. Your inscription, however, is quite wrong in implying, even facetiously, that I, by this time, may be "tired of seeing these poems." There has not been a year of the 25 between 1922 and 1947 when I have not re-read your poems, generally not some but all of them. And I could think of no better way of celebrating the 25th year than to read and re-read them again—which I have just been doing. They carry, for me, not only the excitement that, as high poetic art, they intrinsically contain, but the excitement that attaches to them for me personally and is associated with the first days of our individual and mutual ventures. It is an excitement that can never stale or diminish. When I congratulate you, therefore, please remember it is not only the man of 1948 who writes, but the unforgetting young companion of 1922. But the man of 1948 knows, more definitely than ever, that they are great poems and will long, long outlast us both.

In 1946 I sent you Vol. I of *The Tennessee,*[a] but never had any indication that it reached you. For this reason I made no arrangements to send you Vol. II. I have no news of you or your whereabouts, and must address this letter to your publisher. The only news that seems worth giving from my quarter is that there are, as usual, wolves in the next room[b] and that they are also more widely abroad. Packs of wolves, and singles, have been seen and vainly pursued in Maury, Williamson and Robertson counties.

Faithfully yours, Don

200   a. *The Tennessee*, Rinehart Rivers of America Series, vol. 1 (1946), vol. 2 (1948).
      b. Davidson is using the words of Tate's poem "The Wolves."

201/ALS   New York City
                                                       12 February 1948

Dear Don:

It's a fine letter, and I appreciate it. I got the book out with misgivings because there were so few new poems; but my *excuse* was the limited edition of *The Winter Sea*; and I thought it legitimate to combine that book with the old poems, which have been long out of print. Your loyalty and your praise have touched me deeply: there's nobody in the world from whom I more desire them.

After some six months of seclusion Caroline and I are coming back to the world again, and to a normal life. I only allude to our abysmal troubles: they are over, I trust, and a new life awaits us if we can seize it. I have quit Holt,[a] and now have more leisure than I've ever had along with freedom of mind. Financially we're in excellent condition, but I fear we shall have to stay in N.Y. to remain that way, at least for a year or two. We are both at work—for the first time in four years.

I was in Memphis last week for three days visiting Nancy and her family (2 grandsons) and I wanted to come by Nashville, but there was no time for it. My excuse for the trip was an honorary D. Litt. from the Univ. of Louisville, which I blush to say I accepted. I had always supposed I would decline such an "honor," but when it came to the decision I imagined that Kentucky as the place of remembrance could not be denied.

No, we never received Vol. 1 of *The Tennessee*. I will now get both volumes and read them.

Aff. yrs. Allen

P.S. I congratulate you on the "wolves in the next room." While I was a publisher the beasts were only jackals.

P.P.S. Some time I'd like to know how my new poem "The Eye" struck you. I saw it, in the writing, as man in the universe of nuclear energy.

201   *a.* Tate was an editor for Henry Holt from 1946 to 1948.

202/ALS

Nashville, Tenn.
24 February 1948

Dear Allen:

I am sorry to be a little late in answering your February 12th letter. I am deeply pleased to have the good news that it contains. It makes me happy to hear from you in this way, and to know that you and Caroline are at work, as of old, together and with favorable auspices, even though in New York. This news relieves the distress that has gnawed within my mind for some time.

You were quite right in accepting the honorary degree. I am glad you did not reject it. I heartily congratulate you, and I foresee more honors of this kind for you. As you say, Kentucky could not be denied. In a similar situation, two years ago, I accepted an honorary degree from Cumberland University. Few people know about this. I would have been glad to get out of it, for I knew the occasion would be painful; but I could not refuse L. L. Rice, then president, with whom I had cordial relations dating far back. The occasion *was* painful. It was tragic. It was the old man's last appearance as president. He was turning over the institution, which had failed, to the Baptists. His farewell address contained as much bitterness as I ever heard from the lips of a public speaker, but I think I was one of the few who realized that.

I noted at once the "The Eye" is a new poem. It is a most remarkable poem. The Greek prescript belongs; for the poem, as to language, is Greek in its precision, though modern in its tropes. I feel unable to make a decent comment, at present. I will have to wrestle with it awhile—I mean as Jacob wrestled. I shall give it close attention, you may be sure. I can still read your poems. Strangely, I cannot read Ransom's any more, and I cannot take as much pleasure as I would expect in Red's—though some of his still hold good for me. Your Greek is one of the great things that make your poetry different. Ransom is too much engaged, still, with Shakespeare. He has made a terrific mistake in counting Homer "out"—in behaving as if Homer never existed. I can see little reason, truly, for studying poetry at all, if Homer has to be left out.

I am much surprised that you never received Vol. I of *The Tennessee*. I just looked at my old list, and it indicates that a copy was to be sent by Rinehart to you at the Henry Holt address, the only one I knew at that time, 1946. I'll see if I can persuade Rinehart to attend to Vol. I, and I am sending you, from my own hand, Vol. II. Of course I would not think of omitting to send you my books, if you can bear the sight of the damned things. Vol. II has been favorably received *outside* the South, but nearly all the Nashville, Chattanooga, Knoxville, Memphis reviews have sneered at my "prejudices" and done their best to injure me. They hate me because in Vol. II I do something they can't endure—i.e., tell the plain, true story of Civil War, Reconstruction, later agitations, and TVA.

I don't know whether I told you that I am on leave of absence from Vanderbilt, and *may* ask to have the leave extended. We spent most of the autumn at Marshallville, Ga., where John Wade again found space for us refugees. And we also traveled extensively in the Carolinas, Alabama, & Mississippi (as far south as Natchez). We had to come back to Nashville because Theresa has to teach, this term. I am supposed to be writing but haven't got beyond first sketches as yet. I have resumed acquaintance with the guitar after not having touched one for 30 years or more. I use my mother's old guitar, and I am teaching myself to devise modal and lute-like arrangements for folk-tunes. I can also strum, hill-billy style, but that is not so interesting.

Regards to you both, from us both.

Affectionately Don

203/ALS

New York City
27 February 1948

Dear Don:

I am glad to get this news-letter from you and to know that you've had the winter off. I wish we could get some time "off" from New York, but as I wrote you, the financial advantages are so great that we must stick it out for a while. (I teach one evening, Caroline, an afternoon and evening, and together we make more than I made at Princeton!) I am not sure where I ought to be (unless I had an independent income!) but I am sure that neither publishing nor regular academic work is for me: the Sewanee story was much more complicated than it seemed, and my personal situation was not the main factor in my leaving.

I wish I *did* have some real Greek! I am trying to do a study of Longinus and stumble over his quotations, which I cannot evaluate stylistically. I haven't read Homer in years but I shall read him next fall for a series of lectures and will tackle the Greek again.

I am glad about the guitar. I keep at the fiddle a little, not practicing but playing pieces. This evening I am to play with Gladys Brooks, V. W.'s wife and a fine player. V. W. is a nice man whom I've grown to like, though I can no longer read him. He has forgiven me my public digs at him.

The Holt office was not very reliable about packages; so doubtless Vol. 1 of The Tennessee went to some other desk. I look forward to reading both volumes the moment I finish Longinus.

The local reaction to your book was to be expected. How can they square it with the political revolt of the South? Why couldn't the Southern Governors have got together long ago on *fundamentals* instead of waiting to let cheap political tactics by Truman force them to act? Maybe you know how to answer this question. I don't.

Aff. yrs. Allen

204/TLS

Princeton, N.J.
18 February 1950

Dear Don:

This is like a breath of old times—to get a poem from you.[a] And a mighty good piece of work it is. This is a field in which you are entitled to be called an expert. You were the first person so far as I know who said that the damned scientists would split the atom; and now they've gone and done it. What else they can do we must modestly await. When they set up the chain reaction that they cannot stop, and thus convert Magna Mater into a Nova, it will be too late for us to reflect upon what has happened. That seems to be the only complete relief in sight.

We are pretty well satisfied with our present routines. We like our house, and we like living in Princeton better than ten years ago; it is a great advantage to have no official connections locally; and at New York University I see nobody but the students, and I see them only in class. Caroline likewise, at Columbia. In the past two years we've made more money than ever before, but it does us no good because it is all frittered away; and we are getting old. I am struggling with a book on Poe, and with odds and ends of criticism. I am very pleased to see as epigraph to your poem Poe's words. Poe's Nervous Man is our ancestor, however clumsily he creates him; and that is the main argument of my book.

If you will be in Nashville between July 1 and 15 we shall hope to see you. We may run down for those two weeks, and visit around a little. We were saying the other day that a time comes when we must get back, if only for a few days. Caroline joins me in love to both of you, and in the hope that you all are in good health. We're tolerable.

Yrs. Allen

204   *a*. "The Nervous Man," *Virginia Quarterly Review* (Spring 1950).

205/TLS

Princeton, N.J.
15 May 1950

Dear Don:

You can't imagine how grateful we are for your fine, generous letter. I must tell you that the book[a] is really Caroline's. She did twelve of the fifteen commentaries, and a third of the back matter as well. I wanted to put a story of hers in, but she felt that it would be improper. Tom Walsh[b] feels that the sale ought to be good, but you know the calibre of the profession. Tom is worried about a rather serious error: the quotations from A Simple Heart in the Commentary are not from the translation given in the book; but I can't believe that this will seriously injure the sale. We are delighted that you are adopting the book. Your influence will help enormously. I suppose prejudice explains our omission of Jesse Stuart. His dramatization of himself as the Hill-billy, for New York consumption, has disgusted me for years, and I suppose I can't be fair to his work. But in a later edition (if there is one) we can make changes. I agree that The Beast in the Jungle is difficult. We used it because Caroline has made it the center of one of her courses.

You must by all means send us a copy of your speech at Miss. State College.[c] I need to hear strong words about the South. I can imagine what David Cohn said.[d] He is a very bad person, thoroughly trivial and corrupt. I wish the people in Mississippi would invite me to one of their Festivals. I am getting more and more jittery in this part of the country, and I need to be renewed.

Ever since Dick Beatty wrote me about Mrs. Cowan[e] I have wanted to confer with you about the Fugitive files. The material I have consists entirely of letters from you, JCR, and Red, and it is a question how much of it should be opened to inspection. I should have to get the consent of the three of you in any case. I wonder whether it would be the right thing to do to send your letters to each of you, and ask you to check what you are willing to reveal to Mrs. Cowan. Of course, on your recommendation I would be willing to let her see any of my letters that you thought relevant. (I believe that John and Red have not saved their correspondence with us.) In the case of Mrs. Cowan we seem to have the best opportunity to get a scholarly history written.

When do you go up to Breadloaf? Will you be driving up? We will be here until June 15th, and we hope you'll come by to see us. This would be our only chance in the near future to confer on many matters.

Ever yrs. Allen

205 a. The House of Fiction (1950). b. An editor at Scribners. c. "Why the Modern South Has a Great Literature," Vanderbilt Studies in the Humanities (1951). d. Cohn, a Mississippi journalist, appeared on a Southern Literary Festival program with Davidson. e. Under the direction of R. C. Beatty, Louise Cowan is writing a dissertation on the Fugitives, later in revised form published as The Fugitive Group (1959).

206/ALS

Nashville, Tenn.

4 June 1950

Dear Allen:

I spent most of last Friday going through some of your letters to me, with Mrs. Cowan. It was quite an experience for me, as I had not looked at those letters for many years. Some of them, perhaps a lot of them, I probably hadn't re-read since I first received them from you, long ago. A few of them display your ebullient youth ("calidus juventa" and all that) and are written in that chaffing style you used for a short time. But most are of quite a different sort—extraordinarily fine in every way, really wonderful letters. Of course I remembered them as being such. But the realization came on newly, with tremendous force, and left me, when the day was ended, feeling rather stunned by over-powering memories.

Aside from what they reveal of you personally—which in every way does you honor—they clearly show (and I was struck by this) that *The Fugitive* adventure was only a phase of your (and of our) numerous activities and interests. It ought to be clear now to Mrs. Cowan (it is certainly clear to me) that those letters as a whole belong to the biography of Allen Tate and that they shouldn't be explored too extensively for so modest a project as the present one, but should be reserved, in the main.

In sampling them with Mrs. Cowan I tried to select those that bore rather particularly on Fugitive matters, but I let her take some notes on a few others of a broader range. It seemed worthwhile for her to realize that, after you went to New York, during the later years of Fugitive publication, things were quite different from what they had been, say, in 1921 and 1922, when we were just starting. I have charged Mrs. Cowan to show you her notes and to secure your approval for whatever she thinks she may use. Perhaps this can't be absolutely determined now, but you should have a good idea what is in prospect. Please consider, among other things, the difficult question of how far she ought to go in describing the argument—principally centering on John Ransom—about the "editorship" of the magazine, the public credit for it, and so on (you will remember all that). Several of your letters speak very shrewdly in diagnosis of Ransom's ambitions. I read parts of these to her, but did not allow her to take notes at the ticklish points.

You may not have time to go heavily into my letters to you, with

Mrs. Cowan. But perhaps the fact that she has the dated extracts from your letters to me will expedite the process, so far as your file of my letters is concerned. Of course I leave the procedure entirely to your judgment.

I understand that Mrs. Cowan is leaving tomorrow for Princeton. You are not expected, of course, to house her; she may or may not make the trip with her husband; at any rate she (or the couple) will find quarters; and she understands that you are getting ready to leave and will have to arrange interviews as best you can.

I hope you will like her. I am sure that you will find that she has an excellent mind, and I believe she has a sufficient insight into poetry and criticism. She writes superbly well. The chief mystery about her, to me, is how she happened to choose this difficult project. The answer given, so far, is that, in the work of the Fugitive-Agrarian group, she found something that, for the first time, "gave her her bearings," or something like that. She is a Texan—perhaps Beatty told you this— and I think of German parentage, with some middle Tennessee ancestors somewhere in the reckoning. She wears "slanted" spectacles, which don't become her very well—but there's no other oddity about her that I know of. I have found her very sensible and agreeable, and I trust you and Caroline will.

Perhaps you can help advise her how she can reach John Ransom for a visit. That is an important problem that remains unsolved.

Your brother Ben was here for Commencement, but I didn't see him. He has been nominated for membership on the Board of Trust. but I don't think he was elected, this round.

Much more might be said, but I'll stop here.

Faithfully, Don

207/ALS

Nashville, Tenn.
26 January 1951

Dear Allen:

...I have been reading the first draft of Louise Cowan's Fugitive thesis, which is now in a fairly complete shape up to about 1923. She is doing very well indeed. I am amazed at the way she has been able to work out a pattern of treatment that has meaning and perspective, despite the mass of detail that might have thrown a fog over everything if wrongly handled. It's good fortune for her that the Fugitive group formed rather gradually and that she can treat the various members as they appeared, almost one by one, upon the scene; but she also shows a degree of insight that rather surprises me, although, knowing her, I ought to have been prepared for it. I think it will be a thoroughly good piece of work. But I earnestly hope that you, above all others—together with John, if he will help—will read all you can of her thesis and assist in the process of correcting and filling out on points of fact and fundamental interpretation. Your memory and judgment are needed. I don't want her to be relying on me from now on to the extent that she has been relying in the process of getting started.

The news has come—from several sources—that you have joined the Mother Church. (Maybe "joined" is not the right word; it has a deplorably Protestant flavor!) That step is certainly one that I can well understand and, if it weren't so personal a matter, I could say, "support." I have many times thought of just that step for myself. But, aside from inertia, one of the things that always held me back was the question of whether, in the last analysis, the priest would be any more tolerable than the preacher. (The Pope presents no difficulties to me.) It's the preachers—and probably the priests—that keep me out of the communion of any church at present. But in general, the only churches I respect are the Catholic and, say, the Primitive Baptists (to name an oldfashioned fundamentalist sect). But Lord deliver me from the Methodists, the Baptists in general, from most of the Episcopalian lot, the Presbyterians, and the rest.

Theresa joins me in regards to you both.

Faithfully yours, Don

208/TLS

Minneapolis, Minn.
27 October 1951

Dear Don:

We were very much amused to get the clipping about the lady social worker who was about to review The Strange Children for the Centennial Club. But we were also a little sad that Theresa didn't undertake to suffer vicariously for Caroline by going to the meeting so that she could report it to us. It must have been a rare occasion.

I think your decision about the money from Harpers is a wise one.

There isn't enough to go far if divided up. I am glad I'll Take My Stand will be back in print. That book still holds its own. I don't know anything about Peter Smith except that he is the son of the ineffable Harrison Smith.[a] I do know that he has reprinted some good books.

We like this place tremendously—the place itself, the University, and the people. There is a great deal of nonsense in the University—which is to be expected—but curiously enough there is also an encouragement of quality; and the English Department has about as little internal strife as any I've seen or heard about. I am assured and I believe that there is no resentment of my presence—a pervasive air that I've always felt elsewhere. Sam Monk tells me that when my name came up last year the full professors voted for me unanimously. Thus, for some reason, the breach between the man of letters and the scholars seems to have closed here.

We have Joseph Beach's house, across from the campus, a large ramshackle, gloomy, dingy dwelling with four bedrooms. We like it very much, particularly after the close quarters at Princeton. Caroline has so much free time that she has already begun her new novel. I teach five hours a week—all in the afternoon: my mornings are free! And—quite between us—I get the largest salary in the Department—a boon that I inherit from Red's tenure. And nobody seems to resent this either.

What news of the Vanderbilt front? Write us how things go.

Yrs. ever Allen

P.S. We've been twice to St. John's Abbey near here, now the largest Benedictine community in the world. Their most cherished sacred relic is the complete skeleton of St. Peregrinus, the 14-year-old martyr of the reign of Commodus. He lies in a glass case (very much like the Sleeping Beauty) in a Roman costume of his period which was piously made by the Benedictine nuns. As you know, we are under no obligation of faith to believe that these bones are Peregrin's, but it is pleasant to be engaged by the perspective opened up by the possibility. To say nothing of the strange fate of a young Roman martyr's bones lying in repose in Minnesota!

208   a. Peter Smith expressed an interest in reprinting *I'll Take My Stand*.

209/TLS

Minneapolis, Minn.
8 March 1952

Dear Don:

I'm mighty glad to get yours of the 5th. I haven't heard from Shenandoah, but this morning Caroline had a letter from them asking her to write a review of a book about Faulkner. She is declining only because she is back at her novel and doesn't want to break the stretch of work. I remember Ashley Brown[a] very well.

I propose a brief theological argument. You say that if you could get up at five and write poetry you might feel again like one of God's children. Haven't you reversed the causal sequence?

However that may be I am sending you another section of the poem I'm working on.[b] I may have read you part of this, but it is now twice as long and entirely rewritten. I wish you would do an old-time job on it. Since it's the introductory section (I plan seven in all) I must make it as right as I can.

I am going to the University of Kentucky to give two talks, March 24–25, and it will be a great temptation to drop down to Nashville; but I must resist it.

I wish you'd write us the Nashville news. I take it that the Chancellor's rosy dream of a great Reunion of the Fugitives faded at cockcrow.

Yrs. Allen

209   *a.* At this time a Vanderbilt graduate student writing a dissertation on Caroline Gordon.   *b.* "The Maimed Man," *Partisan Review* (May–June 1952).

210/ALS

Nashville, Tenn.
30 March 1952

Dear Allen:

I have read & re-read "The Maimed Man" various times and can find very little in it to criticize. You are moving at the level of Vergil and Dante, vision and verse-instrument truly both one, and completely yours and you, all indistinguishably. So it is not possible, as in our salad days, to venture with rude hand among your lines. The laurel you invoke is on your brows, and what can I do but salute you, and await the fulfillment of the great journey you have begun?

Besides, you are doing the all-but-impossible thing in English verse—making *terza rima* work at the sublime level. And if I pick at any of the stitches of the seamless coat, I risk causing you to dislodge more texture than a criticism would really intend, the irreplaceable along with the replaceable—the possibly replaceable. Nevertheless, I have dared to raise some rather hesitant questions at the bottom of page 3—you will see the comments there. I was inclined also to question "football coach," on the preceding page, as being possibly too vulgar in its present associations for your purpose, and also as being a reference that may "date" too easily and therefore too soon fall out of common apprehension; but I'm not certain that this doubt is justified. The kind of reference implied in "football coach" is certainly what you want.

The query as to the appropriateness of "glass swirled by old blowers" is entirely provisional, depending on how you mean the character of the protagonist to develop. My personal associations may enter too much into my reaction. In recent years I have been in too many antique shops, in Vermont and elsewhere, and have heard too much talk of "old glass," "antique mirrors," etc. So my question does not necessarily have merit.

The punning passage which follows does seem to me to raise serious questions. I have never been able to accept Donne's supposed pun on *die*, for example, as valid to the extent to which you argue for it in "Understanding Poetry."[a] His pun, if intended, seems like an injection of something frivolous at a point where I am expecting to be serious, if not grim, in the context of the poem; it does not seem to be a bantering sort of poem. On the other hand, the puns of various kinds made in the ordinary Petrarchan vein seem to me to belong in the line of bantering compliment or teasing; they hardly intend to be anything but wit in the courtly sense, and one cannot therefore charge the poet with being frivolous, when frivolity was aimed at. Shakespeare's puns on his own name, in the "Will" sonnets, are just that sort of thing, angrily or even bitterly rendered; and so I don't hold those sonnets are to be rejected as "poor." But if Shakespeare had punned on "Will" for a lofty religious or philosophical purpose, then I would feel doubtful as I am about your "I"—"iambics"—"eye"—"I" sequence. But I may be missing something in the passage, of course. I would like to have your own comment. It may not be possible to escape from saying "I mean by *I*" in that one line—I certainly like "God's image made uncouth."

The only other comment I have is that you are evidently composing a long poem which must be taken as a whole. Therefore no criticism can really be relevant, or of much use to you, at this point. It would never do for me to niggle at small cruxes in a work of large scope. Augustus was right (though whether for the right reasons who can know?) in setting aside Vergil's wish that the *Aeneid* MS. be destroyed. It could never have been as "polished" as one of the Eclogues, even if Vergil had lived another decade! I am implying something that I hardly know how to describe, about the necessities of the "large" poem. But your venture already begins to illustrate what I am talking about, and it shows how far you now are beyond the point when, in Fugitive days, you temporarily accepted John Ransom's argument (though it wasn't only his) for the "minor" poem. John, following that too narrowly conceived theory has ended up by offering invalid criticisms of Shakespeare's sonnets—and by being unable, it would seem, to write even "minor" poems (polished "microcosms"). But here you are, writing the "major" poem. Go ahead—and please let me see more! I'm waiting, prayerfully & trustfully, & wishing I, too, could start a new long poem.

I accept your theological rebuttal. If I were as much a child of God as I would like to be, I could get up—perhaps—at five A.M. & write poetry, like you. I suppose that would also mean that, as a child of God, I could peacefully go to sleep at 10 P.M., as I cannot now, being in the grip of secular if not satanic urgencies. . . .

I intended to tell you, before this, that Mary and her husband (Dr. Eric Bell) have been very active in the coalition group of Young Republicans, States Righters, etc., that have been doing some political ground work here, partly for the present campaign, partly for larger purposes, including a fight *against* the Communists & socialists and *for* religion. When Paul Blanshard was brought here recently by a group of Protestant ministers, to make one of the anti-Catholic speeches that he is giving all over the country, this group went into action with some effect. They were not able, of course, to cause Blanshard to cancel his speech, but they did force two or three prominent ministers to withdraw their sponsorship, and they made a considerable drive on various other prominent persons & organizations.

My son-in-law Eric, by the way, is now a Catholic convert. He had been inclining that way for some time, and joined immediately after the Blanshard affair.

I ought not to be taking time to write at such length, for I am overwhelmed with work. Our opera is now in rehearsal here[b]—and Bryan & I had to get busy and also provide script & score for another

tryout production at Middlebury in May. I heard the orchestra re-
hearse Friday, for the first time. It is glorious music. You will be playing
it on your violin some day. I still have not had time to get a script
ready to send you, but will do so as soon as possible. While in the midst
of this delirious excitement, I have to revise my freshman textbook for
Tom Walsh and do other not particularly pleasant things, and am very
nervous and hard-run.

Affectionately, Don

210   *a.* The essay referred to is "Understanding Modern Poetry," *English Journal*
(April 1940). *b. Singin' Billy, An Opera in Two Acts,* music by Charles F.
Bryan, drama and lyrics by Donald Davidson. This folk opera has never been
published.

211/TLS

Minneapolis, Minn.
4 April 1952

Dear Don:
      Your letter revives the old days. I knew I could depend upon you
alone for the old kind of close reading. You have put your finger on
all the questionable spots, the punning and the wavy glass: I will have
to work at those passages again. But I am relieved that you seem to
approve of the over-all intention and effect. In fact, the perspective you
see the poem in is the very one I *thought* it was in: "vision" poetry,
quasi-allegorical. You have been so generous that I am making bold to
send you another part—Part III; but please look at it, if at all, at your
leisure.
      Well, this sort of exchange of letters is merely a continuation of
a correspondence that began exactly thirty years ago—as I am reminded
by Mrs. Cowan's dissertation, which I finished going over yesterday. To
see it all set down there, as it began, gives me the little shudder that
comes of sensing the presence of another world at one's elbow. She
makes it all "history," as if it were over; and yet it obviously isn't over.
      I think, by the way, that Mrs. Cowan has on the whole done a
fine job. The writing ought to be improved; but whether she can improve it, and whether for her purposes it needs to be much better, are
not questions for me to take up with her. I have amplified the biographical section about me, short of going into the financial collapse of
my father about 1915, a fact that would no doubt throw light on the

uncertainties and perhaps some of the aberrations of my life up to about 1925; and I have urged her to omit, or merely glance at, the row between John and me in 1923. I do hope that you will be able to see this matter as I do, and will advise her accordingly. There is no reason why, at some later time, this quarrel cannot be approached quite easily as a fact of literary history—though not a very significant one. But her reader, not knowing anything about the friendship that developed afterwards and that has now run without interruption for more than 25 years, would get entirely the wrong emphasis. In fact, the scope of Mrs. Cowan's dissertation does not permit her to tell the story of the healing of the breach. There is also a technical reason for minimizing this episode: it did not take place in the pages of The Fugitive, and has no bearing upon the direct narrative. After John and I are dead somebody may want to tell the whole story, and that will place the row in proper perspective, where it will have little importance.

We are much moved by Eric's conversion, and thank God for it. By the way, I didn't mean that I personally am one of the children of God, and can therefore get up at five and write verse. That would make it sound a little too easy. No doubt I get up at five for *naturalistic* reasons, because I am Poe's Nervous Man in your poem.

Affly yrs Allen

212/ALS

Nashville, Tenn.
18 April 1952

Dear Allen:

I was delighted to receive the copy of another section of your long poem. It's masterly and fine. I'll have to wait, awhile, however, before subjecting it to the close scrutiny I gave the other. At the moment I'm heavily engaged in matters pertaining to operatic productions—which, a few years ago, I would have thought the most unlikely of all possibilities.

As to Louise Cowan's thesis, I feel very much as you do. I have talked to her at some length about the questions you bring up, and I feel sure she will tone down both her treatment of the Mims factor (about which I had earlier cautioned her) and her account of the Ransom-Tate public literary "combat." About the latter I was by no means as well informed, either at the time it occurred or later, as her thesis treatment now makes possible. I don't think it can be passed over altogether, but I do believe her treatment should be somewhat reduced, and also that she should discover in it evidence of the tough, "no quarter" type of criticism to which we constantly subjected each other in private, and of which this "quarrel" was the only example (so far as I remember) to get aired in public.

It bothers me, too, to look at the record, all set down in past tense with such a look of finality. In fact, I've about got to the place where I can't read her chapters without feeling disturbed by just such thoughts as you express; at times I fell into such a swound of reminiscence that it was totally impossible for me to read her work critically. In fact, I have asked to be relieved—and have been relieved—from the committee that is "directing" her thesis; and so am now a "source" rather than a "director." And I absolutely refuse to "sit" on her examining committee, as I have told her. I do what I can, however, to watch for factual errors and wrong emphases or coloring. I don't think the thesis, as such, could possibly be a good literary performance. The task of piecing together all the bits of the mosaic would, of itself, almost prevent that. In fact, she told me she felt ill at ease as to the writing itself; she said she had never before tried to write "history" and was having to learn how to do it. She is more at ease—and writes far better—in straight literary criticism. When the thesis task is done and she can view the whole, I think she can do a *book* that will be better than the thesis.

It was impressed upon me how grateful we ought to be to her—and how necessary her work is—when I had a visit recently from Henry Wells of Columbia University. He is writing a book about Merrill Moore, apparently with only such attention to the Fugitive group as a whole as will enable him to orient his treatment of Merrill with reference to that group—in Merrill's "early stops." He seemed a pretty sensible man, on the whole. But of course, having as he does only Merrill's slant as to the group, his book is bound to be wrong about the group, however "right" it may be as to Merrill the doctor-and-sonnet-diary writer. (Wells says that Merrill's sonnets should be regarded as a "diary.") Until a book is available to set off against such partial views, all views of the Fugitive "group" will be partial.

I would like to expand somewhat on those incidents of Fugitive days that your letter brings to mind—but the night wears on, and I'll wait till another time. I don't think you should feel any embarrassment or dismay as to the presentation Louise Cowan gives of you. She admires you intensely; and I think her treatment of you, throughout, is in general splendid. It is undoubtedly you as you then were—calidus juventa—and very fine in that gallant occupation! It never hurt your poetry, your critical intelligence, your soul.

I am sending you and Caroline the promised script of *Singin' Billy*. Since it is copyrighted as an "unpublished dramatico-musical composition," we can't give away or otherwise distribute to the "public" any copies; but all loaned copies have to be returned in order to avoid any seeming of "publication." (Stage presentation is not "publication." We paid a copyright lawyer to find out about all this and more.) This is the full version, as I wrote it. We had to cut it somewhat for presentation here. I had, in fact, "overwritten" it to some extent, as it was not clear, during my writing, just how much music Bryan would produce. He produced a lot—a piano-vocal score of 153 pages! So we had to cut to bring the whole within a playing-time of 2 hrs. and a half, or a little over. Please keep in mind that the dialogue is intended to be spoken and the "lyrics" to be sung. You can't, therefore, really judge the "lyrics" without the music. You must believe me when I tell you that they "sing" extremely well; and Bryan's music is really extraordinary.

I have carefully woven into lyrics and dialogue some things that you and Caroline, as Catholics, Confederates, and symbolists, may notice—I don't think "everybody" will. I say "carefully woven"—but it isn't quite true. The thing just happened and I can't explain it.

I suggest that you try reading some of it aloud. And return it, with any comments, in the envelope provided.

We "open" the production here Wednesday night, Apr. 23. Think some prayerful thoughts for me.

Faithfully, Don

213/ALS

Nashville, Tenn.
1 May 1952

Dear Allen:

After about ten days of almost complete delirium—dress rehearsals plus five performances of *Singin' Billy*—I am gradually coming back to normal, and will write you as soon as possible about your fine poem.

The theatrical life is TOUGH! Up till 2 A.M., every night, from Sunday night, a week ago, through last Monday. After-theatre parties, consultations, work, etc.

I enclose a program. *Singin' Billy* sold out, almost at once, for the four nights originally scheduled and was held over for another night, when we again had a good audience. Branscomb brought the Board of Trust over for the Friday night performance. Many visitors came from distant points in neighboring states. The newspaper accounts were just "publicity"; they never caught on. But *Singin' Billy* was a word-of-mouth sensation. We could have had good audiences for some more nights—but we had to let the boys and girls (and professors) get back to their "studies." From the general audience reaction, as well as from comments that have come to Bryan & me, I judge that folks came expecting nothing much and got one of the big surprises of their lives; they are still trying to figure out what happened. Bryan and I feel extremely well pleased, for though it was not a perfect production, and under the circumstances couldn't be, the 40 gallant and beautiful boys & girls of the cast & chorus gave such a lively and stirring rendering that you couldn't help but be enchanted. I felt so enchanted and so full of rather weepy gratitude that I wrote some verses of thanks; and Charles Bryan arranged to have me put them on a "ditto" sheet, which he signed with his thanks in a bar of music, and we gave copies to the whole lot at the end of the last show. . . .

John Wade and his wife, with the Richard Dodds, came up from Marshallville for two days and were here for the "first night." How I wish you and Caroline could have been here. If you'll bring your violin to Bread Loaf, we'll play through the *Singin' Billy* score.

As ever, Don

214/TLS

Minneapolis, Minn.
1 May 1952

Dear Don:

Yours of April 18 was much appreciated, as was the script of Singin' Billy. I confess that I have been able only to glance through the libretto and admire some of the fine lyrics. I have been under terrific pressure for three weeks, and there will be no letup until after June 2nd. I will not bore you with details, except to say that I've had to write a Phi Beta Kappa address (for delivery here) tonight, and make a précis of it (about 1/3) to give in Paris on May 21![a] I will explain. There's an organization which you doubtless know about, The Congress for Cultural

Freedom, which is holding an International Exposition of the Arts in Paris all this month. Writers from all non-Communist nations are invited (i.e., Western nations); I am one of six Americans. We travel round-trip 11,000 miles to speak twelve minutes; hence the précis of the longer speech. I might add that the American branch of the Congress was founded to oppose and discredit the infamous Waldorf Conference in 1949. It is the only "organization" I've ever joined, because it is the only international group opposed to Communism that means business. It will doubtless amuse you to know that Red was invited to go, but Yale wouldn't give him leave! The others (about whom I will make no comment) are Faulkner, Farrell (reformed Marxist), Glenway Wescott, Katherine Anne Porter, and Auden. The curious thing about this list is that my old friend Archie MacLeish is not on it. Ten years ago his name would have led all the rest. A change has come over the spirit of these "Conferences." Think of an old reactionary like me being there. I have an extra carbon of my précis which I will enclose. I decided, as usual, to let 'em have it. . . .

A brief closing glance at Mrs. Cowan's reconstruction of those days. I can't tell you how moved I am by the solid evidence of your kindness and loyalty to me when I most needed your support. Well, it is to the honor of human nature and ad majorem Dei gloriam.

Affly Allen

214 *a.* "The Man of Letters in the Modern World" appeared in the Autumn 1952 issue of the *Hudson Review.*

215/TLS

Nashville, Tenn.
4 May 1952
Dear Allen:

I never heard before about the organization before which you are to speak in Paris, but I am glad you were chosen and will have the opportunity to deliver the true and powerful gospel as you have set it down in the copy you sent me. If you don't mind, I would like to read it to my writing class. What you say, also, about your addressing Phi Beta Kappa is good news—the first good news I've had of anything relating to Phi Beta Kappa in a long time. You know, of course, that the headquarters organization was taken over by the communist or pro-communist crowd at least as early as 1940. About that time I read my

Phi Beta Kappa poem at Williamsburg and had to endure the humiliation of knowing how it was dismissed with contempt while the applause went to Marjorie Nicholson, who made the "address." You know what her address was like. It was the same kind of thing I heard MacLeish give at Bread Loaf in those years. I'll say no more here, except that I hope the day of influence of such people is beginning to end, but the damage they have already done is beyond all estimate. I urge you to read Whittaker Chambers' book, every bit of it, at the earliest opportunity. I have read it. An advance copy was sent to me. I don't understand, by the way, why you think it "curious" that MacL. is not on the list of speakers on which you are included. The only thing curious to me about MacL. is that he retains any shred of reputation. I have never forgotten that he was a leader in the "merchants of death" anti-munitions-maker drive, which was communist-managed. Alger Hiss was counsel for the Nye committee.

Good luck to you on your trip. As to the "Singin' Billy" script, do whatever suits you best. If you don't want it cluttering up the place, mail it back now. You can read it when you are at Bread Loaf, with the score, if you'll only stay with us long enough. I would like to say, in regard to "Singin' Billy," and my connection with the dramatics and the music Bryan wrote, that the whole episode, from the beginning of the composition through the production here, afforded me the highest, truest joy, the most profoundly stirring moments I've known since the Fugitive days, with you. I say "with you" for reasons that you know. The part of the Fugitive days that was with you is the only part that has lasted, with me, in the highest and warmest levels of memory. John Ransom instructed me—and finally rejected me. You both instructed me and moved me. I'll not forget.

Yrs. Don

216/TLS

Minneapolis, Minn.
6 May 1952

Dear Don:

All that humming hive of operatic activity in Nashville, with you in the limelight, must portend a new renaissance. Would that we had been there for the great opening!

I am going to send the script back because I don't know otherwise when I'll get a chance to send it; and I can't do it justice now. I've looked at it enough to see that you, having reached the ripe age of 58, are able to tap a new and vigorous vein. I want you to sing some of the lyrics at Bread Loaf. But I will not be able to bring my fiddle: it is too fragile for the long trips and the changes of temperature.

I'm glad you're insisting that Louise Cowan *show* what she has quoted from letters to the authors. You're quite right: the original permission was *general*. But she's a fine conscientious girl, as I see her, and I am sure she will do the right thing.

I leave here Friday (9th) for Princeton, and then take off for Paris on the 12th. I will be back on June 2nd. More later.

Yrs. Allen

217/TLS

Minneapolis, Minn.
7 May 1952

Dear Don:

I can scarcely do justice to your good letter: I'm just two days from my departure. By this time you've got my letter of yesterday.

Yes, indeed, read the excerpt from my Phi Beta Kappa speech to your class. The complete version will appear in the Fall issue of the Hudson Review. I was amazed when some of the professional liberals around here told me that they had been "deeply moved" by the speech; some of them even wrote me letters.

On second thought, I will send you the complete version later to-day or tomorrow. It will be too long to read to your class, but I want you to read it.

Yes, I'd heard all about Spears[a] and the S.R. I think he'll make a good editor, though perhaps a little on the academic side. As to filling his place, I had already written Spears about J.V. Cunningham at Chicago. A first-rate classical scholar and one of the best Renaissance men in the country. I just thought that in view of Curry's imminent retirement, some reshuffling might be done, and Cunningham groomed for Curry's place, and an 18th century man brought in too. I didn't write this direct to Curry because nobody likes to be reminded of approaching retirement. Cunningham's new book *Woe or Wonder?* is a study in the backgrounds of Elizabethan tragedy, and to my mind a critical as well as scholarly masterpiece. Curry knows his work. He has written about Curry.

In haste, Allen

217 *a.* Monroe Spears has been appointed editor of the *Sewanee Review*, and Davidson has requested that Tate recommend someone to replace him at Vanderbilt.

218/TLS

Marshallville, Ga.
1 December 1952

Dear Allen:

At last I have had the right kind of chance to read "The Buried Lake."*a* I gave most of the evening, yesterday, to reading and re-reading it, and that was a good way to let November, '52, pass on. Allen, this poem is just about perfect. You can go no further than this in blending marvelous simplicity of diction, perfect firmness yet flexibility of prosodic scheme, and rich complexity of emotional-metaphysical experience. I don't say, of course, that I've mastered the meaning; and until the whole sequence is in hand, I don't think I could. So I'll let that part go, and be merely technical for the present. Really, I have no criticisms worth anything, but just to keep up the principle I will raise one or two small questions: (1) Is there possibly a slight difficulty of construction in lines 3–4, in the use of the verb "let" with the phrase "of living blood?" The normal construction would be: "let blood with your fleam." (2) In Stanza 5 I am just a little bothered by the use of the word "abort." It gives you one of your characteristic metaphors in "abort a world of snow," but that doesn't seem to work well with "In childhood, etc." Of course "abort" is the adult's vocabulary, I understand that. But I would prefer a word that might be assimilated to "childhood" more readily. I have no other blue pencil marks to make. It is wonderful poetry. I think it succeeds better than "The Winter Sea"*b* which was also in this general vein. The last two pages are particularly fine: a summit so high that you will do well indeed not to slip from it. But you will do well, and not slip, I think. I have only one more thought. The suggestion doesn't apply to this section, necessarily, but when you have finished the whole long poem you may want to look back and see whether, for a poem of this scale, you have too often accented the laurel, myrtle, and so on. Since I don't know what the scale of the poem is, I can't offer this as a criticism—only as something I asked myself about.

I would like to dwell on the subject of poetry, but must get on with this letter. I have thought some, but written no further as yet on the poem of mine that I mentioned.ᶜ But I have been reading Homer's Greek about Odysseus' meeting with Circe—all that part, which bears on my poem. I am doing without a translation—as much as possible without a dictionary. There is something in all that part that has been passed by too easily. Did you happen to see an article somewhere, perhaps in The Classical Journal, about "animal dances"? I got from it, I don't know whether justifiably or not, that the men transformed into animals might belong to a "cult"—that they "represent" animals. If so, it is religious mysticism of a kind, not "magic," that is involved, or that underlies the Circe business. . . .

Recently I read, for Univ. of S. Carolina Press, a manuscript about DuBose Heyward (pretty badly done). In it I discovered something—a copy of a letter from John Bennett to Heyward. When Ransom's "Armageddon" won the S.C. prize, there was a great scandal and uproar in the Poetry Society of S.C., because many members thought John's poem "blasphemous," "radical," and in various ways offensive. They threatened to resign from the Society if this poem was published in the Yearbook. Bennett and Heyward debated whether to publish the poem and lose their supporting membership, or not publish the poem and face another kind of difficulty. They decided not to publish it in the Yearbook but in a *separate* brochure. So that was why John's poem was published in that form. I didn't know anything about all this. Did you?

We are very pleasantly located in John Wade's little green house, where we started our Georgia experience 20 years ago. John has not been very well in recent months, and he has a very bad cold now. All the same, he has laid out, back of his fine place, a Great Garden, of a historical-symbolical nature, of a kind that only John could think up and carry through. We walk, every day, over its 10–15 acres. I wish you and Caroline could see it. It is going to be one of the rare sights of the country. And I wish you could, some time, see John Wade and have a visit in these parts.

I am going to quit this business of writing letters if all my letters to you have to be long ones and from you I get only short notes in reply. Remember that, in the future. You are not particularly communicative, Allen, except in poetry.

Theresa joins me in regards to you both.

As ever, Don

P.S. We expect to be at Marshallville until Christmas.

218 a. In the *Sewanee Review* (Summer 1953). b. *The Winter Sea: A Book of Poems* (1944). c. Apparently "Old Sailor's Choice," *The Long Street* (1961).

219/TLS

Minneapolis, Minn.
14 January 1953

Dear Don,

I've been so harassed that I haven't been able to write a letter longer than three lines; and I'm still hard-pressed. We are now rather definitely expecting to go to Italy late in the summer for a year—University of Rome—and because I can't send money back to pay on the mortgage and other debts I've got to do readings and lectures all I can. Between now and the end of April I have nine engagements, and I hope to accumulate enough money to cover the obligations while we are away. There's also the income tax. Of course, we'll be able to live like princes in Italy because all the money I get must be spent there.

Your comment on my poem not only encouraged me; it was, as in the old days, extremely useful. I've done a lot of rewriting with some of your criticisms in mind, and I think it's improved. What encouraged me was your feeling that at last I had got the diction simple along with a complex subject. What I've been trying for in the past five or six years of practice is an approach to the objective analogical method which dominated poetry up into the Renaissance—in which what looks to us today like metaphor was actually a generally accepted relation between the physical world and the invisible. We have no such generally accepted relation. All that I can do is to try to tone the language down and to juxtapose objects in such a way as to make them symbolic objects while remaining in the full sense physical objects. After some experimenting I found that for me the formal terza rima gave me the best chance to do this in a poem of any length. The ten-line stanza I worked out for Seasons of the Soul was useful only for moderate lengths.

I wish you would send me any more or less finished parts of the poem you told me about. I have an idea that we lose very little in intervals of silence, and that it is often better not to write at all for long periods: we come back to it not only with new insights and subjects, but with old habits of technique discarded; for it is these technical habits, repeated daily, which bind us to subjects that have ceased to be active for us.

I was very much amused recently by John Ransom's leading article in the New Republic on T. S. Eliot's new Collected Poems.[a] There is, first, a completely cranky and untenable point which distinguishes poetry from religion. Religion and the "mysteries" are for people who have a sense of sin. Poetry is "appearances," presumably for people who delight in the sensible world without sin. John rejects religion and takes poetry. I wondered whether he felt that he was without sin; at any rate he seemed to be casting a stone. But there was one extremely good point. He alluded to our old views of the late twenties when we were rebelling against modernism, and pointed out that we never got much further than Nostalgia because no historic faith came into consideration. I think there's a great deal in that. We were trying to find a religion in the secular, historical experience as such, particularly in the Old South. I would now go further than John and say we were idolaters. But it is better to be an idolater than to worship nothing, and as far as our old religion went I still believe in it.—All this as preface to saying that I hope I'll Take My Stand can be reissued. I too like Rubin.[b] I wish we could find a university where he could take the Hopkins Review—the best little magazine going today. Can't you do something at Vanderbilt? I would try here but a state university is not the place for such a magazine. They would want to make it scholarly and official. —I was annoyed recently by an essay in the Hopkins Southern symposium about the sense of "place" in Southern fiction writers. Caroline wasn't mentioned. The sense of place is more powerful in her books than in any other Southern writer. Herbert Read saw that when he agreed to publish The Strange Children in England. Even an Englishman could see it. The Strange Children by the way has had a great success in England.

I have had to break with Scribner's. Since the death of Charles Scribner Sr. the policy has changed; they are getting commercial in the regular hard-boiled way. They turned down my new book of essays. Henry Regnery in Chicago will publish it this spring.[c] It is very pleasant not to be told that I am being done a favor. They will publish my long poem and everything else I write.

I am going to Burlington again this summer—June 15–28—and I will hope to see you and Theresa on the way back to Princeton. Things have worked out in the past few years so that we never seem to go South, and I don't like it. But I don't know what I can do about it.

Send me the poem and write me the news.

Yrs. Allen

P.S. The Buried Lake will be in The Sewanee Review in April. If you have time I hope you will tell me how it sounds to you then. The following passage from the Little Office of the BVM I am using as an epigraph to The Buried Lake:

Ego mater pulchrae dilectionis, et timoris, et agnitionis, et sanctae spei.[d]

219   a. Ransom's review of *The Complete Poems and Plays of T. S. Eliot* appeared in the *New Republic* (December 8, 1952). b. Louis D. Rubin, Jr., then at Hollins College. c. *The Forlorn Demon: Didactic and Critical Essays* (1953). d. The shorter service of the Blessed Virgin Mary: "I am mother of beautiful esteem, and of fear, and of recognition, and of sacred hope."

220/ALS

Bread Loaf, Vt.
16 July 1955

Dear Allen:

I don't know where you are this summer and am sending this to the St. Paul address, the latest one of which I have record.

Though I haven't heard from you directly, I'm most gratefully conscious of your ministrations in behalf of my projected publications; first Louis Rubin wrote me about the special edition of the essays; now Russell Kirk writes that you'll take a hand in the reprint of *The Attack on Leviathan* that Regnery is considering. Naturally I'm most joyful and willing to have your hand in such enterprises, editorially, critically, sponsorially,—any way. I could wish for nothing better. It is a great lift to know of your concern and realize that I won't be left merely to consult my own spectre.

The *Leviathan* book is no great problem. I certainly concede that it should be shortened, and wrote Kirk to that effect. The essays, however, are going to take some work on my part if I am to finish up those that so far are only in a kind of academic-lecture state. I shall also probably be puzzled to know how much to include of the old ones, of which there is enough, good, bad, and only middling, to make a couple of books. I hope to get a passable MS, however, by the end of this summer. I am not teaching; just living at Bread Loaf and trying to get over a horrible case of fatigue.

I had hoped when next I wrote you to be able to send you a poem, fairly long, that I have been working on. Have returned to it, after a lapsus, with a good prospect of finishing. If it gets done, I'll send it later. . . .

I hope you and Caroline are well. Theresa joins me in affectionate regards to you both.

As ever Don

P.S. I don't have the strength, right now, to write more than this one-page letter. A few days ago I had word of the unexpected death of Chas. Bryan, my collaborator in the opera.

221/ALS

Nashville, Tenn.
22 May 1956

Dear Allen:

Your letter raises my spirits. I have been miserable in the aftermath from the very frustration you refer to.[a] We should have been allowed some time to unbutton. As it was, we were being buttonholed every minute by some watch dog or other for posterity. Yet the "Reunion" was, as you say, a success. On the public side, it was tremendous. There is no question that the large crowds came out of other reasons than mere curiosity, though some were merely curious, of course. Something has happened, over the years—a belated growth, maybe. I would say, however, that it's in Nashville, Tennessee, and the South rather than in the present Vanderbilt, which is mostly as indifferent and ignorant as the dominance of social science and a non-Southern faculty can make it. The students nevertheless caught on, during the Reunion, and have been beleaguering me with questions and comments ever since.

I was so greatly moved the first afternoon, when you and Red and

Andrew spoke, that I needed a kind hand to wipe away my tears. At
other times I felt greatly excited, but what you and Red were saying
revived deep feelings that haven't possessed me for many years. The audience could grasp only a part of what you meant. Naturally it had to
be said in the language of hidden implication. I felt as if we were having
a thoroughly private conversation in full public hearing without the
public knowing what was going on. You spoke better than I have ever
heard you speak—and that is saying a heap. I have never heard a speech
in my life like those brief words of yours. . . .

If we have another gathering, I would hope that the successive
generations of Vanderbilt writers since 1930 could be brought into it.
That is what I urged upon Rubin, also Randall,[b] from the first, but
could make no impression. They deserve entry and the benefits of "conference"—as some of those admitted to the closed circle did not. In any
such future meeting, too, I would think that the major writers assembled
should *not* be invited on the basis of whether they were "members" of
the Fugitive or Agrarian group, but simply because of their achievement and worth as "Vanderbilt writers." In that way, frivolous and
empty distractions could be kept out. What do you think?

I so much regretted not having one real chance to talk with you
and Caroline. I did *not* know about the Kansas City people. Who the
devil are *they*, to come between us?

Please take care of yourself, Allen (my old entreaty!). I felt concerned that you seemed thin and fatigued, though otherwise so completely your old self. I can't bear the thought of your being ill.

We go to Bread Loaf in late June and shall be there until some
time in the fall. I hope to get some writing done. Also to get some
strength back. Right now, I'm a wreck.

The volume of collected essays is now in the hands of L.S.U. Press
and is to appear in the fall.[c] I hope to do some more poems. I resented
JCR's repeated references to our being finished as poets—or something
like that. How did John get *that* idea?

I want you to finish the new poem—the long one.[d] I put it ahead
of the "Ode"—more so than ever since I heard you read it.

You must come back to Vanderbilt—at any rate to Tennessee. The
feeling you have had since May 5 is the voice of your *good δαίμων*.[e]

As ever, Don

221   *a.* The reunion has just been held. See edited transcript: *Fugitives' Reunion,
Conversations at Vanderbilt,* ed. Rob Roy Purdy (1959).   *b.* Randall Stewart

had planned the Fugitives' reunion and had originally planned to edit the symposium transcript. *c. Still Rebels, Still Yankees and Other Essays* (1957). *d.* "The Swimmers," *Hudson Review* (Winter 1953). *e.* Daimon.

222/TLS

Nashville, Tenn.
22 March 1958

Dear Allen:

I will have to write briefly now, but hope to expand later. What you say about Bradbury's book[a] is rather appalling. I have not yet read it, but had all the time expected the worst, because of his connection (isn't he at Union College, Schenectady?) and because of his obvious impudence in attempting the subject without any real inquiry into it. From what you say, he must be a plain fool or else a deliberate assassin. I shall have to read the book, I suppose, if only to check on his historical-biographical excursions that you mention, but I hate the idea of getting into it. As to his use of poems without permission, the copyright question may actually be somewhat complex where the original copyright was in the name of the "Fugitive Publishing Company" and was not validated by a book-publisher's or other subsequent copyright. The "Fugitive Publishing Company," you see, did not renew its copyright at the end of the first 28–year period—that is, the magazine copyright. Perhaps that is something I should have done—actually it never occurred to me to see to it. Maybe it would have been somewhat complicated; second-period renewals have to be in the name of the author. . . .

I am struggling with my Bowdoin lecture and will send you either a sketch of it or a carbon of the tentative MS between now and April 1st.[b] I would suggest that we divide the field by letting me concentrate on the "non-literary" features of the Southern situation (though I can't entirely exclude the "literary", of course), and you take the "literary" (without excluding the "non-literary"). That is a division already implied in the topics, of course. My position will be that I have already lived through two or three "New South" periods, yet "the South" is persistent through them all, and my task is to distinguish that South and define what is actually "conservative" about it; also what bearing that "conservatism" has on the general scene. I intend to be somewhat reminiscent, as in the Mercer lectures. And, since it is futile to try to *convert* the audience, I'll try to be more of a reporter and analyst than an advocate—though, of course, without yielding any ground on fundamentals. Rossiter and such recent writers provide me with some context which I suppose I can assume as familiar.

I enclose a carbon of my review of your Jackson, which Kirk says he likes and will publish.[c] The review isn't all I would wish it to be, but I had to let it go as it is. A large essay is needed.

I am concerned about what you say about your health. Please take care—rest—don't let those ulcers generate another attack—obey that doctor. Don't let the Bowdoin thing fatigue you; you already have plenty of ammunition for it.

As ever, Don

222 *a.* John M. Bradbury, *The Fugitives* (1958). *b.* Later published in revised form as "The New South and the Conservative Tradition," *National Review* (September 10, 1960). *c.* Davidson reviewed the reprint of *Stonewall Jackson, The Good Soldier* in *Modern Age* (Fall 1958).

223/ALS

Nashville, Tenn.
28 March 1958

Dear Allen:

I have done about 15 pages of my Bowdoin lecture and had hoped to send you a carbon of at least that much, but I am dissatisfied with some of my tergiversations and elaborations of expression, and will have to do some revising before I start sending it to you. I should finish this first draft by Sunday and will plunge right into the rewrite and send you a carbon, probably in installments, as fast as it takes on some finish.

This is the shape it is taking. I have to deal with the "New South" somehow before I can develop the part about "Conservatism." I define *two kinds* of "New South"—one, with a small "n," is the more or less "natural" process of change affecting the whole country and *crossing* sectional patterns—as, for example, in Andrew Jackson's period, perhaps in the Wilsonian (1912–20). Jackson represented a "new South" that got plenty of support in the North. Schlesinger is something over a hundred years late in recognizing some of its unfortunate elements, but makes various wrong inferences about it.

The other kind of "New South" is to be defined as the expectation the North generates of a South that it *wants* to come forth. It's a dream-vision—a fantasy. But some Southerners will always join up with it; for the South is never unanimous in its opposition to the North. Now a cycle starts, and I try to trace the natural history of this cycle in abstract, analytical terms, without particularizing as to the issues involved. The Southern New South-ers immediately acquire influence out of proportion to their numbers and weight, because of the support (subsidy) they get from the North. Now the North begins to pay for its own self-deception. Of course it is to the advantage of the New South-ers to convey a misleading report to the Northern Maecenases. But soon they encounter the South's "conservatism" (the constant element that differentiates the actual South from the "New South" and the "Old South," both of which, as understood by the North, are fantasies). The cycle ends with a vast distortion of the moral reform which was launched from the North in the first place. The defense mechanism of the "New South-ers" leads them into a vulgar kind of myth-making. The general result is to put the "problems" into a new context, without solving them; and the sectional disagreement never reaches any settlement satisfactory to both sides.

The "Old South" fantasy built up by the Henry Grady liberals is an example of the working of the defense mechanism. It is still imbedded in Northern thinking. It is the straw man that they and the more recent Southern liberals occupy themselves with attacking. And our concern in *I'll Take My Stand* was to clear away all this nonsense and get down to realities and principles.

I thought that the "cycle" idea might have some weight with that Bowdoin audience. It relieves me of the burden of arguing on specific issues such as slavery and the race question. Also I believe it's valid historically and socially. It gives me a chance, too, to deal with "conservatism" as a fairly constant, at least a steadying principle amidst the flux. If it is allowed a voice, then the South can participate in national affairs in a positive way, without having to wear the two masks forced on it by the New South cycle—in which it is invited, if not commanded, to disown its character and at the same time is defamed for having a character it never possessed. But if the South isn't allowed a voice, the situation stays always out of balance and compressed; for the liberals can never acquire full leadership on the terms proposed; the conservatives of the higher type stand aside in disgust; and the leadership goes, in one period, to the Cole Blease, Vardaman type, in another to the Bilbo, Heflin, Huey Long type. These are a product of the New South cycle.

I won't touch the literature except for brief illustrations. I am using Grady and his crowd to illustrate the "sentimental" picture of the

"Old South"—and I'm giving them a reminiscence of Bob Taylor's "Fiddle & the Bow" lecture (which I heard about 1907) to show them in dramatic terms how it worked!

Another reason for taking this approach—I am guessing at the line that probably will be taken by Woodward (who is certainly "liberal" if not radical), Mrs. Hodding Carter, and the NAACP official, and hoping to offset it. Whoever planned that Bowdoin program must surely have had a purpose in giving you and me the last word. Perhaps we have friends at Bowdoin.

This approach of mine leaves lots of room for you. I'm eager to know what strategy you are using. If you can give me some idea of what you will say, it will help immensely in my final rewrite. And I want your criticisms of my line of attack—by all means—the sooner the better.

Faithfully, Don

P.S. Any sketch or summary of your lecture would help—at least to avoid useless contradictions or overlapping on major points. And you have to send that publicity man something anyway, don't you? He's been after me.

224/TLS

Nashville, Tenn.
19 October 1958

Dear Allen:

Belatedly, I have decided to ask for a Guggenheim grant—a five-to-six months one, the fall semester of next year, plus whatever I can salvage from the summer, for I don't think I could manage a full year. This would be to finish up things started, especially poetry, that I will never finish prior to ossification unless I can break away from commitments and routine. Would you permit me to give you as "reference?" I hate the idea of asking for assistance from the Guggenheim people, and one of the things I specially hate about any such application is the having to burden—perhaps embarrass—friends with a request to say something in my behalf. However, this will be the one and only time. I suppose I shall never have another chance. But I almost perish now at the prospect of making out—and mailing before Nov. 1—the application blanks, and of compiling information for the foundation bureaucrats. And then maybe getting a refusal!

I enclose a small poem. This one seems finished. I have another one, several pages long, which requires some touching-up before I would dare submit it to your strict eye. This past summer, though utterly defeated physically and in various other respects, I started writing poetry again. The impulse seems to be lasting, in fact gaining, and I had better go ahead with it while the momentum lasts. The poems I did this summer start from a Vermont background, except for one long one that promises well, so far; it starts from Gilmore Simms' "Woodlands Plantation." I *may* have a small new volume ready soon; also I want to see what can be salvaged of the old things for some kind of collection.[a]

Sorry I couldn't join you at the Harvard affair;[b] but it's a good thing I didn't venture. I felt terrible until mid-August or later, then recovered somewhat, but in Nashville recovered only a beat-up feeling.

A former student of mine, James W. Rowe, sent me a thesis that he did, on the "Tennessee Agrarians," for his M.A. in political science at George Washington University. It is the fairest, most discriminating thing of the sort that I have seen. Rowe is brilliant. And now I have Marion Henry's[c] son in a class at Vanderbilt (Elmer Hamner)—the class of about 100 to which I am trying to teach Yeats, and soon will try Eliot. At times I find myself wondering whether Yeats was indeed a great poet or a great fool, but the class (I hope) is not in such a mental quandary. I will join you in holding that at his best Yeats is a great poet, and nothing can beat him down; but at some points he is appallingly near to pretentious trash. Would you agree? I hope you are well. Theresa joins in regards.

As ever, Don

224   *a.* These poems were published in *The Long Street* (1961). *b.* To honor Ransom on his seventieth birthday, Davidson sent a poem, "Meditation on Literary Fame." *c.* Marion Henry Hamner of Clarksville, Tennessee, a relative of Caroline Gordon.

225/ALS

Oxford, England
21 November 1958

Dear Don:

You see where I am!—Yours of Oct. 19th was long delayed in forwarding, so you must forgive what only seems a late reply. The Guggenheim people ought to be ashamed to ask *you* for testimonials from your friends, and you ought to be ashamed of not just going ahead and giving my name without asking permission.

I wish I could have an old-age renascence like yours. I like "A Barren Look" very much. Yet in the historical perspective I am a little uncertain: was this poem written by a Southerner or a Yankee?[a]

I am housed very comfortably in this luxurious college. But the Fulbright commission keeps me constantly on the go, talking and reading publicly till I am blue and numb.

I wish you'd write (between poetic seizures) a new essay on Yeats. The trashy element ought to be put in its place.

I should very much like to see James Rowe's thesis. Couldn't he send me a carbon? And what has happened to the Fugitive Reunion volume? Has Randall become discouraged? There's a book in it, but somebody would have to do a lot of work.

Write me your news. Send more poems.

Affly, Allen

225   *a.* "Of the good sort." [Tate's footnote.]

226/ANS

Minneapolis, Minn.
22 October 1959

Dear Don,

The poem is a subtle and cunning device, and deeply moving.[a] I remember an evening at Benfolly when you and Theresa and the Owsleys, and certainly Andrew but not, I think, John, were there; it was a chilly fall day and we sat round the fire in the dining-room, downstairs. All that is evoked by the poem so vividly that I can hear our voices now. It must have been around 1932. But apart from what the poem evokes from our common past, it is a very fine poem. You have never surpassed it in your lyric style. The third stanza is magnificent; the fourth very fine but properly subdued before the climax of the fifth and last. How can I ever thank you, my dear old friend?

There are other, personal matters that I want to write you about, but not in this letter. You know me so well that you must know that I never think people esteem me, even my closest friends. I am touched almost to tears.

Affectionately, Allen

226   *a.* Davidson has just sent "Lines Written for Allen Tate on His Sixtieth Anniversary," *Sewanee Review* (Autumn 1959).

227/ALS

Nashville, Tenn.
26 October 1959

Dear Allen:

The poem is my "letter" for the occasion and for much more, and so I don't write this as a postscript to the poem but simply to say (like one of Hemingway's characters brought to near speechlessness) that I *feel good* to have your letter, your actual letter. I *felt good*, too, while I was writing the poem and thinking of you through all the years— back and back as well as now and now. Yet I had much mental pain and anxiety all the time for fear that I couldn't make the poem carry all I wanted it to carry to you as poet and dear friend, and also be the *public* tribute you should have—for all time if I could hope for so much for any few lines from me. Well, now I have your letter.

Possibly J.C.R. was not present at the particular gathering you recall. For me those evenings, those afternoons, tend to merge into one. I can recall as you do the fireside circle—and I can hear the voices, especially yours. But I want to remember all as present—it's my inaccurate wish thinking yet has a truth in it.

I am writing—or trying to write—poetry nearly every day now that I am not teaching.

Let me hear from you when you can write more amply.

As ever, Don

228/LS

Minneapolis, Minn.
23 November 1961

Dear Don,

What a fine book it is! I have been reading and rereading for several weeks.[a]

First, the old poems. You have selected very cannily, and I miss only one favorite of mine—Corymba. I am astonished at the vitality of these old pieces. For example, Fiddler Dow. In the old days I was so hot on my own scent that I could not look to right or left, and I am only now, nearly forty years late, appreciating this poem. Likewise Prelude in a Garden and The Old Man of Thorn.

Now, the newer pieces. The Greek that you and Theresa have been reading more and more in the past twenty years has had its effect. Your finest are A Touch of Snow; Woodlands, 1956–1960; Hermitage; and Lines Written for A.T. (By the way, I admire greatly Louise Cowan's fine commentary on that poem.) In all these poems there is still the romantic nostalgia but it's disciplined by a hard precision of phrase which I'm sure is "classical"; and perhaps the romantic nostalgia is classical too! [b]

You have some "difficult" poems. I admire without quite understanding The Ninth Part of Speech.

Andrew was up here recently, as you doubtless know, and he is conspiring to get some things said about The Long Street in the SR; and I'm in on the conspiracy. [c]

I wish I could see you soon, but I don't see an opening at present. I couldn't come to your annual literary shindig last April, and now that I could come this year I will probably not be invited. Bear in mind that I have written a long introduction to the Complete Poems of Paul Valéry (for the Bollingen project), and I can use it as a lecture in the next year, since the book will not come out till early 1963.

Affectionate congratulations on the book; and my love to Theresa.

Yours ever, Allen

228   *a. The Long Street* (1961). Louise Cowan's essay referred to below is "Donald Davidson: 'The Long Street,'" in W. E. Walker and R. L. Wekler, eds., *Reality and Myth: Essays in American Literature in Memory of Richmond Croom Beatty* (1964). *b. Sunt lacrymae rerum; et mentem mortalia tangunt.* Tate's Latin note, which may be translated as: "There are tears of things, and they touch the heart of man." *c.* Tate reviewed *The Long Street* in the *Sewanee Review* (August 1962).

229/TLS

Nashville, Tenn.
29 November 1961

Dear Allen:

Your letter makes me very happy. It's a surprise that you like some of the old Fugitive poems. I was afraid they would be the very sort you would deplore, or else pass by politely. I did not put in "Corymba" (which I knew you liked) because it appeared in my first book—the poor *Outland Piper*—and for this book I used only poems that I had not included in a volume of mine. These old Fugitive poems would have been included in the *Lee in the Mountains* volume, but Houghton

Mifflin made me cut them out. Such is my recollection. For this new book I did revise them, here and there. The romantic nostalgia, or whatever it may be called, is certainly incurable. One must admit that, if it lasts till age 68. But if Vergil had it (and I certainly think he did) why not you and I? Of course it can be guarded somewhat. I learned that from you. But really, do we have to be as icily on guard as is Valéry? I have been reading him, too, at intervals—for the first time seriously —and some of the French commentary on him, while I have also been reading Vergil, the Greeks, and (don't forget) Tate. I am specially pleased that you like the "Woodlands" poem. It was intended to be a group of several related poems; I finished only two, and am still not sure the second of the two is really finished. In general, I feel better about some of the new poems than anything I've ever written in verse, but at the same time have been depressed to face up to the obvious truth that it's a pretty thin sheaf to harvest after all these years. But your letter helps. Immensely!

The plans for our April literary shindig are only now beginning to be discussed. There's been delay partly because Randall Stewart and Walter Sullivan hatched up a scheme to get me more heavily involved than I should be (I asked my doctor about it). I don't know just exactly how the affair is to be arranged, but am sure that the invitation to you is scheduled to be renewed, either for the spring occasion or some other time this year. The Valéry lecture would be the very thing.

I hadn't known about any "conspiracy"—but I was mystified by some sly words John Ransom dropped. He didn't enlarge when he saw how mystified—or scared—I looked. John is sharing my office, but I don't see enough of him.[a] I have not seen Andrew. He wrote me briefly—also vaguely. Similar talk from John Wade, whom Theresa and I just visited, Thanksgiving week. Dear friends, you are the law and the prophets to me, as of old. I cannot say more here. Theresa joins in affectionate regards.

As ever, Don

229 *a.* Ransom has come back to Vanderbilt to teach for the first semester of the 1961–62 school year.

230/ALS

Nashville, Tenn.
4 January 1962

Dear Allen:

We are happy that you will be here for the April "Symposium."
John Wade has accepted. However, Reginald Cook of Bread Loaf
School and Middlebury College, whom we invited as our "Yankee"
member this year, wrote that he couldn't come, on account of heavy
academic and administrative duties.

Could you suggest someone for that place? In recent years we've
had such people as Austin Warren, Warren Beck, Richard Weaver,
Cleanth Brooks. (Dick Weaver & Cleanth came in as "Ringers," you
might say, or maybe galvanized Yankees. We ought to have some *real*
Northerner like Cook or Warren or Beck.) Christopher Dawson has
been mentioned as a possibility—some one thought he still might be at
Harvard.

Harper's "Torchbooks" editor just wrote me that the paperback
edition of *I'll Take My Stand* is now scheduled, definitely, for July
publication. She (Miss Jakob) also sent me a copy of Louis Rubin's
Introduction. It is soft and nice and "moderate" and praises us to the
skies as literary persons, etc., etc. but on the whole seems to me defensive
in a way that I can't much like. . . .

As ever Don

231/ALS

Nashville, Tenn.
11 March 1962

Dear Allen:

Thanks very much for the copy of the Lillian Feder article on your
use of classical literature.[a] It's good. I have been reading it with absorbed attention. She might have said that you are far more "classical"
than Eliot, but not only on account of the quoted prescripts, assimilated
narrative, symbolic material, and so on, which she expounds so well.
She does not quite realize, it would seem, that the Vergilian world not
only "provides an ideal" against which you "measure the present," but
that that world is *in* the present, however much unacknowledged, as a
submerged reality. This is what keeps you from being merely "nostalgic"
(as some fool is always saying of us all) or "romantic" as Keats was in

his "medievalism" or his spurious "classicism"; for him those terms had no present, active meaning. And this, too, is what gives the poems Feder discusses their tremendous substantial reality. It is something that Archie MacLeish or M. Cowley could not possibly understand. But I had better not go on like this. I am grateful to Lillian Feder for forcing important matters on my slack attention, among them especially the passage from Homer—what Glaucus says to Diomede. It had never occurred to me to connect it with your "leaves" refrain.[b] I'll accept Feder's "gloss" on this, no matter whether or not you had Homer in mind.

All this is a subject I would like to dwell on. But time presses, too much so. Theresa and I are now definitely planning to have that Fugitive meeting at our house, the evening *before* the Symposium; that is to say, we are counting on you for dinner the evening of April 24th, and after dinner will further count on you to read a poem, as of old! Or more than one, if so provided. John Wade is arriving that afternoon. Jesse Wills, with his wife Ellen, is pretty sure to be on hand, and have a poem. (Jesse has a travel schedule—business affairs—that has to be adjusted.) I have not yet reached Alec Stevenson. Probably he and Elise are in Florida—where they recently invested in a house. A Marshallville friend of John Wade's—and mine—may come with John: the one and only Dick Dodd. Since our house is small, the assembly of that evening will be limited to those named, unless some other one of our old friends turns up unexpectedly, in which case we'll squeeze and manage somehow. This is a "Fugitive" meeting—or "Fugitive-Agrarian."

As ever, Don

231   *a.* "Allen Tate's Use of Classical Literature," *Centennial Review* (Winter 1960).
         b. In "Ode to the Confederate Dead."

232/ALS

Nashville, Tennessee
24 October 1962

Dear Allen:

Coming home from the Vanderbilt campus (what's left of it) after a long and very exhausting day, I read your review of *The Long Street* and found in it the finest draught of restorative ever poured for me by any hand. I'm deeply honored—and pleased—that it is your hand that poured it; the more so, Allen, because I have a pretty sure conviction that it's as much as a man's literary life is worth (so to speak) to make even a slight gesture toward restoring me, much less the South. I feel especially appreciative at what you say about the people who "place" me so glibly—or more likely ignore me. But most of all I'm deeply touched, and made most warmly grateful, by what you say in your very last sentence,[a] and in what leads up to it. I don't know how I can ever live up to what you say. It is such a thin little sheaf of poems, as you noted. I must write more, somehow, and will if I can get freedom to do so—a fairly long poem that I have had in mind, and some shorter ones, hanging now in an unfinished state. But in this volume I didn't intend to put all the poems I "want to keep." I thought of it only as a new book of poems, with some old ones, never gathered up before. This is what I meant to say or imply in the brief Foreword. (I wonder if the pages were left uncut at that point in your copy.) My notion was that, if this volume should be at all well received, perhaps I could persuade a publisher to bring out a "collection" or "selection" ranging back through the years.

I miss in this public criticism the stern admonishments that you've given me in private, from the beginning, and that have always hit the mark, to my eternal benefit. You have let me off easy this time. That's a pleasant sensation! But I *need* that rap on the fingers and hope you won't forbear to administer it—in discreet privacy—when occasion demands.

The middle portion of your review is something for me to ponder and discuss with you later. It is in part an excursus into historical surmises. I hope you'll believe me when I assure you that I truly haven't done much historical surmising. But I won't go into that subject here. When I can get some free time I'll try to write down some views about the matters you bring up; and also, more particularly, will try to give you a "report," as nearly factual as I can make it, on the Mississippi troubles, referred to in your recent letter, and on the general Southern situation *now*, as I see it. I will do this unless interrupted by missiles from Cuba or elsewhere.

"At the Station" is a quite old poem. I wrote it, in practically the present form, when we were in Wesley Hall, but don't remember whether I offered it to *The Fugitive*. I'm interested that you should single it out for mention. . . .

As ever Don

232   *a.* "To bring one's affection and admiration together, so that these emotions,

rare even in isolation, are indistinguishable, is a privilege enjoyed not more than three or four times in one's life," *Sewanee Review* (Autumn 1962), p. 673.

233/TLS

Minneapolis, Minn.
23 November 1962

Dear Don,

I can scarcely believe that your good letter of October 24th has been here a month. In that period I had to deal with a virus, and in the midst of that a minor operation. I'm feeling better now.

I'm sorry I got mixed up about the scope of The Long Street. It may confuse some of the readers of my review. But at any rate I'm glad you liked what I wrote. Now Scribners should get out a Collected Poems. Is Tom Walsh still there? Could I do anything in support?[a]

As to the Mississippi situation, my views come down to a kind of stoicism. I don't see how the Federal Government can be opposed. The South has nothing to oppose it with, except sporadic violence.—If you can't lick 'em, join 'em, might well be the Southern slogan; that is, take over integration and do it gradually the Southern way. I have always been annoyed that the Southern Way of Life becomes a popular cause only when race relations are upset. If there isn't more to the Southern way of life than this, it is not worth fighting for. The people in Mississippi who opposed Agrarianism enthusiastically invited Northern industrialists to come down and exploit the poor whites, and now they affirm the Southern way by rioting.

I wish I could get down to Tennessee for a good talk. I'm always going East or West. But maybe we can meet this summer.

As ever, Allen

233   a. Tate assisted Davidson in finding a publisher, the University of Minnesota Press, for his *Collected Poems, 1922–1961* (1966).

234/ALS

Nashville, Tenn.
21 December 1962

Dear Allen:

I've been hardly able to think of anything but your poetry for the past two or three weeks. After reading you faithfully—and often—for forty years, I now read you more *intensely* than ever. It would be 24 hours a day if poetry were in complete control of the day and this body. That's what teaching does. As J.C.R. said to me last fall, "You never really know a poet till you write about him"—or teach him, I would add. Poor teacher as I am, simply incapable of getting up a 'lecture' of the regular academic sort, it seems to be going well. But I won't fully know until I see the students' papers. They are taking you very seriously, anyhow.

Meiners[a] is a help. Yet I feel he allegorizes too insistently at some points. And he doesn't see the *four* parts of "Seasons of the Soul" as reflecting *throughout* the disastrous implications of World War II; he brings that up in connection with "Summer," then neglects it. I can't forget the time when you wrote these poems (and sent parts of them to me, I'm sure—during the war some time). And all the poems in your *Winter Sea* volume seem closely related to the "Seasons," as your other dream-poems, for me, connect rather closely with 'Autumn.' Theresa, by the way, though she had not read your 'Autumn' or heard it read in a long time, remembered it with extraordinary vividness. So that when you began to read last spring, all was familiar and also exciting; she 'followed' you because she 'knew' what was coming.

In two weeks and a little over, we have studied *only* Sections I & II of your poems. Every line has been read in class—and discussed—and often read again—for the poems can't be exhausted. We have not quite two weeks more, after Christmas, and will have to be selective, in class discussion, about the remainder. But it nearly all has been 'assigned', and I think they will read without fail the 'assigned' poems and probably more. For a written exercise prior to final exam., I'll give them some options (since time is short). *Among* the various options is a study of (1) versions of "Ode to the Confederate Dead"—that is, the 1928 one compared with the present one; and (2) the present "To the Lacedemonians" compared with the 1932 one—I have the Richmond *Times-Dispatch* front page, of that date, you'll remember. These won't be dry "collations." I won't stand for that. They must say what the difference is, & why—in short, study your *art*. I hope you won't object to this. It's one way of forcing students to be specific and to look hard at poetry.

So for the teacher—well, the teacher learns, too. I feel an enormous relief in coming to your poems, after wrestling with W. B. Yeats & Eliot, earlier in the semester. Some time I'll try to tell you what I've learned.

That next two weeks I'll be catching-up with various neglected commitments, with very little time out, except to spend Christmas Day with Mary and her family—and perhaps go to 9 o'clock Mass with them at St. Henry's Church—which is not very far from Nine Mile Hill. We used to gather chestnuts on Nine Mile Hill, and think of it as far out in the country.

As ever, Don

234   *a.* R. K. Meiners, *The Last Alternatives: A Study of the Works of Allen Tate* (1962).

235/ALS

Nashville, Tenn.
1 January 1963

Dear Allen,

... Your letter made me happy. Theresa and I spent a good part of last evening reading "The Eye." I was bound and determined to track your λαιδρὴ κορώνη prescript to its source, and with Theresa's help found it.*a* Now, I am *almost* tempted to connect the λαιδραὶ κορωναὶ at the end of the poems not only with the strife between the Laurel and the Olive of Callimachus' *Iambus* but with the three ravens of the Old English ballad who in the "realistic" Scots and American versions become the malevolent and disloyal peckers-out of the slain knight's bonnie blue eyes. But that may be imposing entirely unnecessary complications?

Earlier I located without any trouble the Propertius prefix to the *Oenia* series, and read that Elegy thoughtfully—for the first time in my life: I never studied Propertius, and so didn't recognize the passage offhand. I have to be *ready* to propound if a student asks a question, even if I don't quite get around to a discussion of these early poems of yours—all of which I can now far more knowledgeably value than I could 40 years ago. They are still good—even the slightest of them.

None of your commentators that I have so far read or scanned have taken notice of the close correspondence between Lacy Buchan's vision in Part III of *The Fathers* and your "Records I."

It does me good, somehow, to jot down these bits in a letter to you, but don't feel obliged to write an answering comment unless you definitely feel like it. I hope the after-Christmas "paralysis" (which also afflicted me) has departed and left you in good health & spirits.

As ever, Don

235 *a.* Davidson is referring to the prescript to Tate's poem "The Eye." The Greek prescript " λαιδρὴ κορώνη, κῶς τὸ χεῖλος οὐκ ἀλγεῖς;" may be translated "Impudent crow, why doesn't your beak feel pain?"

236/TLS

Minneapolis, Minn.
10 January 1963

Dear Don,

Your letter of the 1st came the day before we went East for four days; and I'm back now with bronchitis worse than ever. I suppose it's this foul climate. If I live two more years I shall try to retire, and leave.

Literary cunning could go no further than you and Theresa have taken it in your gloss on the Laidre Korone. If I remember rightly Callimachus meant only that the "lip" of the crow should "ache" because he caws all the time. But I definitely made the transfer that you suggest: it aches from pecking out eyes; this crow becomes one of the crows of the Twa Corbies. This pleases me ENORMOUSLY, that you and Theresa should have detected the shift. Nobody else has. As to the Propertius, I have completely forgotten what I meant; so I'll leave that to you too!

I *think* that Arthur Mizener spotted the relation of my Records I to Lacy's vision; but I'm not sure. In a sense that early poem was the spring-board for The Fathers.

I am deeply grateful, my old friend.

As ever, Allen

P.S. I can't resist telling you that yesterday I received from Florence the Medaglia d'Oro della Società di Dante Alighieri for 1962. This is given annually to a poet of any nationality. A couple of my terza rima poems were put into Italian a few years ago; so I reckon this is the result. Other recipients have been Guillen, Montale, Sbarbaro, Jean-Jouve. Pretty high company for an ex-Fugitive! I confess this pleases me more than any so-called honor I've ever had.

237/TLS

Nashville, Tenn.
15 January 1963

Dear Allen:

The good news in the P.S. of your letter ought to have been in the Ante Scriptum—it was too good to keep until I turned the sheet over. But it crowned the letter all the same. I greatly rejoice that the Dante Society Medaglia d'Oro has come to you, and send warmest congratulations on behalf of Theresa and myself. Of the other recipients you name, Guillen is the only one of whom I have the slightest knowledge. I met him years ago when he was at the Middlebury College Spanish School, and used to come up to Bread Loaf with Salinas. But since we have Claudio Gorlier of Turin here this semester—as "visiting scholar", on an A.C.L.S. grant—I soon managed to get informed through him. (Didn't you meet him, some years past, when you gave a lecture at Turin?) On Monday, my class was having its last meeting of the semester, and the last session on your poetry. So it was a very happy moment when I could mention your award—a fine climax (the best possible) to a month's close study by those young folks and me. I asked Gorlier to speak to the class for a few minutes about the award and whatever else he might like. He made a charming short talk of the sort that only a literary European can make, graceful in compliments, and both witty and wise. Gorlier emphasized the antiquity of the Dante Society and said, among other things, that the award surely was not merely for your excellence in terza rima but also for general reasons—as it had been for Montale ("our best poet," he declared, "in Italy"), and for Guillen, et al. He also told the intently listening class that affiliation with a place had much to do with the universality that the Fugitives were achieving; and that he was convinced that the Trojans, in their farther westward flight, did not land at Plymouth, Mass., but in the South.

Theresa and I are hugely pleased to have your confirmation of the suggested gloss on the Laidre Korone as becoming one of the Twa Corbies. We are continuing to discuss that poem, "The Eye." Indeed, we had it for lunch today. Theresa is exceedingly helpful in discussion of your poems because she is a very close reader and comes to a poem without troublesome preconceptions. As to the Propertius prescript, I don't think we have very much to offer. In that particular elegy, Propertius (in case you don't remember offhand) brings various reproaches against Cynthia: in fact, he compares her, not by way of praise, with Lais, Thais, Phryne, and such famous courtesans, hints that she is too fond of being in houses that have dirty pictures on the walls, that she has too many *falsos ... propinquos* who claim the *ius osculi*,ᵃ and so on. It seems to me that it's chiefly the last lyric of the series that carries the point of your prescript, and maybe in some lines echoes Propertius a little. On the whole the Oenia group seem to me definitely Tatian, light-hearted Tatian—and I've always liked them.

Arthur Mizener refers to Last Days of Alice in his Introduction to The Fathers, not to Records I. So, at least in the Sewanee Review printing of his Introduction; I have not checked the Alan Swallow edition. But of course that's all in an important line of interpretation. I would be inclined to take it further and bring Death of Little Boys into that same line. Abstraction threatens, is indeed imminent, but does not quite prevail at the funeral of Lacy's mother, in The Fathers. In Death of Little Boys, it has prevailed; the result is raw fear rather than grief; the "guests" turn down their palms to repress indecorous (unmodern) manifestations of grief; people, place, objects lack identification and connection; in the end there is "calm" but not consolation. In discussing Death of Little Boys with the class it seemed to me a good idea to note that it should be contrasted with Ransom's Dead Boy, in which the scene is particularized, though the only symbolic object with a name is "Virginia's aged tree." I began to wonder—though I did not tell the class this—whether you wrote the poem as a somewhat deliberate counterpart to John's. I never thought to ask you the question, long ago, and don't mean to belabor you with it now, but it's very interesting to think about. . . .

As ever, Don

237   *a.* "False hangers-on" who claim "the right of the kiss."

238/TLS

Minneapolis, Minn.
22 January 1963

Dear Don,

Our correspondence has been most interesting for me, but I am now becoming a little embarrassed. It has been all about *me*. May we change the subject?

For example, your Collected Poems. When we were in New Haven two weeks ago, I saw John Hall Wheelock. I asked him whether he thought Scribner might publish such a book. He has been long retired, but he still has great influence. He said he would support the project with great enthusiasm. So I think you ought to go ahead. I need not say that I will support it too. You will know whether to start with Tom Walsh. Let me know what you decide to do, and when you will do it.

I am deeply touched by the attention you gave my poems in your class. And please thank Claudio Gorlier for his part on the last day. I remember him very well, but I had lost track of him in recent years. He is right: Aeneas didn't go to New York. He went to Virginia. Caesar went to New York.

Have you heard that Edna Lytle's cancer has returned? This time, to the oesophagus. Andrew didn't say that this meant the end, but I infer that it did. This is a sad note to end on.

Ever yrs. Allen

239/ALS

Nashville, Tenn.
20 February 1963

Dear Allen:

I was glad to deliver your telegram to Dr. Sanborn.[a] The enclosed clipping will give you an idea of the little party we arranged—with the help of Ivar Lou Myhr (Mrs. Duncan), Annie Lee Cooney, Isabel Howell, *et alii*. Dr. Sanborn was calmly typing at his desk when I came in to see him at the very beginning of the "surprise party," and in his usual manner ran the gamut from jovial exchanges of wit to philosophical-scientific speculating during the course of the occasion. When I began to recall his German student days to him by repeating part of "Alt Heidelberg, du feine" he carried right on through the old poem— and sang it, too, clearly and in tune. He complained only of some trouble with his back and indeed was somewhat bent-over, but straightened up when the photographer asked him to.

Thanks to you for wiring the greetings. Apparently, the news spread pretty well. Six former students phoned from Washington, for a group-conversation. Jimmy Stahlman[b] and others sent flowers. It was a success as the news story indicates.

Winter weather has been *very* hard on us here, with little surcease, but Monday the 18th of February was by good fortune a beautiful, mild day.

Take courage—snowdrops are blooming on our terrace, and the yellow crocus, too.

As ever Don

239   *a*. Congratulating Herbert Sanborn, professor emeritus of philosophy at Vanderbilt, on his ninetieth birthday.   *b*. Publisher of the *Nashville Banner*.

240/TLS

Minneapolis, Minn.

21 April 1963

Dear Don,

Either you or Tyree Fain must have sent me my copy of *The Spyglass*, and I am very grateful for it. Tyree has done a first-rate job of editing, and I have so written him.

Well, I didn't know how good The Spyglass was—or its various other headings—Critic's Almanac, etc. You may remember that I was in New York and France from 1924 to 1928, and saw your column only at intervals. You were a prophet in those days. I am amazed at the accuracy of your judgment of the Southern novelists. You saw the virtues of Stark Young and Elizabeth Roberts before anybody else did (not the virtues that NY saw), and you put people like Heyward in their permanent place. I believe you err in only one prophecy, that T. S. Eliot would write no more poetry. I am astonished too how in dealing with the historians you develop the main theme of I'll Take My Stand before any of the rest of us did. I didn't know this, couldn't have known it at the time. I think that this book should have been published long ago. We are all indebted to Tyree for prodding you into it.

What you say of my Jackson, along with the article you wrote in 1957, gives me permanent pleasure. I wish I could redo parts of it, but what I still like is what you liked in 1928.

I simply didn't remember that I had written so many as 27 reviews for you! They weren't very good. You are six years older than I, but at the same time you had no right in those days to be so much more mature than I was.

I wrote a little while ago to Charlie Scribner about your Collected Poems. He is always slow, but he will reply.

When are you and Theresa leaving for Bread Loaf? I expect to come to Tennessee on June 6th or 7th to stay five or six days, first in Nashville, then at Monteagle with Andrew.

Ever yrs. Allen

241/TLS

Nashville, Tenn.
4 May 1963
Dear Allen:

I felt very bad that I could not join you and others who were with Andrew last Sunday.[a] Theresa was knocked out by a hard attack of laryngitis, and missed the Symposium events entirely; got up Friday, only to be back in bed again Saturday. I was completely exhausted, by the week-end, and didn't dare make the trip to Sewanee. Walter Sullivan told me about the funeral. When Andrew was here on Thursday, I had the good fortune to get him apart from the crowd, and we talked for some time—the first real talk I have had with him in years. I have never known a braver spirit than Andrew, and that knowledge of him came upon me more deeply than ever during that Thursday, when we all knew the crisis might come at any time. Theresa and I never got to know Edna very well—or Andrew's children. We have felt upset and anxious about their situation, for years. Walter said you were urging Andrew to spend some time with you on Cape Cod this summer. That would be a fine thing. If Andrew is able to come, maybe you'll all find a chance to run up and see us at Bread Loaf. Did you know that Cleanth Brooks and Louis Coxe will be teaching there this summer?

This is a disjointed kind of letter, but I can't help it. Until Tyree Fain checked the file, I didn't realize, any more than you did, how many reviews you wrote for the Book Page. This whole resurrection is in fact a big surprise to me. I wrote those things, back yonder, mostly at top speed, and at all hours, and after the page was discontinued I had some vague notion that some kind of book could be got together from them. I even assembled some clippings, I think. But whoever it was that I showed them to didn't encourage me in the book direction, and I dropped the idea, and put the whole thing out of my mind. . . . I'm happy that you like it, and will give me a good score on all but the Eliot prediction. On that, I believe, I hedged a *little*. But I still can't help feeling, at times, the glassy stare of that monocle. As to who was more knowledgeable, my impression has consistently been—and still is—that I could never possibly catch up with John, who was born in '88 or with you, born in '99, who leaped ahead of both John and me in manner most unbecoming in a young Victorian! For you, too, Allen, are Victorian!

I have written to Tom Walsh and said, among other things, that I will be trying to work out a collected poems volume this summer and would like to submit one to Scribner's by early fall. No word from them as yet, but I hardly expect anything definite, soon. If I am to get up a collected volume, I will badly need some advice as to what to include. When I look back, I get the shakes. . . .

I have had another surprise recently. By careful scientific inquiry—including no doubt the use of the new Computer—it has been discovered that I am *the* senior member of the entire University faculty (in point of service), and for that reason (I suppose) I have been asked to say a few words, as representative of the Faculty, at the inauguration of Chancellor Heard next fall. Isn't that like asking the oldest Barnacle to speak for the Ship?

I hope that we will still be on hand when you visit Nashville in early June. That's the time when we are either taking off for Bread Loaf or in awful fury of getting ready to do so. Let me know your plans, as exactly as possible.

As ever, Don

241 *a*. At the funeral of Edna Lytle, Andrew's wife, in Monteagle, Tennessee.

242/TLS

Minneapolis, Minn.
9 February 1965

Dear Don,

I am mighty glad to have yours of the 5th. If the question of the size of the book comes up, am I authorized to tell Jack Ervin that you will consider omitting a few poems?*a* Or will you write him that? It might be better for him to have this information before the board meeting on the 23rd, lest they come to an adverse decision based on cost of printing, and then hesitate to reverse it.

I am extremely proud to be the subject of one of your lectures. If you are writing the lectures, I hope I may see them. The series looks like a book in the making.

Certainly Tom Inge should be given permission to see your letters to me. I am opposed to unknown persons examining our private correspondence, but this is an entirely different matter. And of course Inge may see my letters to you if he needs them. Just ask him to write to Alexander Clark at the Princeton Library; Clark will clear it with me.

I have read your "Decorum in the Novel"*b* all too hastily and I am not certain what I think of your argument. Some form of censorship is absolutely necessary but what agency, government or church, should enforce it I do not know. I think your indictment fails to discriminate between works like *Ulysses* and *Lady Chatterly*. The latter I think is definitely an obscene book, but I do not think that *Ulysses* is, in spite of the dirty language, which is dirtier than anything in *Chatterly*. The intention and the effect are the crucial things. In your comment on Mark Schorer's essay you put Flaubert and James together. I see no connection. James is not "neutral"; his "central intelligence" puts the moral struggle *inside* the main character; and there is always perfect propriety of language. I don't see James as in the "scientific" naturalism of Zola, etc. There has always been obscene literature, but the problem today, in this disordered society, is to keep it out of the hands of the young. The breakdown of family and religious authority are responsible for the trouble, and as you say the commercialism of the publishers in an "open" society. It seems to me that the only genuine solution is not in sight; we shall have to get worse before we can get better, if we ever can get better; for that solution is *moral* authority vested in certain institutions, not police authority. For the police and the courts have no access to the kind of classical decorum that is the heart of your argument. The entire matter is too much for me. Your essay I will go back to, for it may help me think it out.

I'm still swamped with unanswered letters. But let me hear from you about the poems.

Yrs. Allen

242 a. The University of Minnesota Press is planning Davidson's last collection of poetry, *Poems 1922–1961* (1966). b. *Modern Age* (Winter 1964–65).

243/TLS

Nashville, Tenn.
11 February 1965

Dear Allen:

Your Feb. 9th letter has just come, and I'm happy to have it. Indeed you are authorized to tell Mr. Ervin that I will consider shortening the book by omitting a few poems—perhaps especially the two long ones placed at the end—"The Case of Motorman 17" and "The Deserter: A Christmas Epilogue," and maybe some more. I haven't thought that through and faced up to the possibility of cuts because I *hoped* for an inclusive volume. I wrote Mr. Ervin, when I sent in the MS that it is tentative in its present form and that I hoped "to retain the long poems in Part v if possible." At the time I didn't say more, lest he consider it an "invitation" to urge cutting, right away. I would be much obliged if you could tell him that I am willing to make omissions. You advised me—wisely, too—to send the Ms. to him in the first place, and I would hope very much to have your advice about the omissions if they turn out to be necessary.

I would surely have done better, through the years, if I could have had your advice more often. That would apply also to the "Decorum in the Novel" article. My main difficulty in writing it was that I had to compress into one article (kept under a space-limit) what needed the room of a book—or a good-sized monograph. So I didn't attempt literary criticism of the works under discussion. If you will look again at my reference to James, p. 44, you'll find that it appears in a favorable context. Of course James would never have confused the "objectivity" that he cultivated with scientific objectivity or the quasi-objectivity of the Naturalists; and I don't believe he would agree with Schorer that technique *alone* "objectifies the materials of art." That sort of doctrine, unless properly qualified, pulls James into line with Zola, Lawrence, Henry Miller et al. Any little *sale bête* who has some cleverness and facility can *claim* to be "objective" and under present conditions doesn't get called down either by the Courts or the critics. I don't advocate censorship. I just gloomily foresee that the *sales bêtes* with their cheap dirt that simulates literature will bring on censorship. Isn't it one of the things that happens in a society that's degenerating as rapidly as ours is?

There is now a good chance that Theresa and I may get a trip to Europe next fall—not from the Fulbright people, but through help from another quarter. If it works out, we will leave from Montreal Sept. 9, make some brief stops in the places where we have friends or that Theresa may want to see (as in Germany—the ancient seats of her family being in such places as Aachen, Blankenheim, etc. She had an uncle, or great-uncle, who was a professor at Heidelberg). Then we'll spend the main part of our time in Italy and Greece and sail from Piraeus on the Greek Line, Nov. 16, for Halifax, and subsequently drive home.

As ever, Don

244/TLS

Minneapolis, Minn.
29 May 1965

Dear Don,

I thank thee, my friend, for the fine commentary on my To the Lacedemonians. I needed this "boost" after reading that very bad book by John L. Stewart.[a] I am glad that he likes Red best, but not pleased that he seems to like you least. Red is more nearly the liberal. He seems to approve of us in this descending order: Red, John, Tate, and you. But his liking or not liking is beside the point. He doesn't understand any of us. And I am both bored and annoyed by his humorless beating of dead horses, such as my juvenilia; and I am more than annoyed by his deductions, from my Mother and Son and A Dream and a Vision, about my mother's character. You and I are reduced to the Yankee stereotype: we are worshipping the vanished glories of the Old South. There is no evidence of this in any of our writings. But enough. I have written him a rather severe letter.

You are the only critic who has ever given serious attention to To the Lacedemonians. And I am grateful for your perception of the significance of the revisions. You are exactly right about them.

More later.

Ever yrs Allen

244   a. *The Burden of Time: The Fugitives and Agrarians* (1965).

245/ALS

Nashville, Tenn.
4 June 1965

Dear Allen:

I'm happy that my piece on "To the Lacedemonians" pleases you[a] —glad, too, that I didn't make any errors of the sort for which one would have to rush out a "stop-the-press" plea. *Southern Review* just sent me proofs, a few days ago. In print the piece looked better to me than I had anticipated, from my prolonged staring at the typescript.

Stewart's book came to me not long ago, with a letter from him, partly apologetic, but largely defiant in a sort of Ivy League way. He knows how bad it will make me feel (he says), is sorry to have his book be the cause, but is grateful for this-and-that, and I am to understand that his critical position is objective and a matter of conscience, etc.,

etc.—not those words, but that's the idea of his curious letter. How can I answer such a letter—how comment in any way on such a book? I knew it would be bad. His Ph.D. thesis, of the 1940's, was a forewarning; so was his letter of last summer when he wrote me for permission to quote —but only from things written up to 1930 or thereabouts. Still, I hardly expected such a large-scale demonstration of myopia & dislike. His critical opinions are his own business. His carelessness about facts is something he—and, for that matter, Princeton Press—is surely account-able for. There are gross errors on many, many pages. I've not read the book through—only scanned it—and his errors, his imaginings, are in-credible. What "readers" could Princeton Press have used for Stewart's MS? Maybe I can find out something from Carlos Baker by simply call-ing a few of Stewart's worst errors to his attention. Should I try that? Carlos is probably still on the "committee" or whatever it's called, of the Princeton Press.

Stewart's far too effusive acknowledgments to me in his foreword bother me even more than his criticisms: he thus involves me in *his* irresponsibility.

Clearly his critical judgements are on a straight ideological basis. Ransom, Red Warren, M. Moore, as "defectors" to the North—to the Ivy League—liberal North—are "good" writers. You and, above all, I, not having defected to the same extent as our three friends, are "bad" by definition.

What a shame!—since there might have been some sense in connect-ing "Agrarian" principles, etc. with the literary performance. I suppose the book will do some harm in those quarters where such a treatment as Stewart's will be welcomed. But no matter—he can't prevail. Let us think of him as an Ivy League (now Big Californian) version of Rufus Griswold.

We'll leave in a few days for Bread Loaf. Should have left *before* now.

As ever Don

245   *a.* The reference is to a paper Davidson read at Hampden-Sydney College in April 1965, a part of which appeared in the *Southern Review* (July 1965).

246/TLS
                                                    Nashville, Tenn.
                                                    1 February 1966
Dear Allen:

I am happy to have your letter and get you located again. The English department has a copy of the Inge-Young book all ready to send you, and I was going to write to Andrew to make sure of your address. This is one of 100 copies of the "limited edition." Somebody said you got a copy of the trade edition when you were here. Now you'll have the "de luxe" also, which is the same thing only different—in binding, etc., and in being signed by Inge and Young, numbered, and so on. I think I told you the circumstances of the origin of this book and how it got started as a kind of English department project before I knew what was going on.

Russell Fraser, the new head of the department, told me just a few days ago that he was expecting or at least hoping to have you here for a semester. I'm terribly glad it has all been worked out. You should have been here years and years ago. Isn't it so often true that a new man, stepping in, can get things done that nobody could put over before, despite the obvious need for doing what was urged by the old members? It will put a new look on everything for me to have you here. And I'll stir up your reminiscences for your literary memoirs if you'll stir up mine! There are some blank—or vague—spots in my memory that I'm sure you can fix up. I am vastly pleased that Kermode cornered you and got you started in a reminiscent direction. Should I suspect that you were already halfway in the notion?

Our European trip was fine all the way. We were lucky in the weather everywhere, except at Halifax, upon our return. In Ireland we visited with Bryan MacMahon—whose unusually fine stories you may have seen—both in Dublin and at his home in County Kerry. In London we were with Cleanth and Tinkham[a] for parts of two days. Cleanth had been suffering from an unexpected attack of the gout, but was in good spirits—though both he and Tinkham can think of little now but getting through with his pesky duties and returning to the U.S. Your recommmendation as to hotel in Rome—Inghilterra—worked out very well for us. They served the worst continental breakfast we had anywhere, but the location was good, our room was good, service was all right. We actually liked Milan better than Rome, for reasons that I can't really quite understand. Our three weeks or more in Athens was the best part of our whole trip in many ways. But I didn't expect to see the Greeks picking cotton on the plain of Thebes, and I found the mountains simply terrifying. Nothing had prepared us for them—or for the really threatening ruggedness of the Acropolis. Since getting back here in December we have been tired and stodgy to the nth degree, and feel the pains and anxieties of old age invading us, sometimes stealthily, sometimes with abrupt force.

I am glad you like the looks of *Poems 1922–1961.* For my part, I'm delighted with the general make-up of the book and with the Minnesota Press, all of whose staff have been very good to me. I owe you thanks, once more, Allen, for introducing me to John Ervin and his publishing house. Let's don't think about the reviewers. They will certainly do the chop-chop act, plenty of times.

As you see, I am having typewriter trouble. It's a new typewriter. My old lucky World War 1 model folding Corona is locked up in a closet in our house at Bread Loaf. We intended to bring it and various other items when we stopped in Vermont to pick up our car, but it was like an ice-house in that shuttered-up place, and we fled before we could carry through our plan.

As ever Donald

246   *a.* Mrs. Cleanth Brooks.

247/TLS

Nashville, Tenn.
20 February 1966

Dear Allen:

Perhaps you were sometimes (though rarely) 'mean' thirty years ago, but not about the "Lee." All your suggestions there were helps, truly, and I'm glad you don't mind that the Young-Inge book makes evident my indebtedness to you. It is a rather strange combination, isn't it, of an "essay" that is a collation of texts with an extensive bibliography containing so much that might well be ignored if not forgotten? I have wondered what will be really thought, if not said, about it. Yes, there was a dinner occasion, for Theresa and me. Andrew turned up, though he was hardly expected, I was told. Jesse and Alec were there. Tyree Fain, too. If I can get hold of one of the "programmes" I'll send it.

I have a letter from Virginia Rock about the reworking of her thesis[a] for the book that she is making out of it for Louis Rubin's LSU series, and I imagine you have heard from her too. Now, in the midst of too much already to do, I have to try to think of what corrections I had in mind once and what advice to give her now, since she solicits it. I would hope that, if she can do some needful revision, her book will do something to offset Stewart's massacre of the subject.

Rashly, I have promised to write a kind of review article on Edmund Wilson, basing it mostly on his latest, *The Bit Between My Teeth.* I have read Wilson fitfully, through the years: *Axel's Castle, To the Finland Station, The Wound and the Bow, Memoirs of Hecate,* and, more recently, *Patriotic Gore,* but have not followed him through his so-called chronicles. I won't quote you—but do you think that he is a "man of letters" or "literary critic" in the best sense of those terms? I find him being described now as our "first" (i.e. top) man of letters— astounding overstatement, to me! He seems more a kind of journalist, a high-grade one, fascinating to read, and I think honest, though maybe not as honest with himself as he thinks he is. What solid foundation does he really have to stand on, now that Russian Communism has soured for him? And why couldn't Wilson, with all his learning and sense, see from the beginning that Communism was not a solid foundation? Now, since he has no religion, and since his society is shot to pieces, he has nothing but books to hold to, as far as I can see, and no experience now but in books, nothing much to write about but writing. An eclectic? A reporter? What? Certainly a fine example of alienation. By the way, were you the Mr. Charles or Cousin Charles of Tennessee that Wilson dismissed with a gesture during his travels across the continent—in the Depression period or thereabouts? Don't feel obliged to answer such questions, but if you have time to jot down a note or two, I'll be grateful.

As ever, Don

247   a. "The Making and Meaning of *I'll Take My Stand:* A Study in Utopian Conservatism," University of Minnesota (1961).

248/TLS

Ripton, Vt.
2 October 1966

Dear Allen:

I'm not sure where you are this fall, so am sending this to Monteagle in care of Andrew.

It's too bad to have to unload such a large Fugitive affairs bulletin upon you, but the past keeps pursuing the fleeing Fugitives. It seems quite often to catch-up with slow-footed me first. This is my cry for help.[a]

Theresa and I hope to stick it out here through October, then return to Nashville. Theresa insisted on our getting electric heat (baseboard type) installed, so that the old man won't have to carry wood and stoke fires so much as formerly. I yielded—with some regret. For one of the few things I can do successfully and take pleasure in is to build a fire. The *Poems, 1922–61* has hardly been noticed, critically, but to my great surprise has sold well—for a book of poems that's also a book of mine—during the first six months. I hope you have done some good work on your long poem and whatever else you may be writing. My bread-and-butter revision of a textbook, a painful labor, is nearly done. Little else, though. Theresa joins me in our best.

As ever, Don

248   a. In regard to a projected reprinting of all numbers of the *Fugitive* by Peter Smith.

Appendix A

🌿

The Fugitive-Agrarian Movement

The continuity of the movement is seen in the following lists of contributors, beginning with the four Fugitives who continued with the group through its Agrarian phase. See also Appendix G.

The Fugitive (1922–25)	*I'll Take My Stand* (1930)	*Who Owns America?* (1936)
Donald Davidson	Davidson	Davidson
John Crowe Ransom	Ransom	Ransom
Allen Tate	Tate	Tate
Robert Penn Warren	Warren	Warren
	Lyle H. Lanier	Lanier
	Andrew Lytle	Lytle
	Frank Lawrence Owsley	Owsley
	John Donald Wade	Wade
	John Gould Fletcher	Herbert Agar
	Henry B. Kline	Hilaire Belloc
	Herman Clarence Nixon	Cleanth Brooks
	Stark Young	T. J. Cauley
		David C. Coyle
		Henry C. Evans, Jr.
		Mary Fisher
		Willis Fisher
		Douglas Jerrold
		George Marion O'Donnell
		John C. Rawe
		James Waller

Appendix B

❦

TLS

Clarksville, Tenn.
24 July 1930

To the Contributors to the Southern Symposium:

I. I submit that the present title of the Symposium, "I'll Take My Stand," is an unfortunate one, for the following reasons: 1) Its implications will not be immediate for the general, particularly the "foreign," reader. 2) Even if they should be, they are likely to rouse antagonistic prejudices corresponding to the sympathetic ones latent in the Southern reader. In the former case, the title becomes a disadvantage; in the latter, it is neither here nor there, since the stirring of vague prejudice butters no parsnips. 3) *I don't like it.* This, for me, is the overwhelming objection. It makes my ears burn. It is a breach of decorum in my mind beyond any rationalization. It is a perfectly gratuitous breach, for it has no definite purpose, and does not justify itself on the ground of breaking a law of taste in order to set up a better one. 4) It is an emotional appeal to ill-defined beliefs; it is a *special plea.* The essays in the book justify themselves *rationally* by an appeal to principle. It thus falsifies the aims of the book.

II. The title was selected in an irregular manner: 1) It was not put to a formal vote. Thus any active or latent opposition at the moment was not called forth simply because it was not apparent that a final choice had been made. 2) This state of affairs continued until through sheer inertia we drifted into accepting the title uncritically. 3) Objections on the part of the opposition were not seriously met. Ridicule of other suggestions, refusal to see the issue, and postponement of discussion, met the objections.

III. I therefore ask the contributors to take a vote whether I shall or not be permitted to run the following note on the first page of my essay: "By permission of the other contributors to the book the writer of this essay wishes to point out that the title, I'll Take My Stand, does not set forth his own aims, and that in so far as he understands the aims of the book at large it does not set these forth either."

Yours in the faith, Allen Tate

TLS

Nashville, Tenn.
5 September 1930

To Allen Tate, Robert Penn Warren,
and Andrew Lytle, Esquires, Clarksville, Tennessee.

Gentlemen:

The undersigned members of the group taking part in the publication of a book called, for the present, "I'll Take My Stand," are strongly opposed to the sending to the publishers of any letter relating to the title, and strongly in favor of keeping the present title.

For two reasons: 1) It is too late now to raise this question with the publishers. They have advertised and sold the book already under the given title, in the innocent presumption that a group of Southern gentlemen would not embarrass them at a late moment by changing their minds. If you are sensitive about public opinion, we are sensitive about the proper conduct of our business with the publishers. Our book is already well known locally under the given title. In at least four newspapers the book has had prominent notice under this title. The book is already delayed in its preparation through our own remissness, since we are in the position of having submitted our manuscript some five or six weeks later than we gave the publishers to understand in advance. Under these circumstances it is not highly becoming to raise further difficulties.

Furthermore. 2) We favor the title on its merits. To us it does not connote the same ideas that it does to you. It means: "A statement of convictions by Southerners; take them or leave them; specifically, we unite Southernism with agrarianism, on grounds both historical and philosophical." We are not startled by the consideration that the phrase is lifted from a song named "Dixie," and that in its immediate context appears the expression, "to live and die for Dixie." The full title is: "I'll Take My Stand: The South and the Agrarian Tradition." Observe that the colon is one of the subtler marks of syntax that could not possibly occur to a frenzied and uncritical patriot—there is infinite protection for us in that colon. But if we must be accused of being frenzied and uncritical patriots, let us be accused. When you fight, you must not be too squeamish; you are *sure* to be misrepresented. As historians you will know that one of the means of destroying effective group action is by the hyper-sensitivity of individual members. We hold that we are not quoting the whole of the song Dixie; that the song Dixie is not so disreputable as you suppose; and that even the full total of all the associations of the song Dixie, both private and general, which an enemy might seek to fasten upon us, will not do any particular damage. The title-phrase is strong, clear, homely, and mostly Anglo-Saxon from the point of view of language; and historically it is apt.

Referring to the argument in Paragraph 2 of your proposed letter. "If the Southern tradition stands for anything valuable, that value is also universal." Do you mean that you want nothing local in your title? You still have it in the title of your proposing; you have it plentifully in the book at large. Or do you mean that you want the universal ground of the local to stand immediately beside it? You have it under the old title: "the Agrarian Tradition." As for exclusiveness, any historic principle that has been fought for will have that; we mean to be exclusive of all false principles; that is, of all Southern principles that are not agrarian, and of all universal ones that are not agrarian likewise. As for emotionalism, if our title inspires the wrong emotions, they will probably subside when the emoted reaches the definition in the subtitle. And our belligerency *might be* a vague one against Yankees, but it happens to be immediately disclosed as a precise one against non-agrarians.

We might add: The alternative proposed could not serve for our book. The issue of communism is a good one that we might have made central to our exhibit, but did not. Actually, we only have one brief reference to that issue. If you take the title you name, you will have to arrange for a full-length paper to be included in the contents, which will elaborate the issue advertised. The book as it stands at present will have only the slightest relation to such a title.

Respectfully,
Donald Davidson
John Crowe Ransom

Appendix C

🌾

TCC

Clarksville, Tennessee
17 November 1933

Eugene F. Saxton, Esq.
Harper & Brothers
New York City

Dear Saxton:

We have completed definite plans for another symposium, and we hope of course that Harper's will wish to publish it. We should like to see it published in the spring. We can have a complete manuscript ready for the printer by January 15th. The terms of the contract for our former book would be satisfactory to us.

The new book will have two new features. First, it will be geographically less restricted in scope, and it will be more definite in aim and program. Secondly, it will contain essays by writers who are not Southerners, but who participate in our ideas in their universal implications.

The general purpose of the book will be to define what at present we are calling a genuine Conservative Revolution: we are in the midst of a revolutionary process in this country, but to what extent is it defined in the mind of the Administration? Is it the familiar American procedure of tinkering with the parts, and letting American society drift, or does the outlook include a specific notion of the kind of society America should have? That is the question the book will try to answer. We oppose to the notion of "planned economy" the notion of "planned society." We cannot see that anybody in power or likely to be in power has a conception of a great American society: there is only the attempt to bring up incomes a little, and to be all things to all men. We shall, in the various essays, canvass the historical background for the possibility of a "planned society," and try to find a possible direction for it in the present state of affairs.

Our present list of contributors is as follows:

1) John Crowe Ransom: Relation of Land to Industrialism. A survey of the present state of the land in the line of an essay appearing in the October number of The American Review.

2) Frank L. Owsley: Scottsboro: After and Before. A full and absolutely forthright discussion of the Negro question.

3) Lyle H. Lanier: The Sociologists, or the Idea of Abstract Planning. The general thesis of this essay will be that humanitarian sociology corrects no fundamental evils, but rather makes the position of the wage-slave more hopeless than ever; it does nothing to restore him to property ownership and only aims at making his serfdom contented, an aim that inevitably fails in the cycles of depression.

4) Donald Davidson: University Education. The demoralization of the colleges under the influence of a predatory economic system. Examination of Flexner's thesis; an attempt to find the causes of the abuses observed by him.

5) John Donald Wade: Some Anti-Liberals in the Post-Bellum South. A discussion of the point of view of some Southerners who opposed the liberal reconstruction program of men like Page, etc.

6) Andrew Nelson Lytle: Some Ante-Bellum Planners of Society. Chiefly a discussion of John Taylor of Caroline; historical background of the thought of the men in preceding essay.

7) Robert Penn Warren: Some English Agrarians. Background: William Cobbett, Arthur Young. Victorians: Ruskin and his group. Reason for the failure of Ruskin's ideas to take hold: romantic mediaevalism. Their positive critical value.

8) T. S. Eliot: The Pseudo-Religious Character of the Extreme Determinists' Ideas of Economics.

9) Allen Tate: The Union and the Machine. The superstition of Technological Determinism examined. Derivation of this superstition from concealed political will to power. The idea that the machine cannot be controlled a part of the "drift-economics" of capitalism. History of the superstition in America. Its connection with the idea of the sanctity of the Union, which is not a real Union, in this view, but a vast possibility of industrial exploitation.

10) Herbert Agar (a new contributor, author of "The People's Choice," Houghton-Mifflin, 1933). "Crisis Legislation vs. the Planned Society." This will be the specific essay on the general question dis-

cussed in the book. The general thesis is that industrial capitalism is capable only of crisis legislation; abstract profit has destroyed concrete society. Dehumanization of economics.

11) John Gould Fletcher: The Return of a Twenty-Year Exile. Changes in America since 1912. A general survey of American life in that time.

12) Herman Nixon: The Tenant Farmer in the United States. The twice-forgotten man: forgotten by the old planter, and finally crushed by industrial capitalism. Plight of tenant farmer a phase of the general tendency of capitalism to reduce the population to servitude.

This is our prospectus. Most of the contributors are already at work upon their essays. Perhaps some of them would be available for Harper's Magazine. Most of the others will appear in the pages of the American Review. Since we published the first book, we have acquired a considerable following. The most prominent evidence of this is The American Review. Mr. Collins abandoned the Bookman for the express purpose of giving a joint hearing to the English Distributists and to our group. The publicity following from this would be of considerable value to a publisher.

May we hear from you at your earliest convenience? With kindest regards,

Yours very sincerely, [Allen Tate]

Appendix D

❦

TCC

TO THE ARMY OF TENNESSEE

"General, I am ready and have more hope in the final
success of our cause than at any time since the first
gun was fired."—Major-General Patrick R. Cleburne,
C.S.A., killed in action at Franklin, Tennessee,
November 30, 1864.

Where the road turns between the cedar groves
And the blue waves of hills lap all the distance,
Stop, look back, remember, for all is clear.
Leaves of November are falling on Winstead Hill
And before us, stark as Franklin field, the past
Is stripped to enduring boughs of memory
And of glory, what still remains.

No sound of guns. The silence drags its haze
Over the sunken breastworks where the bones
Forget their names and only the rich earth
Utters fragments we know not how to reap.
No sound of guns. But an echo is on the air
Repeating, summoning still where undying smoke
Thunders around lost city roofs and the cannon
Dog the tired cannoneers who now too late
Flinch from the lanyard. Now the years take back
The spoils they gave here, and the laurels blast.
Autumn, a mouldering blaze, drags down the nation
To the abyss chosen, defined by seventy autumns
Dropping their hollow fruit in the victor's hand.
Not yet is the Union saved, not yet do the waters

Run unvexed to the sea, not yet is freedom
Seated upon her thousand hills. But they
Who most proclaimed these now are most cast down.
And I hear beyond Winstead hill a lamentation
A lamentation arising from crooking backs
And aimless fingers picking, reaching, clutching,
And the dry throats speechless, the slack arms clasping
And meeting but air—And I hear the Angel of the Lord
Crying with a strong voice Fallen Fallen
And the too shaken multitude crying Alas
For that city for in one hour is thy judgment come
And the unshaken earth crying aloud O Come
Come out of her, my people. But their ears are stopped
Their eyes are dazzled with a hungry glitter of eyes
Their ears are deafened with steps that murmur and follow
No command. And no sword leaps up. And no tongue,
But only confusion of tongues, the wrack
Of Babylon that falls, a twilight clutter.

But here a twilight not of dissolution burns.
By Winstead hill, by the low Harpeth valley
This twilight is renewal of old vows,
An incantation, seized again, by which
The old corruption puts on incorruption,
And men may see the body of their faith.
From the marrow of Alabama, Tennessee,
From Georgia hearts here battered and redeemed,
From this once resolute Southern dust I gather
Steps of an army, Confederate bugles calling
Fulfillment of old pledges stronger than death.

And now across the four-years-trampled fields
The still defiant flags toss to the yell
Of a ravelled army breaking the thicket's edge.
This is the last charge of the old brigades
Whose battles rocked the west with thunder-names:
Shiloh, deadliest Sabbath, where the river
All but received the memory of their foe;
And Murfreesboro, where the cast of fate
Mocked at the wasted blood, the frozen field;
The lunge of Chickamauga and the moon

Of stormy gatherings tossed from ridge to ridge
On the red hills of Georgia. These have marched
To the sound of guns forever and forever,
Not tiring, not surrendering even
To their own generals. The axe
Blunted in hands that could not heft its strength
Hoarded or nicked by clumsy strategists
Who never swore an oath or cleft a skull
Like the true woodsman, Forrest. Oh, these have charged,
Retreated, charged, retreated, charged again.
And now the viking arm of Hood, berserk,
Sweeps north again: One great charge more, my brothers.
Rake the South free from burnt Atlanta's walls
North to Ohio, east to the camps of Lee
Till the red hand of Sherman marches in vain.
One charge more. Well, General, if you say so—
We have hard riders who know how to lead the way
And men with guns who can bite a cartridge yet;
Call up Adams, Granbury, Gist, and Strahl,
Call up Pat Cleburne. We will follow on.
Oh, sound the bugles, dress the ranks, and charge.
The Army of Tennessee knows how to charge.

I see the November sunset redden their starry banners,
St. Andrew's Cross towers on Harpeth valley.
I see the brigades form line of battle.
The veterans are supple, steady.
They know their places, they move intent as panthers.
I see brown necks bare, rifles poised, cartridge boxes unlatched.
They are rusty of beard, the brighteyed valorous.
And the generals, alert, in the chieftain's place.
They walk or ride the line, waving forward with sword or hat.
And Pat Cleburne gallops front in his sock feet.
He gave the boots to a barefoot soldier; his smile
Went up to Hood in the last salute, saying:
General, I am ready . . .
And I see the skirmishers go out, the lean hunters
Giving the dare. And the ranks move slowly at first.
The guide is centre—hold the Columbia Pike.
And yonder the town, white and red among dusty trees.

The cotton gin, the locusts, the hills behind
And I see young Carter angrily looking and crying
The Yankees have got my house . . . my [folks?] are there.
He is on furlough, but who can deny him this charge?
He hurries to join the moving ranks . . . to die
On his own ground.
And I hear the soldiers saying Farewell.
Farewell, comrades, farewell you blue-grass fields
On which we look our last. Farewell
To all of our great captains:
To Albert Sidney Johnston, he was our first,
To Braxton Bragg, Lord help his shaky hand,
To Joe Johnston, he was our Fabius,
To Bedford Forrest, he was our sword of Gideon.
And you too Farewell, John Hood, for you have read
One good conclusion written on our brows:
Better to die and never see the end.
Better to die while the South is still the South
Than live without arms to strike, and witness her shame.
Under the grass, when the Old Republic withers
(As wither it must if this our strength shall fail)
Our bones will sleep unknowing what will come
Remembering that our country still was here
Where still our arms, our flags advance
This day in 'Sixty-four, when on these fields
Shoulder to shoulder with our kin we stood.
The charge quickens. I see the enemy now.
There, there are the Yankees. Yell, gray lines.
The Army of Tennessee knows how to charge.
Not how to surrender, but how to charge, to die.

Fated, valorous army, who watches you
In this last darkling grapple? Who cheers you on?
You walk in the valley of death without parade
Knowing the taste of blood, the choke of defeat.
But hands of mourners will come to gather you
Under the maples by MacGavock House
Which presently like you will moulder and sink
Hearing but pilgrim steps, the pelt of leaves
That litter your ranks . . . your graves.

                              A circle of fire
Glows from river and town. The live darkness
Unyielding stabs the Southern ranks.
The flags plunge and fade. The thick smoke drifts.

Farewell, Army of Tennessee.
The leaves fall but the boughs of memory
Keep your rough glory for the flesh obeys
Not the dropped leaf but the root, which silent as earth
Feeds forever the sacred vow, the touch
Of a late comrade sworn to remember you.
Farewell, but as I turn, and again the motor
Throbs for the quick descent from Winstead hill
And the dim road hurtles backward into night
The fading breastworks, the hill, the Carter house,
I know that only the dust returns to dust
But the vow lives on and can await its season.
What are the faces alive on city streets?
What are the accents? What the hands that beckon?
I have known you of old, O young Confederate soldiers,
The likeness of you in uniform of gray,
The very flesh of the fallen, unsubdued.
You, at Shiloh, lifted the sagging banner.
You in the thickets of Chickamauga raced
Up to the cannon's mouth. And you, my comrade,
Marched with us all one thunderous night of summer;
At dawn we passed the river and came into action
And till dusk fought on. Your eyes remember this.
And now when old friends gather against the night
We take not little counsels from a time
That gives men nothing to die for, but reclaim
The privilege of our fathers who could hold
Something more precious than life itself, and remember
The Army of Tennessee knows how to charge
And so come home to camp ground at last.

                                          Donald Davidson

"I think I was foolish to attempt this, and I know I'm foolish to send
it in this unfinished state. I don't know what is the matter with me—
but here it is for you to gobble up, Grandpapa Wolf!" [Davidson's
note to Tate.]

Appendix E

✤

Clarksville, Tenn.
24 May 1937

An Open Letter

Chancellor James H. Kirkland
Vanderbilt University
Nashville, Tennessee

My dear Sir:

This letter will reach you as the intrusion of a stranger, yet I hope without impropriety. I am an alumnus of Vanderbilt and I take interest in her affairs.

It is now common knowledge that Mr. John Crowe Ransom is about to leave Vanderbilt to join the faculty of a college in Ohio. I know nothing of the reasons that may prompt Mr. Ransom to go, after twenty-five years at his Alma Mater, to another institution. If he goes it will be a calamity from which Vanderbilt will not soon recover.

Mr. Ransom is, I fear, a little more famous internationally than locally. He is one of the most distinguished men of letters in the world today. Where Vanderbilt is known outside her Alumni Associations and similar groups of persons whose enlightenment of interest is not quite perfect, she is known as the institution where John Crowe Ransom profoundly influences, through his teaching and writing, the course of modern literature. I need not cite any of his more brilliant achievements, but I should like to bring to your attention two recent incidents that illustrate the far-reaching character of his reputation. The Lowell family of Boston and Harvard University has just sent one of its sons to Nashville to study poetry with Mr. Ransom—I do not say Vanderbilt, because young Mr. Lowell will follow Mr. Ransom to Ohio. In the past few months a correspondent of mine at Cambridge, England, has informed me that his fellow students repeatedly express a wish to study under John Crowe Ransom.

I am sure that you have applauded the notable revival of letters in the South and that you have felt in it a proprietary interest, since the center of this revival has been Vanderbilt University. I can only ask you to imagine Harvard University, at the height of the New England revival, letting Charles Eliot Norton go to a small college in the Middle West.

I know that college officials labor under peculiar difficulties. Occupied as they must be with organization and finance, they are infrequently in a position to judge the value of certain members of their faculties. If this is true of the officials, it is even truer of boards of trustees, which, I believe, are as a rule composed of business men who tend to look upon professors of even the first distinction as mere employees. If you are not aware of Mr. Ransom's distinction, which is of the very first order, the sources of your information have been faulty, and I am sure that you will see it as your duty, in view of the gravity of the occasion, to correct them. But if you, as the head of a great university, are indifferent to the grounds of this expostulation, then I can only pity you, and meditate upon emotions that I shall not easily get my own consent to express. The literary historians of the future will express them for me.[a]

Very truly yours, Allen Tate

[a]   See T. D. Young, "In His Own Country," *Southern Review* (Summer 1972).

Appendix F

✤

Chronologies of Donald Davidson and Allen Tate

Donald Grady Davidson

1893   Born April 18 in Campbellsville, Tennessee, to William Bluford and Elma Wells Davidson.

1901   Enters Lynnville Academy, Lynnville, Tennessee.

1905   Enters Branham and Hughes School at Spring Hill, Tennessee.

1906   Family moves to Columbia, Tennessee.

1909   Is graduated from Branham and Hughes in June, after completing four years of Latin, three of Greek, and four of English and mathematics; family moves to Bell Buckle, Tennessee; in September enters Vanderbilt University on "$100 loan and a little odd cash"; meets Ben and Varnell Tate, older brothers of Allen.

1910–12   Accepts teaching position at Cedar Hill Institute, Cedar Hill, Tennessee, where he teaches Greek, English, arithmetic, plane and solid geometry, Latin, and history; writes words and music for an operetta based on the Pandora myth.

1912–14   Teaches at Mooresville Training School, Mooresville, Tennessee; during summer works on farm of Sawney Webb, headmaster of the Webb School, Bell Buckle, Tennessee.

1914–16   Returns to Vanderbilt in fall and accepts part-time position teaching English and German at Wallace University School; enrolls in English courses with Edwin Mims, Walter Clyde Curry, and John Crowe Ransom; also has Herbert Sanborn in philosophy; meets Alec B. Stevenson, William Y. Elliott, Stanley Johnson; at the apartment of Sidney M. Hirsch participates in informal meetings which develop into the Fugitive group; contributes a few poems and essays to the Vanderbilt *Observer*.

1916–17   Teaches at Massey School, Pulaski, Tennessee; enters officer candidate school at Fort Oglethorpe, Georgia, on May 12; receives bachelor of arts degree, in absentia, from Vanderbilt in June; John Crowe Ransom is in same camp and together they read manuscript for Ransom's *Poems About God*; commissioned second lieutenant of infantry on August 15 and assigned to 81st Division, Camp Jackson.

1918   Transfers with division to Camp Sevier in May; promoted to first lieutenant; on June 8 marries Theresa Sherrer of Oberlin, Ohio, whom he had met two years earlier while she was teaching Greek, Latin, and mathematics at Martin College, Pulaski; in July is transferred to Camp Mills and hence overseas; serves in France in the Bruyeres area, in active combat for about six weeks; after armistice moves to billeting area near Chatillon-sur-Seine.

1919   Daughter Mary Theresa born March 26; leaves France for United States in June; discharged at Camp Sherman, Ohio, in July; attempts to secure teaching position at Vanderbilt and newspaper position in Cleveland, Ohio, before accepting position at Kentucky Wesleyan College in September.

1920–21   During summer works as a reporter for Nashville *Evening Tennessean;* accepts position as instructor of English at Vanderbilt and begins teaching and graduate study in September; regular meetings of Fugitive group begin in September at home of James M. Frank, 3802 Whitland Avenue; for summer employment sells wall maps in Alabama; in November invites Allen Tate to attend Fugitive meetings.

1922   On April 12 first issue of the *Fugitive* appears; Davidson represented by "A Demon Brother," "The Dragon Book," and "Following the Tiger" under the pseudonym of Robin Gallivant; receives master's degree from Vanderbilt in June; spends summer as counsellor at Camp Kawasawa near Lebanon, Tennessee.

1923   Publishes poems in *Folio, Double Dealer, The Yearbook of the Poetry Society of South Carolina,* and the *Fugitive; An Outland Piper* accepted by Houghton-Mifflin; serves as editor of *Fugitive*.

1924   *An Outland Piper* appears; begins, on February 24, to edit book page for *Nashville Tennessean* in which he publishes the early criticism of Tate, Ransom, and other Fugitives; promoted to assistant professor; first important critical essay, "Certain Fallacies in Modern Poetry," appears in the *Fugitive*.

1925   Last issue of the *Fugitive* appears in December; "Joseph Conrad's Directed Indirections" appears in *Sewanee Review*.

1926   Wins first prize in South Carolina Poetry Society Contest for "Fire on Belmont Street"; exchanges letters with Tate and Ransom regarding defense of southern culture.

1927   *The Tall Men*, his second volume of poetry, is published by Houghton-Mifflin.

1928   Book page syndicated in *Memphis Commercial Appeal* and *Knoxville Journal;* contributes to *Fugitives: An Anthology of Verse;* "First Fruits of Dayton, The Intellectual Evolution in Dixie" appears in *Forum*.

1929   Promoted to associate professor.

1930   Contributes "A Mirror for Artists" to *I'll Take My Stand; Tennessean* book page is discontinued.

1931   Begins summer teaching at the Bread Loaf School of English, Middlebury College, Vermont, where he is to teach almost every summer for the rest of his life; *Bookman* publishes "Criticism Outside New York," the story of his seven years experience as a book reviewer and editor for the *Tennessean*.

1932   Wesley Hall, where he lives on Vanderbilt campus, burns; spends academic year, from September until June, at Marshallville, Georgia, the home of John Donald Wade, where he is to spend many holiday periods through the years; contributes "The Southern Poet and His Traditions" to *Poetry;* participates with Ransom, Tate, Lytle and others in discussions with Seward Collins regarding the publication of the *American Review;* completes first draft of "Lee in the Mountains" in early September and two more completely revised versions of the poem during fall and early winter.

1933   "Sectionalism in the United States" appears in *Hound and Horn;* "The Rise of American Cities" appears in *American Review* in April; during next four years contributes nine "agrarian" essays to this journal; in December "Still Rebels,

Still Yankees," his most widely anthologized essay, appears in *American Review.*

1934   "Lee in the Mountains" is published in *American Review* for May.

1935   "A Note on American Heroes" is published in *Southern Review,* the first of six essays to appear here; contributes "The Trend of Literature: A Partisan View" to *Culture in the South,* ed. W. T. Couch; *"I'll Take My Stand:* A History" appears in *American Review.*

1936   Contributes "That This Nation May Endure: The Need for Political Regionalism" to the second Agrarian symposium, *Who Owns America?*

1937   Promoted to professor of English at Vanderbilt.

1938   *Lee in the Mountains and Other Poems, Including the Tall Men* published by Houghton-Mifflin and *The Attack on Leviathan: Regionalism and Nationalism* by the University of North Carolina Press.

1939   *American Composition and Rhetoric* published by Scribners. He is to publish four more editions of this book, which becomes one of the most widely used textbooks in America during the next three decades.

1941   Publishes "Yeats and the Centaur" in the *Southern Review.*

1942   *Readings for Composition from Prose Models* (in collaboration with Sidney Erwin Glenn).

1943   His poem "Hermitage" appears in *Virginia Quarterly Review.*

1946   Publishes *The Tennessee: The Old River, Frontier to Secession* (Rinehart's Rivers of America Series), Volume 1; awarded honorary degree by Cumberland University.

1948   *The Tennessee: The New River, Civil War to TVA,* Volume 2, is published; awarded honorary degree by Washington and Lee University.

1952   Collaborates, as librettist, with Charles F. Bryan, composer, in writing and producing a folk opera entitled *Singin' Billy.*

1955   *Twenty Lessons in Reading and Writing* published by Scribners; accepts state chairmanship of the Tennessee Federation for Constitutional Government.

1956   *Still Rebels, Still Yankees and Other Essays* published by Louisiana State University Press; Fugitive reunion at Vanderbilt May 3–5.

1957	Delivers Eugenia Dorothy Blount Lamar Memorial Lectures at Mercer University, November 20 and 21.
1958	*Southern Writers in the Modern World* (Eugenia Dorothy Blount Lamar Memorial Lectures) published by University of Georgia Press.
1959	"Lines Written for Allen Tate on His Sixtieth Anniversary" appears in *Sewanee Review*.
1961	*The Long Street*, his fourth volume of poetry, is published by Vanderbilt University Press.
1962	*I'll Take My Stand* reissued in Harper Torchbook edition.
1963	Publication of *The Spyglass: Views and Reviews, 1924–30*, containing a selection of about fifty reviews and essays from the *Tennessean* book page.
1964	Retires from teaching and becomes professor of English emeritus at Vanderbilt.
1966	*Poems: 1922–61* published; awarded honorary degree by Middlebury College, Vermont; edits, and writes introduction for, *Selected Essays of John Donald Wade*.
1967	Writes introduction for the Peter Smith reprint of the *Fugitive*.
1968	Dies in Nashville, Tennessee, on April 25.

John Orley Allen Tate

1899	Born in Winchester, Clark County, Kentucky, to John Orley and Eleanor Varnell Tate.
1906–8	Lives in Nashville at intervals while brothers Ben and Varnell in Vanderbilt; enters Tarbox School in Nashville; remains only three months.
1909–12	Attends Cross School, a private academy emphasizing Latin and rhetoric, in Louisville, Kentucky.
1912–14	Public high school in Ashland, Kentucky.
1915	Half-year in public high school, Evansville, Indiana.
1916–17	October 1916 to April 1917 in Cincinnati. Conservatory of Music; studies violin under Jean Ten Have and Eugen Ysaÿe; enters Georgetown Preparatory School to prepare for Vanderbilt admission.
1918	Admitted to Vanderbilt for fall with provision that he pass

a third-year Latin examination; taught English by W. C. Curry and John Crowe Ransom, philosophy by Herbert Sanborn, Greek by Herbert Cushing Tolman.

1919–20   First published poems, "Impossible" and "Red Stains," appear in *American Poetry Magazine*; joins Calumet Club in which fellow members are Ransom, Curry, Davidson, and Alec B. Stevenson.

1921   Publishes "A Ballade of the Lugubrious Wench" in *Jade*, humor magazine of Calumet Club, of which he is president; invited by Davidson to informal discussions with group that later published the *Fugitive*.

1922   In April, in first issue of the *Fugitive*, publishes under Henry Feathertop pseudonym "To Intellectual Detachment" and "Sinbad"; from June to September in Valle Crucis, North Carolina, for reasons of health; in fall and winter works in family coal business in Ashland, Kentucky.

1923   Returns in February to Vanderbilt to complete degree; meets Robert Penn Warren and rooms with him and Ridley Wills; places "Calidus Juventa," "Euthanasia," "William Blake," and other poems in *Double Dealer*; with Ridley Wills writes *The Golden Mean*, privately printed in a two-hundred-copy edition; in August is graduated magna cum laude; exchanges letters with Ransom in the *Literary Review* on *The Waste Land*; assistant editor of the *Fugitive*; remains in Nashville during fall expecting scholarship for master's degree in classical studies.

1924   In February accepts position as English teacher in Lumberport, West Virginia, High School; meets Laura Riding Gottschalk in Louisville; in New York meets Hart Crane, Gorham Munson, Slater Brown, Edmund Wilson, and others; returns in July to Guthrie, Kentucky, to visit Warren; there meets Caroline Gordon, whom he marries in the fall; returns to New York and rents apartment at 30 Jones Street; begins career of free-lance writing with the *Nation*, the *New Republic*, the *Herald Tribune*, and other periodicals.

1925   Accepts position with Climax Publishing Company, publisher of *Ranch Romance* and *Telling Tales*; Nancy Tate born September 23; Tate moves to larger flat on Morton Street; meets John Peale Bishop; rents part of rural house in Patterson, New York; Crane lives with the Tates.

1926   Tate working on "Ode to the Confederate Dead"; moves to
        27 Bank Street, New York City, where he does janitorial work
        in building to assist with expenses.

1927   "Poetry and the Absolute," first important critical essay, ap-
        pears; helps find publisher for *Fugitive* anthology; meets
        Ford Madox Ford.

1928   Contributes to *Fugitives: An Anthology of Verse;* publishes
        Mr. Pope and Other Poems and *Stonewall Jackson: The
        Good Soldier;* receives Guggenheim fellowship; in London
        from September to November; meets T. S. Eliot, Herbert
        Read, and, in Oxford, L.A.G. Strong; in Paris on Thanks-
        giving Day; meets Julian Green, Morley Callaghan, Sylvia
        Beach, Ernest Hemingway, Gertrude Stein, and others; lives
        rent-free for six months in Ford's apartment at 32 rue de
        Vangirard; Warren, then a Rhodes scholar, visits him; estab-
        lishes friendship with John Peale Bishop; writes "Mother
        and Son."

1929   Publishes *Jefferson Davis: His Rise and Fall*; writes "Message
        from Abroad."

1930   Sails for New York, January 1; leaves for Tennessee in
        February; in April is given by his brother Ben an antebellum
        farm house near Clarksville, Tennessee, about forty-five miles
        from Nashville; Caroline and Allen christen home "Ben-
        folly"; contributes "Remarks on Southern Religion" to *I'll
        Take My Stand.*

1931   "Sonnets of the Blood" appears; begins work on a biography
        of Lee, never completed.

1932   Becomes southern editor for *Hound and Horn;* publishes
        Poems: 1928–31; writes "To the Lacedemonians" for the
        Confederate soldiers' June reunion in Richmond; edits south-
        ern number for *Poetry;* in France from June 1932 to Febru-
        ary 1933 (Caroline Gordon has Guggenheim award); writes
        "Picnic at Cassis" (later entitled "The Mediterranean").

1933   Becomes friends with Herbert Agar and invites him to sub-
        mit articles to the *American Review;* receives Midland Au-
        thor's Prize from *Poetry;* "The Immortal Woman," a short
        story Davidson found "repulsively Jamesian," appears.

1934   With Herbert Agar explores possibilities of establishing a
        midwest-southern political weekly; "Sonnets at Christmas"
        appears; becomes lecturer in English at Southwestern, re-

placing Warren, and moves to 2374 Forrest Avenue in Memphis.

1935   In July makes first appearance at a writers' conference, at Olivet College, Michigan; "The Profession of Letters in the South" is published.

1936   Edits, with Agar, *Who Owns America?* to which he contributes essay "Notes on Liberty and Property"; publishes *The Mediterranean and Other Poems* and *Reactionary Essays on Poetry and Ideas;* resigns from Southwestern and returns to Benfolly; takes summer job as lecturer in English at Columbia University; "Narcissus as Narcissus" published; with Anne Goodwin Winslow does dramatic version of *The Turn of the Screw* entitled "The Governess."

1937   Publishes *Selected Poems;* Ford Madox Ford spends summer with Tate at Benfolly; Robert Lowell visits; becomes involved in the controversy over Ransom's leaving Vanderbilt for Kenyon; participates in writers' conference at Olivet College.

1938   Accepts position as professor of English at the Woman's College of North Carolina and moves to 112 Arden Place, Greensboro; spends summer at Scoville Cottage, West Cornwall, Connecticut; completes *The Fathers* there on July 21; novel appears in early fall; "Tension in Poetry" appears; becomes advisory editor of *Kenyon Review.*

1939   Lectures at St. Johns College, Annapolis, Maryland, and considers position there; participates in a writers' conference at Savannah, Georgia; becomes resident poet in Creative Arts Program at Princeton; spends summer at "Westwood Cottage," Monteagle, Tennessee, where he finishes "The Trout Map," in September and moves to 16 Linden Lane, Princeton; impressed with professionalism at Princeton and the fact that the creative program is separate from the English department; begins work on "Miss Emily and the Bibliographer."

1940   Begins to appear as panelist on CBS program "Invitation to Learning"; declines offer to become consultant in poetry to the Library of Congress; "Understanding Modern Poetry" appears.

1941   Publishes "Literature as Knowledge: Comment and Comparison" and *Reason in Madness, Critical Essays.*

1942   Submits unsuccessful application for commission in U.S. Naval Reserve; with John Peale Bishop edits *American Harvest;* edits *The Language of Poetry* and *Princeton Verse Between Two Wars;* publishes "*The Fugitive, 1922–25,* A Personal Recollection"; resigns at Princeton and returns to Monteagle, where he writes "More Sonnets at Christmas"; Robert Lowell and his wife, Jean Stafford, join Tates there.

1943   Completes draft of "Jubilo" on January 20 and "Winter Mask" in February; begins "Seasons of the Soul"; translates *Pervergilium Veneris* and writes "More Sonnets at Christmas"; in September moves to Washington to accept position as consultant in poetry at the Library of Congress; edits, with the assistance of Frances Cheney, *Sixty American Poets, 1896–1944, A Checklist;* becomes involved in the activities to save the life of Ezra Pound.

1944   John Peale Bishop dies April 4; begins work on Bishop's manuscripts to prepare the collected edition of his poems, not completed until 1948; in July moves to Sewanee, Tennessee, to become editor of *Sewanee Review.*

1945   On January 23 consults with Archibald Macleish about position of cultural attaché to the American embassy in Paris; resigns from the *Sewanee Review* October 15; publishes "The New Provincialism, with an Epilogue on the Southern Novel."

1946   In January receives divorce from Caroline Gordon; visits her in New York in February and in March they agree to remarry in April; sells Benfolly; moves to apartment at 108 Perry Street, New York; becomes editor of belles lettres for Henry Holt and Company; T. S. Eliot visits Tates in May.

1948   Publishes *Poems, 1922–1947,* "Longinus and the New Criticism," and *On the Limits of Poetry, Selected Essays 1928–1948;* leaves Henry Holt to become lecturer at New York University; becomes a fellow of the Kenyon School of English; serves on jury which awards Bollingen prize to Pound and states reasons for voting for Pound in *Partisan Review.*

1949   Publishes *The Hovering Fly and Other Essays;* serves year as visiting professor of humanities at University of Chicago; buys home from Louis O. Coxe on Nassau Street in Princeton; for Ben Tate, who had paid for it, house is called "Benbrackets."

1950   Joins Roman Catholic Church.

1951   With Caroline Gordon publishes *The House of Fiction;* pub-
        lishes "To Whom is the Poet Responsible?"; accepts appoint-
        ment as professor of English at the University of Minnesota
        and in September moves to Joseph Warren Beach's old house
        at 1409 University Avenue, Minneapolis.

1952   Delivers "The Man of Letters in the Modern World" as Phi
        Beta Kappa lecture at Minnesota; delegate to the Congress
        for Cultural Freedom in Paris, where he delivers a shortened
        version of "The Man of Letters in the Modern World"; in
        August delegate to the UNESCO conference in Venice;
        granted audience by Pope Pius XII; publishes "The Angelic
        Imagination: Poe and the Power of Words," "Is Literary
        Criticism Possible?" and "The Symbolic Imagination: A
        Meditation on Dante's Three Mirrors."

1953   In summer, lectures in the American Studies Program in
        Oxford under auspices of Fulbright program; during fall
        and winter is Fulbright professor at the University of Rome;
        publishes *The Forlorn Demon: Didactic and Critical Essays.*

1955   Tate and Caroline Gordon separate.

1956   Arranges lecture for T. S. Eliot at University of Minnesota;
        Fugitive reunion at Vanderbilt May 3–5; lectures in India
        during fall for Fulbright program; returns by way of Europe
        and lectures in Turin, Rome, Milan, Florence, Paris, Lon-
        don, and Nottingham; receives Bollingen Prize.

1958   Fulbright lecturer at Oxford University, from which he re-
        ceives honorary master of arts degree; lectures at the Uni-
        versity of Leeds in spring and Harvard University during
        summer.

1959   Is divorced by Caroline Gordon and on August 27 marries
        Isabella Gardner; autumn issue of *Sewanee Review* is de-
        voted to a celebration of his sixtieth birthday; Ransom,
        Davidson, Eliot, and Read are among those offering tributes;
        publishes *Collected Essays.*

1960   Publishes *Poems;* publishes "A Southern Mode of the Imag-
        ination."

1961   Receives the Brandeis University Medal for Poetry.

1962   Receives *Medaglia d'Oro di Società Italiana di Dante Ali-
        ghieri* at Florence, Italy.

1963   Receives $5,000 Fellowship Award from the Academy of
        American Poets.

1964   Elected to American Academy of Arts and Letters.

1965   Elected to American Academy of Arts and Sciences.

1966   Isabella Gardner is granted a divorce on March 28; made Regents' Professor of English; marries Helen Heinz on July 30; teaches at University of North Carolina at Greensboro during fall semester.

1967   Teaches spring term at Vanderbilt; twin sons, John Allen and Michael Paul, born August 30.

1968   Serves as president of the National Institute of Arts and Letters; retires from University of Minnesota in June and moves to Sewanee; Michael dies in July.

1969   A third son, Benjamin Lewis Bogan, born December 18. *Essays of Four Decades* is published by Swallow.

1971   *The Swimmers and Other Selected Poems* is published by Scribners and Oxford University Press.

1974   Delivers principal address on centenary of Robert Frost's birth, March 26, Library of Congress.

Appendix G

❦

The Fellow Fugitives of Davidson and Tate

Walter Clyde Curry

Referred to in the letters as Doc, Doc Curry, W. C., and W.C.C.; he received his Ph.D. degree from Stanford University in 1916 and was a member of the faculty when the Fugitive meetings began. His interests were more scholarly, perhaps, than those of the other members. He later published distinguished studies of Chaucer, Shakespeare, and Milton, and succeeded Edwin Mims as chairman of the Vanderbilt English department.

William Yandell Elliott

Referred to as Bill Elliott; influential in introducing principal figures to the Fugitives before World War II; he rejoined the group after study at the Sorbonne; a Rhodes scholar, he later became a professor of government at Harvard University.

James M. Frank

Usually referred to as "Mr. Frank"; the Fugitives' meetings were held in his home near Vanderbilt; he remained a Nashville businessman.

William C. Frierson

Returned to the Fugitive discussions in 1921, after completing his Rhodes scholarship; he later taught English and modern languages in several colleges and universities.

Sidney Mttron Hirsch	Referred to as "Dr. Hirsch"; James Frank's brother-in-law; a mystic and a Rosicrucian, he presided at many of the Fugitive meetings.
Stanley Johnson	Referred to as Stanley; he was studying for a master's degree in English during the meetings of the early 1920s; his wife, Will Ella, was head librarian at Vanderbilt during the days of the *Fugitive;* two months after Johnson left Vanderbilt, his novel *The Professor,* satirizing college life, was published.
Merrill Moore	One of the younger members of the group; his sonnets appeared in the first number, however, and his poetry was praised by Davidson; he practiced psychiatry and continued to write sonnets until his death in 1957; he is best known for *The Noise that Time Makes* (1929) and *One Thousand Autobiographical Sonnets* (1938).
John Crowe Ransom	Referred to as J. C., Johnny, John, and J.C.R.; he received the bachelor of arts degree from Vanderbilt in 1909 and the *Literae Humaniores* degree from Oxford University as a Rhodes scholar in 1913; during the earlier part of his twenty-three-year tenure at Vanderbilt (1914–37), he taught most of the Fugitive group; his most important publications are *Poems about God* (1919), *Chills and Fever* (1924), *Two Gentlemen in Bonds* (1927), *God Without Thunder* (1930), *The World's Body* (1938), and *The New Criticism* (1941).
Alfred Starr	Little mention of him in the letters; although he attended meetings of the group, he was listed as a member only in the last two issues of the *Fugitive;* he later was president of the Bijou theater chain.
Alec B. Stevenson	Son of a professor of Semitic languages at Vanderbilt, he was editor of the Vanderbilt

Observer, an undergraduate literary magazine, and was instrumental both in bringing
the Fugitives together and in arguing for the
"new poetry"; he made a career of investment
banking in Nashville.

Robert Penn Warren

Referred to as "Red"; as a seventeen-year-old
sophomore he began attending Fugitive meetings in the spring of 1923 and officially became
a member of the group early the next year.
After receiving the B.A. (Vanderbilt, 1925),
the M.A. (University of California, 1927), and
the B.Litt. as a Rhodes scholar (1930), he
taught at Southwestern, Vanderbilt, Louisiana State, Minnesota, and Yale. Author of
more than twenty books of poetry, fiction,
and literary and social criticism, he is the only
writer to win the Pulitzer Prize for both fiction and poetry.

Ridley Wills

A lively if not very serious member of the
group; he left Vanderbilt after receiving the
B.A. degree in June 1923 to become a news-
paperman in New York.

Jesse Wills

Cousin to Ridley Wills and an important
member of the Fugitives; Tate thought him
the most talented of the group during the
early meetings; he also assisted in the editorial chores of the magazine while working
for the National Life and Accident Insurance
Company, in Nashville; his three volumes of
verse are *Early and Late: Fugitive Poems
and Others* (1959), *Conversation Piece* (1965),
and *Nashville and Other Poems* (1973).

Index